Private Law in China and Taiwan

Past research and literature suggest that legal institutions drive economic development. Yet China has grown for decades without the fundamental legal infrastructure that was once considered necessary: A phenomenon that is known as the "China puzzle" or the "China myth." By carefully comparing the four key branches of private law in China and Taiwan – a jurisdiction that grew with modest legal institutions and shares a similar legal and nonlegal culture – this collaborative and novel book demystifies the "China puzzle." Top scholars in the field use an economics-focused analytical approach to explain how and why the laws have taken such paths over the past four decades. Comparing property, contract, tort, and corporate laws in China and Taiwan, these authors delve deeply into key doctrines to provide a meaningful account of the evolution of private law in these two jurisdictions.

YUN-CHIEN CHANG is Associate Research Professor and Director of Center for Empirical Legal Studies at Academia Sinica, Taiwan. He was a visiting professor at the University of Chicago and elsewhere. He has (co-)authored and (co-)edited eight books and more than 70 journal articles and book chapters, in English and Chinese.

WEI SHEN is Dean and Professor of Law at Shandong University Law School, and Global Professor of Law at New York University School of Law. He is the author of seven books and over one hundred journal articles in English and Chinese.

WEN-YEU WANG is a law professor at National Taiwan University and has authored over 100 academic books and papers in Chinese and English. Notable among them are: "Corporate versus Contractual Mutual Funds: An Evaluation of Structure and Governance" (1994) and "The Best of Both Worlds? On Taiwan's Quasi-Public Enforcer of Corporate and Securities Law" (2015).

Private Law in China and Taiwan

Legal and Economic Analyses

YUN-CHIEN CHANG
Academia Sinica, Taipei, Taiwan

WEI SHEN
Shandong University Law School, China

WEN-YEU WANG
National Taiwan University, Taipei, Taiwan

CAMBRIDGE
UNIVERSITY PRESS

CAMBRIDGE
UNIVERSITY PRESS

University Printing House, Cambridge CB2 8BS, United Kingdom

One Liberty Plaza, 20th Floor, New York, NY 10006, USA

477 Williamstown Road, Port Melbourne, VIC 3207, Australia

4843/24, 2nd Floor, Ansari Road, Daryaganj, Delhi - 110002, India

79 Anson Road, #06-04/06, Singapore 079906

Cambridge University Press is part of the University of Cambridge.

It furthers the University's mission by disseminating knowledge in the pursuit of education, learning and research at the highest international levels of excellence.

www.cambridge.org
Information on this title: www.cambridge.org/9781107154247

First published 2017

A catalogue record for this publication is available from the British Library

Library of Congress Cataloging-in-Publication data
Names: Chang, Yun-chien, editor. | Shen, Wei, editor. | Wang, Wenyu (Law teacher) editor.
Title: Private law in China and Taiwan : legal and economic analyses / edited by Yun-chien Chang, Wei Shen, Wen-yeu Wang.
Description: New York : Cambridge University Press, 2016.
Identifiers: LCCN 2016026237 | ISBN 9781107154247 (hardback)
Subjects: LCSH: Civil law – China. | Civil law – Taiwan. | BISAC: LAW / Civil Law.
Classification: LCC KNQ500 .P75 2016 | DDC 346.51 – dc23
LC record available at https://lccn.loc.gov/2016026237

ISBN 978-1-107-15424-7 Hardback

We together dedicate the book to
our private law teachers and students

Contents

Figures

Contributors

Yun-chien Chang: Associate Research Professor, Institutum Iurisprudentiae, Academia Sinica. J.S.D., NYU Law.

Saul Levmore: William B. Graham Distinguished Service Professor of Law, University of Chicago. Ph.D. (Economics), J.D., Yale University.

Bruno Deffains: Professor of Law and Economics, University Paris 2 Panthéon Assas. Ph.D. in Economics, University of Nancy.

Jing Leng: Professor of Law, East China University of Politics and Law. J.S.D., University of Toronto.

Wei Shen: Dean and Professor of Law at Shandong University Law School. Ph.D., London School of Economics and Political Science.

Wen-yeu Wang: Professor of Law, National Taiwan University College of Law; former President, Asian Law and Economics Association. S.J.D., Stanford Law School.

Wei Zhang: Assistant Professor, Singapore Management University. Ph.D. in Jurisprudence and Social Policy, UC Berkeley School of Law.

Tze-Shiou Chien: Research Professor, Institutum Iurisprudentiae, Academia Sinica; Professor of Law, National Taiwan University College of Law. DCL, Georgetown University Law Center.

Shitong Qiao: Assistant Professor, Hong Kong University Faculty of Law; J.S.D., Yale Law School.

Ruoying Chen: Associate Professor, Peking University Law School. J.S.D., the University of Chicago Law School.

Ching-Ping Shao: Professor, National Taiwan University College of Law. J.S.D., UC Berkeley School of Law.

Acknowledgments

This book originated in the symposium held during the 2014 Asian Law and Economics Association Annual Meeting when two of us took leadership roles in the Association. We thank all participants of the conferences, especially the presenters, commentators, and chairs in each panel. The financial support from Taiwan's Ministry of Science and Technology, the College of Law at National Taiwan University, and several other organizations is greatly appreciated.

Introduction

YUN-CHIEN CHANG

This book explores the evolution of property, contract, tort, and business organization laws in China and Taiwan. Given the drastic changes in the two jurisdictions in recent decades, the book covers not only the current laws, but also how these laws evolved into their current forms. Moreover, this book does not merely restate black letter laws – it also offers economic analysis of the driving force behind the legal evolution and examines whether the legal changes are economically efficient.

Given China's dazzling economic development during the past three decades, few would question the importance of studying China, particularly the four basic legal fields that will shape the future of the Chinese regime and greatly affect the interests of foreign investors. But why Taiwan? To put China's legal changes in context, one has to find a proper benchmark. Hong Kong and Singapore are ruled by Chinese people, but their laws are fundamentally shaped by English common law, and they are both much smaller than Taiwan. Macao is in a similar situation, except that it has imported Portuguese law, which has hardly any influence on laws in China. By contrast, in the property, contract, and tort laws of China and Taiwan, the doctrinal structures are both civil law, whereas in business organization law, the US law is the main inspiration. Moreover, in many ways, private laws in China and Taiwan are heavily influenced by German jurisprudence, making the comparison even more meaningful. There is also strong evidence that Chinese scholars and legislature, in formulating these four areas of laws, widely consult laws and legal scholarship in Taiwan. Therefore, putting Taiwanese laws and Chinese laws in the same volume helps readers have a better understanding of the uniqueness (or the lack thereof) of Chinese laws. To put it boldly, the future transformation of Chinese law might resemble the evolution of Taiwanese law. Furthermore, Taiwan and China are culturally similar, so proponents of the "Chinese characteristics" theory (laid on the foundation of the Chinese, or Confucian, culture) would need to find support in Taiwanese law.[1] The Taiwan laws in this volume thus provide valuable information.

One goal of this volume is to offer a concise summary of black-letter private law in China and Taiwan. Chinese laws change fast. At the time of writing, the Property Law of 2007, the Labor Contract Law of 2007, and the Tortious Liability Law of 2009 are less than ten years old. The Contract Law of 1999 has not reached "adulthood" either. The Company Law of 1999 was recently amended in 2013. In addition, this volume covers new Judicial Interpretations in the fields that constantly reshape the legal landscape.[2] Private law in Taiwan has undergone a tumultuous fifteen-year span as well. The Taiwanese Civil Code, originally enacted in China in 1929, was infrequently amended during the first few decades of its implementation in Taiwan. The early revisions focus almost entirely on family law and succession law. Then, in 1999, the Book of Obligation in the Taiwanese Civil Code, which contains contract law and tort law, among others, underwent a major overhaul, as if to prepare the Civil Code for the new millennium. Between 2007 and 2010, the Book of Things in the Taiwanese Civil Code, which contains property law, was updated.[3] As one major vehicle for the capitalistic market in Taiwan, the Company Act has been revised on multiple occasions since its inception, most recently in 2015. This book, which gives an up-to-date overview of the relevant laws and judicial decisions, enables English readers to get a better grasp of the laws in China and Taiwan.

Another aim of this book is to unite a powerful and dominant legal analytical approach with important legal issues in China and Taiwan. Very few comparative law scholars or China experts see laws in China and Taiwan through the lens of law and economics. In his final book, *Why China Goes Capitalist*, which he co-authored with Ning Wang, Ronald Coase made a rare attempt to analyze the legal institution in China from an economic viewpoint. But Coase and Wang (2012)'s book does not explore the details of the law. In line with the law-and-economics paradigm, this book will offer insights into the general evolution of law, particularly the evolution of private law in China and Taiwan. Contributors use economic theories either to explain why a certain field evolved toward its current form or to evaluate whether a specific statutory stipulation or a judicial decision is economically efficient.

This book contains ten chapters, in addition to an Introduction and a Conclusion. The first two chapters are more theoretical in tone. Authored by Saul Levmore and Bruno Deffains respectively, they provide theoretical groundwork for the economic analysis offered in the eight following chapters. Levmore's chapter draws on the eight chapters as evidence both for and against his thesis. Deffains' theoretical framework for legal harmonization and transplantation offers insights into understanding the evolution of private and company laws in China and Taiwan. The eight application chapters will discuss one by one property, contract, tort, and company laws in China and Taiwan.

More specifically, in Chapter 1, Saul Levmore argues that legal evolution, and variety within and among legal systems, can sometimes be explained as the product of disparate strategies for solving social problems. A *concentration* strategy is one that focuses rights, responsibilities, or both on a single party in order to encourage that party to take precautions or otherwise solve a problem. In contrast, a *distribution* strategy is one that scatters incentives in order to encourage multiple parties to behave as a team. Within this framework comparative negligence gives an example of the latter and strict liability for defective products an example of the former. The concentration–distribution tension, or choice, is developed through examples from tort, contract, property, and corporate law in the United States, China, and Taiwan. With respect to complex social problems, contemporary law and politics often look to the government to be the problem solver, and government control can then be understood as an emerging concentration approach. In turn, in a kind of second step of problem solving, the government might assign tasks, through its lawmaking power, in either distributed or concentrated fashion. Emerging reactions to climate change and other large-scale problems can be expected to follow this pattern.

In Chapter 2, Bruno Deffains addresses the economics of harmonization and legal convergence. Harmonization obliges different national legislations not to be contradictory with regard to common aim. It seeks to coordinate legal systems by eliminating major differences and creating minimum requirements or standards. Unification, by contrast, refers to the substitution of multiple rules by a new legislation at a supranational level. Unlike unification, which contemplates the substitution of two or more legal systems with one single system, the harmonization of law seeks to promote coordination of different legal provisions or systems. From an economic perspective, convergence imposes a debate about two different questions: Should legal systems converge? And, if the answer is positive, how can convergence be obtained? This chapter begins with an economic evaluation of the benefits and limits of convergence (costs of legal fragmentation, natural and functional convergence, and institutional isomorphism). The chapter then goes on to analyze different ways to achieve convergence (imitation and herding behaviors, legal competition, legal transplant and coordination). The third part of the chapter considers the question of legal convergence when preferences are endogenous. When legal problems have solutions that can be ranked according to their efficiency and when the optimal solution is unique, unification occurs in the long run because all countries tend to choose the optimal rule. Legal preferences change in the same way that this optimal rule is the preferred rule in the long run.

Chapter 3, co-authored by Jing Leng and Wei Shen, describes international conventions (such as the "United Nations Convention on Contracts of International Sales of Goods," known as CISG) and local characteristics that shape the contours of Chinese contract law. Important topics, such as the distinction between default rules and mandatory rules, contract interpretation, and three types of remedies, are also included. Among other interesting dimensions of Chinese contract law, two features stand out. First, in contrast to other civil law countries, China prioritizes damages over specific performances. Second, administrative agencies have always been present in shaping (sometimes directly censoring) the contents of various contracts.

Chapter 4, penned by Wen-yeu Wang, reviews the inadequacy of the way in which the Taiwan Supreme Court and contract law scholars interpreted contract laws and contracts. In addition to several other matters, this chapter points out that several features of the system have persisted throughout the past decades and showed no signs of moving toward increased efficiency. First, while Taiwanese contract law covers both private and business contracts, the development of Taiwanese contract law, in terms of both its statute and case law, is heavily skewed in the direction of consumer contracts, while the legal development to accommodate the complexity of business contracts has been largely ignored. There is an overarching driving force of consumer protection that indiscriminately applies not only in consumer contracts but also in cases of business-to-business (B-to-B) transactions. The principal driving forces behind business transactions (B-to-B contracts), such as common industry practice and the nature of transactions, are seldom explored or considered in legal scholarship or in courts. Second, in the absence of any substantial modernization of Taiwanese contract law, the courts tend simply to resort to the mechanical application, by way of analogy, of the default rules contained in the Taiwan Civil Code without taking into consideration the true intentions of the parties and basic principles of contracts such as party autonomy. Such stoic interpretations and applications of the already outdated Civil Code make it impossible for Taiwanese contract law to be efficient in the face of the ever-evolving business landscape. This chapter critiques three important Taiwan Supreme Court cases to demonstrate the aforementioned points.

Chapter 5, contributed by Wei Zhang, delineates the enormous changes in Chinese tort law since the formal legal rules came into being in 1986. The most salient feature of the evolution of torts in China in the past three decades is the growth of a liability system moving predominantly in favor of tort victims. This feature, however, has eluded previous introductory works on Chinese tort law written in English. In addition to using the major civil statutes to demonstrate this point, this chapter also surveys the administrative laws and regulations as well as the judicial interpretations that also shape the contours of the Chinese tort law. An equal emphasis on the latter is another unique contribution of this chapter. After an overview of several aspects of tort law that shows an expansion of injurers' liabilities, this chapter assesses the efficiency implications of the evolution of tort law in China. Given the exceptionally low point at which the increment of victim protection in tort law started, the change of rules in China is, by and large, moving in the direction of cost internalization as required by efficiency. However, the potential improvement in efficiency is perhaps a by-product of the development of tort law in China. The motivation behind the rule change is more likely to be loss redistribution rather than efficiency upgrade.

Chapter 6, written by Tze-Shiou Chien, begins with a description of tort law in Taiwan, an integral part of the Civil Code of 1930. Liability for damages has been based on the fault principle. There are three basic categories of tort: infringement of rights, *contra bonos mores*, and violations of protective laws. Types of strict liabilities were added to the Civil Code in 1999. The Consumer Protection Law ushered in products liability in 1994. Insurance and other nontortious compensation institutions that affect tort law have also found their places in Taiwan. Courts, as the interpreter of the law, have played a significant role in the development of tort law in Taiwan, although not to the extent they have played in common law systems.

Chapter 6 offers a critical examination of this evolution of tort law in Taiwan, as articulated by the Taiwan Supreme Court, from an economic perspective – specifically the Coasean view, rather than the Pigovian or Posnerian views. Standard law and economics would characterize tort law as legal measures to deter injuring persons from engaging in activities that cannot be justified on the grounds of cost. The criterion for the liability for damages is the level of physical capacity to prevent accidents. This, however, is an *ex ante* regulatory measure. It does not fit with the idea of tort law as an *ex post* compensation mechanism. Chapter 6 sees tort law as a set of default rules which are *ex ante* agreed upon by the injuring persons and the injured persons to be applied *ex post* in the concrete cases of accidents. The injuring persons and the injured persons would make a deal agreeing on a set of fault-based liability rules to allocate the loss because the rules are beneficial to both the injuring persons and the injured persons. Whether the damage is foreseeable to the injuring persons is the key. The law as a norm must be recognized by the ruled. Liability for damages must be foreseeable to the injuring persons, otherwise tort law would lose its normativity and thus also its legitimacy. Based on the human nature of cognition, the foreseeability of damage depends upon the riskiness of activities in which the injuring persons engage. The more risky the activities are, the more likely the injuring persons will be liable for damage. The riskiness of activities, then, would depend upon the physical capacity to prevent accidents of the injuring persons. The less capable the injuring persons are, the more risky the activities in which they engage. As a result, the less capable the injuring persons are, the more likely they would be at fault and then liable for the damage. In the fault principle, there exists a built-in incentive to improve the physical capacity to prevent accidents because this would increase the scope of activities that the injuring persons may engage in without being held liable for damage.

Chapter 7, authored by Shitong Qiao, engages the debate on the nature of property rights through the lens of Chinese property law, real estate law in particular. Qiao engages the important debate on whether property rights are better characterized as a bundle of rights or *in rem* rights. Traditionally, the *in rem* nature of property was widely recognized, at least since Blackstone. Later, however, legal realists succeeded in promoting a rival conception – property as a bundle of rights. Coase (1960) reinforces the realist picture by conceiving of property as a list of particularized use rights. Merrill and Smith (2001; 2012) push back the realist conception and contend that property rights are *in rem*. Qiao's chapter moves the ball forward by engaging this debate in the context of a huge developing country – China.

Set against the backdrop of Chinese land reform, Chapter 7 argues that the path of Chinese land reform reflects the "bundle of rights" picture rather than the *in rem*ness picture of property rights. The two main achievements of Chinese land reform, i.e., the establishment of transferrable land use rights in the urban area and the establishment of the household responsibility system in the rural area, this chapter argues, are examples of the "stick by stick" approach (in property jargon, a bundle of rights and a bundle of sticks are interchangeable). This chapter develops its argument by reviewing the main property laws and policies introduced over the past three decades. The basic contours of the Chinese property system are thus revealed.

In Chapter 8, I first give an overview of the several types of limited property rights allowed by the Taiwan Civil Code and provide statistics as to how often property owners in Taiwan utilize these forms. The Book of Things in the Taiwan Civil Code was overhauled between 2007 and 2010. Chang coded the amendments and found: (1) 97 percent of the proposals by the taskforce (composed of property scholars and judges) were accepted verbatim by the legislature and (2) property laws in Japan, Germany, and Switzerland heavily influenced this round of amendments. The unconventional story behind the legal changes is that scholars and judges are the "interest group" that drives these amendments. The business world is generally uninterested in changing the abstract Taiwan Civil Code. Generally speaking, the new law, as proposed by this interest group, is more efficient than the old law. For instance, the new law decreases information costs for third parties in several respects. The findings also have implications for the debate regarding the evolution of property rights and the long-term efficiency of the common law versus statutes.

Chapter 9, written by Ruoying Chen, provides an overview of a few of the major issues in business organization laws in China, consisting of four principal topics: (1) the broad economic and political background of the legislative history of the core body of business organization laws, i.e. company law, which has closely tracked the steps of, and been largely driven by, the reform of state-owned enterprises; (2) issues relating to the limited liability company, such as piercing the corporate veil and the recent abolition of the statutory minimal registered capital; (3) corporate governance issues, especially those unique to China, such as shareholder supremacy driven by protection of state-owned assets; and (4) duties of corporate officers, such as the judicial and regulatory implementation of the duty of care and shareholders' derivative lawsuits. Each section provides a critical introduction to the legal framework and current legal issues, and also aims to highlight recent research development. With respect to rules and the legal framework, special attention is paid to judicial practice as well as regulatory activities. Meanwhile, the broader economic, political, and social background is taken into account in an attempt to shed light on the institutional origins of legal rules and the potential driving force for the implementation of law, which is indispensable to understanding both law in action and its future development. Unlike the existing literature on corporate law in China, this chapter incorporates recent statistical studies of judicial practice in this field, in addition to theoretical inquiries in the traditional fashion. These social science studies demonstrate that the corporate law in action in China leaves many questions that are not yet well addressed by traditional theoretical inquiries.

Chapter 10, contributed by Ching-Ping Shao, argues that the Taiwan Company Law adopts a blockholder-centric model. This approach is evident in both the board hegemony rule incorporated in 2001 and the shareholders' right of proposal transplanted in 2005. This chapter focuses on the underlying reasons for the evolution of the juridical-person shareholder rule and the mandatory cumulative voting rule, both rarely seen in comparative corporate governance nowadays. As concentrated ownership structures are ubiquitous in most jurisdictions, the Taiwanese experience imparts valuable lessons for scholars and policy makers alike. More specifically, Chapter 10 first observes that in the corporate governance world, Taiwan is an outlier when it comes to the selection method for the board of directors. According to the Taiwan Company Law of 1946, a juridical-person shareholder of a company could skip elections in shareholder meetings and designate its representatives to serve as directors. The number of directors that the juridical-person shareholder can single-handedly appoint is proportionate with its shareholding with respect to the total outstanding shares of the company. The Taiwan Company Law of 1966 abolished the designation power of juridical-person shareholders and adopted mandatory cumulative voting. Furthermore, juridical-person shareholders can send natural-person representatives to participate in elections and replace their representative directors at will. These new rules maintain the overwhelming influence of juridical-person shareholders. While the cumulative voting rule was changed from a mandatory rule to a default rule in 2001, it remained in practice a sticky default. This permissive form of rule did not last long. The Taiwan Company Law of 2011 revived mandatory cumulative voting.

In the concluding chapter, Wei Shen and Wen-yeu Wang identify the commonalities and differences in Chinese and Taiwanese laws and flush out the meaning and implication of the Chinese characteristic theories. The comparative setting is a very interesting tool in understanding why two jurisdictions that share the same origins and cultural backgrounds are moving into two diverging directions.

References

Chang, Yun-chien. 2012. Property Law with Chinese Characteristics: An Economic and Comparative Analysis. *Brigham-Kanner Property Rights Conference Journal* 1:345–372.

Chang, Yun-chien, Weitseng Chen, and Ying Chieh Wu. 2016. *Property and Trust Law in Taiwan*. Alphen aan den Rijn: Wolters Kluwer.

Chen, Lei. 2010. Private Property with Chinese Characteristics: A Critical Analysis of the Chinese Law on Property of 2007. *European Review of Private Law* 5:983–1004.

Coase, Ronald H. 1960. The Problem of Social Cost. *Journal of Law & Economics* 3:1–69.

Coase, Ronald H., and Ning Wang. 2012. *How China Became Capitalist*. New York, NY: Palgrave Macmillan.

Huang, Yasheng. 2008. *Capitalism with Chinese Characteristics: Entrepreneurship and the State*. Cambridge: Cambridge University Press.

Kennedy, David, and Joseph E. Stiglitz, eds. 2013. *Law and Economics with Chinese Characteristics: Institutions for Promoting Development in the Twenty-First Century*. Oxford: Oxford University Press.

Li, Xiang, and Jigang Jin. 2014. *Concise Chinese Tort Laws*. Berlin: Springer.

Ling, Bing. 2002. *Contract Law in China*. Hong Kong: Sweet & Maxwell Asia.

Liu, Chengwei. 2008. *Chinese Company and Securities Law: Investment Vehicles, Mergers and Acquisitions and Corporate Finance in China.* Alphen aan den Rijn: Wolters Kluwer.

Merrill, Thomas W., and Henry E. Smith. 2001. What Happened to Property in Law and Economics? *Yale Law Journal* 111:357–398.

2012. Making Coasean Property More Coasean. *Journal of Law and Economics* 54(4):S77–S104.

Shi, Chenxia. 2012. *The Political Determinants of Corporate Governance in China.* New York, NY: Routledge.

Sommers, Amy L., and Kara L. Phillips. 2012. *Real Property Law in China: A Guide to Foreign Investment.* Chicago, IL: American Bar Association.

Stein, Gregory M. 2012. *Modern Chinese Real Estate Law: Property Development in an Evolving Legal System.* Farnham: Ashgate.

Wang, JiangYu. 2014. *Company Law in China: Regulation of Business Organizations in a Socialist Market Economy.* Northampton, MA: Edward Elgar.

Notes

1 Scholars are fond of using "Chinese characteristics" in the titles of their works, though not always endorsing the theory that social phenomena or laws in China are unique and have to be so. See, for instance, Chang (2012), Chen (2010), and Huang (2008). Another recent book, *Law and Economics with Chinese Characteristics: Institutions for Promoting Development in the Twenty-First Century*, edited by David Kennedy and Nobel laureate Joseph E. Stiglitz (2013), contains critical reflection on the general theory of law and development as applied to China

2 For books written in English on Chinese private laws, see, e.g., Ling (2002), Stein (2012), Sommers and Phillips (2012), and Li and Jin (2014). For books written in English on Chinese company laws, see, e.g., Liu (2008), Shi (2012), and Wang (2014).

3 For writings in English on Taiwanese private laws, see, e.g., Chang, Chen, and Wu (2016).

PART I

Foundation

1 Concentrated and Distributed Law

Observations on Legal Evolution in China and Taiwan

SAUL LEVMORE

1 Concentration and Distribution Strategies in Law

There are several ways to compare law across jurisdictions – and many of these can be associated with theories about the evolution of law. Laws can be imitated or transplanted (Watson 1993); they can be driven by function and thus converge at notable points (Levmore 1987); they can be driven out if economically inefficient; and they can be the product of power structures, including interest group pressures (Levmore 2002). The theories undergirding these possibilities are usually conceived on a grand scale, though there are implications for specific legal rules. There is room, however, for theories that operate on a more modest scale and that share the stage with other influences on legal evolution. One such theory, or subject matter, concerns harmonization, or the tendency of legal systems to converge on a rule where doing so economizes on transaction costs among trading partners. Just as neighboring states might agree on a currency, so too they might agree or naturally develop similar or even identical commercial laws in order to encourage trade or, more defensively, in order not to lose ground to other jurisdictions (Levmore 2013a). In some cases, jurisdictions might strategically delay or refuse to harmonize, in the hope and expectation that other jurisdictions will do the work associated with harmonizing change. These and other aspects of harmonization are discussed in Chapter 2. Still, harmonization is surely part of the evolutionary story, albeit more so with respect to commercial law than other areas of law or even entire legal systems with little cross-border trade or where the strategy is to occupy a niche.

Another, perhaps unrecognized and somewhat limited, theory begins with alternative strategies for overcoming collective action and other problems where several parties could take precautions or otherwise solve a problem that might, at least in general terms, have been predicted. One can begin with a highway accident involving more than one vehicle, or a commercial law dispute between the original owner of stolen property and its later, "good-faith," purchaser, but inasmuch as much of the literature on legal evolution concerns property rights, the discussion here begins with a simple example from property law, familiar to all lawyers: the management of a resource such as water, fossil fuels, arable land, or timber. The social problem, that is, the task for law, is the efficient management of the resource, though, of course, a minor manifestation of this problem might come to court when two parties clash over its use. Here, conventional property rights are easily and commonly understood as an efficiency-promoting tool. The owner of a fee simple interest, for example, is in a position to invest in the property in a manner that is consistent with the best, or wealth-maximizing, long-run use of the property. Ownership – backed by a legal system and its rules against theft and trespass – is the opposite of the tragedy of the commons, with its well-known collective action problems among actors who look out for themselves and have little reason to help achieve the socially desirable result. Property ownership, or "strong" property rights, can therefore be thought of as an illustration of a *concentration* strategy; rights or responsibilities (or both) are concentrated by law in the hands of a single decision-maker. With such concentration, law focuses its incentives on one well-situated party. There are, to be sure, alternative explanations of strong property rights, and reasons to think that some strong property rights reflect interest group pressure rather than efficiency concerns, but it is likely that many concentrations of rights and responsibilities evolved because of their efficiency.

In sharp contrast, the emergence and growth of comparative negligence in tort law can be understood as an illustration of a *distribution* strategy within legal systems. In these settings, rather than concentrating on a single player, law spreads its threat of liability, or other remedy, on multiple parties in order to encourage socially desirable behavior through what amounts to a kind of teamwork. In the case of comparative negligence, post-accident accountability makes good on these threats of liability, so that parties who can contribute to the socially desirable outcome have reason, in advance, to behave well. In principle, this tension or choice between concentration and distribution – two strategies with strong law-and-economics foundations – depends on the making of some judgment about the relative competence of legal institutions and private parties to gather information and determine the details of efficient precaution taking. The less information available to lawmakers in advance, and the fewer the contractual connections among parties, the more attractive it will be to deploy comparative negligence, or another rule reflecting distributed responsibility with retrospective accounting.

The present chapter advances two points. First, it introduces this tension between concentrated and distributed strategies as a tool for understanding the evolution of law in many subject areas and in many parts of the world. Nearly every claim in the preceding paragraphs is controversial, but a modest form of the concentration–distribution thesis presented here should be easy to accept as an explanation of one influence on the evolution of law. The aim here is to set forth and illustrate such an explanation. Second, and relatedly, it emphasizes the increased reliance on governments as problem solvers and puts this evolutionary phenomenon in a new light. As governments take responsibility for such things as consumer safety, highway accidents, industrial innovation, and even climate change, concentration has increased in importance. Law can be understood as emerging to solve problems that were previously left to the private sphere or simply regarded as beyond the competence of law. This emergence, or advance, can be attributed to improvements in the technology for gathering and dissecting information. Concentration and distribution are both sensible strategies, and it is no surprise – although it is a source of some confusion – to see that law often uses both. Most important, although problem solving is increasingly concentrated in the hands of government, this government will often use its lawmaking power to allocate responsibilities in something approaching, or reminiscent of, a distributed fashion. These points are applicable to lawmaking in general, but in the present chapter they are illustrated with references to the evolution of law in China and in Taiwan.

2 Tort Law

Tort law offers the most straightforward example of the evolutionary tension between the concentration and distribution strategies. In one legal system after another, we observe the emergence of comparative negligence, which is a means of allocating responsibility among multiple parties that could have solved a social problem. The problem is one that could be solved through *concentration*, by designating a single party, sometimes known as a least-cost-avoider, but is instead normally and increasingly solved with a multi-party *distribution* strategy.

Consider a simple illustration in which an automobile, A, and a bus, B, crash in a manner that injures a pedestrian, P, and cause 100 in damages. Ignore the damages sustained by the bus and automobile or imagine that they nearly crashed, and to avoid one another, they swerved and hit the pedestrian. Imagine further that A could have avoided the accident at a cost of 30, perhaps by greatly reducing its speed; B could alone have prevented the accident at a cost of 20; and the two together could have avoided the accident by spending 10 and 5, respectively. Perhaps if the automobile had gone somewhat slower and the bus had used highly visible lights, then the accident would have been avoided through this sort of joint care at a total cost of 15.

There are a great many ways for law to encourage the parties to avoid the 100 loss, or accident, suffered by P. Buses involved in pedestrian accidents could be held strictly liable, in this case for the full 100 loss suffered by P. The idea behind such a liability rule, which could be defended as a least-cost-avoider rule, might be that pedestrians are often embarking or disembarking from buses, or perhaps bus drivers are to be viewed as professionals whose experience makes them good candidates to be the focal points of tort law designed to reduce injuries. Faced with this liability rule, which obviously reflects a concentration strategy, we might expect the bus in the present example to slow down, which is to say spend 20. If the bus driver, or owner, had some means of communicating with the driver of the automobile, the bus might pay the automobile driver 12 to slow down (at a cost of 10) and then the bus would have spent 5, all to solve the problem at a cost lower than 20. But this sort of bargain, inspired by the Coase Theorem, seems difficult and unlikely, inasmuch as it is difficult to identify and then communicate with the driver of a car one might crash into in the future.

Note that lawmakers might err and follow the concentration strategy by assigning full liability to the driver of the car, A, rather than to B. It is an apparent error because in this case B's precaution costs are lower than A's though, of course, still greater than those comprising the joint care solution in which A and B together avoid the accident. It is easy to imagine that this case is representative of the precaution costs generally faced by automobiles and buses. On the other hand, it might be that in other cases automobiles can more easily avoid buses.

Alernatively, perhaps if liability were placed on automobiles, their owners would be more likely to take mass transit or to refrain from buying vehicles in the first place. Once the activity of automobile driving is taken into account, it could well be that a concentration strategy of the sort described here is socially efficient.

It must be apparent that there is an alternative strategy to follow here in the form of liability according to comparative fault. It is a prototypical distribution strategy and is, of course, commonly used in the event of a multi-party traffic accident. Typically, responsibility is allocated by inquiring into the comparative negligence of the driver of the car, of the bus, and even the pedestrian, whom we previously assumed to be passive, nonnegligent, and the only injured party. Comparative negligence calculations are prepared, of course, to relax all three assumptions. It is useful to pay attention to the variety of rules available to the distribution strategist. A good starting point is to imagine situations in which the legal authorities know all the precaution costs faced by the parties. Imagine, for example, perfect information about bus and car operations, and video footage of the roadways. In such a setting the most straightforward thing for law to do would be to inform the driver of the automobile that he must spend 10 (in the manner known to be part of the low-cost precaution solution) and the driver of the bus that she must spend 5, again in the specific manner known to the lawmaker either before or after the accident. The idea that the lawmaker might have this capacity before the accident will seem like a bit of science fiction, though there are cases where law can discern such joint-precaution strategies in advance. But following an injury to P, it is easy to imagine a lawsuit in which P brings both A and B to court. Note that we can set aside the evolution of contributory-to-comparative negligence because the example involves a plaintiff who has done absolutely nothing wrong.

There is an interesting pair of nested evolutionary questions associated with the present example. If the law evolves to a comparative negligence, or distributed, approach with respect to such cases, how exactly should this comparative negligence be executed? If the socially desirable result is to avoid the accident illustrated here by expenditures of 10 (by A) and 5 (by B), then what should be the allocation of legal (tort) liability if neither party takes the desirable precaution? One intuition is to look at the shortfall in inputs: A's shortfall is twice B's, 10 compared to 5, so A will be made to pay twice as much as B. A pays

67, while B pays 33 under this view, and this is likely the most common understanding of comparative negligence. An opposite intuition is that B is more reprehensible, for B took no precautions at all, even though so little was required of B. The idea might be that one who fails to lift a finger is more at fault than one who fails to make a very large expenditure, albeit one that is socially desirable in cost–benefit terms. In the United States, jury instructions ask that liability be allocated according to the relative fault of the parties, and this gives some latitude for an interpretation of culpability. Perhaps it is B who should pay 67 out of the 100 in damages suffered by P. Alternatively, comparative negligence could focus on relative causation rather than relative fault, or on some combination of the two. The bus has more mass than the automobile and a fact-finder might reason that as between the culpable, or negligent, parties, B is likely to have been the more significant cause of the result. Again, B would pay a larger share.

At first blush, a law-and-economics approach would seem to require the first of these three approaches. After all, the idea is to get A to spend 10. If the injury were 20, rather than 100, and A need only pay one-third, as under the second approach, then A might prefer to be liable than to take the proper precautions – even though the injury of 20 can be prevented by precautions totaling 15 in cost.

The preceding reaction is short-sighted. B, after all, will have the incentive to spend 5 (to avoid liability of two-thirds of 20) in order to do B's share of the cooperative solution; if B spends 5, B will presumably be found not negligent and then A will (or should) pay the entire 20, or 100 (depending on which example of P's damages is on the table). By reasoning backward, then, A can see that he had better spend 10 or he will be left to pay the entire loss, because B will surely take the pro-social precaution. Following this logic, there is the surprising conclusion that it does not much matter how law carries out the comparative negligence process. As long as at least one wrongdoer is immediately encouraged to take the socially correct precaution, the others will fall into line. As an evolutionary matter we might expect to find any of these rules, because every one of them will do the job. In the language of comparative law as well as evolutionary theory, we expect convergence, or uniformity, where there is a functional imperative. But where a range of rules will do, or where the rule does not matter from a functional, or efficiency, perspective, variety might be found. Instead of being puzzled by the obscure and often incomprehensible jury instructions offered by state law in the United States, one might instead marvel that the fact-finder is left to do as it likes just where it does not really matter what rules it uses, functionally speaking. The trick is simply to have every party think that socially cooperative behavior on its part is a good idea, because it will pay some fraction if others are also at fault, and it will pay a great deal if others are later found not to be at fault. Within a range, almost any version of comparative negligence will work and, sure enough, we do not find many legal systems specifying the operational details. In sum, the distribution strategy is widely and increasingly followed, but the details of distribution across the relevant parties do not converge.

These points are borne out in Chinese and Taiwanese law, as Chapters 5 and 6 will show. Thus, there is a *res ipsa* presumption against a motorist in Chinese law, unless the accident is with another motorist. There is also a comparative negligence rule for medical malpractice (because other health care providers as well as patients can contribute to a loss), but it exempts, or excludes, a provider who can show that he or she took appropriate precautions while the patient did not comply with the requirements of the treatment provided. These and other rules can be understood as accommodations to fact-finding problems – but ones that are well within the range where any version of comparative negligence encourages identical and efficient outcomes. Somewhat similarly, Taiwanese law, not unlike American law, piggybacks on criminal violations to generate civil liability. One who violates a criminal statute is regarded as per se negligent when it comes to a tort suit. Chien is critical of this quick and easy use of what might be a casual "conviction," but it might economize on fact-finding costs and, in any event, is not inconsistent with a distribution strategy.

And then there are other areas of tort law where the concentration strategy has dominated. The best known is products liability law where strict liability for defective products, in effect an insurance scheme on top of one designed to deter fault, focuses liability on the manufacturer of most products. A version of this rule has been found in most American jurisdictions for some time, and it is also found in many other jurisdictions around the world. Among the reasons to think that such liability reflects a concentration strategy is that the manufacturer is in a good position to contract with other parties who may be responsible for the defect. Thus, an automobile manufacturer may really be an assembler, incorporating tires, wheels, brakes, airbags, and many other parts that originate from disparate sources. The vehicle is then transported to a dealer where some adjustments and add-ons might be made and incorporated. Nevertheless, a consumer experiencing a personal injury, traceable to some defect in the vehicle, can collect from the manufacturer. Tort law thus provides a super-warranty, and the manufacturer has an incentive to take or contract for efficient injury-reducing precautions.

This concentration approach is especially notable in evolving Chinese law, as is apparent in Chapter 5. The 1993 Product Quality Law holds producers and sellers liable for "defective" products – meaning those that are unreasonably dangerous or simply do not conform to regulatory or industry standards. There is also an obligation to recall defective products. Taiwanese law, by contrast, appears to work with presumptions rather than strict liability (in the sense that the term is used in US law); the manufacturer can escape liability by showing that it exercised reasonable care. The rule is thus one of negligence, but with the burden of proof on the manufacturer rather than the plaintiff (Taiwan Civil Code, Art. 191-1).

The evolution in this area toward a concentrated solution is slightly imperfect, but in ways that emphasize the theme advanced here. First, the concentration strategy would be even more obvious if the injured party could sue the manufacturer and could *not* collect from the dealer or another party. Instead, the American evolutionary path, at least, traveled through a requirement of privity – a doctrine limiting the consumer to suit against the party with whom he had a direct contractual relationship – before settling on the manufacturer. Inasmuch as the consumer can sue the manufacturer or the dealer (from whom he purchased the automobile, for example), there is something just short of a concentration strategy at play. In fact, the consumer has no reason to sue the dealer and, in any event, the dealer and manufacturer are close contractual partners who can easily allocate precaution-taking tasks between them. Moreover, the penultimate evolutionary step requiring privity (and thus precluding suit against the manufacturer or distant vendor, however negligent) can also be thought of as reflecting the concentration strategy. Rather than having the injured party sue the dealer, manufacturer, wheel-maker, and so forth, in the hope of finding one culpable party or finding that law would spread liability across these parties in proportion to their respective fault, litigation, and responsibility are focused (concentrated) on one party. Modern products liability law simply relocated the focal point from the dealer to the manufacturer, but the strategy of concentrating responsibility was already in place. One way to understand the growth of product liability law in jurisdictions that had the privity constraint is that there was eventual convergence, or concentration, on a particular problem solver.

It is noteworthy that even where concentration is the strategy of choice, as in modern product liability law, it gives way to, or is refined by, distributed solutions in subfields. For example, the seller of used goods is often relieved of strict liability and, indeed, in just such situations comparative negligence is often the rule. A person injured by a defect that could have arisen long after manufacture is likely to sue the manufacturer, used goods dealer, occasional repair person, and anyone else likely to be incorporated into a comparative negligence lawsuit. Essentially, following the injury, courts will need to determine the precautions that all these parties should have taken.

On the other hand, the evolutionary theory offered here suggests that we might expect a concentration strategy to arise where distribution had previously been the rule. One of many such examples is found in Chapter 5, where we learn that Chinese law assigns responsibility for contaminated blood to the hospital in which it is transfused to the injured patient. More generally, Chinese law now places residual liability on hospitals, presumably for injuries arising out of apparent malpractice. Of course, it remains to be seen how this innovation will be applied, and whether it will obviate the need or inclination of families (on occasion) to storm a hospital and demand compensation when a loved one seems to have died unnecessarily. Hospitals are another well-situated problem solver, much like manufacturers, and they, too, have contractual connections with other possible wrongdoers as well as precaution-takers. Observers of American law will recognize the opportunity; some jurisdictions in the United States have imposed strict liability on blood banks regardless of whether the technology was already available to screen for the problem that proved injurious.

It is apparent, at least with the power of *ex post* rationalization, why tort law has chosen, or evolved, a distribution strategy in some cases and a concentration strategy in others. Concentration is most appealing when there is a party that can direct others to take precautions in its place, or where the party itself will do the job. The manufacturer is likely to know or be able to discover various parties' precaution costs –

and to be superior to any court in this regard. In contrast, the automobile, bus, and pedestrian in the earlier example have no special information about one another's precaution costs and no ability to bargain with one another in advance of the accident. We might wonder whether tort law would choose a concentrated or distributed approach if it were required to choose one for all of tort law. But the evolution of tort law has not been constrained in this way. No single feature emerged across all tort law environments. Apparently, there is enough doctrinal and contextual flexibility for law to deploy a concentration strategy in products liability law and a distribution strategy – indeed, instructions of various kinds but all captured by the comparative negligence label – in most other settings.

It is unlikely that this choice, or tension, between concentration and distribution will be resolved in favor of one or the other strategy. As a matter of moral intuitions, both strategies are attractive and there is no reason to think that one will completely displace the other. From the perspective of efficiency, it seems that where transaction costs are high and there is but modest knowledge in the hands of the *ex post* fact-finder, a scattered distribution of liability is more attractive. Ideally, each party knows whether it is part of the joint care solution and it knows that if it does its part in this sort of teamwork, it will, *ex post*, avoid liability, with the remaining liability shared only by those who did not do their part in the efficient joint care solution. On the other hand, the more the parties can bargain, and the more the fact-finder will have trouble ascertaining the joint care solution even *ex post*, the more it might make sense to assign one party as the best problem solver, with the identity of this party known in advance, and force that party to take the precaution (or not) and to contract out for teammates. There is every reason to think that both situations, or extremes, will continue to be found and that law will have no reason to choose decisively between the two strategies. If so, there will be evolution toward a mix of concentrated and distributed responsibilities.

3 Contract and Property Law

For the most part, and across a variety of legal systems, the assignment of rights and responsibilities in contract and property law reflects a concentration strategy. In property law there is often a starting point of the single owner. In many economies this is an individual, though overtime law recognizes various forms of collective ownership without quite returning to the commons of prehistory. But in some economies the single owner is the state and this too, as emphasized below, can be conceived as a concentration strategy. The evolution of this concentration strategy, culminating in fee simple ownership, is an important landmark in the literature on the evolution of property rights.

The owner of a fee simple property right is heralded by the law-and-economics literature as in a good position to contract or assign responsibilities and benefits in a way that maximizes value. Legal assignment followed by bargaining (and its enforcement) for further or corrective assignment is the strategy. It is a pattern that is also found in riparian rights, intellectual property's use of monopolies, and elsewhere. There are exceptions, but the pattern and evolution of these exceptions go in both directions. An owner controlling a large tract that was once a tribal commons can be seen as an intermediate step in an evolutionary process that might one day produce a kind of return to the commons in the form of a state-protected park occupying the site. More commonly, the evolutionary process will bring about many small parcels, condominiums, various options, drilling rights, rentals, and much more. All these might be understood as evolutionary steps beyond the simple concentration strategy, whether fueled by efficiency pressures, by the desire to extract taxes, or by both. Inasmuch as this is an important and awkward step in the argument about concentration and distribution, it is useful to dwell on it.

Consider first the single owner of a tract of land who decides to build a large structure. It is easy to marvel at the advantages of single ownership; the concentration of rights and responsibilities encourages the efficient development of the property. The single owner will consider potential conflicts among users of the building. The building might be fashioned as a residential structure, or perhaps some floors will be residential while others will be designed for retailers or for office space. But it is unlikely that a noisy workshop will be located adjacent to residential space. Similarly, elevators and structural components will be designed to maximize the value of the building as a whole. A concentrated strategy of ownership is consistent with this aim and perhaps the easiest way to achieve it. But once the building is up and running, it is plausible that agency costs make ownership of individual units more desirable than allowing them to be rented. The original owner might offer condominiums or other ownership interests that provide superior incentives for the ongoing residents or users of the building. To be sure, this distribution of rights and responsibilities is a product of private contract and not mandated by law, but the devolution of concentration to distribution is significant. Moreover, law sometimes, if not often, subtly encourages or discourages distribution by contract. Real property is rarely infinitely divisible and alienable; tax law makes some legal structures more or less desirable; government spending and regulation encourage large holdings in some spheres and smaller ones in others. The more rights and obligations are distributed *because* of law, whether directly or through private arrangements, the more we can think of evolutionary patterns in concentration–distribution terms. A further elaboration of the present example illustrates the common sense of this approach. Imagine that the owner of a large residential or commercial building reacts to a rent control statute by subdividing ownership interests and creating condominium (or other) owners where there had been tenants. In such a case it would be misleading to think of the evolution from concentration to distribution as having occurred through private arrangements rather than through law.

The preceding example offers an opportunity to emphasize the recurring problem, or reality, of competing theories of the evolution of property rights. The optimistic theory is that the evolutionary path traces or even enables efficient transformations. The owner of a tract of land can farm it efficiently, while one of many people living in a commons can never be sure that he will reap what he sows. No wonder private ownership evolved, goes the argument. In contrast, it is possible that the emergence of ownership in some settings has little to do with efficiency, and could turn out to be desirable or undesirable. Property rights, especially of the concentrated kind, might derive from violence, from an appeal by an interest group to a ruler who monopolizes violence, or simply from the ruler's desire to extract taxes or other rents. In this regard, the Chinese experience is especially noteworthy because of the importance of local governments. Chapter 7, on Chinese property law, convincingly argues that local governments in China – once the driving force toward stronger property rights – now often oppose concentration because further concentration reduces their influence over the terms and frequency of transfer of land from agricultural to other uses.

Before turning to contract law it is useful to concede that the ideas of concentration and distribution in property are relative. As legal systems evolve, or perhaps and more simply as populations become more dense, even the simplest form of concentrated ownership is best understood as a bundle of rights – where plenty of rights are missing from the bundle and allocated elsewhere. The owner of a fee simple property interest cannot stop an airline from flying far overhead; the owner must pay taxes to the government for various collective goods; the owner is subject to nuisance and liability suits from neighbors; and zoning and other laws might limit the owner's uses of the property. A skeptic might say that there is no concentration strategy at work and that different legal systems simply distribute rights and responsibilities differently. There is even room for the argument that property law often encourages joint care, and in these cases abandons the concentration strategy. For example, Chapter 8 shows that Taiwanese property law encourages an owner to object in timely fashion when an intruder builds on his land; better teamwork is rewarded with a property rule rather than mere damages. Correspondingly, where there has been an unintentional trespass, Taiwanese courts have discretion to switch to a liability rule. This skeptical view regarding the strength of the concentration strategy in property law is not inconsistent with the evolutionary story advanced here. In any event, it is most useful to evaluate property rights in relative terms, in which case it is sensible to think of some as more concentrated than others. To be sure, the evolutionary path has not been a simple story of triumph of the concentration strategy, as evidenced by the many developments in law have caused the evolutionary path to wind back toward the commons.

These two stories about the evolution of law do not carry over easily to contract law, where nothing neatly matches the attraction of fee simple ownership or the inclination of interest groups (which are likely to find most contract doctrines helpful in some cases but costly in others). As such, the prevalence of the concentration strategy in contract law is notable. The starting point in contract law is the observation that the simplest, and therefore the most common, contracts find parties allocating rights and responsibilities to one or the other. But the more interesting feature of contract law from an evolutionary perspective is that even when faced with difficult disputes, courts and legislatures are strongly inclined to "winner-takes-all" rather than distributed results. There are exceptions, of course, but a few examples of the concentration strategy will be illustrative.

As a first example, consider a mainstay of the literature on comparative law, the "good-faith" purchaser of stolen property, where the thief is unavailable. Almost all legal systems choose the original owner *or* the purchaser as the winner, and very few divide the item (or loss) between the two, even though it is plain that both can take precautions and that joint care is almost surely optimal. It is a concentrated approach rather than a case-by-case *ex post* evaluation of precaution taking. Even the occasional system that splits the loss does so in an *ex ante* property rights fashion, with no *ex post* evaluation.

Other examples abound. The very concepts of consideration (in some legal systems), specific performance, mistake (and even mutual mistake), and duress are features of contract law that ought to be associated with the concentration strategy. These doctrines generally make one party bear responsibility where law might have distributed responsibility after the fact in order to encourage dual precaution taking. For example, a party that is awarded specific performance is essentially awarded a property right. And one that loses a case because a court finds that there was no consideration, and therefore no enforceable contract, essentially is without a right in some legal systems, though in others parties can share a loss. In any event, sharing can also occur in the shadow of contract law by way of restitution, which often gives partial recovery and thus can be seen as carrying out something of a distribution strategy. Within contract law there certainly are contexts, or areas, like requirements contracts and other "relational contracts," where law-and-economics scholars have encouraged judges to follow a distribution strategy because teamwork seems required to achieve the best result. By and large law has rejected these suggestions and stayed the course with a single winner, or concentration approach.

It is interesting that some of the contested areas of Chinese contract law are at this margin where law can evolve to take modest distributionist steps in order to encourage teamwork. Anticipatory breach is one such area, and the two legal systems, as discussed in Chapters 3 and 4, appear to be on separate evolutionary paths in this respect. Note that by always requiring buyers to inspect goods upon receipt, Chinese law takes another (if unusual) step toward a distribution strategy, because the buyer is required to take a precaution for which it is well-suited.

Where contracts and commercial law grapple with collective action problems with collective and, perhaps we might say, distributed remedies, the logic is plain and there are "exceptions" or highlights with strong concentration schemes. Consider, for example, the law of bankruptcy and, in its shadow, that of security interests. Bankruptcy law is anything but a concentrated system of responsibility – unless we think of the bankruptcy trustee that way – but it would be difficult to use a concentration strategy without making great sacrifices in efficiency. The well-known idea reflected in that area of law, after all, is to promise equal treatment to creditors so that they do not prematurely rush to disassemble the insolvent debtor, when the debtor might be worth more to the collective as a going concern. Against the background of the proportional sharing rule, or distributed rights, however, is priority for secured creditors. It is very rare for several creditor-claimants to real estate, or to a piece of equipment, to share. They take a security interest, or concentrated focal point, at the outset, and then prevail, at least against most creditors who could have easily learned of the security interest. Of course, securitization and a thick market in these interests allows a kind of distribution in modern markets, though it may be fairer to say that there is distribution of some rights and outsourcing, in very concentrated fashion, of the work or responsibilities of monitoring the debtor and the original transaction. I will return to this below with a brief discussion of the evolution of corporate law.

It is unimportant for the larger thesis here whether we think of contract law as guided by a concentration strategy, with some exceptions that can be rationalized, or simply as reflecting a mix and tension between the two strategies. The central thesis is that the evolution of law is often about these opposing pulls, and I am not making a claim about the triumph of one of the other in tort, contract, or other law. In the remainder of this chapter, I do make just such a claim about a class of complex problems, but thus far the argument is about the choice between the two strategies with occasional suggestions about the forces that favor one or the other strategy. Products liability as opposed to comparative fault in tort law presents as good an example as any of the tension and the forces that seem likely to push evolution in one direction or the other. The forays into contract and property law are meant to show that the concentration and distribution strategies are hardly limited to tort law.

Prior to introducing the idea of governments as the "new" concentrated problem solvers, it is worthwhile to note another area of law where private arrangements, rather than law itself, reflect the concentration–distribution trade-off. The area is that of corporate law and, unsurprisingly, it will be apparent that the private arrangements enabled or tolerated by corporate law do not come about in a vacuum but are associated with evolutionary steps in law. This pattern was introduced in the earlier discussion of property law and it repeats here.

4 Corporate Law

A solo entrepreneur who is eager to expand his enterprise has a number of ways of assembling capital, and one of these requires a means of promising a share of upside returns without entirely giving up control. Owners are inclined to think of investors as free-riders of sorts, and would prefer to gain investors who do not second-guess or unseat them, and who do not object when new innovations earn more for the entrepreneur than for the latecomers. Eventually, law developed or enabled a web of contracts, known as a corporation, which enabled the controlling shareholder to run the show and be held responsible only for true misbehavior and not for merely mistaken judgments. New ideas and opportunities must be shared only if they are found to be within the business promised to the shareholders. It might be fair to say that the concentration strategy implicit in an ownership structure with heavy reliance on bondholders and other debt gave way to distribution, not in the interest of encouraging teamwork among many monitors or precaution takers, but rather in the interest of creating a thick market. Market pressure and profit opportunities would then give an incentive to able monitors, usually in the form of third-party providers. The stock market gives feedback to outsiders as well as to managers and helps shareholders (and the law) keep an eye on their agents. At the same time, debt became more concentrated, both through the proliferation of security interests, noted above, and with the growth of major creditors. Over time the concentration on the credit side has also evolved, as securitization and other means of spreading debt have developed. This can be thought of as evolution in favor of distribution – but the distribution is through markets rather than through anything like comparative fault. Private parties are free to manage the level of concentration and distribution by buying up debt.

Taiwanese law is especially sensitive to the needs of large shareholders, as is apparent in Chapter 10, where it is called a "blockholder-centric" approach. In turn, Chapter 9 draws attention to the importance of SOEs, or state-owned enterprises, in Chinese law. It is tempting to think of the accommodation of, as well as the limitations on, controlling shareholders as reflecting a concentration strategy inasmuch as the ownership structure is less distributed than elsewhere. On the other hand, other legal systems also enable controlling shareholders, even though the evolutionary process has produced more widely held corporations. If law is the cause of the concentration–distribution mix, then it is likely to be through a combination of tax law, government contracts, regulatory policy, and too much more to specify here.

In any event, there is more going on here than a simple mixture, or private choice, between concentration and distribution. Things like the 2008 Recession and housing crisis in the United States caused lawmakers to think again about securitization and the proliferation of various financial instruments. Some observers yearned for the old days when the local bank really inspected and monitored the homeowner who sought a mortgage. Now it is all about homogeneous loans which are sliced and diced and sold in the market – although there is a move to bring back centralized government agencies that would service or own the bulk of the mortgages. But by and large concentration has given way to distributed interests, and they are so dispersed that only the mega-market is there to give some signals about what is in need of investigation. Thick, global markets are in this way the evolutionary product, or stage, beyond earlier concentrated owners. It will not be surprising if in the next stage these markets serve as interest groups that force governments to be much more involved in investigating and guaranteeing the original mortgages or other interests. If there is so much distribution of liability, as we might call it, then the push for regulation by a central authority becomes stronger. Moreover, at some point the distribution strategy can fail because of its own weight; liability or other features are so dispersed that each possible precaution taker has little to gain or every reason to think that others have taken the necessary precautions. No liability is hardly an improvement, but concentration in a single party, or the government itself, is attractive. Most optimistically, an eager politician will appeal to the dispersed parties and promise to take action on their behalf. In concentration–distribution terms, the government can be seen as the new, single, concentrated precaution taker and insurer, especially if politicians can gain by appealing to interests in need of help and, most especially, if these markets and the private entities within them are regarded as too big to fail.

5 The Concentration Strategy of Government

I have suggested that the government might emerge as a concentrated problem solver in corporate law. This possibility reveals some definitional problems, or gaps, in the evolutionary story advanced thus far. Concentration is described as one of two legal strategies, but the claim is not that these are law's only two tools. In different areas and jurisdictions, these strategies have been developed by courts, legislatures, authoritarian governments, and private actors. In the private sphere most organizations also mix concentration and distribution strategies, as they try to encourage and exploit both leadership and teamwork. It should not be confusing, therefore, to think of law as sometimes assigning responsibility to a local or central government, even though this government might itself be a source of law. An assignment of responsibility to the central government can be by authoritarian fiat, by democratic means, or by pressure from below. The idea here is to be less concerned with the source of authority as with the strategy for solving a social problem.

The concentrated strategy associated with modern governments is easily seen in tort and related law. A good place to begin is with negative externalities, like pollution, because they quickly reveal the choice between a tort system and a more centralized administrative system. With a little thought it becomes apparent that many social problems facing the modern state can be met with either (or a combination) of these tools. In turn, my claim is that while the private law system chooses between concentrated and distributed strategies, the administrative state is almost, by definition, a concentrated strategy, but then this concentrated legal power often delegates work, or outsources, to distributed entities. The two do not usually add up to the same thing. The very reasons a central authority is attractive imply that information is available to it, so that a command and control system, often with some distributed tasks, is preferred to an "after the fact" allocation of responsibilities.

The fact that central authorities often delegate tasks to multiple parties should not distract from the observation that law's strategy is essentially of the concentrated sort. Consider in more detail the problem of pollution in an ecosystem or a single river. A modern, conventional tort system allows an injured downstream user to recover from unreasonable upstream polluters. There are, of course, problems with this tort-based approach to environmental harm; the victims may be dispersed and may even have difficult gaining standing or proving damages. An otherwise well-situated plaintiff may have trouble proving which upstream defendants caused the plaintiff's injury. These are all reasons to expect evolution toward an administrative solution, especially if the social problem seems to grow with more intensive uses of the river. But for the moment consider the likely evolution of law in a jurisdiction that tries to solve the problem with private suits. Note that a distribution strategy is more likely than a concentrated approach. It is easy to imagine, as happened in some jurisdictions, law enabling comparative negligence or even restitution-style suits by plaintiffs against a number of defendants. The burden of proof might effectively switch to defendants to show levels of causation or wrongdoing. A private law-based concentration strategy is harder to imagine. There is no obvious single party to hold liable, and certainly no party with ready means of contracting for precautions with other polluters. If conventional tort law is to provide deterrence against polluters it will do with a distribution strategy.

Consider now a political shift such that the government takes responsibility for this environmental problem. It may do so with respect to a single river or with respect to clean water more generally. The political impetus might come from the failure of private law, an environmental disaster, or simply political pressure arising out of the citizenry's discontent with the status quo and with injuries from polluted water. Perhaps a politician or interest group calculates that it will benefit from cleaning up the environmental damage. Again, this spur, or evolutionary impetus, could be – but need not be – in the direction of efficiency or improvement. It is not hard to imagine the government taking charge of the environmental problem because many governments have done so over the last half-century. The methods of environmental control are, therefore, familiar. An administrative agency might inspect all potential polluters and decree acceptable levels of emissions from each source. A market-oriented government might calculate an emissions tax and apply it to all firms, thus encouraging optimal reductions. Alternatively, or additionally, a government agency might influence behavior with an *ex post* (but public law) system. Periodically, investigators could estimate the cost of cleanup and divide these costs among all polluters in some formulaic fashion. The choice among these (and other) alternatives is likely to be based at least in part on the capacity of the government to acquire information of one kind or another. In many cases the concentrated versus distributed choice is the same as an *ex ante* versus *ex post* rulemaking decision. *Ex post* assignment might bring about rent-seeking, but still there is a choice between concentration and distribution.

The last alternative, in which the government decides on a level of cleanup and acceptable pollution and then allocates costs retroactively, most resembles a private law tort system following a distribution strategy, except that it overcomes conventional problems of standing and perhaps causation and fault-finding as well. Nevertheless, following the categories introduced here, we can regard all these schemes as beginning with a concentration strategy, inasmuch as the government is out to solve the problem, and then distributes obligations through one means or another. A superconcentrated strategy might find the government cleaning up the river, compensating injured parties, and also taking over the firms or banning further industrial activity. But this extreme form of concentration is unusual, except perhaps in wartime, and in any event requires tax or other revenues that are themselves allocated in some distributed manner. The more the government relies on private decision-making (as with an emissions tax), the more the strategy should be regarded as one of distribution. The point is simply that an administrative system is not necessarily more concentrated than a private tort system, but it begins with a concentration strategy and proceeds from there. An industrial organization scholar might insist that the government is no different from a large, centralized firm. The private firm must also choose a method of organization and whether to let its subsidiaries or divisions operate independently or follow instructions from the center (Williamson 1975). But this is not quite the parallel that should concern us here. Instead, the idea is that organizations and legal systems must choose whether to concentrate responsibility or encourage teamwork by distributing it.

In short, the concentration label can be applied to strategies designed and largely carried out by the government (which is to say the legal system itself). This central manager takes upon itself a role similar to that of a fee simple owner and then delegates tasks. It is a central authority rather than a libertarian starting point. In some cases it taxes, in others it commands and controls, and so forth. It uses different tools based on political and efficiency pressures.

6 Illustrations of the Role of Government in Legal Evolution

The role of government as "single owner" of sorts is best understood through additional examples. Consider, for instance, the rather common role of governments in building infrastructure or even just roads. There has been evolution all over the world toward central planning and road-building, where there was once a commons or even private ownership. Almost necessarily, when the government takes charge of road-building it makes decisions about the safety and efficiency of these roads. A legal system might enable a private tort system for accidents on these roads, especially when the "cause" is thought to be negligent driving, but an enormous part of the activity level and safety level associated with travel depends on the government's (concentrated) strategy with regard to road-building, speed limits, police deployment, gas prices and taxes, minimum driving ages, insurance requirements, and other restrictions. Most governments will also use a tort system with dispersed liability to control speed and other behaviors, but as a descriptive, evolutionary matter, virtually every government now controls roads more than any single owner or agent controlled them before. There is some distribution of responsibilities, but overall the picture is one of concentration.

The extension of government control to more areas, which is to say one important kind of concentration strategy, is familiar, but not always easy to understand. Politicians may like power, but this is hardly a new preference, and the task is to explain increasing concentration. Moreover, politicians do not prefer a dissatisfied citizenry and every time the government takes control of a problem it opens itself up to failure and rejection. One possibility is that technological change has made some problems larger and more apparent; negative externalities on a large scale are difficult for governments to ignore, and they can overwhelm most private law systems. My intuition is that technological change has dramatically improved law's ability to assign responsibility and assess precaution taking. There are better tools and a greater ability to monitor the behavior of others. It took a long time to develop the technology of figuring out who set a fire, but by now we are able to ascertain the origins of most fires. The same is true for pollution, tainted food, and building collapses. These improvements also make private law systems work better, but there is at least the possibility of sensible command and control. In the production of benefits or surpluses, there seems to be something of an evolutionary pendulum as command and control gains popularity but is then diminished when governments figure out the value of the free market and of unleashing human ingenuity and effort. On the other hand, where negative externalities are concerned, so that the main issue is the assignment of precautions, people need to be motivated by responsibility for losses or other means. Here, the choice among command and control (speed limits, for example), outsourcing to a single well-situated party (like a manufacturer), and threat of liability assigned to multiple players after the fact (liability in proportion to negligence in causing environmental damage for example) is the stuff of current law (and interest groups) and there is no reason to expect one to emerge as the evolutionary winner. There is reason to expect some concentration in the sense of a government-provided solution, if only because interest groups will see that the information necessary to solve the problem is available, but the details of this concentrated strategy are less predictable. In the final section, two additional illustrations expand on this idea about the evolutionary tension between concentration and distribution. The first example recasts the tension between concentration and distribution, while the second example capitalizes on the information technology and collective action problem in order to offer a prediction about the increased reliance on a concentration strategy in one important setting.

Consider, penultimately, the role of government in promoting innovation. Many countries use patents and other grants of monopoly power to stimulate investment and innovation. Setting aside the government's decision to reward and stimulate in this way, this might appear to be an obvious deployment of what I have called a concentration strategy. The government creates a single owner, albeit not to solve a looming problem, but to reward a past success. At the same time, governments give grants to researchers, run universities, and so forth. These tools are generally decided upon by a central agency which then distributes benefits. The example shows how easy it is to confuse concentration and distribution. A centrally managed prize system is *more* concentrated than a patent system in that it requires more information and decision-making on the part of the central authority. It is less concentrated than the patent approach in the second step, because the patent system allocates benefits to a single, some might say concentrated, winner, who then makes decisions about licensing and so forth.

There is a healthy literature on the substitution of prizes for patents because, in principle, a prize can be just as encouraging as a patent, without subjecting consumers to monopoly pricing and deadweight loss (Levmore 2013b). Prizes are often designed to reward second- and third-place finishers, and, more generally, are less beholden to the concentrated, single-winner idea in the second stage. Moreover, the authority to award prizes can also be delegated to many decision-makers in distributed fashion. Many prizes can be offered with regard to a single aim, and the second-place effort can get a reduced prize and so forth. If it is true that concentration is favored over distribution in evolutionary terms when there is more information in the hands of the central authority, then over time we might expect some growth of the prize system at the expense of the patent system. This conclusion holds constant the impact of interest groups which, as previously emphasized, might provide an alternative explanation for the rise or fall of property rights.

Note that prizes can track patents by allocating them according to the actual market share of the innovation in question. Just as a patent holder earns more as his innovation succeeds in the marketplace, so too prizes can be based on sales. In contrast, market success and other information can be gathered with prizes then awarded *ex post* based on judgment about how various parties contributed to an innovation. Instead of a "winner-takes-all" patent, or one or more prizes distributed according to a set formula or some assessment of the likelihood of future success, performance can be evaluated after the fact and prizes allocated to all who contributed to it (Levmore 2013b). Put this way, a prize system can follow a distribution strategy. Indeed, if the prizes were to be awarded by judges or juries on an episodic basis, this imagined prize system would be as close a relative as one could imagine to a court-based, comparative fault, tort system.

Consider next, and finally, climate change, a topic replete with negative externality issues of the largest kind. We do not know where it will take law over the next one hundred years. It could bring about larger political units. It might stimulate large cross-country agreements on taxing carbon. There are as many possibilities as pundits. But if the main points of the present chapter are correct, we might expect a mix of concentration and distribution strategies. Two predictions come out of the two parts of this chapter. First, it is almost inevitable that as the costs of climate change become apparent there will be increased pressure on the central government to take charge of the situation and "solve" the social problems it presents. This is a case where technological change, available information and data processing, large-scale externalities, and even cross-border collective action problems all point to a concentrated strategy.

As we have seen, however, the fact that the government might be seen as the best problem solver does not mean that the government will solve the problem on its own. At the very least, the government is a concentrated solver in the manner that a manufacturer is assigned the task in product liability law. The manufacturer contracts with various precaution takers, and then does some insuring on its own. Somewhat similarly – though surely by law rather than by contract – the government assigns tasks to various firms and citizens. It does so with mandates and with incentives of kinds not often available to mere manufacturers, but the mixture of concentrated responsibility and distributed precaution taking is quite familiar. One way to be reminded that this will be no mere return to a distribution strategy is to recognize how unlikely it is that the prototypical distribution strategy, comparative fault, will be used in adjusting to climate change. No one expects a central government to announce that every few years juries or judges will be assembled to look back on shortfalls in precaution, evaluate damage to the environment, and allocate compensation for the latter on the basis of the former. Among other reasons, the information required to do this is unavailable or too complex to be processed by such fact-finders. Similarly, but more trivially, no government will assign the task to a single problem solver; the problem cannot be put in the hands of a fee simple owner, any more than all accidents could have been avoided by a rule holding General Motors, or any other single party, strictly liable for all injuries. Neither a pure concentration strategy nor a straightforward distribution strategy will materialize. Neither can do the job efficiently, and neither is likely to emerge as a result of interest group pressure.

We can, however, make two easy predictions. One is that political pressure will bring about a concentrated solution in terms of process; the government will be thrust into the position of solving the problem. In terms of actual precautions, however, we can expect the government to use a variety of tools, many of which are drawn from the distribution strategist's toolkit.

Imagine, as it is easy to do, that governments grapple with climate change by enacting a combination of regulatory schemes. Perhaps there will be a carbon tax along with recycling requirements, subsidies for some energy sources, penalties or stiffer requirements with respect to others, and so forth. In addition, governments are likely to undertake substantial public works projects ranging from more efficient power plants in some countries to seawalls in others. In concentration–distribution terms this is certainly not akin to stronger property rights (indeed higher taxes can be understood as consistent with weaker and less concentrated property rights). When the plan includes the command and control of utilities or high energy-consuming industries, then obviously there is concentration at work. But inasmuch as a carbon tax encourages firms to consider alternative methods on their own, it should be understood as part of a distribution strategy. Finally, large spending programs generally involve very specific instructions, in part to encourage noncorrupt competitive bidding, and are thus the stuff of concentration. Overall, then, the first step of problem solving, which might be called its procedure or setup, is of concentrated form, and then the implementation is a mixture of concentration and distribution. Ideally, this mixture depends on relative information costs and competencies, though in reality there are no doubt political considerations. The choice between concentration and distribution may be at some level like the choice between two states vying for a government project. There may well be an efficient location for the project, but political considerations also enter into the decision as various constituencies may need to be satisfied in order to bring about any project at all.

In the end, the only constant in the concentration–distribution evolutionary pattern is the growth of the bureaucracy. Here there is a steady evolution toward a single problem solver, but that solver might use taxes, regulatory controls, and various outsourcing techniques so that at the level of implementation there is no straight and steady evolutionary path. Concentration and distribution may remain in tension, as they do in the doctrines of tort law, with various substrategies falling in and out of favor. As always, this favor may be a combination of efficiency and interest group satisfaction. The efficiency-based story will emphasize the technological capacity to gather information and use tools that reflect the relative advantages of concentrated and distributed mechanisms. But we must remain aware of the less optimistic evolutionary story, that interest groups rent-seek and exert pressure in order to be free of costly responsibilities. Thus, the government might assign responsibility through taxes or commands to X because Y and Z "paid" to be left free. It might employ V to build seawalls (at great profit) because it was the most politically successful rather than the most efficient provider. In short, even where we predict and understand the evolution toward a form of concentrated ownership, we cannot be sure that this evolution is something to be celebrated rather than questioned.

References

Levmore, Saul. 1987. Variety and Uniformity in the Treatment of the Good-Faith Purchaser. *Journal of Legal Studies* 16:43–65.

2002. Two Stories about the Evolution of Property Rights. *Journal of Legal Studies* 31(S2):S421–S451.

2013a. Harmonization, Preferences, and the Calculus of Consent in Commercial and Other Law. *Common Market Law Review* 50:243–260.

2013b. The Impending iPrize Revolution in Intellectual Property Law. *Boston University Law Review* 93:139–162.

Williamson, Oliver E. 1975. *Markets and Hierarchies: Analysis and Antitrust Implications*. New York: The Free Press.

Watson, Alan. 1993. *Legal Transplants: An Approach to Comparative Law*. Athens, GA: University of Georgia Press.

2 *The Economics of Legal Harmonization and Legal Convergence**

BRUNO DEFFAINS

1 Introduction

This chapter studies the law and economics of harmonization and convergence between legal systems. The goal of harmonization encourages different national legislations to adopt similar approaches to the pursuit of a common aim. Harmonization co-ordinates different legal systems by eliminating major differences and creating minimum requirements or standards. Unification, by contrast, refers to the substitution of multiple rules by a new legislation (or the substitution of one legal rule for others) at a supranational level. Unification focuses upon substituting or combining two or more legal systems and replacing them with a single system.

Unlike unification, which contemplates the substitution of two or more legal systems with one single system, the harmonization of law seeks to promote the co-ordination of different legal provisions or systems. Harmonization is generally synonymous with "convergence of law." However, harmonization is usually regarded as being an "active" process, achieved through the enacting of legislation whereas convergence is generally associated with a more "passive" approach such as a natural convergence of law through custom and the frequent use of the same legal principles. Among the most prominent recent examples of harmonization are those given by the UNCITRAL (United Nations Commission on International Trade Law) or the "EU directives" to set common goals and standards across the countries of the

* This paper was presented at the 10th Annual Meeting of the Asian Law and Economics Association held at National Taiwan University College of Law on June 20–21, 2014, and at the Asian Law Institute Annual Conference held at National Taiwan University College of Law on May 20–21, 2015. The author thanks the participants of the Conference for helpful comments, and, in particular, Yun-chien Chang, Saul Levmore, and Ariel Porat.

European Union. Convergence imposes a debate about two different but related questions:[1] Should legal systems should converge? And, if the answer is positive, how should convergence be achieved? In this presentation, we develop a Law and Economics perspective on these two questions.

One can readily observe the importance of these questions for the evolution of legal systems around the world at the global as well as regional levels. Chapters 5, 8, and 10 in this book give interesting perspectives about the evolution of legal solutions in the different fields of liability, property, and corporate law.

2 Benefits and Limits of Legal Harmonization

2.1 Costs of Legal Fragmentation

Law is a fundamental instrument of international economic integration: Different legal systems increase transaction costs in cross-border businesses, particularly in terms of the acquisition and understanding of legal information and uncertainty concerning national legal procedures. Clermont and Eisenberg (1996) show how foreign plaintiffs need to present stronger cases to win in US courts, which implies that foreign firms are likely to be, to a certain extent, deterred from engaging in cross-border contracting. Rodrik (2004) observes that the diversity of national arrangements is the most significant source of transaction costs in international exchanges. His evaluation is that they account for about 35 percent in ad valorem terms, compared with the 5 percent due to typical trade barriers. The European Commission regards legal uncertainty as the main reason to explain why European integration develops more slowly than might be expected and desired (Communication to the European on European contract law of September, 2008). An empirical study by Ben Butter and Mosch (2003) finds that the similarity of legal systems may be able to produce roughly between 50 and 80 percent more cross-border trade, using data drawn from 25 OECD countries. Turrini and van Ypersele (2006) conduct an empirical study of the "border effect," assuming it might result from legal differences. Even within a single country, trade between two regions is higher when subjected to the same court of appeal. The authors also estimate that legal similarity can increase trade among OECD countries up to

65 percent, controlling for transportation costs, common culture, language, and so on. Thus, encouraging laws and legal institutions to converge may actually produce different benefits.

First, it contributes to the elimination or reduction barriers to cross-border productive activities subject to legal rules, and thereby fosters investment, trade, mobility, and competition. Second, it improves the functioning of national laws and institutions also for purely national activities, spurring development and growth: the right choice allows greater welfare due to domestic activities. Third, it is characterized by a self-reenforcing mechanism. The development produced both by the cross-border and the domestic sector growth improves the institutional possibility frontier and thus allows for further advances.

2.2 Natural Convergence

The principal reason for convergence is the reduction of legal uncertainty and, consequently, transaction costs. In a way, the process of globalization demands the harmonization of legal systems to increase the importance of transnational markets and to eliminate the "border effect." For instance, the WTO is pushing countries toward a faster harmonization of the law because standardization aims to render uniform the legal responses to the same situations. As already observed by John Henry Merryman (1977): "In some cases the desire for convergence of legal systems merely expresses a preference for simplicity. It responds to popular discontent with complexity and seeks to impose order where there is untidy diversity."

This approach to legal diversity would hardly merit recognition and discussion, since it is little more than an expression of frustration at the fact that the world is complicated, disorderly, and uncertain, were it not so firmly rooted in human psychology. It is closely related to an exaggerated demand for certainty in the law. In other words, convergence facilitates international transactions, increases the level of general welfare, promotes the diffusion of culture, and promotes international understanding. The idea of "simplification" and "better understanding" leads Merryman et al. (1994) to develop the idea of "natural convergence" as a unique solution to a given legal problem. Countries could converge spontaneously toward the same rule when they are faced by the same legal problem, even without any interactions among them. Different nations have a tendency to have similar problems, and to arrive at similar legal ways of dealing with them.

2.3 *Functional Convergence*

Considering the "natural convergence" hypothesis, complications could exist if a legal problem has multiple solutions. It is a well-known topic in comparative law that different legal rules can solve the same problem. In such cases, "functional convergence" could occur even if formal rules diverge.

Levmore (1986) was one of the first scholars to look for regularities more than differences. In addition, legal convergence could appear as inevitable in the sense that it is the efficient response to common problems (Easterbrook and Fischel 1991). This point also refers to the debate about the efficiency of common law (see e.g. Priest 1977; Posner 1979). "Classical" Law and Economics considers that if laws in different countries are meant to provide solutions to very similar problems, they have to be similar in content. As a result, there are only two possible justifications to comparative variation: a disagreement about the optimal solution and the functional equivalence of different solutions. Essentially, saying that different rules in different countries are functionally equivalent is to say that there is no real variation between them.

2.4 *Institutional Isomorphism*

Scholars in international relations (Pollack 2007) and international public law (Goodman and Jinks 2004, 2005, 2008, 2013) argue that a key factor in legal convergence is the change in the perception of the world that policymakers experience either by frequent interactions at the international level (i.e., international socialization) and/or by feeling an obligation to comply with a dominant culture (i.e., acculturation).

International interactions generate a convergence of legal preferences which leads, in turn, to legal convergence that could be interpreted as an institutional isomorphism according to Goodman and Jinks (2005). This approach seems particularly relevant in relation to the evolution of public rules of law (regulation and competition rules) as well as for private practices such as corporate governance characterized by a broad consensus on general principles for firms' objectives and management methods.

2.5 Limits to Legal Harmonization

Despite its overall desirability at the global level, advantages brought by reduced legal diversity produces winners and losers both at the domestic and the international levels, which triggers opposition to harmonization. Strategic moves also contribute to a distortion of the process. Defensive measures after the adoption of harmonization efforts may result in even worse outcomes. Different types of redistributive effects can result from legal harmonization: incumbents protected by disparity, established powers obtaining rents from disparity, economic agents who benefit from legal diversity per se. Reductions in legal disparity also entail a series of important direct costs: the costs of departing from local preferences (including different cultures, worldviews, etc.) as to how to resolve issues and produce legal outcomes, the costs of the disparity from specific local circumstances (since legal solutions are often contextual), the costs of the harmonization process itself, the costs of failing to find the right harmonized set of rules and institutions, error costs, and legitimacy (democratic or otherwise) costs.

The debate about legal origins and the "institutional frontiers" is interesting to note at this analytical stage. The "legal origins" project suggests that the lawmaking institutions are carried over from historical incidences and thereby have an effect on economic outcomes. Evidence from this body of work suggests that "civil-law" countries have less efficient governments and courts, less secure investor rights, and stricter market regulation than "common law" countries (La Porta et al. 2008). The impact of this view has been significant during the last decade via the World Bank Doing Business Project. The main intuition of the "legal origins" approach can be expressed from a comparative perspective (Djankov et al. 2003).

The authors define the "Institutional Possibility Frontier" to compare common law and civil law countries (i.e., England versus France). They observe that whether common or civil law is transplanted, the equilibrium dictatorship and disorder increase because the institutional possibilities are less attractive. Relative to the efficient choice for a developing country's Institutiional Possibility Frontier, transplantation leads to excessive intervention and regulation, and relatively more so in civil than in common law countries. Because of the substantial risks of public abuse of business, developing countries need less regulation for efficiency. But when legal systems are transplanted, they end with as much relatively speaking, and more in absolute terms, than do the origin countries. This problem is most severe in civil law countries, which end up being especially over-regulated relative to efficiency. The evidence shows that the levels of regulation are generally excessive in developing countries. The transplanted regulatory systems appear excessive for the countries that use them.

However, some scholars argue against the legal origins project. For instance, according to Guerriero (2013), transplanted lawmaking institutions have in fact been changing over time and this wave of reforms reflects the welfare-maximizing choices of societies. Building on data detailing the history of the legal order of 156 countries, he finds evidence that pro-case-law reforms – in nations where "statute law" was imposed by colonizers – are more likely with a weaker democracy and a broader cultural heterogeneity. On the other hand, moves toward statute law in England's former colonies are found where the cultural differences among subgroups are the smallest.

Dari Mattiacci and Guerriero (2015) demonstrate empirically that culture is the main driver of divergence between legal institutions. The legal origins effect seems to be weak. In addition, recent psychological studies suggest that humans have well-defined preferences over the harshness of punishment for dangerous actions, and that these tastes are modulated by the cultural biases of the group to which individuals pertain. The rationale for this pattern is the fact that the main driver of legal changes is the ability of the legal system to select those laws that satisfy the cultural biases of the largest part of the population.

3 How Should Legal Systems Converge?

There are different techniques to achieve legal convergence. The main distinction is to be drawn between noncooperative and cooperative ones. Following Gomez (2011), we propose to characterize the different methods as belonging to three different models: uncoordinated convergence, voluntary coordination, and political fiat from a superior authority.[2]

3.1 Uncoordinated Convergence

The jurisdictions come closer in terms of legal outcomes through processes that are not coordinated or agreed, and are not fostered or mandated by a higher or external power to the countries themselves. The players in the harmonization game act independently and noncooperatively to reach some spontaneous uncoordinated convergence.

3.2 Herding Behaviors

The first mechanism refers to "imitation and herding behaviors" in the lawmaking process. When facing a choice of legal regime under conditions of limited information about what the best solution would be, legal systems lacking a strong determination for one or the other option may simply follow the steps of other countries who have been earlier movers. The economic models of herd behavior and informational cascades show the old parable of the "blind leading the blind": an equilibrium in which all players adopt the same action, which is generally suboptimal.

Some of the examples listed by Gomez (2011) are relevant for our purpose here: Corporate governance alarms post-Enron. Soon after those events the United States adopted the Sarbanes–Oxley Act, and many European countries followed suit promptly, despite the substantial differences in terms of the types of firms, and also in the style of corporate law and corporate governance to be found on the opposite sides of the Atlantic. In Federal systems, studies show that states or regions that approve first pieces of legislation in a given matter are imitated, to a large extent, by later lawmakers in other states or regions, with theoretical models of deference to judicial precedent causing herding behavior in courts.

3.3 Legal Competition

The second mechanism is "legal competition." Individuals or firms "consuming" a legal product (a corporate form, a set of legal rules for an economic or personal transaction, an interpreter and enforcer of a contract) may be able to choose from among different alternatives offered by diverse legal systems: Choice may be physical (exit, relocation) or purely "legal" (choice of Law). Competition among jurisdictions may force them to improve the quality of the legal rules to satisfy the preferences of the "consumers" or "buyers" of legal rules (firms, contracting parties, marrying couples). The "sellers" (i.e., the jurisdictions) will be under competitive pressure to adopt rules that provide maximum benefits to the customers of the legal system. Competition would produce the legal solution that maximizes the satisfaction of legal customers. Given that the efficient solution would be – roughly – the same for all jurisdictions, assuming the relevant median preferences are similar across countries, the competitive process would push all jurisdictions to choose the uniquely efficient legal regime.

Interesting evidences are given by the Delaware dominance with regard to the incorporation of large firms in the United States or by dominance of New York legislation with regard to financial contracts and M&A agreements among US listed companies. Another example is the widespread adoption of English legal structures in the European market for debt and derivatives contracts. Prevalence of ICC arbitration rules in the European context, or the AAA arbitration rules in the context of the Americas, or ICSID arbitration for disputes over foreign investments.

3.4 Legal Transplants

The third mechanism is the "legal transplant." Comparative lawyers use the term "legal transplant" to refer to this import of legal rules, doctrines, and institutions. Those in charge of lawmaking in a given jurisdiction (i.e., legislators, courts, administrators in public agencies) may learn and acquire knowledge about how to properly design the legal rules for a certain area of the law. Law is, among others, a technical and specialized field of human knowledge, and techniques may travel, and can be taught and learned across countries. Usually comparative lawyers mix together voluntary and involuntary (especially colonial) transplant.

An interesting example is given by the adoption of German civil code by the Japanese and Turkish legal systems. Similarly, many Latin American countries have adopted US rules on judicial structure. Another illustration is the European Constitutions adopting the Kelsenian model of a Constitutional Court to control legislation or post-communist countries adopting laws and institutions from neighboring noncommunist countries.

To conclude, one can observe that all of the former mechanisms are uncoordinated: in these instances no visible hand leads towards the increased harmonization of legal rules. Similar or identical contents in substantive legal rules and in legal institutions may also be the result of cooperative or coordinated actions taken by the affected jurisdictions: international conventions, uniform laws, model laws, etc. The larger or smaller degree of harmonization that may be achieved through these processes will be the outcome of a coordination game played by the different jurisdictions, and with different entrepreneurs in the process: international organizations and agencies, intergovernmental structures, NGOs, private institutions, firms and industry associations (see, e.g., self-regulation in the financial sector), to name just a few.

4 Elements for a Debate

Concerning the choice between cooperation and noncooperation, different arguments have to be considered.

4.1 Political Pressure

According to Macey and Colombatto (1997), it is not nations that decide to cooperate or forge international agreements. Rather, this is carried out by regulators, bureaucrats, and politicians within nations and in doing so they respond to political pressure and to self-interest. When this happens, the regulators in a given country will have strong incentives to engage in activities such as international coordination in order to survive. Even if regulators would prefer not to cede or to share authority with their counterparts from other countries, technological change, market processes, and other exogenous variables may deprive the regulators in a particular country of the power to act unilaterally. Sokol (2011) develops a public choice approach to explain why many antitrust issues have been addressed internationally through soft law. The political context impeded the WTO's hard law solution, and led instead to the creation of soft law's institutional alternative: the International Competition Network (ICN).

4.2 Legal Preferences

Evidence exists that preferences for most legal questions are not uniform around the world or even in different parts of the world.

Many scholars have asserted the advantages of legal competition between governments to deal with the diversity of citizens' preferences, something that has been the subject of particular study during the debate over the possible introduction of a European Constitution (Frey and Eichenberger 1996, 2001; Bodenstein and Ursprung 2005; Feld 2005).

However, preferences are not purely exogenous. The recognition of endogenous legal preferences appears through the notion of international socialization in international relations literature. Pollack (2007) reviews how policy- and lawmakers' preferences change by interacting and socializing at an international level, inducing changes in their vision of the world. Persuasion, for instance, is often used by representatives or nongovernmental organizations to change their foreign colleagues' preferences. Goodman and Jinks (2008, 2013) use the term "acculturation" to describe the general process by which actors adopt the beliefs and behavioral patterns of the surrounding culture. They remark that a complex social process is driven "by identification with a reference group which generates varying degrees of cognitive and social pressures to conform with the behavioural expectations of the wider culture." Acculturation works even if there are no physical international interactions. For example, important foreign constitutional and legislative provisions can cause domestic internalization. Foreign practices are thus examined by a national court not for the legal reasoning of a specific foreign court, but as evidence of a norm that is widely accepted by other states. The US Supreme Court's reasoning seems to witness such a process of acculturation (Pollack 2007).

4.3 Legal Culture and Adaptation Costs

In comparative law literature, legal harmonization and unification are frequently seen as threats to the legal culture and history of a country (see, e.g., Legrand 1996, 1997). Legal traditions may be so divergent from one another that society would simply resist the proposed legal change. Therefore, huge adaptation costs may make convergence impossible. Even law and finance scholars who argue that common law systems perform better than their civil law counterparts explicitly recognize that it would be economically impossible for France or Germany to change their legal system in favor of common law mechanisms (La Porta et al. 1998).

At the international level, decentralized policies can only lead to a durable legal status quo. Achieving legal convergence would thus require international coordination. But legal uniformity might not be the best legal distance between countries. However, the recent work of the "Cambridge Group" finds little support in longitudinal data for the legal origins theory. While shareholder protections and corporate governance standards have been strengthened worldwide, these legal changes have not resulted in more dispersed share ownership and increased stock market activity, as predicted by Legal Origins Theory. According to Armour et al. (2009), these considerable legal reforms suggest that "lock-in through legal origin has not been much of an obstacle to the formal convergence of systems."

4.4 Theoretical Literature

There is at present an important literature on the subject of legal convergence. What is particularly absent is the dynamic view about convergence and the fact that there is no distinction between harmonization and unification. Authors generally analyze the trade-off faced by lawmakers who seek to benefit from adapting their legal systems to the foreign legal systems while minimizing the cost of any change. Loeper (2008, 2011) compares decentralization with unification and highlights the importance of patterns of jurisdictional interdependence. He finds that if external costs are sufficiently high then no uniform policy Pareto-dominates decentralization. In these circumstances there is a self-disciplining effect which induces local jurisdictions to choose similar policies. Carbonara and Parisi (2007) show that if, before cooperating, countries can increase their legal switching costs so as to shift the burden of legal adaptation to their partners, two outcomes are possible. First, there may be less legal convergence with endogenous switching costs than without (whether or not nation-states cooperate). Second, with endogenous switching costs, no legal cooperation may be preferred to legal cooperation. This is what they call the "paradox of harmonization."

Crettez, Deffains, and Musy (2013) develop a dynamic model with two nation-states. In their model, the preferences of nation-states are such that it is costly to change their laws, but it is also costly to have a legal system that differs from that in the other nation-state. At each time, both nation-states must decide whether or not to adapt their legal systems. They balance the advantage of adapting their legal system to the other nation-state with the cost of any such change. The model confirms that cooperative legal arrangements are not necessarily the dominant strategy to observe convergence between legal systems. No cooperation can dominate temporarily or even definitively to achieve convergence. The emergence of more cooperative decisions essentially has an impact on the speed of convergence, but not on the fact of that convergence. The more drastic form of convergence, which takes the form of an immediate unification of legal systems, is an optimal solution for nation-states only in very specific cases. In general, such convergence is dominated by the process of gradual harmonization.

This approach seems particularly relevant in evaluating legal convergence within the European Union context. During the first decades following the ratification of the European Treaty in 1958, the directives, as a harmonization mechanism, were so complete and precise that they were quasi-equivalent to a unification process. There was no real degree of freedom for Member States to introduce such directives. In the 1980s, we observed a significant change in favor of "minimum" harmonization, i.e., a move towards no cooperation on the continuum of international legal strategies. This is the "new approach" of directives that only define the "essential requirements" for Member States (Officiel Journal of the European Union – Information and Notices, 26 July 2016). Although directives will continue to be used to set the basic requirements, they have to be limited to the setting of essential requirements which are necessary to ensure general interests. The formal introduction of subsidiarity and proportionality into policymaking by the Maastricht Treaty and later in the Amsterdam Treaty protocol is the main evidence of such an evolution.

5 Legal Convergence and Endogenous Preferences

The current study of legal dynamics lacks an analytical framework to understand the joint evolution of national preferences and national legal rules, and the conditions leading to legal convergence. To fill this gap, Crettez, Deffains, and Musy (2014) develop a two-country model of legal dynamics in which each country's social welfare depends on its actual law, its culturally ideal one (i.e., legal preferences), its efficient one and the law of the other country.

Countries are better off when all these legal rules coincide. Moreover, in each country the actual law and the cultural biases of the population respond to three kinds of costs: the cost of legal diversity; the cost of the divergence between the actual law and the culturally ideal law; and the cost of divergence between actual and efficient laws. While international socialization and acculturation by Goodman and Jinks (2013) are essentially sociological notions, they have many features in common with the concept of endogenous preferences as it has developed in economics (see, e.g., Kuran and Sandholm 2008; Alesina and Reich 2013).

Crettez, Deffains, and Musy (2014) develop some empirical evidences of endogenous preferences in different fields of law, from the abolition of the death penalty in European countries to the protection of shareholders around the world. In fact, assuming that legal preferences or norms are endogenous is not a new idea in Law and Economics (see, e.g., Huck 1998; Kotsadam and Jakobsson 2011). Levmore (1986) gives some credit to the possibility of endogenous legal preferences: "The discussion that follows... most readily supports a position that combines an emphasis on law as a device shaped by the members of society in response to internal conditions in the search for ways and means to translate their basic social postulates into action with a view that changes are stimulated when a culture's rules are not consonant with its survival."

In a way, it is possible to conciliate the notions of international socialization and acculturation with economics and rational choice theory. Let x_t^i and π_t^i denote, respectively, the actual law and the legal preferences of country i ($i = 1, 2$) at date t ($t \in N$). We assume that there is initially no legal uniformity, i.e., $x_0^1 \neq x_0^2$ and $\pi_0^1 \neq \pi_0^2$. All these numbers are always common knowledge. At each date, both countries decide simultaneously the magnitude of change of their laws and, when possible, their legal preferences. The decision horizon of a country is one period ahead, as if there were nonoverlapping generations of lawmakers. Crettez, Deffains and Musy (2014) propose two definitions concerning the issue of legal dynamics:

Definition 1 (Legal Convergence). There is legal convergence at date t if the legal distance at this date decreases with respect to the previous period: $|x_t^i - x_t^j| < |x_{t-1}^i - x_{t-1}^j| (i \neq j)$

Definition 2 (Legal Uniformity). There is legal uniformity at date t when the legal distance is nil, i.e. $|x_t^i - x_t^j| = 0 (i \neq j)$

The preferences of lawmakers are described by a utility function which is the sum of two continuously differentiable subfunctions, all defined in R^2: $U^i(x^i, x^j) + V^i(x^i, \pi^i)$, $i, j = 1, 2$ and $i \neq j$. The first subfunction, U^i, describes the cost of divergence of country i's law from the other country j's law. The second sub-function, $V^i(x^i, \pi^i)$, $i = 1, 2$, describes the cost of the divergence of country i's laws from country i's own legal preferences.

5.1 Legal Preferences are Constant Across Time

The lawmaker of country i chooses the value of its law x_t^i in order to maximize his utility function. In a Nash equilibrium, the first-order conditions are as follows:

$$U_1^1(\bar{x}_t^1, \bar{x}_t^2) + V_1^1(\bar{x}_t^1, \pi^1) = 0$$
$$U_1^2(\bar{x}_t^2, \bar{x}_t^1) + V_1^2(\bar{x}_t^2, \pi^2) = 0$$

Each of these conditions reflects a trade-off between decreasing the cost of legal distance and decreasing the cost of the divergence between the actual law and the culturally ideal law.

Proposition 1. When legal preferences are fixed and are initially different ($\pi^1 < \pi^2$), legal convergence stops at a given date and legal uniformity never occurs. Moreover, national laws are closer to each other than national legal preferences:

$$\pi^1 < \bar{x}^1 < \bar{x}^2 < \pi^2$$

The distance between laws is smaller than the distance between legal preferences. Moreover, once the laws x^1 and x^2 are chosen by national lawmakers at date 0, there is no more convergence because a steady state is achieved. As a consequence, we observe a strong legal origins effect (Deakin et al. 2007): the distance between laws remains constant over time and legal uniformity never takes place. These results arise because there is a trade-off between reducing the legal distance and increasing the gap between the actual laws and the national preferences. Legal uniformity does not occur because it is costly for countries to depart from their legal preferences, even though it is also costly to have laws different from those of other countries. The equilibrium values of the laws are then different from the culturally ideal ones.

5.2 Legal Dynamics with Endogenous Legal Preferences

We add a new subfunction in the utility function of the lawmakers $W^i(\pi_t^i, \pi_{t-1}^i)$, that describes the cost borne by country i from changing its preferences. This function is at its maximum when preferences do not change, i.e., when $\pi_t^i = \pi_{t-1}^i$. It is increasing with respect to π_t^i when $\pi_t^i < \pi_{t-1}^i$ and decreasing with respect to π_t^i when $\pi_t^i > \pi_{t-1}^i$.

The result of countries' interactions at date t is given by the Nash equilibrium $(\bar{x}_t^1, \bar{\pi}_t^1, \bar{x}_t^2, \bar{\pi}_t^2)$.

Proposition 2. Assume that legal preferences are initially different, i.e., $\pi_{-1}^1 < \pi_{-1}^2$. Let a sequence of Nash equilibria be given. Then both laws' legal preferences tend to be more alike across time. Moreover, at each date t, the legal distance is smaller than the distance between legal preferences:

$$\bar{\pi}_{t-1}^1 < \bar{\pi}_t^1 < \bar{x}_t^1 < \bar{x}_t^2 < \bar{\pi}_t^2 < \bar{\pi}_{t-1}^2$$

The sequence of legal systems and legal preferences $(\bar{x}_t^1, \bar{x}_t^2)$ and legal preferences $(\bar{\pi}_t^1, \bar{\pi}_t^2)$ converges respectively to the same limit – that is, infinity. In other words, legal uniformity is realized in the long run.

This result captures the idea that socialization and acculturation make legal systems and legal preferences more alike across time (what Goodman and Jenkins call institutional isomorphism). Proposition 2 shows that the cost of legal diversity as well as the cost of the distance between actual laws and legal preferences within countries are key factors for legal convergence in the long run. Differences in legal preferences prevent laws from converging instantly and from eliminating the cost of legal diversity. This difference is a key reason why countries are continuously induced to adapt their legal preferences.

Even in the absence of legal cooperation, legal convergence and legal uniformity can occur in the long run, via a step-by-step process of adjustment of both legal rules and legal preferences. This leads to a continuous process of legal convergence, ending, in the long run, in legal uniformity. This contrasts with Proposition 1 because when legal preferences can change over time, we should assist to a "weak legal origin effect." Legal rules can be different in the short run if they are initially different, but they tend to become identical in the long run, because countries also gradually converge in terms of their culturally ideal laws. International convergence of social values is then necessary to have international convergence of legal rules.

5.3 Endogenous Legal Preferences and the Natural Convergence Assumption

We now take into account in the model the cost of not choosing an efficient legal rule. We add a new subfunction $Z^i(x_t^i, x^i)$, where x^i is the efficient rule for country *i*. With these preferences, the function is maximized when $x_t^i = x^i$; it is increasing with respect to x_t^i when $x_t^i < x^i$, and decreasing when $x_t^i > x^i$. Suppose first that the optimal legal rule is unique. In a Nash equilibrium the first-order conditions are as follows:

$$
\begin{aligned}
&U_1^1(\bar{x}_t^1, \bar{x}_t^2) + V_1^1(\bar{x}_t^1, \bar{\pi}_t^1) + Z_1^1(\bar{x}_t^1, x) = 0\\
&V_2^1(\bar{x}_t^1, \bar{\pi}_t^1) + W_1^1(\bar{\pi}_t^1, \bar{\pi}_{t-1}^1) = 0\\
&U_1^2(\bar{x}_t^2, \bar{x}_t^1) + V_1^2(\bar{x}_t^2, \bar{\pi}_t^2) + Z_1^2(\bar{x}_t^2, x) = 0\\
&V_2^2(\bar{x}_t^2, \bar{\pi}_t^2) + W_1^2(\bar{\pi}_t^2, \bar{\pi}_{t-1}^2) = 0
\end{aligned}
$$

Proposition 3. Let $(x_t^1,\ x_t^2, \pi_t^1, \pi_t^2$ be a sequence of Nash equilibria. Then the laws and legal preferences of both countries converge and legal uniformity is achieved in the long run. Moreover, the limit law is the unique efficient one.

Both countries finally adopt the efficient rule. Proposition 3 is similar to Proposition 2 in the sense that endogenous preferences allow for legal uniformity in the long run. But here the long-run value of the legal rule is the (unique) efficient one. It always pays to change a country's legal preferences so as to make them closer to the efficient legal rules. Suppose now that each country has specific optimal legal rules. We have to analyze legal dynamics when the efficient legal rule is country-dependent (we denote by x^i the efficient legal rule of country *i*, $i = 1, 2, x^1 \neq x^2$)).

As stated by Deakin et al. (2007), "legal rules are endogenized by local economic conditions and political context. This is a theme common both to modern comparative legal doctrine of functional analysis and to the varieties-of-capitalism approach. The same effect might be achieved in one system by a rule of law and in another by self-regulatory instruments of soft law." For example, an efficient labour law can be country-specific because the weight given to job protection is not the same everywhere.

In a Nash equilibrium the first-order conditions are as follows:

$$U_1^1(\bar{x}_t^1, \bar{x}_t^2) + V_1^1(\bar{x}_t^1, \bar{\pi}_t^1) + Z_1^1(\bar{x}_t^1, x^1) = 0$$

$$V_2^1(\bar{x}_t^1, \bar{\pi}_t^1) + W_1^1(\bar{\pi}_t^1, \bar{\pi}_{t-1}^1) = 0$$

$$U_1^2(\bar{x}_t^2, \bar{x}_t^1) + V_1^2(\bar{x}_t^2, \bar{\pi}_t^2) + Z_1^2(\bar{x}_t^2, x^2) = 0$$

$$V_2^2(\bar{x}_t^2, \bar{\pi}_t^2) + W_1^2(\bar{\pi}_t^2, \bar{\pi}_{t-1}^2) = 0$$

Proposition 4. In a steady state, we have $x^1 < \bar{\pi}^1 = \bar{x}^1 < \bar{x}^2 = \bar{\pi}^2 < x^2$. In that case, the actual laws coincide with legal preferences. Moreover, in each country the actual law differs from the corresponding optimal legal rules.

There is no legal uniformity in a steady state. Moreover, in each country the actual laws coincide with its legal preferences. These preferences, however, do not coincide with the efficient legal rules. The distance between the laws remains positive but smaller than the difference between the country's efficient legal rules.

There is a compromise between the efficiency loss and the cost of legal distance. In some specific cases (see, e.g., quadratic functions in Crettez, Deffains, and Musy 2014), we show that whatever the initial values of the laws and legal preferences in a given country, their values converge to the same number, which is country-dependent, and which lies between x^1 and x^2. Legal uniformity does not occur in the long run (the legal distance remains constant).

Siems (2008) provides a detailed comparative law analysis of the process of legal convergence in shareholder law. He highlights some trends of converging changes in national legal cultures (civil law and common law, Western and Asian law) and some trends of natural convergence in shareholder law. According to him, this diminishing distance between legal views and legal rules of different countries is driven partly by the internationalization of the economy and partly by the pressures of specific groups (companies, shareholders, foreign countries, and international organizations) to converge.

6 Conclusion

The approach of legal evolution developed in this presentation implies that the speed of legal convergence differs from law to law, depending negatively on the magnitude of the costs of change, and positively on the importance of the process of acculturation/socialization. The speed of convergence could be lower when the costs of change are high and when international interactions are infrequent, or do not induce a process of international socialization. The ongoing process of globalization and internationalization of cultural and moral values should then increase legal convergence.

When legal problems have solutions that can be ranked depending on their efficiency and when the optimal solution is unique, unification occurs in the long run because all countries tend to choose the optimal rule. Legal preferences change in the way that this optimal rule is the preferred rule in the long run. An optimal solution, however, is not necessarily unique. For instance, choosing between the death penalty or a life sentence, or whether or not to legalize same-sex marriages, depend fundamentally on the cultural and moral values of people, of norms within a given country, rather than discussions on the intrinsic efficiency of the rule.

In such cases, theories of legal evolution that build on natural convergence cannot explain the process of legal evolution. Convergence cannot occur by this means. Yet convergence is still often observed for these kinds of rules. We can explain this fact by the effects of acculturation/socialization. From this viewpoint, international socialization can explain the process of legal convergence, even when there is no legal rule intrinsically preferable to others.

References

Alesina, Alberto F. and Bryony Reich. 2013. *Nation Building* (February 2013). NBER Working Paper No. w18839 (available at SSRN: http://ssrn.com/abstract=2226811).

Armour, John, Simon Deakin, Priay Lele, and Mathias Siems. 2009. How Do Legal Rules Evolve? Evidence from a Cross-Country Comparison of Shareholder, Creditor, and Worker Protection. *The American Journal of Comparative Law* 57:579–629.

Balas, Aron, Rafael La Porta, Florencio Lopez-de-Silanes, and Andrei Shleifer. 2009. The Divergence of Legal Procedures. *American Economic Journal* l:138–162.

Barkow, Jerome H., Leda Cosmides, and John Tooby. 1995. *The Adapted Mind: Evolutionary Psychology and the Generation of Culture*. New York, NY: Oxford University Press.

Bebchuk, Lucian Arye, and Mark J. Roe. 1999. A Theory of Path Dependence in Corporate Ownership and Governance. *Stanford Law Review* 52:127–170.

Bisina, Alberto, and Thierry Verdie. 2001. The Economics of Cultural Transmission and the Dynamics of Preferences. *Journal of Economic Theory* 97:298–319.

Bodenstein, Martin, and Heinrich Ursprung. 2005. Political Yardstick Competition, Economic Integration, and Constitutional Choice in a Federation. *Public Choice* 124(3):329–352.

Boranbay, Serra, and Carmine Guerriero. 2012. Endogenous (In) Formal Institutions. *Amsterdam Center for Law & Economics Working Paper* 2012–04.

Bowles, Samuel. 1998. Endogenous Preferences: The Cultural Consequences of Markets and Other Economic Institutions. *Journal of Economic Literature* 36:75–111.

Carbonara, Emanuela, and Francesco Parisi. 2007. The Paradox of Legal Harmonization. *Public Choice* 132:367–400.

Clermont, Kevin M. and Theodore Eisenberg. 1996. Xenophilia in American Courts. *Cornell Law Faculty Publications*. Paper 237. http://scholarship.law.cornell.edu/facpub/237.

Columbato, Enrico and Jonathan Macey. 1997. Lessons from Transition in Eastern Europe: A Property-right Interpretation. *Journal for Institutional Innovation, Development and Transition* 1:10–17.

Crettez, Bertrand, Bruno Deffains, and Olivier Musy. 2013. On Legal Cooperation and the Dynamics of Legal Convergence. *Public Choice* 156:345–356.

Crettez, Bertrand, Bruno Deffains, and Olivier Musy 2014. Legal Harmonization with Endogenous Preferences. *International Review of Law and Economics* 39:20–27.

Dari-Mattiaccia, Giuseppe, Bruno Deffains, and Bruno Lovat. 2011. The Dynamics of the Legal System. *Journal of Economic Behavior and Organization* 79:95–107.

Dari-Mattiacci, Giuseppe, and Carmine Guerriero. 2015. Law and Culture: A Theory of Comparative Variation in Bona Fide Purchase Rules. *Oxford Journal of Legal Studies* 35:543–574.

Deakin, Simon, Priay Lele, and Mathias Siems. 2007. The Evolution of Labour Law: Calibrating and Comparing Regulatory Regimes. *International Labour Review* 146:133–157.

Den Butter, Frank and Robert Mosch. 2003. The Dutch Miracle: Institutions, Networks, and Trust. *Journal of Institutional and Theoretical Economics* 159(2):362–391.

Djankov, Simeaon, Edward Glaeser, Rafael La Porta, Florencio Lopez-de-Silanes, and Andrei Shleifer. 2003. The New Comparative Economics. *Journal of Comparative Economics* 31:595–619.

Easterbrook, Frank H., and Daniel R. Fischel. 1991. *The Economic Structure of Comparative Law*. Cambridge, MA: Harvard University Press.

European Parliament. 2008. Communication to the European on European contract law of September, 2008. www.europarl.europa.eu/sides/getDoc.do?type=TA&reference=P6-TA-2008-0397&language=EN).

Feld, Lars. 2005. The European Constitution Project from the Perspective of Constitutional Political Economy. *Public Choice* 122(3):417–448.

Frey, B.S. and R. Eichenberger. 1996. *FOCJ: Competitive Governments for Europe. International Review for Public Economics* 16:315–327.

Frey, Bruno S., and Reiner Eichenberger. 2001. Metropolitan Governance for the Future: Functional, Overlapping and Competing Jurisdictions. *Swiss Political Science Review* 7:124–130.

Garoupa, Nuno, and Anthony Ogus. 2006. A Strategic Interpretation of Legal Transplants. *Journal of Legal Studies* 35(2):339–363.

Garoupa, Nuno, and Carlos Gomez Liguerre. 2011. The Syndrome of the Efficiency of the Common Law. *Boston University International Law Journal* 29:288–335.

Gómez, Fernando Pomar. 2011. The Economics of Harmonized Law-making in Private Law: Mechanisms, Modes and Standards. Pp. 1–28 in *The Foundations of European Private Law*, edited by Professor Roger Brownsword, Professor Hans W. Micklitz, Leone Niglia, and Stephen Weatherill. Oxford: Hart Publishing.

Goodman, Ryan, and Derek Jinks. 2004. How to Influence States: Socialization and International Human Rights Law. *Duke Law Journal* 54-3:621–703.

Goodman, Ryan, and Derek Jinks. 2005. International Law and State Socialization: Conceptual, Empirical and Normative Challenges. *Duke Law Journal* 54:983–998.

Goodman, Ryan, and Derek Jinks. 2008. Incomplete Internalization and Compliance with Human Rights Law. *The European Journal of International Law* 54:725–748.

Goodman, Ryan, and Derek Jinks. 2013. *Socializing States*. Oxford: Oxford University Press.

Guiso, Luigi, Paola Sapienza, and Luigi Zingales. 2008. Social Capital as Good Culture. *Journal of European Economic Association* 6:295–320.

Guerriero, Carmine. 2013. Endogenous Legal Traditions. *Working paper*.

Hansmann, Henry, and Reinier Kraakman. 2001. The End of History for Corporate Law. *Georgetown Law Journal* 89:439–468.

Herings, p. Jean-Jacques, and Arnald J. Kanning. 2008. Harmonization of Private Law on a Global Level. *International Review of Law and Economics* 28:256–262.

Huck, Steffen. 1998. Trust, Treason, and Trials: An Example of How Evolution of Preferences Can Be Driven by Legal Institution. *Journal of Law, Economics, and Organization* 14:44–60.

Kotsadam, Andreas, and Niklas Jakobsson. 2011. Do Laws Affect Attitudes? An Assessment of the Norwegian Prostitution Law Using Longitudinal Data. *International Review of Law and Economics* 31:103–115.

Kuran, Timur, and William H. Sandholm. 2008. Cultural Integration and its Discontent. *Review of Economic Studies* 75:201–228.

La Porta, Rafael, Florencio Lopez-de-Silanes, and Andrei Shleifer. 2008. The Economic Consequences of Legal Origins. *Journal of Economic Literature* 46(2):285–332.

Legrand, Pierre. 1996. European Legal Systems are Not Converging. *International and Comparative Law Quarterly* 45:52–81.

Legrand, Pierre. 1997. The Impossibility of Legal Transplants. *Maastricht Journal of European and Comparative Law* 4:111–114.

Lele, Priya, and Mathias M. Siems. 2006. Shareholder Protection: a Leximetric Approach. *Journal of Corporate Law Studies* 77:17–50.

Levmore, Saul. 1986. Rethinking Comparative Law: Variety and Uniformity in Ancient and Modern Tort Law. 61 *Tulane Law Review* 235.

Loeper, A. 2008. *Coordination in Federal Systems* Working Paper.

Loeper, A. 2011. Coordination in Heterogeneous Federal Systems. *Journal of Public Economics* 95(7):900–912.

Merryman, John H. 1977. Comparative Law and Social Change: On the Origins, Style, Decline & Revival of the Law and Development Movement. *The American Journal of Comparative Law* 25:457–483.

Merryman, John Henry, David S. Clark, and John O. Haley. 1994. *The Civil Law Tradition: Europe, Latin America and East Asia*. Charlottesville, VA: LexisNexis.

Nunn, Nathan, and Leonard Wantchekon. 2009. The Slave Trade and the Origins of Mistrust in Africa. *NBER Working Paper* 14783.

Palepu, Krishna, Tarun Khanna, and Joseph Kogan. 2002. Globalization and Similarities in Corporate Governance: A Cross-Country Analysis. *Strategy Unit Harvard Working Paper:* 02–41.

Pollack, Mark. 2007. Rational Choice and EU Politics. Pp. 31–56 in *The Handbook of European Union Politics*, edited by Knud Erik Jørgensen, Mark Pollack, and Ben Rosamond. New York, NY: Sage Publications.

Posner, Richard. 1979. Utilitarianism, Economics, and Legal Theory, *Journal of Legal Studies* 8:103–131.

Priest, Georges. 1977. The Common Law Process and the Selection of Efficient Rules. *Journal of Legal Studies* 6:65–99.

Quinn, Dennis P., and A. Maria Toyoda. 2007. Ideology and Voter Preferences as Determinants of Financial Globalization. *American Journal of Political Science* 51(2):344–363.

Rodrik, Dani. 2004. Globalization and Growth – Looking in the Wrong Places. *Journal of Policy Modeling* 26(4):513–517.

Roe, Mark J. 2000. Political Preconditions to Separating Ownership from Corporate Control. *Stanford Law Review* 53:539–606.

Siems, Mathias M. 2008. *Convergence in Shareholder Law*. New York, NY: Cambridge University Press.

Siems, Mathias M. 2011. Measuring the Immeasurable: How to Turn Law into Numbers? Pp. 115–136 in *On Law and Economic Growth*, edited by Michael Faure and Jan Smits. Cambridge: Instentia.

Sokol, Daniel D. 2011. Explaining the Importance of Public Choice for Law. *Michigan Law Review* 109(6):1029–1048.

Turrini, Alessandro Antonio and Tanguy, van Ypersele. 2006. Legal Costs as Barriers to Trade. *CEPR Discussion Paper 5751*.

Zweigert, Konrad, and Hein Kötz. 1998. *An Introduction to Comparative Law* Vol. 3. Oxford: Clarendon Press.

Notes

1 This essay is based on the different models developed by Crettez, Deffains, and Musy (2013 and 2014).

2 Political fiat from a superior authority is principally a reference to the colonial situation which is not discussed in that paper.

PART II

Application

3 *The Evolution of Contract Law in China*

Convergence in Law but Divergence in Enforcement?

JING LENG* AND WEI SHEN**

1 Introduction

This chapter provides an overview of the contract law system in the People's Republic of China (PRC). The central theme is that while the black letter contract law has indicated a trend of convergence moving toward some basic norms which appear in other countries' contract laws and international conventions, the enforcement of contract law shows a visible trend of moving toward a hybrid regime combining features of both formal and informal enforcement mechanisms. This paradigm of evolution reveals the intricacies and complexities in China's contract law regime as well as the country's rule of law movement in general. This chapter will demonstrate how this peculiar pattern of legal development has been formed and how it could inform our understanding of possibilities and ramifications of legal convergence and persistence in an increasingly globalized world.

2 Legislative History and Structure of Contract Law

2.1 *Legislative History*

Before the initiation of the reform and opening-up era in PRC there had been only contractual practices but no legislative activity in relation to contracts. It was not until the early 1980s that China started to enact laws on contracts, beginning with the promulgation of the Law on Economic Contracts of 1981, which was followed by the Law of

* Professor Leng thanks Jianxing Li and Longyan Ni for research assistance.
** The authors thank Huihui Zhang for formatting the article to conform to the citation style.

Foreign-related Economic Contracts of 1985 and the Law of Technology Contracts of 1987, each of which dealt with particular types of contracts based on the nature of business as well as the identity of parties. In addition, the General Principles of Civil Law (GPCL), promulgated in 1986, are also applicable to contractual activity. As a significant development, the Contract Law of 1999 replaced the three earlier statutes to unify the nation's contractual legislative framework which had been fragmented for almost two decades (Wang 1999, p. 7; Ling 2002). The 1999 Contract Law achieved a degree of uniformity in China's contract law regime. The fact that the Contract Law abolishes the differential treatment of domestic and foreign parties and applies equally to them conforms to the national treatment principle, the core pillar principle under the General Agreement on Tariffs and Trade (GATT) and its successor, the World Trade Organization (WTO). In subsequent times, China further enacted two other contractual statutes – the Law of Rural Land Contracts of 2002 and the Law of Labour Contracts of 2007.

As the Contract Law is the centerpiece of China's legislative output in the field of commercial law, it is worthwhile recounting the historical background in which it was enacted, which offers a glimpse into the social and economic settings at earlier stages of China's transition to the market economy which was the context for the legislative efforts. As the fragmented structure of the contractual legislation at the time had increasingly been proven costly and outdated, there was a strong need for a unified contract law to remove discrepancies and inconsistencies among various contract codes. In 1993, the building of a socialist market economy was formally endorsed by the China Communist Party with the goal of deepening economic reforms. This heightened the agenda for legislative endeavors on contracts.

In 1993, the initial drafting work was undertaken by academics in 12 research institutions, including established universities and the China Academy of Social Sciences, which were entrusted with the task by the Standing Committee of the National People's Congress (NPC) (Liang 1996). The draft statute was polished several times after heated discussion and debate in the circles of legislators and academics before being settled as a final text. The NPC passed the law in 1999, which, signaling a high degree of legislative sophistication and foresight, has remained unchanged ever since. Importantly, there have been three subsequent judicial interpretations issued by the Supreme People's Court

(SPC) in 1999, 2009, and 2012, respectively, that have helped substantiate the implementation of the Contract Law. In addition, the SPC has also issued a number of judicial interpretations on specific types of contract, such as contracts on sales of goods, sales of commercial housing, constructions, transfers of state-owned land use rights, subcontracting of rural land, foreign-related civil and commercial issues, urban house leasing, financial leasing, foreign-invested enterprises, travelling, and informal financing (Han 2011b, pp. 19, 369–378, 706; Tian 2013, p. 5; China Legal Publishing House 2015, pp. 18–19).

With regard to the enactment of the Contract Law, there were several important considerations underlining the meticulous drafting process (Hu 2010). First, under the then fragmented framework of contractual legislation, domestic economic contracts, foreign-related economic contracts, and technology transfer contracts were governed by different sets of legal rules. The stratification was prone to gaps in application and enforcement, reinforced by broad-brushed stipulations which lacked operative details. Second, there was a need for additional rules to combat increasing contractual fraud in market transactions which had infringed upon the interests of the state, collective units, and citizens. Third, previous legislation had left out multiple types of contracts, such as contracts on financial leasing, commission, and brokerage, calling for a significant expansion of the legislative coverage. Finally, as contents in the previous three statutes corresponding to the characteristics of a planned economy had become obsolete when the country was moving toward a market economy, a unified new contract law was expected to remove those out-of-date provisions. In particular, the legislative purpose was clarified as upholding the lawful rights and interests of parties, not ensuring the execution of economic plans. This goal was enshrined in the principles of freedom of contract, fairness, as well as honesty and good faith which were incorporated in the text of the Contract Law, as opposed to emphasizing government oversight of contracting activity through administrative monitoring and sanctions under the previous statutes (Liang 1999a, pp. 26–27).

2.2 Legislative Style

The development of the socialist market economy has given rise to the concept of commercial law as a relatively distinct area of law, with contract law being one of its core elements. A widely shared consensus in academic circles is that China practices the fusion of civil law and commercial law (*minshang heyi*) in legislative activity, in the sense that there need not be a commercial code in addition to a civil code even though the enactment of a long-awaited Civil Code has been protracted for many years. Instead, it is believed that the general principles and rules of civil law provide the foundation for commercial law, which builds on the basis of the more specialized principles and rules in the civil law applicable to the relationships and the activities among profit-making business entities of equal legal status (Chen 2011, pp. 161, 316, 318). As a result, in PRC there is no Commercial Code but only a quasi-civil code titled the General Principles of Civil Law (GPCL), as mentioned above.

The GPCL spells out baseline principles and rules in relation to the regulation of personal and property relations arising from all kinds of civil acts, including contracting. The GPCL consists of three central elements – subjects of civil law (including individuals and legal persons), ownership and "obligations" (*zhaiquan*), and supplementary elements concerning "legal acts," proprietary rights, agency, limitation periods, and compensation for loss (Chen 2011, pp. 161, 316, 318). The section on "obligations" provides some basic guidelines governing contractual relationships, but is very general and scanty in substantive prescriptions. The vast room left unaddressed by the GPCL for regulating contracts is primarily filled by the Contract Law.

2.3 Types of Contracts

In the Contract Law, 15 types of contracts are addressed separately, called "named contracts" (known as "typical contracts" in Taiwan; see Chapter 4), each occupying an individual chapter. The 15 types of named contracts cover the following areas: sales, supply and use of electricity, water, gas and heating, donation, loans, lease, financial leasing, hiring for work, construction, transportation, technology, storage, warehousing, commission, brokerage, and intermediation (Zhang 2006, pp. 11–12, 87, 132).

Other types of contracts not covered in the Contract Law are nevertheless recognized as "unnamed contracts," which are less frequently used in practice. Unnamed contracts are also subject to the Contract Law through the practice of "application by analogy" (Zhang 2006, pp. 11–12, 87, 132). This means if there is a certain type of contract that is not listed in the Contract Law, it shall still be governed by the provisions in the statute that are most closely related to such contracts (Article 124).

3 Influence of Foreign Law and International Conventions versus Local Characteristics

The Contract Law displays traits of a strong influence of foreign law and international conventions as well as of local characteristics reflecting peculiar domestic needs.

3.1 Influence of Foreign Law and International Conventions

Legislative techniques and particular legal mechanisms from both civil law and common law systems were incorporated in the drafting of the Contract Law. This attitude of openness to advanced overseas experience permeates the text. For example, the law has instituted the mechanism of "unrest defense" traditionally used in the civil law system on the one hand (Articles 68 and 69), and the notion and practice of "anticipated repudiation" originating from the common law system on the other (Article 94(2), Article 108). Another example is the deviation in the Contract Law from the principle of liability at (presumed) fault in attributing liability for breach of contract. This principle has traditionally been used in civil codes across civil law jurisdictions, including France, Germany, Japan, and Switzerland. China instead adopts the common law principle of strict liability to protect the interests of the innocent party via extended scope of liability for breaches, as emphasized below.

The other issue concerning learning from overseas experience relates to alignments with international conventions on contracts. The first of the guiding principles on legislating for contract law made it clear that China should make broad references to successful practices, judicial precedents and scholarship in advanced market economies, participate in international markets, adopt common rules underlying the inner workings of the modern market economy, and stay consistent with international conventions and commercial customs (Liang 1999b, p. 121). Here, "international conventions" primarily refer to the United Nations Convention on Contracts for the International Sale of Goods (CISG), which has been in effect in China since 1988.

There are several aspects of the influence of the CISG on the Contract Law.

First, the law has incorporated key contents in the CISG in relation to the formation of contract, such as definition of offer, definition of invitation for offer, validity of offer upon arrival, revocation of offer and its restrictions, expiration of offer, definition of acceptance, validity of acceptance upon arrival, validity of late acceptance, revocation of acceptance, as well as validity of both written and oral contracts. China was the tenth signatory state to the CISG, which came into effect in China's territory on January 1, 1988. It has generally been agreed that the CISG had a crucial influence on the development of Chinese contract law (Blase 2000, p. 95). However, it is not clear from the legislative documentation why the CISG was used as a template for drafting the Contract Law. The literature appears to suggest that the CISG was often viewed by Chinese scholars and government authorities, in particular, the then Ministry of Foreign Trade and Economic Cooperation, the predecessor of the Ministry of Commerce, as a more advanced international convention on contract law rules (Ding 1999, p. 25) as it represents a great success to harmonize the differences in contract law norms and principles among various legal families. Given the fact that China is one of the largest trading nations in the world, relying on a more harmonized contract law code helps generate lower transaction costs and reduce potential disputes. Modeling its Contract Law on the CISG also means that the transplant would be easier and less costly for China compared to other options. In this sense, China's borrowing of the CISG to unify and upgrade its Contract Law was an evolution toward efficiency.

Second, as to the conditions triggering the termination of contract, the Contract Law has accepted the doctrine of "fundamental breach" prescribed in the CISG, although with minor variations in wording (Han 2011a, p. 11). The law also follows the CISG in recognizing the validity of amendments to, or termination of, contract by consensual agreement. There is also no difference in the prescriptions on consequences of termination of contract between the CISG and the Contract Law.

Third, on liability for breach of contract and exemptions from liability, there are also signs of convergence with the CISG. For example, while the CISG incorporates both notions of "anticipatory repudiation" at common law and "unrest defense" (*Unsicherheitseinrede*) in the civil law tradition, the Contract Law recognizes both of these notions to the same effect. Under the CISG, the establishment of liability of the breaching party for compensating losses suffered by the other party does not require fault, but comes with possibilities of exemptions from liability. Such a system is called "strict liability" and has been written into the Contract Law as it is widely regarded as one of the overwhelming tendencies for contract law development around the world, although some civil law jurisdictions still adhere to the principle of liability at fault. In addition, in calculating losses as the basis of damage compensation, the Contract Law follows the CISG in adopting the rule of foreseeability.

3.2 Reflections on Local Characteristics

The Contract Law is heavily reflective of the transitional environment and dynamics during the period of economic and social reforms in the PRC. It shows clear signs of trying to deal with a distinct set of problems and conflicts faced by contracting parties in the country's gradual transition to a market economy.

For example, the "right of subrogation" (Article 73) has in particular been instituted for mitigating the problem of "triangular chains of debts" (*san jiao zhai*) in practice where the difficulty of collecting debts is colored by multiple, intermingling contractual relationships. A common scenario is that A is the creditor to B who is, in turn, the creditor to C, with C being the creditor to A. This problem of revolving debts had been pervasive in the early years of the reform of state-owned enterprises (SOEs) when the double identity of both creditor and debtor was so commonly observed in the state sector.

Other examples of China-specific provisions include the following (Liang 1999a, p. 27):

- The "right of cancellation" targets debtors who tried to evade or repudiate debts by transferring properties to a third party (Article 74).
- The obligation of the seller to transfer ownership of the subject matter to the buyer is aimed at remedying previous mishandling of cases by authorities (courts or administrative agencies) where a sales

contract was nullified due to lack of formal registration of ownership transfer (Article 135).

- Multiple assurances for overseeing the formation and performance of construction contracts triggered by the particular difficulty in ensuring high-quality projects in a business environment where honesty and professionalism are often overshadowed by a thirst for profit. The requirement of an open tender for the formation of construction contracts and the adoption of a compulsory supervision system are responses to the serious social problem of poor-quality construction projects that had resulted in personal injuries and property damages (Article 271 and Article 276).
- To address abuses of attribution of liability to third parties for breach of contract in adjudicative practice, the law enshrines the doctrine of "privity of contract" by holding the breaching party liable despite of a third party's culpability (Article 121).

Another of the unique mechanisms specific to the country's transforming social and economic settings is the set of rules for establishing the validity of contracting acts by "legal representatives" of legal persons and other organizations in the context of ultra vires (Article 50). Unless the counterparty knows or ought to have known that the legal representative had overstepped his or her authorized scope of powers, the contract so concluded shall be valid (Liang 1999a, p. 29).

So far we can see that the Contract Law has taken into consideration both well-established international practices and pertinent domestic demands. Why should a legal convergence of this kind ever occur? The main reason is that interactions of different legal systems increase transaction costs in cross-border businesses, particularly in terms of collecting and understanding legal information and the uncertainty concerning national legal procedures. The main function of legal convergence on contracts is the reduction of both legal uncertainty and transaction costs in both international and domestic trade (Chapter 2). This applies equally to the PRC in its incorporation of foreign rules and international conventions into the Contract Law when the country in the late 1990s was starting to unify its previously fragmented domestic product market held up by local protectionism and to tap the global market of trade and investment.

In this process, unique problems of contractual difficulties arising from transitioning and still underdeveloped legal and business environments nevertheless required local solutions not attended by foreign law and international conventions. This is primarily why the PRC Contract Law has shown signs of both convergence toward international norms and persistence with local practices.

3.2.1 Public Policy

As pointed out above, the recognition of international standards and norms has not led to the disregard for local conditions and particularities. Chinese Contract Law, at least on occasions, is reflective of strong local flavors albeit with the CISG's liberal imprint. One of the features of the Contract Law is its room for subjecting the party autonomy to public policy. Although no explicit expression of "public policies" is found in the Contract Law, scholars nevertheless argue that the expression "public interests in society" in Article 52(5), which shall not be violated by contracts, can be rephrased as "public policies," which could be interpreted to include both public order and public morality (Wang 2011, p. 660). Because contracts that violate public interests would be held null and void, by the same token, contracts that disrupt public policies shall also be invalidated. Public policies can enter the inner system of civil law through the so-called "transferring clauses" (Su 2005, p. 8).

The existence of public policy as a legal concept in law and its application in particular cases are quite common in other jurisdictions. In China's context, the situation has two dimensions. First, the concept of public policy is deliberately undefined. Judging from the General Principles of Civil Law, the public policy prevails over international conventions. However, there is no specific interpretation of "public policy," and Chinese law is also silent on the standard by which the "social and public interest" is held superior to the "international conventions." According to the General Principles of Civil Law as well as the Civil Procedure Law, China's "social public interest" may be locked in the objective criterion, that is, whether there is any contradiction to the PRC law. Owing to the ambiguous scope of public policy, the second problem is that the courts often make expansive use of public policy considerations in adjudicating commercial disputes, which creates uncertainty, thereby increasing transaction costs. For example, public policy is expansively used by Chinese courts to practice local protectionism (Long and Wang 2015, pp. 48–59).

3.2.2 Government Intervention

The principle of party autonomy is often compromised by government intervention. It has been widely recognized that the state always plays a prominent role in steering the direction of foreign investment and also of national economic development (compared to a similar phenomenon in Taiwan, described in Chapter 4). Despite the progress in developing greater ties with the international systems of commerce and finance, state control over the direction of foreign investment has been a pronounced norm of the regulatory regime. The extent of state control is best evidenced by the approval regime in the admission of foreign investment. The government authorities are involved in all stages of a foreign investment project, from its formation, through its operation and on to its termination. The approval and/or registration procedures are a prerequisite to foreign investment at almost all stages of a project. For instance, a contract which needs to be approved by the government authority comes into effect only after the grant of the approval. The continuing modernization of the Chinese legal system, institutional infrastructure and institutional designs is moving towards a hybrid configuration involving a strengthening of the state's managerial role and the transformation of a closed society into a liberal and open society. Challenges of securing administrative licenses and business approvals and navigating China's licensing and regulatory procedures have been in existence since the inception of foreign investment regime. The area of law and practice is deeply problematic and unreasonable delays occur too often. The licensing and approval procedures may take much longer than would be expected. Confusion arises frequently when various authorities interpret and apply laws in different ways. Discretionary administrative powers and discrepant local standards often render preparation and paperwork difficult and the results of approval unpredictable. Many foreign investors may have to devote significant amounts of managerial time and resources to handling approvals and licensing issues (US–China Business Council 2007). While the Communist Party has recently shown a determination to allow the market to play a decisive role, removing excessive government intervention from the commercial arena has a long way to go.

3.2.3 Default Rules versus Mandatory Rules

The distinction between default and mandatory rules in contract law is that default rules can be opted out by party autonomy whereas mandatory rules are not subject to exclusion by party autonomy. In the PRC Contract Law, the vast majority of provisions are default rules which can be contracted around, leaving limited room for the legislature to prescribe mandatory rules.

Generally speaking, under the principle of freedom of contract, contract law around the world is commonly characterized by the dominance of default rules, as is the case with the Contract Law. There are also supplementary rules on gap-filling which can be applied when there is no clear indication of the party will. For example, the Contract Law specifies solutions to incomplete or ambiguous contracts by allowing parties to reach supplementary agreements, or to make inferences from existing contract terms or transaction practices, or to follow a set of stand-by standards in the law, if the parties to the contract lack a clear prior expression of will on the relevant aspects of contract (Articles 61 and 62).

As to categorizations of the default rules, the law and economics scholars made a well-known distinction on efficiency grounds between the so-called "penalty default rules" (purposefully set at what the parties would not want), "tailored defaults" (providing precisely what the individual contracting parties would have reasonably wanted in their specific circumstances), and "untailored defaults" (representing what the majority of contracting parties would want) (Ayres and Gertner 1989, p. 91). It was suggested that it may be efficient for courts and legislatures to choose default rules that a majority of people actually object to (penalty defaults) and to intentionally increase the transaction costs of contracting around these rules in order to encourage information disclosure by the more informed party to her counter party and to the court (Ayres and Gertner 1989, p. 95). One such example is the zero-quantity default rule in the Uniform Commercial Code (UCC), under which courts will not enforce a contract when parties did not specify a quantity term *ex ante*. The rationale behind this is that it is less costly for the parties to contract around this default rule by including a quantity term in *ex ante* contracting than for the courts to decide on what quantity the parties "would have desired" in *ex post* litigation (Ayres and Gertner 1989, p. 96). This distinction, however, does not seem to find a similar application under the PRC Contract Law. Under the Contract Law, the parties need to specify a quantity term *ex ante* (Article 12(3)). When the parties failed to specify a quantity term, the statute is not clear as to whether or not the contract would continue to be enforceable (Contract Law, Article 62). The SPC judicial interpretation, nevertheless, fills in that gap by indicating that if the court can decide on the quantity, the contract should be deemed valid (Judicial Interpretation on Several Questions Regarding Application of the Contract Law (Part II), 2009, Article 1). Otherwise, the court may view the contract as being invalid. On balance, this judicial stance is less rigid than that suggested by the UCC. The difference lies in the discretion given by the statute to the court to explore what the parties "would have wanted" when the quantity clause is not specified. Under the UCC, the court can simply leave the matter aside and refuse to enforce the contract (i.e., refuse to calculate on what the parties "would have wanted"). In the PRC, by comparison, the court may come up with a quantity term by exploring what the parties "would have desired" of their contractual dealing, and would only refuse to enforce the contract when it could not decide on the quantity term by interpreting the contract. The judicial position in the PRC contract law regime on the quantity term, therefore, can be understood as adopting a tailored default rule, instead of a penalty default rule.

An even trickier task is to judge (adjudicate) what rules should be characterized as "mandatory." Normally, a primary judgment can be made on the basis of the literal wording of the rules where commands like "shall not," "shall," and "must" appear (Dong 2002, pp. 51–52; Huang 2010, p. 106). Meanwhile, a provision can be understood as "mandatory" if it appears in, or is required by, laws (made by the National People's Congress and its Standing Committee) and administrative regulations (made by the State Council).[1] When it is not crystal clear whether a provision is mandatory or not, the Supreme People's Court has instructed lower courts to make decisions with a comprehensive understanding of the goal and purpose of relevant laws and regulations and balancing conflicting interests.[2]

4 Interpretation of Contract

As another example of convergence, rules on the interpretation of contract in the PRC follow a number of internationally accepted principles and practices, including the highly context-specific rule of making references to commercial customs.

4.1 Contract Interpretation Rules

Article 125 of the Contract Law lays out the general framework for contract interpretation. It suggests that when there is a dispute between parties over the understanding of contract terms, the true meaning of such terms shall be determined by an overall balancing of the literal wording of disputed terms, other relevant contract terms, the purpose of contract, commercial customs, and the principle of honesty and good faith.

First, the priority method used in contract interpretation is literal interpretation, meaning respecting the literal wording of disputed contract terms and their underlying substance.

Second, another method of interpretation is contextual interpretation, which situates the disputed terms in the overall structure of the entire contract in search of their true meaning, especially by taking into consideration the meaning and purpose of other terms (Liang 1995).

Third, the method of interpretation by contract purpose is also encouraged by the law when, as in a number of cases, the literal meaning alone might not be sufficient to form the basis of construing the true meaning of disputed terms.

Fourth, commercial customs may also be consulted in deciding the true meaning of disputed terms. Commercial customs are the commonly accepted practices in particular trades or sectors through longstanding and repeated dealings. They are followed by the players in such trades or sectors largely by consensus. It is therefore desirable that when no agreement can be reached among parties on the meaning of disputed terms, the commercial customs play their role in interpreting the contract. In addition, commercial customs can also serve as references in filling contract loopholes that have rendered parties' rights and obligations vague or ambiguous (Long 2001).

Finally, as the "paramount rule" (or the "emperor clause") in civil law, the principle of honesty and good faith is widely recognized to be the most fundamental moral directive in market economies. This principle is also one of the fundamental rules for contract interpretation across the world, as is the case with the PRC Contract Law.

There are also some mandatory rules for the contract interpretation. For example, the Contract Law requires that "the terms of a contract shall be prescribed by the parties, and generally include . . . quantity, quality, subject matter, and time, place and method of performance" (Article 12). Absent party agreement, some mandatory rules may kick in. When the "quality requirement was not clearly prescribed, performance shall be in accordance with the state standard or industry standard,... in accordance with the customary standard or any particular standard consistent with the purpose of the contract" (Article 62(1)). Similarly, without a party agreement, "a term shall be determined in accordance with the relevant provisions of the contract or in accordance with the relevant transaction customs" (Article 61). The Contract Law then offers greater clarity by setting forth both the baseline quality level and a mandatory hierarchy of default standards.

4.2 Use of Commercial Customs

The Contract Law permits the use of commercial customs in filling contract loopholes. However, scholars have yet to settle on a satisfactory definition of what exactly constitutes commercial customs. Some view customary law endorsed by the state as "commercial customs" in the context of the Contract Law (Luo 2002). Others consider commercial customs as a floating legal concept to be given specific meaning only by judges through case-by-case adjudication (Chen 2011).

Another justification for allowing the application of commercial customs to fill contract loopholes relates to the fact that parties follow them voluntarily. Therefore, in the absence of any contradictory evidence, commercial customs are powerful indicators of the true intent of the parties. An interesting example of courts applying commercial customs to resolve contract disputes is provided by a local court in Shandong province concerning the interpretation of a payment clause in a rural land subcontracting contract. In this case, two parties (the landowner A and the subcontractor B) had agreed that: (1) A would subcontract his land to B for farming purposes; (2) the annual subcontracting fees would be 100 RMB yuan; and (3) the fees should be paid on an annual basis, with each payment made in a lump sum by December 30. What the parties did not specify, however, was whether the annual payment should be made for the use of land during the current year or during the following year. A insisted that the payment should be made *ex ante* before each farming year began while B contended that the payment should be made *ex post* at the end of each farming year. The court ruled in favor of A by resorting to the prevailing commercial custom that it is a common practice for the subcontractor to pay fees prior to commencement of the actual farming activity (Han 2011b, pp. 19, 369–378, 706).

5 Relationship Between Contract Law and Administrative Authorities

There has been an intriguing relationship between the contract law on the one hand, and administrative authorities on the other, which shows a sustained withdrawal of government intervention from contracting activity. This serves as another important indication of China's convergence with international norms and practices with regard to contracts.

Due to its strong affinity with party autonomy, contract law usually does not concern administrative power. That said, in modern contract law, the freedom of contract is still subject to a certain degree of administrative monitoring and oversight by government authorities. Such authorities are either established for the specific purpose of enforcing contract law, or entrusted by the law to exercise an oversight and management function. The enforcement agency for combating antimonopoly violations is one such example.

In the legislative history of the Contract Law, there was strong vigilance to administrative interference and encroachment among the drafters, given the long-lasting influence from the legacy of a planned economy. As a result, the drafters had fought fiercely to remove a proposed article which would give power to the industrial and commercial administrative agencies and other overseeing agencies at various levels of the government to "monitor contracts." This, they thought, would seriously curtail parties' freedom of contract, which would hinder the inner workings of a market economy (Liang 1999c, p. 20).

In debating whether to delete the proposed article, the drafters found that in the decade following the enactment of the Law on Economic Contracts of 1981, a total of 143,000 contracts, involving a staggering amount of RMB 34.2 billion yuan in transaction values, had been nullified by the industrial and commercial administrative agencies across the country. This pervasive practice of government agencies invalidating contracts was not only rare in other jurisdictions, but also lacked justification in jurisprudence.

Responding to the changing dynamics of economic and social transition, the Contract Law finally resolved to allocate the power for invalidating contracts to the court, removing this power from administrative authorities. Meanwhile, the law also abolished a general contract management system previously enforced by the administrative agencies. With regard to necessary and legitimate government monitoring and oversight, the law provides for a residual power preserved for the government to sanction illegal activity which violates state interests and public interests under the guise of contracts, as well as to pursue criminal liability (Article 127).

Although freedom of contract as an internationally practiced principle has featured prominently under the articles of the Contract Law, there remains a necessary space reserved for the government to conduct commercial regulation and oversight when state and public interests are at stake. This is a tacit acknowledgement of possibilities of market failures and the need for state intervention of abusive contractual activity which cannot be remedied by party autonomy and market mechanisms. How to efficiently allocate powers to sanction the validity of contracts between the courts and regulatory agencies is one of the central concerns in the ongoing development of China's contract law regime, which is still subject to debate, especially in the context of complex financial contracts in the banking, securities and assets management industries.

6 Remedies for Breach of Contract

There are three forms of remedies under the Contract Law: continuing performance, damages, and penalty.

6.1 Continuing Performance versus Damages

Continuing performance allows the aggrieved party to demand that the breaching party continue to perform the contractual obligations if such performance is still possible. Substitute performance is not allowed as the purpose of continuing performance is to have the contract performed as agreed. In this sense, continuing performance is close to the concept of specific performance or actual performance as the non-performing party is compelled to complete the performance of the contract. As continuing performance is compelled by the aggrieved party, it is no longer the same as voluntary performance. Seen from this angle, continuing performance is a legal obligation that is enforced through compulsion. Continuing performance, as a remedy, is commonly applied to monetary obligations. With regard to continuing performance of nonmonetary obligations, the Contract Law has different rules. The law provides that the request for the continuing performance of nonmonetary obligations will not be granted in any of the following situations: (a) the performance cannot be made as a matter of law or as a matter of fact; (b) the subject matter of the obligation is unfit for compulsory performance or the expenses for the performance are excessively high; or (c) the obligee fails to make the request for performance within a reasonable period of time (Article 110).

The first scenario is known as the impossibility rule, which is applied when the continuing performance is rendered impossible either by law or by fact. The second scenario is a so-called impracticability rule, under which continuing performance is impracticable either because of the unique nature of contract or because of prohibitively high costs. Continuing performance is unsuitable when a contract involves personal relationship or personal trust. A partnership contract is a good example of this. The third scenario, also called the time rule, is easy to understand. Continuing performance may not be granted without the request of the aggrieved party but any such request must be made within a reasonable period of time after the breach of a contract by the other party, else the right to make the request will be deemed waived or lost. The time rule has a twofold effect: to maintain a rational relation between the players of business transactions, and to achieve market efficiency.

Remedial measures include repair, replacement, reworking, the return of goods, and a reduction in price or some form of remuneration. The purpose of these measures is to cure the defects in performance and to prevent further losses or damages that may be incurred after the contract is breached. These measures are more suitable to nonconforming performance or performance that does not meet the standard, specification or terms as agreed upon by the parties to the contract. Article 111 is the main clause in the Contract Law dealing with remedial measures. According to Article 111, the aggrieved party can elect to seek remedial measures from the counterparty in light of the nature of the subject matter and the degree of loss when there is no agreement between the parties on the liability for nonconforming quality of performance or such agreement is unclear, nor can the liability be determined by supplemental agreement, contract provisions, or transactional customs. Remedial measures share a similarity with continuing performance as some remedial measures are available to ensure that the contract be performed as agreed upon by the parties.

Damages are the monetary remedy to compensate the loss that the aggrieved party suffers from the breach. Damages are available in most cases when a contract is breached. Damages can be applicable to any case where other remedies are not suitable, available or adequate. This means that damages, as a remedial measure, can be used as a supplement to other remedial measures. This is clarified by Article 112, which provides that if one party to a contract fails to perform the contract or its performance fails to satisfy the terms of the contract, and if the aggrieved party has suffered other loss, the party in breach, after performing his obligations or taking other remedial measures, shall compensate for the loss.

The scope of damages usually covers just property damages. Personal damages, such as mental distress or emotional damages caused as a result of breach of the contract, are not covered. Article 122 supports this stance. It provides that if the breach of contract by one party infringes upon the other party's personal or property rights, the aggrieved party shall be entitled to ask the breaching party to bear liability for breach under this law or to seek tort liability against the party in breach in accordance with other laws. In practice, the aggrieved party is even allowed to change or modify the cause of action after a choice is made pursuant to Article 122 of the Contract Law but before the first instance trial at court begins.[3]

Damages usually only include direct loss and expected benefits (interests). Further, Chinese law does not recognize either reliance interest or restitutional interest. Even though the Contract Law appears vague in terms of the scope of damages, the general view is that direct damages and expectation interests constitute "full compensation" to the aggrieved party. This is a so-called "full compensation" rule.

The Contract Law places no emphasis on any particular form of remedies, which means that all these remedies are optional to the aggrieved party. The aggrieved party may choose from three remedial forms (continuing performance, damages, or penalty) in cases of either nonperformance or nonconforming performance. The breaching party is under legal obligations to compensate the aggrieved party for the loss if continuous performance or other remedial measures are insufficient to cover the aggrieved party's losses (Article 112).

Continuing performance is similar to specific performance. In common law, courts invoke equitable remedies only when they think that legal remedies are likely to offer inadequate relief. In this sense, specific performance is supplementary to under-compensatory damage payments. In China, the general rule is that these remedies are not mutually exclusive. This means that continuing performance (specific performance) may be deemed to be a routine contract remedy. The Contract Law's specific performance rule represents a departure from established rules. First, it departs from China's civil law tradition, which used to prioritize specific performance over damages. Now there is no differentiation between compensation and specific performance in terms of priority in application. Second, it is a deviation from Article 28 of the CISG, which restricts the use of specific performance. The Contract Law provides for specific performance as an explicit remedy under the contract (Article 75).

Characterizing specific performance as a routine contract remedy may achieve higher economic efficiency for several reasons. First, incorporating specific performance as a routine remedy sends a notice to the contracting parties that the contract is to be specifically enforced. The parties then have a stronger incentive to efficiently allocate the risks of loss in the process of negotiating the contract. They would be less willing to leave this task to the court or arbitration tribunal, which is not involved in the contractual formation process and is unfamiliar with the contractual setting. Second, this can promote efficient breach[4] of contract as equating damage payments and specific performance offers the most efficient mechanism for protecting subjective or deal-specific values attached to performance. Third, the post-breach costs of adjusting a contract to benefit the highest-valuing party will be lower as the costs of determining various parties' valuation of performance are borne by those parties in voluntary negotiations. Therefore, the party who is most willing to pay the amount (because of the highest value of performance) is to bear the costs of making the decision. Finally, this can lower the judicial costs of adjudicating subjective values of the performing party, and in turn protect the performing party's deal-specific valuation.

It is worth noting that some empirical research confirms the rare use of specific performance as a contractual remedy in some civil law countries in Europe. This avoidance is largely attributed to the enforcement costs for the actions that need to be undertaken. Taking such actions to enforce specific performance is administratively costly to the aggrieved party. As a result, some countries, such as Denmark, have abandoned specific performance as a legal remedy (Lando and Rose 2004, pp. 473–487). At the normative level, based on the doctrines of efficient breach and efficient enforcement, damages may be used as the chief remedy in contractual disputes. China's Contract Law deviates from the civil-law tradition of prioritizing specific performance and opts for the common-law tradition of using damages as the principal remedies. Based on the efficient breach theory (Posner 1998, p. 145; Cf. Katz 1998, p. 138), China's Contract Law is arguably moving toward efficiency when it comes to remedies.

6.2 The Scope of Damages

Damages can be defined as the monetary remedy to compensate the loss that the aggrieved party suffered as a result of the breach. In contrast to other remedies, damages are universally used (Holmes 1991, pp. 300–301) and can be generally applied to any case where other remedies are not available, suitable or adequate, or can be used to fill the gap left by other remedies or to supplement the loss that could not be covered by other remedies (Article 112).

Compensatory damages are deemed as compensatory because their purpose is to restore the aggrieved party to the same position as the aggrieved party would have been in if the contract had been performed as agreed upon by the parties. Thus, the amount of damages, as stated by the Contract Law, shall be equal to the loss caused by the breach of contract, including the interests that would be expected to obtain if the contract is to be performed (Article 113). Accordingly, the aggrieved party may recover from the breaching party the actual losses and consequential damages (that is, the benefits that are expected). The expectation measure of damages stresses the gain that the aggrieved party anticipated from performance of the contract (Article 113). Consequential damages here are closer to possible consequences, which give the nonbreaching party a greater chance to obtain such damages.[5] The expectation measure is not necessarily economically efficient as the guaranteed profit may induce overreliance by the performing party. The foreseeability rule is therefore used to address this excess expectation issue. The damages are also capped by the probable loss caused by the breach of contract, that had been foreseen or should have been foreseen when the contract was made.

The Contract Law follows the rule of foreseeability when it comes to the issue of causation which concerns the relationship between the fact of breach of contract and the loss. The foreseeability rule requires that the damages be awarded only if they are probable consequences of the breach and such consequences were foreseeable by the parties at the time of contract formation. Accordingly, the breaching party is only liable for the damages that could be reasonably foreseen. The foreseeability rule to some extent keeps the damages within certain boundaries, and lowers the level of damages. The determination of both actual loss and expectation interest is subject to the rule of foreseeability.[6]

But the applicability of the foreseeability rule is not yet clear under the Contract Law. In practice, it is the court that determines what damages are foreseeable. The court may examine the connection between the breach and the loss, and see whether the damages claimed by the aggrieved party are the reasonable and natural outcomes of the breach that would be contemplated by an ordinary person in the same or similar situation at the time of contract formation.

The foreseeability rule effectively lowers the transaction cost by allocating the cost of monitoring risks to the party with knowledge of the risk so that this party can take appropriate precautions or reveal the risk to the counterparty and pay him to assume it. By doing so, the risks are allocated in a more efficient manner.

In contrast to compensatory damages, liquidated damages are provided in advance and take effect when the breach occurs. In addition, liquidated damages are not determined on the basis of actual loss. Rather, liquidated damages are determined by the contracting parties through the provisions of their agreement. Liquidated damages can be made in the form of a specific amount of money or in the form of a particular formula by which the damages are calculated.

6.3 Liquidated Damage and Penalty

There is a ceiling that limits the compensatory damages to the amount not exceeding the probable loss, caused by the breach of contract, that had been foreseen or should have been foreseen when the contract was made. Again, the determination of both actual loss and expectation interest is subject to the rule of foreseeability.

Punitive damages are only permitted under very special circumstances. The key feature of liquidated damages is that the damages are provided by the parties in advance. The parties to a contract may negotiate in their contract a certain amount of damages that the party in breach of the contract should pay as the compensation to the aggrieved party. Liquidated damages differ from the compensatory nature of damages in that they are determined on the basis not of actual loss but of estimated loss by the parties determined at the time of their agreement.

The penalty clause is usually unenforceable in common law jurisdictions. The economic logic behind this "nonenforcement" policy is that the penalty clause would deter efficient breaches and compel inefficient performance as the cost of breach to the contract breaker under a penalty clause is greater than the cost of the breach to the victim (Graves 2013). Thus, the prospective victim has more incentives to provoke a breach so that he can benefit from the breach (such a benefit is greater than the one derived from the performance of the contract). The penalty clause as a remedy is likely to "jeopardize the stability and predictability of commercial transactions . . . and efficient operation of the modern . . . economy."[7] On the other hand, it still makes sense to enforce a voluntarily negotiated penalty clause, which is used to serve other purposes, i.e., convincing the counterparty of the determination to perform the contractual terms. In other words, a voluntarily negotiated penalty clause is more like a credible information channeling device and even then it is only rarely enforced. Instead of deterring efficient breaches, the liquidated damages actually facilitate efficient breaches as the breaching party can easily calculate the price of a breach by quantifying a breach's loss. However, the task of distinguishing between a penalty clause and a valid liquidated damage clause is not straightforward. A problematic liquidated damage clause can be an arbitrary, excessive or abusive one. These types of penalty clauses are defined to be inefficient ones (Ham 1990, pp. 649–671; Kronman and Posner 1979; Hillman 2000, pp. 717–738) and their enforcement will cause the problem of moral hazard.

In China, the liquidated damages are viewed as punitive in nature. The function of the liquidated damages is to deter the breach. The breaching party, therefore, has to face economic punishment. Apart from the liquidated damages, the aggrieved party may be granted other damages.

Article 114 clarifies the relationship between the liquidated damages and actual losses. If the agreed amount of damages turns out to be lower than the loss that was actually incurred, the aggrieved party may appeal to a court or an arbitration body to increase it. The breaching party can also ask a court or arbitration body to reduce the amount of liquidated damages if the amount is proved to be excessively higher than the actual loss. This may distinguish China's liquidated damages from those in the UCC. The readjustment in Chinese contract law is a mandatory mechanism whereas the UCC approach is permissive (Matheson 2006, pp. 329, 370, 382). Further, if the liquidated damages are agreed upon in respect of the delay in performance, the breaching party should be obligated to continue performing obligations within a reasonable time after the liquidated damages are paid.

The liquidated damages that are punitive in nature will not become void automatically. But the liquidated damages shall be made on a reasonable basis, reflecting an honest effort by the parties to stipulate the damages that would be the likely result of a breach. The court or arbitration tribunal will assess the reasonableness of the liquidated damages and may adjust them by either increasing or lowering the amount of liquidated damages. Judicial recognition of liquidated damages is reflective of the respect that is granted to party autonomy. Transacting parties are more familiar than anyone with the subjective value of contractual performance. The penalty clause can serve the purpose of an insurance policy for a risk-averse party who has high subjective value of the contractual performance. To the party obliged to perform (promisor), a penalty clause triggers his extra care in the performance. Through negotiation on a penalty clause, the parties reach equilibrium as the promisee (the party entitled to the performance by the promisor) pays a higher price in exchange for a more credible performance on the part of the promisor. By prohibiting a penalty clause, the court indeed awards a windfall to the breaching party by disallowing a supposed windfall to the nonbreaching party. This could be an efficient arrangement that relies on the transacting parties to decide the amount of liquidated damages, subject to a reasonableness cap. In fact, this approach is close to the court's constrained or restrictive approach in a common law jurisdiction. The judges usually are unwilling to intervene in the transaction by overruling the agreed liquidated damages unless the amount is unreasonable. The rationale of this constrained approach is that the judge was not involved in the negotiation process at any point while the parties were drawing up a contract. Therefore, the judge is less capable than the transacting parties of deciding a more reasonable or appropriate amount of liquidated damage.

7 Enforcement of Contracts

At first look, China's Contract Law does not differ hugely from those operating in other countries due to the legal transplant and strong influences brought by the international conventions and foreign laws. In reality, enforcing contracts is another matter.

There are two opposing lines of thought regarding contract enforcement. Contract formalism contends that a strong and law-based enforcement mechanism supports economic growth. By contrast, contract informalism argues that contracts can be enforced through informal and extralegal sanctions and that a self-enforcing regime still supports economic growth. In the self-enforcing regime, substantial investments need to be made into the relationship-based network. Certainly, long-term and/or repeated transactions are vulnerable in the absence of credible third-party enforcement mechanisms (Williamson 1996, pp. 332, 335–336). The implications of these two hypotheses are related to two stages of economic development. The informal contract enforcement mechanisms can be substitutes for formal ones in a less developed economy. While the economy turns to be mature and developed, a formal mechanism becomes indispensable to sustained economic growth.

However, both of these hypotheses should be scrutinized with caution. Reliance on the contract informalism hypothesis may risk ignoring the importance of the formal enforcement mechanism while the economy is moving to a more advanced level where the market is to witness more long-lived, large-scale, and highly asset-specific investments and complicated contracts. Exaggerating the importance of formal contract enforcement, by contrast, may lead to an overlooking, or even an omission, of the relational contracting mechanisms which exist to a large extent in a less law-based society. Relation-based contracting also facilitates and supports economic growth through less formal enforcement mechanisms consisting of mediators, arbitrators and industrial associations.

7.1 The "China Puzzle" in Contract Law

It is frequently argued that China lacks a functioning legal system featuring a liberal version of rule of law built on separation of powers, that the state structure is fragmented, that the judiciary is less capable of adjudicating more complicated commercial disputes, and that legal processes are less transparent and more arbitrary. Local protectionism, courts' reluctance to use coercive measures in civil cases, the lack of finality of court proceedings, and the inadequate administrative resources at courts' disposal are the most-cited shortcomings and impediments to the effective enforcement of court judgments and arbitral awards (Lubman 1999, pp. 266–269; Clarke 1996, p. 1–91). As a consequence of multiple deficiencies, there has been a low level of satisfaction toward formal contract enforcement institutions among both domestic and foreign investors (Cohen 2005, pp. 31–37).

The importance of courts should not be underestimated as laws and courts are the key components of the institutional framework in which economic reform and economic growth move forward. Even the *People's Daily* expressed anxiety about the situation: "Half of China's civil court rulings remain on paper."[8] This official statement raised a fundamental question: if court decisions cannot be enforced effectively, how can courts implement laws? The conventional wisdom is that the way that Chinese courts operate is not in line with the trend of global convergence. Rather, the day-to-day judicial work has indicated a strong local characteristic reflecting a lower institutional status of Chinese courts in the organization of state power and relationships among government organs. The function of the judiciary is contingent upon the historical origin of the judiciary, administrative influence, economic pressure, social order, and the legal consciousness of local communities (Liu 2006, pp. 75–106). Power and politics may be the most sensible doctrinal framework used to explain why and how the Chinese court system (even the administrative structure) (Li 2013, pp. 119–170) works in such an unsatisfying manner (Clarke 1996, pp. 1–91). Meanwhile, implementing laws through the administrative structure is not free of structural problems and is not necessarily as effective as one may reasonably expect considering the party-state top-down society structure in China. A dynamic recursive framework vividly and insightfully explains the enigma of China's judicial (in particular, enforcement) failure (Liu and Halliday 2009, pp. 911–950) along with the fast-growing economy.

According to the hypothesis of contract formalism, contracts cannot be enforced effectively and economic growth cannot be sustained in the long run if a formal enforcement apparatus supported by state power such as courts is not developed. Nevertheless, the past four decades have witnessed China's unprecedentedly rapid growth in the underdevelopment of a formal contract enforcement regime that would be regarded as conforming to international standards. The widespread existence of relational contracts and networks (*guanxi* or relationship) may explain how fast and long-term economic growth can still be achieved without a mature system of formal contract enforcement mechanisms centered on courts. "Chinese business tends to be conducted through a series of personalized networks based on friendship and trust, which are given substance by long-term relationships and reputation for trustworthiness and reliability, rather than in the open marketplace or in an institutional framework" (Tracy and Lever-Tracy 2002, pp. 65, 71–72). Thus, the ineffectiveness of a formal contract enforcement regime may be supplemented by the reputational enforcement regime in which reputational costs may force the contracting parties to honor and enforce contractual terms.

The literature on law and economics has highlighted several examples of semi-enforcement schemes that were widespread in China's economic development. The "credit commitments" argument (Williamson 1996, pp. 332, 335–336) tried to rely on the social contract between the ruling party and the Chinese population to justify the lack of governance legitimacy in a nondemocratic society. Even without any democracy-based legitimacy, the ruling party and the government are still keen to enforce social contracts with the general public by delivering high levels of economic prosperity. Following this line of thinking, the strongest mechanism for contract enforcement is likely to be employed by government agencies rather than by courts.

Similarly, the "informal/de facto property rights" argument attributes China's success in terms of economic growth to the presence of managerial incentives in non-state-owned enterprises such as township and village enterprises (Clarke 2003, pp. 89, 104–105). These enterprises are not state-owned; they are controlled by local governments and have two principal purposes. On the one hand, these enterprises become the key source of fiscal revenues for local governments to satisfy local spending needs. On the other, these enterprises need to absorb local employees and make profits. Local governments, therefore, have incentives to play a market-preserving role by not becoming engaged in arbitrary confiscation and the expropriation of property rights.

These two examples highlight some aspects of weak formal contract enforcement institutions that went hand in hand with China's economic development. In the early stages of China's economic development, a strong and rule-based enforcement regime did not seem to be the most essential infrastructural component to support China's development. Efficiency still could be enhanced within this enforcement regime. The mysterious force behind this probably is reputation and long-term relationship (Clarke, Murrell, and Whiting 2008, pp. 26–27).

Reputational enforcement is a means of deterring deviation to the contractual terms, and relies on various measures, including collective punishment and moral commitments (Rauch 2001, pp. 1177, 1180–1181, 1183). This, however, does not suggest that networks do not incur costs (Rauch 2001, pp. 1177, 1180–1181, 1183), even though it is claimed that transaction costs may be low in such informal settings (Bardhan 2005, pp. 499, 511–512), but nevertheless remains as a trade-off of private ordering. As a matter of fact, the enforcement of relational contracts may incur information costs due to information asymmetry. While these transactions incur lower fixed costs, the marginal cost of exchanging between unfamiliar parties may be higher than usual (Grief 2006, pp. 88, 311). Without an effective formal enforcement regime, uncertainty still largely exists in contracting. In addition, relation-based governance may only function well in small groups or communities relying on other ethnical or linguistic connections. The other feature of this governance structure is that it works well in repeated transactional modes (Dixit 2004, pp. 4, 66, 80). These advantages can easily turn to be shortcomings – the exclusion of a large number of new entrants or outsiders from entering into business networks (McMillan and Woodruff 2000, pp. 2421, 2425; Gray 1997, p. 14), the discrimination against outsiders (Fafchamps 2004, p. 347), or the lower chance for further expansion in response to welfare-enhancing opportunities (Grief 2006, pp. 88, 311). These drawbacks naturally lead to higher production costs due to the lack of specialization and division of labor in a market limited by the personalized exchange processes (Bardhan 2005, pp. 499, 511–512), as well as higher financing costs as a vibrant capital market is unlikely to be established thanks to the linked but compartmentalized transacting parties (Dixit 2004, pp. 4, 66, 80). This is why the relation-based governance structure may not sustain economic growth in the long run simply because of its lack of dynamic efficiency (Grief 2006, pp. 88, 311). The policy implications of this line of analysis are that an informal contract enforcement regime complements, but cannot substitute for, a system of formal contract enforcement in a dysfunctional legal system (McMillan and Woodruff 2000, pp. 2421, 2423).

China is currently undergoing a profound transition from a planned economy to a market economy. While the onset of economic growth may justify the lack of a functioning institution of formal contract enforcement, sustaining economic development in the long run in the face of dynamic political, economic, and social conditions requires deeper and extensive institutional reform (Rodrik 2003, pp. 8–15). Institutional economics advocates the build-up of higher-quality courts at a higher level of development for those countries which start their growth without good judicial institutions (Glaeser et al. 2004, pp. 271–298). Policymakers need to be aware of the arduous process of institutional evolution (McMillan and Woodruff 1999, pp. 637, 640). Therefore, while China is experiencing its institutional transition from an informal contract enforcement regime to a formal one, it can capitalize on some of the advantages of informal enforcement mechanisms for value-adding and welfare-improving purposes. In Chinese commercial settings, as evidenced by empirical findings, negotiation, mediation, and self-enforcement are used extensively by Chinese businesses (Clarke, Murrell, and Whiting 2008, pp. 26–27). This probably explains the wide use of arbitration and mediation in Chinese courts' adjudication processes. The Civil Procedure Law, for instance, codifies mediation as a required step in civil litigation.

7.2 Role of Informal Mechanisms of Contract Enforcement in Economic Development

Mediation is one of the most extensively used informal mechanisms for contract enforcement in China. In particular, the court-sponsored mediation is frequently used to reach a settlement after commercial litigation commences. The mediator, however, has no power to impose an outcome on the disputing parties. The settlement agreement is a result of compromise made by the parties in the mediation process. Mediation can promote a productive level of emotional expression. The lack of "teeth" in the mediation process itself is also its advantage as the parties can continue their business relationship in the long run.

Mediation can increase the effectiveness of negotiation and help the parties understand each other's views and concerns. The parties can rely more on industrial codes and practices. Negotiation can help the parties realistically assess alternatives to settlement and the outcome can be satisfactory for both parties.

The process can encourage greater flexibility due to low costs. The process is more efficient and cost-effective to the parties as the process may not need professional assistance or third-party involvement. However, mediation exhibits some weaknesses and vulnerabilities in a weak enforcement regime. For instance, mediation is reportedly susceptible to the influence of *guanxi* in both personal and organizational relationships. While mediation is used to urge a more voluntary resolution of disputes, the use of *guanxi* undermines the autonomy of contracting parties. The other problem with mediation is whether it can be used to achieve its optimality in a more litigious society when China moves to a rights-based societal structure.

Meanwhile, some empirical research basically overhauled conventional views on Chinese courts and commercial litigation. Based on intensive interviews and in-depth field investigations in the Pearl River Delta, it was found out that courts in this region were effective and efficient in enforcing commercial judgments. The empirical findings that the enforcement process is relatively efficient, the problem of local protectionism is not serious, the enforcement outcomes are reasonable and the plaintiffs' view on courts is positive challenged the long-standing assumption that Chinese courts were far less than efficient and effective (He 2009, pp. 419–456). Based on some in-depth fieldwork, in contrast to the prevailing view that courts can be notoriously incompetent in enforcement, even courts in some less economically developed areas were able to enforce the majority of debt-collection rulings (He 2011, pp. 253–275). China's efforts in lawmaking and institution-building have been conducive to the adjudication of debt collection cases. These findings not only fill the gap in the existing literature but also affirm the correlation between the functioning of the judicial system and economic development. Further, as far as purely domestic disputes are concerned, the stronger parties (or the Haves), in the sense of possession of rich resources, are more likely to win the cases by a large margin. Institutional litigants fare better than individual litigants (He and Su 2012, pp. 120–145). The fact that the organizational and social status of government-related parties have a greater impact on the outcome of the cases itself triggers a more dynamic interpretation of the roots of the law and the nature of the courts in China.

China's evolving contract enforcement regime is reflective of Dixit's observed model: "it is not always necessary to create replicas of Western-style state legal institutions from scratch; it may be possible to work with such alternative institutions as are available, and build on them" (Dixit 2004, pp. 4, 66, 80). China's tactical reliance on mediation and arbitration in resolving contractual disputes and its systemic combination of alternative dispute resolution mechanisms and courts can be viewed as an effort to incorporate efficient indigenous institutions of contract enforcement into a rule-based modern legal system. This is an effective way to make two enforcement mechanisms complementary to (instead of substituting for) each other. This catch-up path is not only to promote the formal rule of law reform on property rights and contract enforcement (Posner 1998, p. 1), but also to address some concerns over basic civil rights to development (Sen 1990, p. 3). It must be cautioned that formal property rights and contract enforcement may be of little immediate value to some grassroots constituencies in developing jurisdictions.

8 Conclusion

The evolution of China's Contract Law has achieved a number of objectives. First of all, the Contract Law has become less China-specific and more reflective of international rules and practices in nature. The widely accepted legal principles of good faith, the freedom of contract, and the fostering of transactions are embodied in the Contract Law. This paves the way for more cross-border transactions. The party autonomy doctrine is widely recognized and applied in the Contract Law, allowing the parties to "make their own rules" in the contracts. This basically shapes the nature of the Contract Law as conducive to market transactions and accommodating freedom of party will. In addition, the parties are free to make a choice about whether the dispute should be submitted to a foreign or Chinese arbitral tribunal (Article 128). Judging from these indications, the Contract Law laid down a foundation for China's full transition to the socialist market economy.

The Contract Law has achieved a certain level of legislative sophistication, at least in terms of transaction efficiency due to its convergence with widely established contract law rules operating in the rest of the world. The sophistication is threefold. (i) It is evidenced by the adoption of some general principles of international contract law. Such widely accepted principles include fairness, equality, and freedom of contract, even though these principles are adopted with some domestic adjustments. (ii) The sophistication is reflected in various accommodations made by the Contract Law to some traditional contractual norms codified in previous contract law codes in China. For instance, Chinese contract law used to be friendlier to a specific performance remedy. The Contract Law changed this stance and leaned more toward monetary and compensatory damages as a main remedy. This preference is in line with general practices in some European states. The law and economics explanation for this change is based on efficiency considerations. Specific performance is usually more costly given the higher transaction costs involved. Therefore, rendering monetary compensation to the nonbreaching party can be more efficient, not only economically but also procedurally. The rationale behind this change is to reflect the inherent need of a market-oriented economy in pursuit of transaction efficiency. The previous contract law codes designed the rules of liability for breach of contract as a penalty instrument punishing the defaulting party. Under the Contract Law, liability itself is no longer characterized as a penalty, and only the nonperformance of mandatory law leads to punitive damages. Such a change conforms to the party autonomy principle embedded in the market economy and removes some paternalistic elements, which were more consistent with the mandate nature of the previous planned economy. (iii) As pointed out, at the technical level, the Contract Law mandates many sophisticated provisions in all major stages of the contract process as default rules (Hsu 2007, pp. 115–162).

The Contract Law is a hybrid regime not only incorporating China's own legislative and judicial experience but also transplanting a number of norms from the contract law regimes of other countries and international institutions. Convergence in private law has brought a new legal culture to the Chinese society. In the past, contractual freedom was not as commonly recognized in Chinese contract law as in other jurisdictions. Rather, social ethics (termed "public interests") were recognized as predominant norms. The trend of convergence means that Chinese contract law is gradually moving closer to a concept of contractual freedom.[9] Globalization and increasing transnational transactions brought China to a progressive convergence in the field of contract law (Fu 2009, p. 5). In this converging process, both foreign law and international conventions have exerted a substantial influence on the evolution of Chinese contract law. The CISG and the Principles of International Commercial Contract drafted by the International Institute for the Unification of Private Law (the UNIDORIT Principles) were used as guidelines while various contract codes were drafted (Ding 1999, pp. 25, 33). Further, the CISG has been increasingly important in Chinese courts and tribunals' cases (Shulman and Singh 2010, pp. 242–286). It is commonly observed that Chinese courts rely on CISG jurisprudence to interpret the Contract Law (Shulman and Singh 2010, pp. 242–286). This may suggest that international rules, including the CISG, have increasingly become one of the major sources of reference in the adjudication of contract-law disputes in China. Given the transitional nature of China's economy, legal culture and legal institutions, China's evolving convergence with other countries in the field of contract law still shows both its uniqueness and its gradualism (Matheson 2006, pp. 329, 370, 382).

Although the Contract Law does improve China's civil and commercial law and promotes more vibrant and diversified economic activities, there remain marked differences between the Chinese Contract Law and the CISG and other countries' contract codes. Meanwhile, what is less impacted in this convergence process is the legal infrastructure or the enforcement mechanisms. It is unrealistic to say that the enforcement regime for the Contract Law has been in a fixed, static shape. Likely, the Contract Law's maturity and sophistication can be further improved. China's efforts to harmonize its contract law regime both domestically and beyond national borders is a vivid example showing a distinctive application of the convergence or harmonization thesis (Chapter 2). While different national systems have strong incentives to eliminate major discrepancies and conflicts so as to make cross-border transactions less costly, strong indigenous forces support an enforcement mechanism embedded in the local jurisdiction with strong territorial features. Domestic legislatures all move toward an efficient framework by implementing both concentration and distribution strategies with the aim of achieving rights-enhancing and liability-allocating equilibrium (Chapter 1). This serves as a proper explanation of China's contract law regime, which evolved from a fragmented to a unified structure and drew on uniform contract law norms from foreign jurisdictions and international conventions. Nevertheless, the enforcement structure has not evolved in the same direction or at a similar pace as the written rules. Probably, this may be a convenient context to reveal what would happen in the jurisdiction if the government is overconfident about its role in the marketplace without relying on a functioning legal infrastructure (in a wider sense) – traditional practices of relational contracting and enforcement mechanisms still hold a prominent ground in facilitating business transactions.

References in English

Ayres, Ian, and Robert Gertner. 1989. Filling Gaps in Incomplete Contracts: An Economic Theory of Default Rules. *Yale Law Journal* 99:87–130.

Bardhan, Pranab. 2005. Institutions Matter, But Which Ones? *Economic Transition* 13:499–532.

Blase, Friedrich. 2000. CISG and China – An Intercontinental Exchange. *Vindobona Journal of International Commercial Law and Arbitration* 4(1):95–98.

Chen, Albert. 2011. *An Introduction to the Legal System of the People's Republic of China*, 4th ed. Hong Kong: LexisNexis.

Clarke, Donald C. 1996. Power and Politics in the Chinese Court System: The Enforcement of Civil Judgments. *Columbia Journal of Asian Law* 10(1):1–91.

2003. Economic Development and the Rights Hypothesis: The China Problem. *American Journal of Comparative Law* 51:89–112.

Clarke, Donald C., Peter Murrell, and Susan Whiting. 2008. The Role of Law in China's Economic Development. Pp. 26–27 in *China's Great Economic Transformation*, edited by Loren Brandt and Thomas G. Rawski. Cambridge: Cambridge University Press.

Cohen, Jerome A. 2005. Time to Fix China's Arbitration. *Far East Economic Review* 168:31–37.

Ding, Ding.1999. China and CISG. Pp. 25–37 in *CISG and China: Theory and Practice*, edited by Michael R. Will. Faculté de droit, Universitéde Genève.

Dixit, Avinash K. 2004. *Lawlessness and Economics: Alternative Modes of Governance*. Princeton and Oxford: Princeton University Press.

Fafchamps, Marcel. 2004. *Market Institutions in Sub-Saharan Africa: Theory and Evidence*. Cambridge, MA: MIT Press.

Fu, Junwei. 2009. Towards a Social Value Convergence: A Comparative Study of Fundamental Principles of Contract Law in the EU and China. Oxford University Comparative Law Forum. Available at http://ssrn.com/abstract=1564028.

Glaeser, Edward L., Rafael La Porta, Florencio Lopez-de-Silanes, and Andrei Shleifer. 2004. Do Institutions Cause Growth? *Journal of Economic Growth* 9:271–303.

Graves, Jack. 2013. Penalty Clauses as Remedies: Exploring Comparative Approaches to Enforceability. *Touro Law Review* 29(3):681–694.

Gray, Cheryl W. 1997. Reforming Legal Systems in Developing and Transition Countries. *Finance & Development* 34(3):14–16. Available at www.imf.org/external/pubs/ft/fandd/1997/09/pdf/gray.pdf (last visited August 27, 2015).

Grief, Avner. 2006. *Institutions and the Path to the Modern Economy: Lessons from Medieval Trade*. Cambridge: Cambridge University Press.

Ham, Andrew. 1990. The Rules Against Penalties in Contract: An Economic Perspective. *Melbourne University Law Review* 17:649–671.

He, Xin. 2009. Enforcing Commercial Judgments in the Pearl River Delta of China. *American Journal of Comparative Law* 39(2):419–456.

2011. Debt Collection in the Less Developed Regions of China: An Empirical Study from a Basic-Level Court in Shaanxi Province. *China Quarterly* 206:253–275.

He, Xin, and Yang Su. 2012. Do the "Haves" Come Out Ahead in Shanghai Courts? *Journal of Empirical Legal Studies* 10(1):120–145.

Hillman, Robert A. 2000. The Limits of Behavioral Decision Theory in Legal Analysis: The Case of Liquidated Damages. *Cornell Law Review* 85:717–738.

Holmes, Oliver Wendell Jr. 1991. *The Common Law*. New York, NY: Dover Publication.

Hsu, Stephen. 2007. Contract Law of the People's Republic of China. *Minnesota Journal of International Law* 16(1):115–162.

Katz, Avery Wiener. 1998. *Foundations of the Economic Approach to Law*. New York, NY: Foundation Press.

Kronman, Anthony T., and Richard A. Posner. 1979. *The Economics of Contract Law*. Boston, MA: Little, Brown & Co.

Lando, Henrik, and Casper Rose. 2004. On the Enforcement of Specific Performance in Civil Law Countries. *International Review of Law and Economics* 24:473–487.

Li, Ji. 2013. Does Law Matter in China? An Empirical Study of a Limited Case. *George Washington International Law Review* 46:119–170.

Ling, Bing. 2002. *Contract Law in China*. Hong Kong, Singapore, and Malaysia: Sweet & Maxwell Asia.

Liu, Sida, and Terence C. Halliday. 2009. Recursivity in Legal Change: Lawyers and Reforms of China's Criminal Procedure Law. *Law & Social Inquiry* 34(4):911–950.

Liu, Sida. 2006. Beyond Global Convergence: Conflicts of Legitimacy in a Chinese Lower Court. *Law & Social Inquiry* 31(1):75–106.

Long, Cheryl Xiaoming, and Jun Wang. 2015. Judicial Local Protectionism in China: An Empirical Study of IP Cases. *International Review of Law and Economics* 42: 48–59.

Lubman, Stanley B. 1999. *Bird in a Cage: Legal Reform in China After Mao.* Palo Alto, CA: Stanford University Press.

Matheson, John H. 2006. Convergence, Culture and Contract Law in China. *Minnesota Journal of International Law* 15(2):329–382.

McMillan, John, and Christopher Woodruff. 1999. Dispute Prevention Without Courts in Vietnam. *Journal of Law, Economics and Organization* 15:637–658.

2000. Private Order Under Dysfunctional Public Order. *Michigan Law Review* 98:2421–2458.

Posner, Richard A. 1998. Creating a Legal Framework for Economic Development. *World Bank Research Observer* 13(1):1–11.

Posner, Richard A. 1998. *Economic Analysis of Law*. 4th ed. New York, NY: Aspen Publishers.

Rauch, James E. 2001. Business and Social Networks in International Trade. *Journal of Economics Literature* 39:1177–1203.

Rodrik, Dani. 2003. Introduction. Pp. 1–19 in *In Search of Prosperity: Analytic Narratives on Economic Growth*, edited by Dani Rodrik. Princeton and Oxford: Princeton University Press.

Sen, Amartya. 1990. *Development as Freedom*. New York, NY: Oxford University Press.

Shulman, Mark S., and Lachimi Singh. 2010. China's Implementation of the UN Sales Convention through Arbitral Tribunal. *Columbia Journal of Transnational Law* 48(2):242–320.

Tracy, Noel, and Constance Lever-Tracy. 2002. A New Alliance for Profit: China's Local Industries and the Chinese Diaspora. Pp. 71–72 in *Chinese Entrepreneurship and Asian Business Networks*, edited by Thomas Menkhoff & Solvay Gerke. New York, NY: Routledge.

US–China Business Council. 2007. Administrative Licensing and Business Approvals, USCBC 2007 Member Priorities Survey Executive Summary: US Companies' China Outlook: Continuing Optimism Tempered By Operating Challenges, Protectionist Threats. Available at www.uschina.org/public/documents/2007/10/uscbc-member-survey-2007.pdf.

Williamson, Oliver E. 1996. *The Mechanisms of Governance*. New York, NY: Oxford University Press.

Zhang, Mo. 2006. *Chinese Contract Law: Theory and Practice*. Leiden and Boston, MA: Martinus Nijhoff Publishers.

References in Chinese

Chen, Wenhua. 2011. Transactional Customs in Statutory Interpretation: From the Perspective of the PRC Contract Law. *Western Law Review* 2:31–36.

China Legal Publishing House. 2015. *The PRC Contract Law*. Beijing: China Legal Publishing House

Dong, Ansheng. 2002. *Civil Law Acts*. Beijing: Remin University Press.

Han, Shiyuan. 2011a. PRC Contract Law and CISG. *Jinan Journal (Section of Philosophy and Social Sciences)* 2:7–13.

2011b. *The Law of Contract*. 3rd ed. Beijing: Law Press.

Hu, Kangsheng (ed). 2010. *Explanatory Texts on PRC Contract Law*. Beijing: Law Press.

Huang, Zhong. 2010. *On Validity of Unlawful Contracts*. Beijing: Law Press.

Liang, Huixing. 1995. *Studies on Statutory Interpretation of Civil Law*. Beijing: China University of Political Science and Law.

1996. Unsettled Questions in the Process of Drafting PRC Contract Law. *Legal Science* 2:13–15.

1999a. The Unified Contract Law: Advances and Inadequacies. *China Legal Science* 3:25–29.

1999b. *A Study of Theories, Cases and Legislation in Civil Law*. Vol. 2. Beijing: Chinese Academy of Governance Press.

1999c. Successes and Shortcomings of the Contract Law: Part I. *Peking University Law Journal* 6:13–27.

Long, Xingwu. 2001. On Interpretation of Contracts and Its Future Direction. *Transactions of Beijing Institute of Technology (Section of Social Sciences)* 4:58–62.

Luo, Xiaoqi. 2002. Studies of Commercial Customs. *Contemporary Law Review* 2:131–141.

Su, Yongqin. 2005. *State Commands in the Autonomy of Private Law*. Beijing: China Legal Publishing House.

Tian, Langliang. 2013. *Disputes over Contracts on Sales of Goods: Adjudicative Rules and Their Implementation in Cases*. 2nd ed. Beijing: China Legal Publishing House.

Wang, Liming. 1999. China's Proposed Uniform Contract Code. *St Mary's Law Journal* 31:7–17.

2011. *Studies of Contract Law: Volume I*. Beijing: China Renmin University Press.

Notes

1 Supreme People's Court, Judicial Interpretation on Several Questions Regarding Application of the Contract Law (Part II), 2009, Article 14;

Supreme People's Court, Guiding Opinion on Several Questions Regarding Adjudication of Cases of Disputes over Civil and Commercial Contracts under Current Circumstances, 2009, Article 15.

2 Supreme People's Court, Guiding Opinion on Several Questions Regarding Adjudication of Cases of Disputes over Civil and Commercial Contracts under Current Circumstances, 2009, Article 16, which requires local courts to "have a consolidated understanding of purposes of laws and regulations, balance the rights and interests of disputing parties . . . and reach a comprehensive identification of the nature of the normative rules."

3 Supreme People's Court, Judicial Interpretation on Several Questions Regarding the Application of the Contract Law of the PRC (I), Article 30.

4 Efficient breach allows the wrongdoer to profit from his own wrong, which is not morally justified. Economically, efficient breach may induce people to breach the contract so as to allocate the gains from breach to the party in breach.

5 The US's Restatement (Second) adopts the "probable result" language.

6 Also see Article 74 of the 1980 UN Convention on International Sale of Goods.

7 *General Motors Co.* v. *Piskor*, 281 Md. 627, 381 A.2d 16 (1977).

8 "Half of China's Civil Court Rulings Remain on Paper", *People's Daily*, March 13, 2004.

9 European legislatures in recent decades have restricted contractual freedom through antidiscrimination and consumer protection laws.

4 *The Evolution of Contract Law in Taiwan*

Lost in Interpretation?

WEN-YEU WANG

I Introduction

Contract law consists primarily of a legal framework within which parties may create their own rights and duties by agreement. As legal scholars, we are usually concerned with this framework and particularly with the enforceability of promises and the mechanics of agreement. Yet many contract disputes relate, not to such matters, but rather to the nature and extent of the rights and duties that the parties themselves have created. In this context the issue of interpretation arises where there is an ambiguity in the content of a contract. As pointed out by German scholars Canaris and Grigoleit (2010, p.1), interpretation is an omnipresent phenomenon of contract law. Even an apparently precise contract may, under close scrutiny, prove to be in need of significant interpretation.

It is not always possible to solve problems of interpretation by reverting to the wording of the contract or to the clear and concurring intention of the parties. In practice, contracts often contain gaps, either because the parties did not consider the question at all or because they deliberately abstained from dealing with it. In either case, the questions for which no provisions were made need to be solved by applying other methods. In this regard, all Continental Civil Law systems contain supplemental rules or default rules (the "default rules") to complete contractual arrangements. In Germany, for instance, they are called "dispositives Gesetzesrecht." Applied correctly, the existence of these rules may prevent contractual incompleteness and thereby reduce the costs of negotiations and drafting. However, default rules can only achieve their goals if they respond to the typical interests that can be attributed to the parties of the particular types of contract. Ultimately, the interpretation of contracts must comply with the principle of freedom of contract.

Against this background, this article reflects on the Taiwanese Contract Law in practice, and, in particular, misunderstanding and confusion over "the interpretation of contract" and "the interpretation of contract law" by Taiwanese academics and judges. When addressing contractual disputes, this problem results in the tendency to use default rules rather than first interpreting the contract directly. In some cases, Taiwanese courts have either hastily characterized the contract in question as a typical contract without inquiring into its nature or purpose, or rigidly employed a method of analogy to incorporate the corresponding default provisions into the contract in question.

This improper practice of Taiwanese Contract Law is the result of several factors. First, Taiwan is a civil law country and, unlike Germany, it does not have an independent body of commercial law for complex modern business transactions. This deficiency results in confusion between civil contracts and business contracts and an inability to handle modern business arrangements, such as franchise agreements. Second, the Taiwanese Contract Law provides 27 kinds of standard contracts, whose application, in principle, is subject to the parties' autonomous determination. In other words, parties have the right to form a contract that differs from the 27 standard forms. But third, unless the parties explicitly state in their contract that they are excluding the application of such rules, courts in practice tend to classify their contract as one of the nominate contracts or draw an analogy with the nominate forms to resolve the dispute. This route of application largely ignores an examination of the parties' intention and makes the supplementary rules mandatory, meaning that the parties have no choice but to comply with them. Finally, many modern contracts are intentionally incomplete – they deliberately leave room for the parties to adjust the agreement to the rapidly changing business environment. *Ex post* interpretation of the contracts by the court is important, therefore. The contract interpretation issue is especially important in the face of modern business contracts, contracts other than the 27 nominate contracts, and when or how to complete contract lacunae. This article addresses the above intricate issues and suggests possible solutions to them.

II The Background, Structure, and Content of "Taiwan's Contract Law"

This section discusses issues arising from Taiwan's separate Civil and Commercial Law systems which are fundamental to its contract law and the theories derived therefrom. Taiwan's Civil Law system, in fact, does not have a distinct "Contract Law." The relationship between private parties is governed by Taiwan's Civil Code, which is divided into general principles, obligations, property law, and family law. The concept of "contract law" is spread over three sections: general principles, obligations, and property law, the most relevant of which is the part concerning obligations. "Obligations" is the second book of the Taiwan Civil Code, and serves as the basis for remedies arising from all contract obligations as well as torts. In addition to this lack of a distinct contract law, most of the Civil Code's articles are based on abstract contract theories rather than case law, in contrast to the Anglo-American legal tradition. The following subsections provide a general picture of "Taiwan's Contract Law" and point to the main problem with the whole system against the backdrop of contract application in the commercial realm.

The obligations concerning various kinds of contracts are provided mostly in the second chapter of the Code's Book of Obligations. The Civil Code in Taiwan makes no distinction between civil and commercial contracts, and nor does it cover consumer contracts, except for general principles concerning good faith. Most consumer contracts are regulated under the Consumer Protection Law of 1994.

1 A Civil Law Combining Civil Codes and Commercial Codes versus The International Treaty Trend, Namely the UNIDROIT

Contracts can be divided into "civil" and "commercial" contracts. In civil contracts, which include consumer-to-consumer (C2C) and business-to-consumer (B2C) contracts, consumers or parties often lack specialized knowledge in contract formation and an equal bargaining position. Hence, consumer contracts are increasingly been subjected to special rules, mostly of a mandatory character, aimed at protecting the consumers. In commercial (B2B) contracts, on the other hand, the parties are commercial entities with relatively equal bargaining positions and expertise in contract negotiation. As such, commercial contracts would need far fewer default rules and standards than current contract law contains.

In today's fast-paced business environment, where it is difficult for commercial parties to settle their entire contract terms in advance, commercial entities often design innovative terms for adapting their contractual relationship to the actual situation as well as coping with unexpected risks. For instance, in complex contracts such as a corporate acquisition contract, the parties face two significant problems. First, there is the adverse-selection problem; the buyer needs information regarding the quality of what it is buying. Second, there can be a temporal gap between execution of the contract and the closing, and a lot can happen in that period. To respond, the acquisition contract would have to specify on which of the seller's statements the buyer would rely and how the reliance would be protected. Notable examples include the integration clause and the no-reliance clause (Goldberg 2014, pp. 1075–1081).

The Taiwanese Civil Law treats commercial and private contracts in the same manner, despite the different aspects of the contractual situations.

The current international trend suggests a divergence between civil contracts and commercial contracts. The 2010 Principles of International Commercial Contracts exemplifies recent attempts to harmonize the law of international commercial contracts. As indicated in comments 2 of the Introduction Part: "[T]he restriction to commercial contracts is in no way intended to take over the distinction traditionally made between civil and commercial parties and/or transactions. Rather, the idea is to exclude from the scope of the Principles' so-called 'consumer transactions' which are within the various legal systems being increasingly subjected to special rules, mostly of a mandatory nature, aimed at protecting the consumers, i.e., a parties who enters into the contract otherwise than in the course of its trade or profession" (UNIDROIT 2010).[1] Since sophisticated economic actors (e.g., Apple Inc.) can be expected to understand how to make business contracts, contract law should allow them, within constraints, to set their own rules (Schwartz and Scott 2003).[2]

In short, though many countries might not be able to reach agreement on a uniform contract code, many international commercial contract doctrines have sought to unify the various commercial contract practices. Many countries have already modified their contract laws to keep up with international trends and are increasingly making use of the CISG provisions. Recently, countries have also accepted that statutes will play less of a role in regulating parties, and the system should be based on extant trading customs that are coming to constitute a new uniform global contract custom. In contrast, Taiwan's Civil Code does not recognize international trade customs. Consequently, it cannot deal with modern, complex B2B disputes effectively.

2 The Roles and Functions of Typical Contracts

A "typical contract" in Taiwan, also known as a "nominate contract," refers to one of the 27 common contract types codified in the Taiwan Civil Code. In a civil law system influenced by the German Civil Code, these typical contracts are included in the chapter on "Obligations." The "typical contract" provisions are designed for two purposes: first, to supplement the contract; and second, to protect the parties' interests (Wang 2009). The civil law provides in the case of each and every typical contract for compulsory obligations and optional supplemental regulations. Any contract that violates a compulsory rule is deemed to be null and void. However, default rules are aimed at tightening legal loopholes and fulfilling the essential elements of a contract. Parties should be able to override these default rules.

3 Paternalistic Thinking

In the modern market economy, the freedom of contract principle generally plays an important role. Although governments stipulate laws, such as consumer protection laws, to rectify unfair or fraudulent terms and thereby protect vulnerable parties, most governments, even those that emphasize such protection, must avoid excessive intervention in the parties' freedom of transaction. In this matter, Taiwan's government takes an opposite approach (compare a similar approach in China, described in Chapter 3). The authorities provide hundreds of standard form contracts ranging from movie theater tickets to cram school tuition bills, as well as "Dos and Don'ts" for these contracts. The standard form contracts greatly limit the content and form of various daily transactions, certainly a rarity in the world. The reason for such strong intervention is the government's distrust of the market's inherent capabilities. Yet this paternalistic protection not only increases the administrative costs of agreements, but also hinders economic development and innovation. This mentality is also a fundamental problem underlying the interpretation of contracts in Taiwan.

4 The Principles of Contract Interpretation: Articles 98 and 148 of Taiwan's Civil Code

Taiwan's Civil Code does not expressly provide basic contract interpretation principles. Since all contracts involve expression of intentions, Taiwan's courts apply a general provision in the Civil Code to interpret contracts. Article 98 of Taiwan's Civil Code provides that "In the interpretation of an expression of intent, the real intention of the parties must be sought rather than the literal meaning of the words." Although this article is directed at interpreting the parties' intention, the Supreme Court has adopted this article as a general principle of contract interpretation.

In interpreting contracts, textual interpretation is the primary method. If the terms of the contract do not show the real intention of the parties or if the terms are ambiguous, however, the court may then look into the relevant facts and evidence to find the parties' real intention at the time the contract was made. The "real intention" may be subjective, so that errors in wording must not harm the contracting parties' real intention (Chen 2010).

With respect to the principle of good faith, when seeking the parties' true intention, a Supreme Court judgment[3] indicates that transaction practices, purpose of the contract, and noncompulsory rules can all be taken into account, while the "principle of good faith" stipulated in Article 148 of Taiwan's Civil Code, can supplement or modify the meaning in between. How these factors are to be applied in specific cases, including the applicable order and the reasoning, however, remains unclear and can vary from case to case. This phenomenon to some extent reveals the weakness of contract interpretation in Taiwan's judicial practice.

III The Interpretation of Contracts versus the Interpretation of Contract Law

Karl Larenz distinguishes in his legal methods theory between "interpretation of contracts" and "interpretation of law" (Larenz 2008), which includes the "interpretation of contract law." "Interpretation of contracts" focuses on the written or oral declarations among the contracting parties. Each party's true intentions in the contract are ideally revealed. In contrast, "interpretation of contract law" focuses on the legislative intent, social values, and historical materials. In general, contracts and legislation serve different purposes and different parties' interests. The former is designed solely to benefit the contracting parties while the latter concerns the whole society. Therefore, the interpretation principle used for one cannot possibly be applied to the other.

1 Interpretation of Contract Law – The Distinction Between Mandatory and Nonmandatory Rules

"Mandatory rules" and "nonmandatory rules" affect the relationship between the rule of private law and the contractual agreement of the parties. While nonmandatory rules can be set aside by contractual agreement, mandatory rules require the parties' absolute compliance. Since party autonomy and freedom of contract are the most fundamental principles in any liberal system of private law, nonmandatory provisions of law are the general rule whereas mandatory provisions are the exception (Grigoleit 2011).

The distinction between mandatory and nonmandatory rules is based on the purpose of the rules. Normally, rules governing the validity of contracts (e.g., capacity, mistake, or formal requirements) are mandatory rules. They serve the purpose of protecting particular social values, reliance in commercial transactions, and the weaker party in contracts. By way of contrast, nonmandatory rules avoid contract incompleteness and save transaction costs during the contract negotiation and drafting stages (Canaris and Grigoleit 2010). The nonmandatory rules, or what Canaris and Grigoleit (2010) refers to as "suppletive rules," address the parties' typical interests in particular types of contracts by stipulating the standard contract arrangement in advance. The "typical contracts" provided in Taiwan's Civil Law mostly constitute nonmandatory, default rules.

2 The Relationship between Interpretation of Contracts, Filling of Lacunas in Contracts, and Default Rules

The issue of contract interpretation arises when a contract is ambiguous or contains lacunae – lacunae appear in contracts when the parties have not made provisions with respect to certain questions. In fact, as Canaris has pointed out, virtually every understanding of a contract is based on interpretation. Even the mere statement that a contract does not require or allow interpretation constitutes in itself an act of interpretation and the result of such an interpretation.

The main function of contract interpretation is to allow the parties to settle their legal relations as they see fit. This purpose, which derives directly from self-determination and freedom of contract, is the concrete embodiment of human dignity and the right to freely develop one's personality. If a state prescribes every detail of an individual's daily transaction, it will necessarily infringe the person's right to self-determination and thus dignity. Since the age of enlightenment, this notion has won nearly complete acceptance in Europe.

The freedom of contract in connection with free markets also provides for an efficient distribution of resources, leading to a maximization of social wealth. According to the Pareto criterion, the *voluntary* exchange by contract epitomizes economic efficiency. The Coase Theorem suggests that a legal system should allow the *voluntary* exchange of goods and facilitate it by lowering the cost of transactions. Hence the freedom of contracts principle should be respected under all circumstances.

As mentioned above, the interpretation of a contract may address either ambiguity or lacunae. The nonmandatory rules relate mostly to the latter. Lacunae are due to incomplete contracts; they result from the parties' carelessness in considering a specific issue in advance or the parties' deliberate reluctance to do so. In reality, nearly all contracts, by necessity, are to some extent incomplete (Barnett 1992, pp. 821–822). Since parties cannot foresee every future event or know precisely how their own purposes may change, they cannot negotiate terms to cover every contingency. Sometimes, the incompleteness of contracts even serves the parties' interests, because settling foreseeable contingency in advance can be costly. As long as the gap does not affect the contract's fundamental elements, such as the parties, subject matter, and price, the contract is enforceable.

When disputes arise, however, the questions for which no provisions were made can be solved in two ways: fill the gap with nonmandatory (suppletive) rules or interpret the parties' hypothetical intention (Wang 2009). Nonmandatory rules can only be applied when the following two conditions are met: First, the contract contains lacunae; second, no conflict exists between the parties' hypothetical intention and the nonmandatory rules (Kötz 2013). That is to say, after the process of supplementary contract interpretation, if the parties' economic purpose doesn't correspond to the mandatory rules, the courts must not apply the nonmandatory rules.

The application routes to some extent indicate that courts should first apply the hypothetical intention method to determine the parties' interests. One cannot resort to nonmandatory default rules as soon as a contract gap is discovered. Since such nonmandatory rules are designed to save transaction costs and complete the parties' imperfect contract, they must reflect the ordinary intention of the parties. If they do not reflect the ordinary intention, the rule fails to serve its function and thus cannot be applied to interpret the contract at issue.

IV Case Studies

The following three contract cases come from Taiwan's Supreme Court. They either exemplify the improper interpretation of a contract or inadequately apply Taiwan's Civil Law provisions. The first case showcases the Court's neglect in considering the contractual parties' intention, as well as economic interests, before applying the default provisions from the Civil Code, resulting in an inequitable outcome. The second case shows the Court's wrongful characterization of the contract in question based on an approach that severed the parties' intention from the contract, in which a method of analogy is applied to the contractual terms themselves and the default provisions of the Civil Code. It also showcases that a careful consideration of the parties' economic interests may render contract characterization and the subsequent application of Civil Code default provisions altogether unnecessary. The last case is another example of improper characterization, resulting in inequitable outcome similar to the first case.

1 Construction Contract: Taiwan Supreme Court Judgment No. 153 of 2007

In this case, a construction company (referred to as "the Contractor") and a proprietor (referred to as "the Proprietor") signed a construction contract. When the Contractor attempted to perform its contractual obligations the Proprietor failed to cooperate. The Proprietor did not prepare the appropriate working environment that it had promised in the contract to provide to the Contractor. The Proprietor, moreover, didn't pay the Contractor's remuneration. Although the

Contractor continually asked the Proprietor to cooperate and pay the compensation, the Proprietor did not at any time respond to the Contractor's requests. Eventually, the Contractor terminated the contract and sued Proprietor for breach of contract, and requested compensation for damages.

The Supreme Court pointed out that the Contractor had only a "right of rescission" under the Civil Code's "Hire for Work" section and not a right of termination. When the Proprietor failed to carry out its obligation to cooperate, even after the Contractor requested cooperation, the Contractor could only rescind the contract and ask for compensation.

Analysis

The Supreme Court characterized the contract at issue as a "contract of hire for work" under Taiwan's Civil Law. It applied the Taiwan Civil Law Article 507 as the Contractor's only remedy. According to the provision, the Contractor had no right to terminate the contract because Article 507 only allowed cancelation of a contract. However, from the perspective of the parties, especially for the Contractor, the contract is a long-term relational contract, which the parties will execute continuously, and such an arrangement is thus usually characterized as a "Specific Investment." The Court failed to consider that the cancellation of the contract would impose an unreasonably high restorative burden on the Contractor as well as leave the Contractor facing a dilemma over how to reassign resources invested in the construction project to other purposes.

Given the purpose of the contract and the interests of the parties, if the proprietor's action is necessary for the execution of the work and the proprietor fails to perform such action, the Contractor should have the right of termination rather than rescission under Article 507. At the same time, when the proprietor failed to perform, the Court should have properly granted the Contractor the right to terminate the contract. If the Court insisted on characterizing the contract at issue as a "contract of hire for work," it at least should have used a "purposive construction method" to narrow the application of Article 507. If this case were addressed through general principles of contract interpretation as mentioned in Part III.2, as soon as the Court spotted the lacuna in the contract, indicating the parties' failure to negotiate what the Contractor can do when the Proprietor doesn't perform its obligation of necessary help, it should have gone through an evaluation of the parties' interests and determined whether the default rules in the Civil Law could be invoked. Through this process, the Court would have had the chance to examine the parties' interests, the relevant commercial customs, and the suitable economic conditions. After taking such matters into account, the Court would then have been able to reach a conclusion based on the parties' hypothetical intention rather than simply applying the default rules. Finally, the Court would have been able to grant the Contractor the right to terminate the contract, which would have best suited the contract's economic circumstances. In this case, the Court's judgment considered none of these potential – arguably most important – aspects, resulting in an unsatisfactory outcome (Wang 2015).

2 Distribution Contract: Taiwan Supreme Court Judgment No. 362 of 1998

In this case, a software company (referred to as "Manufacturer") and a distributor (referred to as "Distributor") entered into a distribution contract. Article 2 of their contract stipulated that: "Distributor's minimum sales from A shall not be less than 500,000 NTD a month, and an order shall be placed to Manufacturer before the twentieth day of each month; otherwise Manufacturer on its own initiative will deliver products to Distributor and Distributor shall accept these products without any objection." Subsequently, Distributor failed to place an order of 500,000 NTD or more. Manufacturer delivered products to Distributor in accordance with the contract. Distributor, however, refused to accept the delivered products. Manufacturer sued Distributor for breach of contract and requested Distributor to pay the price for all delivered products whether or not Distributor placed an actual order. The main issue in this case was how to characterize "minimum sales." Manufacturer claimed that the agreed amount was the object of this contract, so Distributor had an obligation to place orders which were not less than 500,000 dollars a month. On the other hand, Distributor claimed that this contract was a sales agency contract, rather than a distribution contract. It also argued that the term "minimum sales" was not the object of this contract; the term only gave Manufacturer the right of rescission should Distributor fail to place sufficient orders.

The High Court originally characterized this contract as a hybrid between an agency contract and a sales contract. The Supreme Court decided differently, instead pointing out that the distribution contract in question could be distinguished by its content into one of three types – sales, commissions, or agency. It referred to the default contract rules of "Sale," "Commission Agency," and "Commercial Agents" to determine within which category the individual contract provisions fell, in order to determine the rights and duties between the parties. Although Article 1 of the Distribution Contract used the word "agency," the meaning of other articles were deemed unclear and indeterminate based on Article 1 alone.

Analysis

A lot of time and effort was spent by the courts in categorizing the distribution contract in order to determine the contractual obligations of the parties. Once again, examining the contract closely could have resolved the burdensome categorization and benefitted the hypothetical intention of the parties. The relevant clause stated that the distributor had to purchase goods at the minimum sales amount of 500,000 NTD, or else the manufacturer could still deliver the goods and the Distributor could not object to them.

The issue was whether the minimum sales amount was the essential term of the contract or a condition for when the Distributor failed to meet the minimum sales amount, giving the Manufacturer the right to rescind the contract. The wording " . . . otherwise Manufacturer on its own initiative will deliver products to Distributor and Distributor shall accept these products without any objection" is vague as to the effect of the Distributor's failure to meet the requirement. Yet, since it is not a total failure to deal with the disputed content, the Court should at least try to interpret the parties' possible meaning rather than simply consider the issue as a lacuna in the contract. Sometimes a contract does not have a lacuna, though it has vague terms. The notions of "lacuna in a contract" and "vagueness of contract terms," however, can be difficult to distinguish. In this case, the Court nevertheless ignored this significant process and instead advanced immediately to the characterization issue, thus beginning a long journey of back and forth on this point.

This article submits that the "characterization" process did not contribute to the solution of the case. In fact, in this kind of distribution contract, there is information asymmetry between the manufacturer and the distributor regarding the distributor's actions. In such a situation, the distributor might have an incentive to behave badly by not using its best efforts to promote the products. From an economics perspective, this hidden action is the so-called moral hazard. To prevent this hazard, the manufacturer and the distributor will negotiate a "best efforts clause" to ensure the distributor will do its utmost to sell the products. In this sense, the "minimum sales amount" is a practical criterion. This kind of "best efforts clause" can operate as a risk-shifting mechanism, enabling the manufacturer to predict its monthly minimum sales income and cash flow while giving the distributor certain performance pressure. When the distributor doesn't meet the minimum sales amount, the distributor must take the risk of absorbing the expense between the minimum sales amount and factual sales amount.

Following this logic, if the Distributor refused to pay the agreed price, the Manufacturer should be entitled to terminate the contract and recover the damages for the Distributor's breach of contract. The dispute is thereby resolved, without ever having to characterize the contract at issue. In the end, the Court's resort to the default rules was unnecessary.

Another distribution case presented a similar situation. In that case, the court tried to extract a basis for contract termination by drawing an analogy from the default rules of contracts of "Sale," "Commission Agency," and "Commercial Agents." In the end, however, the court did not indicate the particular provision acting as the basis for the right to terminate the contract. The court merely mentioned that it had drawn an analogy from these three kinds of contracts. The court's thinking was even more farfetched than the previous case. This chapter has already submitted that characterization and the reference to default rules in contract interpretation should be applied cautiously, since the rules do not always reflect the parties' desired interests. Neither of the cited court judgments adopted this characterization approach, but merely made analogies to the default rules to forcefully extract any justification for the courts' finding of a basis for termination of contract. This reasoning by analogy appears to be the prevalent methodology in contract interpretation cases in Taiwan, a truly unique phenomenon.

3 Business Guaranty: Taiwan Supreme Court Judgment No. 584 of 2013

In this case, the Hydraulic Engineering Office of the Public Works Department of the Taipei City Government (referred to as "Government") and the Tein-Tai Construction Company (referred to as "Constructor") entered into an engineering contract. At the same time, Government commissioned JihSun Bank (referred to as "Bank") to issue a "Construction Performance Bond"[4] as a guarantee for Constructor's compliance with the agreement. Article 2 of this bond stipulated, "If Constructor is not in compliance with this bond, Bank shall pay the security deposit to Government as soon as Bank receives such notification from Government. Government, moreover, in dealing with these payments must not go through any legal or administrative proceedings, and Bank voluntarily waived its *beneficium ordinis*[5] without any objection." Subsequently, Constructor failed to carry out the contract. Government terminated the contract with Constructor and requested Bank (the guarantor) to pay over the security interest (performance bond). The main issue at trial was how to characterize the "construction performance bond." Government claimed that the bond was an agreement of "instant payment," which varies greatly from a general civil guaranty.[6] Whereas Bank, with reference to Civil Code Articles 741 and 742, claimed that the guarantor's liability should not be greater than the principal debtor's liability (this concept is known as the "subordinated status" of the guaranty). Furthermore, Bank argued that the warranty period in the engineering contract between parties A and C had expired. According to party B, this terminated the guarantor's liability. Bank would thereby be released from its obligation to pay the money (performance bond).

The Supreme Court held for Government, although the construction performance bond was an alternative to a cash payment for a security deposit, and its essence and legal effect were different from a security deposit. The Court pointed out that the main purpose of the construction bond was to guarantee "instant payment" in case the debtor breached the contract. In regard of Article 2 of the Construction Bond[7] the bond resembled a guaranty of instant payment rather than a general civil guaranty, which would be subordinate to the principal contract. In addition, the Supreme Court highlighted that even if the parties used the word "guaranty" in the bond, it wouldn't change the characterization of the bond. Despite the Supreme Court judgment in this case, other judgments have taken the opposite standpoint: characterizing the construction performance bond as a civil guaranty subordinate to the principal contract. Thus, if the warranty period of the principal contract has expired, the guarantee's liability and obligation also has terminated.

Analysis

A guaranty, in short, is a credit transaction in which one party – the guarantor – specializes in information and monitoring – and another – the creditor – specializes in obtaining loanable funds (Katz 1999, pp. 52–62). The Supreme Court had to decide whether the contract at issue was a typical "guaranty contract" as provided in the Taiwan Civil Code. If the Supreme Court answered the question in the affirmative it had to discuss whether the guarantor could refuse to pay the performance bond based on *beneficium ordinis* and dependency of guarantee. Although the Supreme Court in the end decided that the contract at issue was different from the "guaranty contract" provided in the default rules, the case had already been through several years of litigation on the contract characterization issue. This is yet another case derived from the typical mindset of many courts in Taiwan – to rigidly stick to the default rules instead of properly interpreting the contract by scrutinizing the substantive economic circumstances of the parties. In this case, the contract between the parties was actually a kind of "bank guarantee" which is widely used in the construction industry. The bank guarantee was intended to enhance the credit standing of the construction company.

The commercial activity guaranteed by such a contract is rather important for an enterprise's cash flow. In the case where compensation occurs, the business guaranty ensures a rapid and exact recovery. Therefore, the bank guarantee often contracts terms that revise the rule made by law in order to get out from the procedure of assessing rights and to be convenient to request debt. The liability for the guarantor has deviated from the secondary obligation under the traditional "guaranty contract." The traditional "guaranty contract," compared to the performance guarantee contract, emphasizes the protection of guarantors over the pursuit of efficiency. The regulatory model not only increases the creditor's enforcement costs, but also decreases the efficiency of the risk allocation mechanism. It raises the difficulty of confirming the rights and obligations of parties, and it loses the function of enhancing the credit relationship.

Fortunately, the Supreme Court in this case eventually distinguished clearly between these two, but, before that, many judgments had come to the opposite conclusion – the contract was an ordinary one provided in the "guaranty contract" chapter and hence subject to *beneficium ordinis* and dependence of guaranty. This chapter cites this verdict to remind all legal practitioners: in the case of contract interpretation, especially when applying the default rules, the law must carefully consider the relevant interests of the parties and never simply apply ready-made provisions and therein interpret the contract wrongly. Indeed, such waivers of default are the norm in many B2B commercial credit transactions.

V An Analysis of the Nature of the Problems

The issues in the abovementioned cases flow from several, similar recurring problems: the improper process of contract interpretation, the wrongful determination or even failure to determine whether lacunae exist in a contract, and how to fill a gap in a contract.

As soon as a contract issue arise the Court tends to turn to the suppletive rules rather than to interpret the contract based on its commercial and economic substance. This phenomenon can be dissected from the following points of view.

1 Rules-centric Jurisprudence and an Overemphasis on Default Rules

With respect to the mandatory rules and the nonmandatory default rules, Taiwan's Civil Law does not make a clear distinction between them. As mentioned above, party autonomy and thus the freedom of contract are the most fundamental principles in any liberal system of private law, and therefore nonmandatory provisions of law are the general rule; mandatory provisions being the exception. Any default rules, if desirable in certain situations, must serve the purpose of supplementing the parties' contract and reflecting the ordinary interests of the parties. Thus, the process of determining the true interests of the parties in a specific contract is of crucial importance.

This process of contract determination, however, is also the weakest part of Taiwan's judicial practice. First, though default rules are generally nonmandatory rules, courts in Taiwan do not draw a clear line between mandatory and nonmandatory rules in applying the rules to cases. Second, legal academics and practitioners alike highlight the concept of the basic claim of action, which means one has to base his or her claim on a corresponding provision in the law to claim a contract right. Third, analytical reasoning is widely overused and frequently misused in interpreting contracts. When addressing a lacuna in a contract, the courts should first try to identify the parties' interests in the contract and see if they are the same as the ordinary interests provided in the default rules; and second, to decide whether to apply the default rules or assume the parties' hypothetical intentions. Each of the steps involves a sophisticated gauge of background facts and circumstances.

None of the above-cited articles (i.e., Canaris and Grigoleit 2010) has mentioned the method of analytical reasoning. If analytical reasoning is to be inserted into the overall process of gap-filling, it likely can fit only into the second step: after having decided to apply default rules. Before applying the default rules, however, the courts must carefully consider whether the analogy to the default rules corresponds to the parties' interest distribution. In theory, if the parties' interest distribution differs from the default rules, the courts must not apply the default rules.

Analytical reasoning itself, moreover, is a method of legal interpretation rather than contract interpretation. As Karl Larenz (2008) states in his legal methods theory, contract interpretation is inherently different from legal interpretation. In interpreting contract, the general principle is to ascertain the intention of the declaring party as seen from the perspective of the addressee; by contrast, in interpreting a statute, the court should consider the legislative history and legislative purposes. Unfortunately, Taiwanese courts generally apply analytical reasoning in order to use default rules. As argued by Dworkin: "An analogy is a way of stating a conclusion, not a way of reaching one." (Dworkin 1997). Due to the lack of proper interpretation during the first distinguishing process, default rules are in certain cases applied as if they are mandatory rules.

Taiwan's legal system, for example, allows for both the rescission and the termination of contracts. Logically, most contracts should be canceled under the principle of no restitution and no retroaction (see UCC). The contract law of Taiwan, however, not only applies either rescission or termination in various circumstances, but also stubbornly considers rescission as the rule and termination as the exception. If the parties don't establish clear rules or omit an agreement over the causes of termination (such as the constructional contract mentioned before), the court cannot know whether to grant the right of termination to the parties by interpreting the contract.

In the case of a construction contract, if the court interprets the contract properly, according to the distribution of the parties' interests (the contractor's investment is a specific asset which cannot be used in another way), it should recognize that a contract of hire for work in Taiwan's Civil Law system doesn't grant the contractor the right of termination. In this case, the law articles do not correspond to the distribution of the parties' interests, so the court must not apply the default rules to the parties' dispute. On the contrary, after the court interprets the contract properly, the court should grant the right of termination to the contractor by referring to the parties' hypothetical intentions. In the above case, the Court first regarded the contract at issue as a contract of hire for work under the Civil Law, and then insisted that the Civil Law does not grant the Contractor the right to terminate the contract. Furthermore, the Court characterized Article 507's purpose as: "If the law allows the contractor to terminate the contract, it not only disadvantages the proprietor who does not have its work completed, but also causes severe damage to the proprietor and may lead to the result that no third party can continue and finish the work."

Is such legislation, however, reasonable when the proprietor doesn't perform the obligation of necessary help? Doesn't it give unbridled power to a proprietor who may even fail to assist the contractor? Even though it does, the courts of Taiwan are unwilling to create the right of termination to the parties by interpreting the contracts. The reason is simply because Taiwan's current legal practice does not allow the right of termination through an explanation of the contract. Is the right of rescission and termination under Taiwan's civil law a "statutory cause"? Are these rights mandatory or nonmandatory rules? What shall the courts do when nonmandatory rules are incomplete or do not correspond to the parties' distribution of interest? If the court still insists in applying the article directly, there is no doubt that the rule of "termination equals rescission" will apply. From the perspective of the interpretation of contracts, there is a chance to create the right of termination in such a situation. Taiwanese legal scholars, however, mostly take a conservative attitude toward this point.

The above case typifies the process of classifying the contract in order to seek the basis of claim for the action so that the parties can have a claim to a right. The continuous adoption of this method, however, cannot address every contract issue, as the above case demonstrates. The basic way to solve this problem still lies in adopting a proper mentality toward contract interpretation. We must interpret the contracts appropriately. We must not apply articles arbitrarily. Since the nonmandatory rules are designed to save transaction costs and complete the parties' imperfect contract, they must reflect the ordinary intention of the parties. If they do not reflect the ordinary intention, the rule will fail in performing its function and thus must not be applied to interpret the contract at issue.

2 Vaguely Legislated Articles and Failure to Teach Law Students How to Interpret Contracts

As already mentioned, Article 98 of the Taiwan Civil Law contains a basic principle of contract interpretation. However, the provision's wording, which states that "[i]n the interpretation of an expression of intent, the real intention of the parties must be sought rather than the literal meaning of the words," is difficult to apply given its vagueness. When related judgments fill this gap, courts always use Article 98 as a basis, and then consider other factors, such as nonmandatory rules, the principle of good faith and fair-dealing, business custom, and the purpose of contracting. When courts make conclusions, however, they never clearly state which criteria should apply first. Some judgments only adopt one of the criteria as the explanation for applying Article 98. On the other hand, could the principle of good faith and fair-dealing be the basis for a claim in the action? This issue is yet unresolved. Furthermore, as illustrated in the franchise contract and construction contract case, the practice of law in Taiwan ignores business customs and jurisprudence.

Compared to the German Contract Law, from which Taiwan's law derives, German court decisions tend to emphasize constructive interpretation over nonmandatory rules (McMeel and Grigoleit 2013). According to German law, constructive interpretation requires an unintended gap in the contract and must be based on the parties' individual hypothetical intentions. The method is applied to assume what honest and rational parties would have agreed upon if they had discovered the gap in light of the purpose and nature of the contract and if they had balanced their reciprocal interests according to good faith and fair dealing. For this assessment, the contract itself must primarily (but not exclusively) be taken into account. The courts, by means of constructive interpretation, may only draw those conclusions that can be qualified as mandatory and self-evident consequences of the contracts. As a result, the notion of constructive interpretation must not be used to broaden the subject matter of the contract. Even the German law takes a highly cautious approach to nonmandatory rules in contract interpretation – Taiwanese jurisprudence's heavy dependence on nonmandatory rules thus requires much further reflection. The practice of law in Taiwan has applied nonmandatory rules for many years. This situation has left much to reconsider and reform.

VI PRC Contract Law – A Comparative Note

The People's Republic of China promulgated the Contract Law of the People's Republic of China (hereafter the PRC Contract Law) in 1999. It replaced the previous laws on contract – the Law on Economic Contracts of 1981, the Law of Foreign-related Economic Contracts of 1985, and the Law of Technology Contracts of 1987. The People's Republic of China modeled its General Provisions in the Contract Law after the sale contract chapters in the "United Nations Convention on Contracts of International Sales of Goods" (CISG) and the "Principles of International Commercial Contracts" (PICC) (Chapter 3). Furthermore, the PRC Contract Law contains a Specific Provisions section depicting 15 different typical contracts, ranging from Sales Contracts and Contracts for Construction Projects to Technology Contracts. Many typical contracts in the PRC Contract Law align with current requirements in Contract Law (Chapter 3).[8]

The typical contract chapters in the PRC Contract Law contain mandatory and nonmandatory rules, such as in Taiwan's Contract Law. However, the Supreme People's Court further dissected mandatory rules into mandatory rules on effectiveness and mandatory rules on management. It assigned varying consequences to the mandatory rules. Violations of mandatory rules on effectiveness render a contract ineffective. Mandatory rules on management do not per se render a contract ineffective. Whether a violation of mandatory rules on management leads to ineffective contracts depends on the rule's purpose, the conflicting rights or benefits of the parties, transaction security, and whether the interests of the country or public society are infringed.

Contract interpretation in the People's Republic of China follows Article 125 of the PRC Contract Law. Article 125 states:

> If any disputes arise between the parties over the understanding of any clause of the contract, the true meaning thereof shall be determined according to the words and sentences used in the contract, the relevant provisions in the contract, purpose of the contract, the transaction practices and the principle of good faith.

Chinese legal scholars have deduced the following principles of contract interpretation: (1) objective interpretation over subjective interpretation; (2) systematic interpretation; (3) historical interpretation; (4) teleological interpretation; (5) customary interpretation; and (6) principle of good faith. These principles of interpretation help judges to interpret contracts, and reduce unstructured and arbitrary contract interpretation.

Most of the principles of contract interpretation that the scholars deduced can be found in Article 125 of the PRC Contract Law. However, whether objective interpretation should be favored over subjective interpretation and how the principles ought to be adopted is not among them. Therefore, Judges still have some leeway, which is detrimental to a coherent legal practice.

The legal framework of the PRC Contract Law may, contrary to the scholar's opinion, favor subjective interpretation. Article 125 of the PRC Contract Law comprises the principle of good faith. But objective interpretation and the principle of good faith contradict each other. Subjective interpretation stresses instead the principle of good faith. There is one caveat with subjective interpretation: It may sacrifice predictability.

The PRC Contract Law contains an elaborate system to fill lacunae in contracts. Article 61 of the PRC Contract Law is the first "go-to" section if a lacuna exists. Article 61 of the PRC Contract Law states:

> If a term such as quality, price or remuneration, or place of performance etc. was not prescribed or clearly prescribed, after the contract has taken effect, the parties may supplement it through agreement; if the parties fail to reach a supplementary agreement, such term shall be determined in accordance with

the relevant provisions of the contract or in accordance with the relevant usage.

Supplementary agreements or contract interpretation are the two predominant approaches to fill a lacuna. If contract interpretation has failed, PRC Contract Law contains specific provisions in the typical contracts chapters that suggest how to resolve the lacuna, i.e., Article 139 PRC Contract Law or Article 156 PRC Contract Law. Article 62 PRC Contract Law is the fallback provision when none of the above have resolved the lacuna.[9]

Some scholars suggest that the specific provisions in the typical contract chapters and Article 62 of the PRC Contract Law should prevail over contract interpretation, unless: (1) the application of these provisions would harm the parties' benefits; (2) the analogue application of these provisions for atypical contracts would defeat the purpose of the contract; (3) the contract indicates that the parties did not want these provisions to apply; (4) parties erroneously relied on supplemental specific provisions that contradict the expected application of the specific provisions; and (5) these provisions do not accommodate diverse economical situations.

However, having specific provisions prevail over contract interpretation contradicts the wording of Article 125 of the PRC Contract Law. Individual contract interpretation is more responsive to unique contracting situations than rigid provisions.

Anyway, Chinese judges tend to be more used to the application of the special provisions. In a recent Chinese court case judges applied Article 154, 62 PRC Contract Law without attempting to interpret the contract first (Cui 2013, pp. 72–73).

Analogous application of specific contract provisions to atypical contracts is less common in China than in Taiwan. A judgment by a second instance court in China is particularly noteworthy in this context.[10] The court, contrary to the first instance court's mechanical adoption of specific provisions, held that courts should consider the parties' intent and contractual purpose before applying typical contract provisions to atypical contracts.

VII Conclusions

The freedom of contract principle finds its foundational basis in the notion of personal liberty, and contracting parties may rely on the enforcement of contractual provisions based on such voluntary meeting of minds. But contracts are inevitably incomplete to deal with problems as they arise during performance of the contract. This incompleteness could arise from the lack of consideration *ab initio* of future events, or from contractual calculus to shift the transaction cost of negotiation *ex post*. To perform this contractual gap-filling, then, the derivation of those provisions should find their normative roots in the notion of freedom of contract. Because, after all, it is such freedom that has led to the formation of a contract in the first place.

Taiwan's jurisprudence has long suffered from a systematic disregard, albeit perhaps an unintentional one, of this principle in the courts' haste to level the contractual hole with the default provisions from the Civil Code, grasping at whatever seemed fit prima facie. Though Article 98 of the Taiwan Civil Code stresses the importance of the parties' *real intentions*, a thorough examination of such intentions is systematically neglected by the courts. In the three cases shown, Taiwan's Supreme Court had either hastily characterized the contract in question without much thought into the economic interests that play a vital role in modern business-to-business contract-making, or rigidly employed a method of analogy to implant the corresponding default provisions into the contract in question.

Based on these observations, this chapter further offers some possible explanations and suggestions. To ameliorate this problem, Taiwan's courts should take contract interpretation seriously. It should be stressed that interpretation of contract laws and interpretation of contract are two distinct notions. As observed by this chapter, courts have heavily relied on the former to give meaning to the contract, while Article 98 of the Taiwan Civil Code, and contract-making's normative basis in contractual freedom, would urge an equal reliance upon the latter. By way of comparison, this chapter discusses Contract Laws in the PRC as possible alternatives for when the courts may take up constructive interpretation to advance the notion of contract interpretation.

References in English

Barnett, Randy E. 1992. The Sound of Silence: Default Rules and Contractual Consent. *Virginia Law Review* 78:821–853.

Canaris, Claus-Wilhelm., and Grigoleit, Hans Christoph. 2010. Interpretation of Contracts. Available at http://ssrn.com/abstract=1537169: 19.

Dworkin, Ronald. 1997. *Justice in Robes*. Cambridge, MA: Harvard University Press.

Goldberg, Victor P. 2014. Protecting Reliance. *Columbia Law Review* 114:1075–1081.

Grigoleit, Hans Christoph. 2011. Mandatory Law: Fundamental Principles. *Max Planck Encyclopaedia of European Private Law*, edited by Jurgen Basedow, Klaus J. Hopt, and Reinhard Zimmermann. Oxford, UK: Oxford University Press. Available at http://ssrn.com/abstract=1950670.

Katz, Avery W. 1999. An Economic Analysis of the Guaranty Contract, *U. of Chic. L. Rev.* 66:47–96.

McMeel, Gerard, and Hans Christoph Grigoleit. 2013. Interpretation of Contracts – Prospective European Regulation from the English and German Point of View (March 1, 2013). Pp. 341–372 in *The Common European Sales Law in Context – Interactions with English and German Law*, edited by Gerhard Dannemann and Stefan Vogenauer. Oxford: Oxford University Press.

Schwartz, Alan, and Scott, Robert. 2003. Contract Theory and the Limits of Contract Law. *Yale L. Rev.* 113:541–619.

UNIDROIT. 2010. *Principles of International Commercial Contracts*. Published by the International Institute for the Unification of Private Law ("UNIDROIT").

References in Chinese

Cui, Jian-yuan. 2013. The Interwoven Relationship between Contract Interpretation and Legal Interpretation. *Jilin University Journal, Social Sciences Edition* 72–73.

Chen, Tzu-Chiang. 2010. *Content and Elimination of Contract*. Taipei: Sharing.

Hengyang Intermediate People's Court (Civil, 1), Final, No. 121 (2011).

Larenz, Karl. 2008. *Methodenlehre der Rechtswissenschaft,* translated by Ai-Er Chen. Taipei: Wunan.

Wang, Tez-chien. 2009. *Rules of Obligations*. Taipei: Self-published.

Wang, Tez-Chien. 2009. *The Principles of The Law of Obligations: Basic Theories, Occurrence of Debts, Contracts and Voluntary Service*. 2d ed. Taipei: Self-published.

Wang, Wen-yeu. 2015. Interpretation of Commercial Contract – Analogical Reasoning and Economic Analysis. *The Taiwan Law Review* 236:5, 26–28.

Reference in German

Kötz, Hein. 2013. Dispositives Recht und ergänzende Vertragsauslegung. *Juristische Schulung* 53(4):289, 296.

Notes

1 UNIDROIT Principles of International Commercial Contracts (2010), at page 2; comments 2 titled "Commercial Contracts."

2 Schwarz and Scott (2003) sets out a normative theory to guide decision-makers in the regulation of contracts between firms.

3 Supreme Court of Taiwan Civil Decision (1997) Tai-Shang-Zih No. 1671.

4 "The construction performance bond" is used at the time when contractor was unable to offer a huge amount of security deposit to the principal or client, who approved that contractor could give a bond instead of cash payment. Therefore, the nature of this bond is an alternative security deposit.

5 *Beneficium ordinis* in Taiwanese Law is provided in Civil Code Article 745: "A guarantor may refuse performance to the creditor, so long as the creditor has not filed proceedings for compulsory execution, against the property of the principal debtor, without results."

6 The nature of the civil guaranty lies in its subordinated and supplemental status.

7 "Party B shall pay the security deposit to Party A as soon as Party B receives such notification from Party A."

8 Taiwanese judges and practitioners must analogize the contract on Hire for Work when it comes to Construction Project Contracts (see above), whereas the People's Republic of China can refer to the implemented provisions on Construction Contracts in its Contract law.

9 "Where certain contents agreed upon by the parties in the contract are ambiguous and cannot be determined in accordance with the provisions in Article 61 of this Law, the following provisions shall be applied:

(1) if quality requirement is not clear, performance shall be in accordance with the state standard or industry standard; absent any state or industry standard, performance shall be in accordance with the customary standard or any particular standard consistent with the purpose of the contract;

(2) if price or remuneration is not clear, performance shall be in accordance with the prevailing market price at the place of performance at the time the contract was concluded, and if adoption of a price commissioned by the government or based on government issued pricing guidelines is required by law, such requirement applies;

(3) where the place of performance is not clear, if the obligation is payment of money, performance shall be at the place where the payee is located; if the obligation is delivery of immovable property, performance shall be at the place where the immovable property is located;

for any other subject matter, performance shall be effected at the place of location of the party fulfilling the obligations.

(4) if the time of performance is not clear, the obligor may perform, and the obligee may require performance, at any time, provided that the other party shall be given the time required for preparation;

(5) if the method of performance is not clear, performance shall be rendered in a manner which is conducive to realizing the purpose of the contract;

(6) if the responsibility for the expenses of performance is not clear, the party fulfilling the obligations shall bear the expenses."

10 Hengyang Intermediate People's Court (Civil, 1), Final, No. 121 (2011).

5 The Evolution of the Law of Torts in China

The Growth of a Liability System

WEI ZHANG*

1 Introduction

The formal legal rules governing tortious behaviors in post-Mao China can be traced back to the General Principles of the Civil Law[1] (hereinafter called the "General Principles") promulgated in 1986. Since then, tort disputes have become one of the main types of cases litigated in courts. In 2007, the number of tort cases accepted by Chinese courts totaled about 863,000, and in 2008, this number rose further to 992,000 (Wang 2010, p. 2). Over the same period, a large number of changes have occurred in the law of torts. The transformation of the rules, however, has eluded previous introductory works on Chinese tort law written in English (e.g., Koziol and Zhu 2010). This chapter is devoted to delineating these changes, which present the growth of a liability system moving predominantly in favor of tort victims. Due to the limitations of space, I will focus mainly on the formal rules, with occasional reference to the positions taken by courts in practice. Moreover, my current work looks specifically to the alterations appearing in the law, but does not attempt to present an all-inclusive view of the Chinese tort law. For those who are interested in probing the Chinese tort law in a comparative perspective, this chapter will provide essential information about the mutation of law in a society undergoing economic transition. More generally, students of modern China may also find useful clues in this chapter for understanding the concerns embedded in China's formal institutions, as well as the interaction among different branches of government to address them.

* This research was funded by Singapore MOE AcRF Tier 1 Research Grant (#13-C234-SMU-009).

2 Three Sources of Law

In China, at the national level, three categories of laws[2] are applied in tort litigations: general statutes, special statutes, and judicial interpretations.

General statutes are comprehensive laws governing tortious behaviors, which set down the basic rules applicable to various types of torts. They are enacted either by the National People's Congress (NPC) or by its Standing Committee, and officially dubbed as "law" (*falü*), bearing the highest rank of effect in China's formal sources of law. So far, there are two general statutes on torts, the General Principles and the Tort Liability Law.[3] Chapter 6 of the General Principles, and Section 3 in particular, set forth the rules of torts covering intentional and negligent tortious actions as well as several special types of torts often subject to strict liabilities. The Tort Liability Law, in some sense, is an extension of the rules established in the General Principles and inherited many of its substantive provisions.

Special statutes are laws related to specific types of torts that are usually referred to as "special torts" (*teshu qinquan*) by Chinese lawyers. In most cases, these special statutes do not deal with tort liabilities in particular, but are regulatory rules that apply to specific industries. Some of these statutes are promulgated by the NPC Standing Committee, hence obtaining the status of "law," while others are adopted by the State Council, which are administrative regulations (*xingzheng fagui*) one rank lower than laws in terms of legal effect, or by the ministries of the State Council as departmental rules (*bumen guizhang*) with an even lower rank as a source of law.[4] For example, the Railway Law[5] set down the liability and compensation rules for railway accidents, whereas the Regulation on the Handling of Medical Accidents[6] (hereinafter known as Medical Accident Regulation) includes a chapter devoted specifically to dealing with tort claims of medical malpractices.

Besides the rules provided by the legislative and administrative institutions, the Supreme People's Court (SPC) issues various judicial interpretations on the adjudication of tort disputes. SPC interpretations either take the form of replies to lower courts' requests for instructions pertaining to particular cases or adjudicative problems, or stand alone as general directions on trials of certain types of tort litigations or on certain issues in tort law cases. Whereas the former is usually short and written in an essay style, the latter is closer to laws and regulations in terms of format and generality. Although, in principle, judicial interpretations are not a formal source of law, in practice, they are routinely cited in judgments, especially the legislation-style general directions.

In a nutshell, the law of torts in China started from the General Principles, inviting a wave of special legislations in the 1990s, and was followed by a series of judicial interpretations in the 2000s, before they were consolidated in the Tort Liability Law that took effect in July 2010. However, it is noteworthy that many of the special legislations and judicial interpretations regarding tortious behaviors remain effective after the promulgation of the Tort Liability Law. Thus, where the different sources of law conflict with one another, uncertainty exists in terms of the choice of rules in tort adjudications. This uncertainty may be particularly pronounced when the special statutes differ from the Tort Liability Law since, among the special statutes, quite a few were also adopted by the NPC Standing Committee, hence bearing the same rank of effectiveness as the Tort Liability Law.

3 Expanding the Protection

When asked about the most salient change in the adjudication of tort disputes in China in recent years, a senior judge of an intermediate court in Shanghai answered unhesitatingly, "expanding the protection of victims in torts."[7] His feeling is borne out in this chapter. Since the turn of the century, albeit with some minor exceptions, the law of torts has exhibited a clear trend toward boosting the chances for tort victims to seek legal remedies. This can be detected in a variety of forms as elaborated below.

3.1 Expanding the Scope of Rights Under Protection

Article 106 of General Principles broadly states that "property and personality" are protected against tortious behaviors. This general legislation includes ten sorts of rights over property and seven sorts of rights over personality. It is unclear, however, whether the General Principles are purported to set up an exclusive boundary for the rights protected by tort law. In practice, a wide variety of rights, especially those regarding personality, have been claimed and litigated after the adoption of the law. Sometimes, these novel claims also win support in courtrooms.[8] Indeed, Article 1 of the SPC Interpretation on the Determination of Damages for Pain and Suffering Arising from Torts[9] (hereinafter as "Interpretation on Pain and Suffering") expanded the scope of personality rights by stipulating the rights of dignity (*renge zunyan quan*) and personal freedom (*renshen ziyou quan*), both unseen in the General Principles.

The Tort Liability Law declares, in Article 2, its protection of "civil rights and interests," followed by a laundry list of 18 sorts of civil rights. This contains nearly all the rights mentioned in the General Principles, with four new ones. Although the add-on seems marginal, the scope of protected rights under the new law is apparently open-ended. Moreover, it extends the protection beyond civil *rights* to the notion of civil *interests*. Rights and interests are distinguished in the German law where the latter are protected less generously than the former (Wang 2010, p. 22).[10] A similar distinction was proposed in the course of drafting (Civil Law Office 2010, pp. 153, 166), but the adopted version does not take the German approach eventually. Therefore, under current tort law scheme, the scope of protection has enough flexibility to incorporate a wide range of novel claims when needed.

3.2 Expanding the Scope of Liable Parties

3.2.1 Extending the Joint and Several Liability

Under the Chinese tort law, joint and several liability is extended mainly through the enrichment of concurrent torts (*gongtong qinquan*). The General Principles, in effect, only requires the multiple tortfeasors conducting one tortious action[11] to be liable jointly and separately when they share the intent to injure, are all in negligence, or have a certain combination of intent and negligence (Wang 2010, p. 58). I will refer to this situation as the original type of concurrent torts below. The scope of concurrent torts was first enlarged by Article 148 of the SPC Opinions on Several Issues Concerning the Implementation of the General Principles of the Civil Law (For Trial Implementation)[12] (hereinafter referred to as "SPC Opinions"). It provides for the joint and several tort liability of the person who abets and assists another in committing a tortious action.

In the SPC Interpretation on Application of Law in Adjudication of Cases of Personal Injuries (hereinafter as "Interpretation on Personal Injuries"),[13] the rules of concurrent torts were further extended to three other situations. Based on Article 3 of this interpretation, where some of the injurers do not share the intention or negligence in conducting torts, all the injurers can nevertheless be held liable jointly and severally if their actions are "connected directly" to cause one injury, but severally according to share of negligence or causality if their actions are "connected indirectly." Moreover, Article 4 of the same judicial interpretation sets forth a rule, often referred to as "common risk" (*gongtong weixian*), that the several parties conducting activities potentially harmful to others should be liable jointly and severally if no specific injurer can be identified as the cause of the pertinent harm.[14]

A few words are in order with regard to the "direct connection" mentioned above. According to an eminent Chinese tort law scholar, this means that the actions of the several injurers are so closely linked that none of these actions is dispensable to the occurrence of the harm or differentiable in terms of the contribution to the harm (Zhang 2010, p. 49). For instance, where the victim gets hurt in a traffic accident caused by multiple injurers, courts frequently treat the injurers' actions as directly connected so that they are held liable jointly and severally, e.g., *Yang v. Cai et al.* ((2011) 浦民一(民)初字第40812号).

The Tort Liability Law has preserved most of the above concurrent tort rules, but discarded the distinction between the direct and indirect connections of actions. Instead, when multiple tortfeasors take tortious actions separately but cause one single injury, it looks to whether each individual tortfeasor's action is sufficient to bring about the entire injury. The tortfeasors are liable jointly and severally under Article 11 if the answer is yes; otherwise, they will be liable severally under Article 12. While the effect of this first modification in the new law on the scope of joint and several liability seems ambiguous, the next one has unequivocally extended this scope. Under Article 4 of the "Interpretation on Personal Injuries", in order to avoid liability in cases involving common risk, an alleged injurer only needs to prove that the injury was not caused by his action. In contrast, Article 10 of the Tort Liability Law requires the alleged injurer to produce sufficient evidence to identify the actual injurer who has caused the harm (Wang 2010, p. 67). This is patently a more restrictive condition. Should such evidence be available, there would be no common risk in the first place. Therefore, in case of common risk, it is now easier for victims to hold tortfeasors liable jointly and severally.

Joint and several liability is also extended in some specific contexts. For example, the SPC has dealt with a special type of traffic accidents where the owner of the vehicle causing injuries operates the vehicle commercially in the name of another entity, usually a firm licensed to run a transportation business. This phenomenon is known in Chinese as *guakao* ("hang and lean"). The vehicle owner using another's business name bypasses the regulatory requirements for the transportation industry while the firm allowing others to use its name benefits from charging fees for such usage. In 2008, for example, motor vehicles operating on a *guakao* basis accounted for about 58 percent of the major traffic accidents claiming ten or more lives (Civil Law Office 2010, p. 711). SPC first made it clear in 2001 that the business entity allowing others to use its name for business operation in return for fee payments is liable for traffic accidents caused by motor vehicles conducting business in its name.[15] And in the latest SPC interpretation on traffic accident litigations issued in 2012, such a business entity is liable jointly and severally with the owner of the vehicle causing the accident.[16]

3.2.2 Extending the Vicarious Liability

Vicarious liability is regarded here as the liability borne by one party for the actionable conduct of another, regardless of the former's own fault or the relationship between the two parties.[17] The tort law in China has developed a host of cases subject to vicarious liability over the years.

First, when a minor or legally incompetent person caused harm to others, the General Principles holds her guardian liable for the harm. Even if the guardian has fulfilled the duty of guardianship, his liability will still not be eliminated but merely reduced (General Principles, Art. 133; SPC Opinions, Art. 159). Article 32 of the Tort Liability Law inherited this position. At the same time, both the General Principles and the Tort Liability Law require the minor or the legally incompetent to compensate the victim first by drawing on their own assets (if they own any) with the balance to be covered by the guardian. However, while the General Principles only requires the guardian to cover "appropriately," the Tort Liability Law now demands the full coverage of any shortfall. In addition, the Tort Liability Law also abolished the exception for unit (*danwei*) guardians acknowledged by the General Principles so that they should also cover the deficiency in full.

Second, Article 121 of the General Principles requires firms and public entities to be liable vicariously for the harm to a third party caused by their employees' intentional or negligent activities within the scope of employment. This rule is reaffirmed in the Interpretation on Personal Injuries and inherited by the Tort Liability Law. Whereas the previous rules cover only people employed by the firm, the Tort Liability Law extends the strict liability to individual employers (Tort Liability Law, Art. 35). This latest change in law has echoed the recent development in the Chinese job market, in particular, the surge in services delivered for family instead of firms such as helpers, nannies and tutors (Wang 2010, p. 175). It hence provides broader opportunities for tort victims to seek remedies under the law by meticulously filling a gap in the previous legal rules that may frustrate a legal recourse.

Third, with regard to injuries resulting from the transmission of contaminated blood, Article 59 of the Tort Liability Law allows victims to choose to claim damages from medical institutions even when the latter are not at fault. Conversely, the previous Article 33(4) of the Medical Accident Regulation immunizes medical institutions entirely in similar situations.

Fourth, according to Article 127 of the General Principles, owners or keepers of domestic animals are not liable for harm resulting from a third party's intentional or negligent behaviors, such as sounding a horn next to a horse. Instead, that third party should be liable on his own accord. In the Tort Liability Law, however, this rule is revised. Article 83 of the new law allows the victim to request compensation from the owner or keeper of the animal, and the latter need to pay compensation first and get indemnified later from the third party at fault.

3.2.3 Establishing Complementary Liability

In contrast to the vicarious liability, in China a party bearing a complementary liability needs to compensate the victim only if those who have directly caused the harm fail to pay damages. Usually, complementary liability is proportional to the negligence of the party subject to this liability.[18] Despite these restrictions, it nevertheless serves to increase potential sources of compensation. Complementary liability is not seen in the General Principles, but a creation of the judicial interpretation followed by the Tort Liability Law, and seems unique to China.

Complementary liability is mostly applicable to the situation in primary and secondary schools. According to both Article 7 of the Interpretation on Personal Injuries and Article 40 of the Tort Liability Law, educational institutions bear complementary liability, in proportion to their fault in managing campus, for injuries inflicted by external personnel on students who are minors. This essentially means that schools should be liable secondarily only if the external personnel causing the injury cannot bear the tort liability in full, i.e., judgment proof, and only to the extent of schools' own negligence. In particular, courts are not supposed to compare the fault between external personnel and the school, and hold the latter to bear a certain proportion of the liability primarily. Instead, schools' negligence is determined by looking to the shortfall in precaution compared to their own applicable standard.[19] Consequently, schools are no longer liable after external personnel have paid damages completely. Neither do they have to cover the entire deficiency after external personnel's payment (Wang 2010, p. 217).

3.2.4 Adding Liable Parties to Regular Liability Cases

Apart from the changes in relation to the abovementioned special types of tort liabilities, the Chinese tort law also widens the pool of defendants from whom a tort victim can claim damages in certain cases of regular tort liabilities.

When an injury happens due to material falling off any part of a building or structure, or anything placed thereon or suspended therefrom, Article 126 of the General Principles originally held the owner or superintendent of the building liable unless the owner or superintendent could prove he or she was not at fault. The Interpretation on Personal Injuries took the same position in Article 16. The Tort Liability Law extends this liability to users, usually lessees, of the building in Article 85. Some lessees, especially those of commercial real estates, are wealthy business entities with deep pockets, thus this extension conceivably improves the victims' chance to get compensated.

3.3 Tightening the Liability

3.3.1 Moving Toward Liability Rules Less Favorable to Injurers

In some areas of torts, the negligence rule has been replaced with *res ipsa loquitur* (*guocuo tuiding*) under which the injurer is presumed as negligent unless he is able to prove otherwise.

First, the General Principles does not mention schools' liability for injuries arising on their premises to students who are minors. SPC first set forth a rule, SPC Opinions Article 160, requiring schools to "provide appropriate compensation" if they are at fault for the injuries suffered by minors of no legal competence. Then, in Article 7 of the Interpretation on Personal Injuries, it expands such liability to cover all minors, whether legally incompetent or restrictively competent.[20] Later on, the Ministry of Education also requires schools to be liable for students' injuries when they are at fault, though with an extensive range of immunities.[21] All these previous laws use a negligence rule to determine educational institutions' liabilities. These institutions will be liable only when they breach the duty of care in discharging their responsibilities of managing the campus, and protecting and educating the students. The Tort Liability Law, however, distinguishes injuries to students of complete incompetence from those to students of restrictive competence. Whereas the negligence rule maintains for the latter, *res ipsa loquitur* now applies to the former (Tort Liability Law, Arts. 38, 39). Consequently, where completely incompetent, or younger, students are injured, schools have to prove that they were not negligent in carrying out their duties.

Second, under the General Principles, medical malpractice is a regular tort, and hence subject to the negligence rule. Therefore, plaintiffs are supposed to prove the negligence of medical institutions in order to claim damages for medical malpractices. This rule is inherited in the Medical Accident Regulation. However, according to Article 4(8) of the SPC Provisions on Evidence in Civil Procedures (Zuigao Renmin Fayuan Guanyu Minshi Susong Zhengju De Ruogan Guiding), the burden of proof is shifted to medical institutions in terms of the nonexistence of negligence or causation between medical treatment and injuries. In other words, SPC demands application of *res ipsa loquitur* to medical malpractices. The Tort Liability Law resumes the negligence rule in general medical malpractice cases, but keeps *res ipsa loquitur* for three exceptional situations: (1) violating the provisions of law, administrative regulations or other regulatory rules on medical practices; (2) concealing or declining to present medical records related to the dispute; or (3) faking, tampering with or destroying medical records (Tort Liability Law, Arts. 54, 58).

Furthermore, the negligence rule was substituted with strict liability in relation to traffic accidents. The State Council enacted the Measures to Handle Road Traffic Accidents (*Daolu Jiaotong Shigu Chuli*

Banfa, hereinafter called the "Traffic Accident Measures") in 1991. Articles 17 and 19 of this administrative regulation essentially adopted the comparative negligence rule to handle accidents occurring not only between motorists, but also between motorists and pedestrians or nonmotorized vehicle riders.[22] The Standing Committee of NPC passed the Road Traffic Safety Law[23] (hereinafter the "Safety Law") in 2003. In Article 76, the law restricts the application of the comparative negligence rule to traffic accidents between motorists. As for accidents involving motor vehicles and pedestrians or nonmotorized vehicle riders, the motorist will be liable unless he can prove that the pedestrian or nonmotorized vehicle rider has violated the traffic rules *and* that he himself has taken "necessary and proper measures" to avoid the accident. But even when the motorist satisfies the burden of proof, his liability will only be "reduced" rather than eliminated. Essentially, this is similar to a strict liability rule with a comparative negligence defense. The Safety Law was amended in 2007 to tip the balance slightly back to motorists by reinstating, in Article 76, a 10 percent liability limit for motorists where motorists are not at fault *but* the nonmotorists are. Nevertheless, the strict liability rule remains unchanged (Jiang 2014, p. 4).[24] Article 48 of the Tort Liability Law simply refers to the revised Article 76 for determining the liability in traffic accidents.

3.3.2 Reducing Immunities and Defenses

Tort liabilities have also become greater in China because immunities and defenses applicable to injurers have been restricted in a number of areas.

First, with respect to product liability, Article 122 of the General Principles holds producers and sellers liable for manufacturing or selling products inconsistent with quality standards adopted by the state or industry. Thus, it gives victims no legal basis to seek remedies for losses resulting from products not subject to any such standard. Under the Product Quality Law[25] of 1993, however, producers and sellers are liable for *defective* products, including both substandard products and products that are unreasonably dangerous where no such standards exist (Product Liability Law, Art. 46). The Tort Liability Law does not give an explicit definition of "defective products", but the drafters of the law believe that producers should be liable when their products contain certain features that tend to cause harm, even if the national or industrial standards set for this kind of product do not touch on these particular features (Wang 2010, p. 225). In effect, therefore, after the adoption of the Product Liability Law, the lack of any national or industrial standard is no longer a bar to product liability.

Second, the tort liability for environment pollution is included in the General Principles and the strict liability rule has been applied ever since. However, according to Article 124 of the General Principles, polluters are liable only when discharge violates the government standards. In other words, compliance with these standards could be used to immunize polluters under the original rule. But this immunity was abandoned by Article 41 of the Environment Protection Law[26] in 1989. The Tort Liability takes the same position in this regard. Polluters thus are liable even if the discharge complies with the government standards.

Third, in respect of medical malpractice, the Medical Accident Regulation, as well as its predecessor, provides a variety of immunities to exempt medical institutions from liability. These immunities confine medical institutions' liability to the most serious injuries of death, disability or functional disorders, whereas others allow health providers to avoid liabilities entirely once the patient is in delay or noncooperative otherwise no matter whether hospitals themselves are at fault. Unsurprisingly, these immunities have been criticized for their favoritism toward medical institutions (Civil Law Office 2010, pp. 806–807). In contrast, the Tort Liability Law takes a more balanced position in this regard. According to Article 60, medical institutions' liabilities are exempted only in limited situations such as emergency rescues.

Fourth, immunities and defenses also shrink in certain torts associated with abnormally dangerous activities (*gaodu weixian zuoye*), a phenomenon which is most apparent in two areas: civil aircraft injuries and railway accidents. At first glance, under Article 123 of the General Principles, the strict liability rule is applicable uniformly, with the only immunity of victims' intention, to all business operations of abnormal danger. In practice, however, abnormally dangerous activities are often conducted by certain special industries. In China, these are usually state-owned or state-controlled businesses. Ministries of the central government are charged with both the regulation and the operation of these industries. Therefore, the ministries frequently sponsor special legislations bearing on tort liabilities. Though a blatant challenge to the strict liability rule is rare, quite a few special legislations put in wide immunities and other defenses to bar the claims from tort victims.

In the case of injuries resulting from incidents involving civil aircraft, the Civil Aviation Law[27] passed in 1995 immunizes the airlines from liabilities for personal injuries resulting solely from passengers' health conditions, and also allows their liabilities to be excused or alleviated if a fault on the part of the victims, either by intention or by negligence, either caused or contributed to the injury. Victims' fault is also a defense to claims for property damages during air transportation. Besides, the airlines are not liable for damages, roughly speaking, due to *force majeure* (Civil Aviation Law, Arts. 124, 125, 127). On the other hand, under Article 71 of the Tort Liability Law, civil aircrafts are considered as involving the highest level of riskiness, therefore, their operators' sole defense under this law is victims' intentional behaviors.

Similarly, under Article 58 of the Railway Law, enacted in 1990, railway companies can avoid tort liability completely when personal injuries are caused for "victims' own reason." This clearly includes victims' negligence, and probably even their health conditions or physical features. The broad immunity available to railway companies has led to the cynical remarks that trains are permitted to "hit people for free" (Civil Law Office 2010, p. 252). In 2010, however, SPC adopted a new judicial interpretation on railway accidents, the SPC Interpretation on Several Issues Concerning the Application of Law in Adjudicating Cases Involving Disputes over Compensation for Personal Injuries in Railway Transport[28] (hereinafter known as "Interpretation on Railway Personal Injuries"). Most importantly, SPC restricts the immunity to injuries caused by *force majeure* or victims' certain intentional actions, namely lying on tracks or jumping in front of trains (Interpretation on Railway Personal Injuries, Art. 5(2)).

The final example of curtailment of injurers' immunities or defenses relates to the keepers of domestic animals. While Article 127 of the General Principles exempts these keepers from strict liability when the victim's fault has led to the injury, the present Tort Liability Law, under Article 78, excuses or reduces their liability only if the victim has caused the injury intentionally or through gross negligence (*zhongda guoshi*). In other words, victims' ordinary negligence no longer immunizes domestic animal keepers nor does it even mitigate their liabilities.

3.3.3 Creating New Liabilities

Since the enactment of the General Principles, several new duties have been created for some special entities or individuals, and any breach of these duties can lead to tort liabilities.

Building on the SPC Interpretation on Several Issues Concerning the Application of Law in Adjudicating the Civil Disputes over Computer Network Copyrights of 2000[29] and the State Council's Regulation on Protection of the Right to Network Dissemination of Information of 2006,[30] Article 36 of the Tort Liability Law imposes tort liabilities on network users, and content as well as service providers for the violation of others' private rights. Service providers are jointly and severally liable with content providers if they do not take proper actions after being informed of the violation, or obtaining actual or constructive knowledge of such violation on their own. The Tort Liability Law, however, does not restrict the liability to infringement of copyrights, as the previous administrative regulation and judicial interpretation did, but extends to cover torts against personal or property rights in general (Wang 2010, pp. 188–189).

The duty of operators of public accommodations to protect the safety of people entering their premises was first introduced by Article 6 of the Interpretation on Personal Injuries. Owners of public accommodations, such as hotels, shopping centers, or stations, are responsible for the safety of the public while they are on their premises.[31] The Tort Liability Law, in Article 37, further requires the organizers of mass activities to bear a similar responsibility.[32] Like schools, legal liabilities staying with public accommodations differ according to whether the injurer comes from inside or outside. The public accommodation will be primarily liable when its insiders cause the injury, but only complementarily liable when external personnel cause the injury. In both cases, the public accommodation is liable only if it has breached the duty of safety protection. In other words, negligence is necessary to hold the public accommodation liable, and the scope of liability corresponds with the extent of negligence.

Article 87 of the Tort Liability Law imposes a liability on every user of a building who is likely to commit a tort when objects thrown out of, or falling from, a building cause personal injury and when the particular tortfeasor cannot be determined. In order to avoid this liability, a user has to show that he is not the actual tortfeasor. Otherwise, all users will bear a proportionate share of the compensation to the victim. The users are liable severally so no contribution exists from other users, but they can seek indemnity from the actual tortfeasor if the latter is identified after the compensation has been paid (Wang 2010, p. 429). This liability was not present in any of the previous legislations or judicial interpretations. It was added as a response to a series of legal disputes in the 2000s over injuries caused by anonymous objects falling off from buildings. Oftentimes, these cases involve deaths or other serious bodily injuries resulting in grave consequences on victims and chronic litigations or petitions (Wang 2010, pp. 425–426).

Regarding product liability, producers are now required to prevent harm *ex ante* in addition to paying damages *ex post*. According to Article 46 of the Tort Liability Law, for defects found after the products were put into circulation, producers and sellers shall take such remedial measures as warning and recall in a timely manner. Thus, although the Product Quality Law immunizes producers from tort liability should defects be unidentifiable when products are put into circulation, they will nonetheless be liable if defects are found afterwards and timely warning or recall is not conducted.

Finally, medical institutions' duties are also aggravated in the Tort Liability Law. On the one hand, Article 55 of this law requires hospitals to seek informed written consent from patients, or their close relatives when it is inappropriate to inform patients, before carrying out operations or other special examinations or treatments. And violation of this obligation results in tort liabilities.[33] On the other hand, with the increase in the proportion of examination fees as of the total medical expenses,[34] excessive examinations are regarded as one crucial source of tension between patients and hospitals (Civil Law Office 2010, p. 810). Hence, Article 63 of the Tort Liability Law places a new duty on hospitals to abstain from unnecessary medical examinations.

3.4 Increasing Damages

3.4.1 Adding New Types of Damages

The scope of damages in personal injury cases has been growing continuously since the introduction of the General Principles.[35] The most noticeable change, however, pertains to the addition of two new types of damages.

First, damages for pain and suffering are not mentioned in the General Principles. But SPC adopted the Interpretation on Pain and Suffering that allows such compensation for personal injuries.[36] Under Article 22 of the Tort Liability Law, victims or, in the case of the victims' death, their family members can claim damages for pain and suffering, but this compensation is restricted to those cases involving serious mental distress. In practice, courts routinely award disability or death indemnity together with damages for pain and suffering in cases involving disability or death. According to the SPC interpretation, these indemnities are essentially compensation for the loss of income of disabled or deceased victims. The Tort Liability Law also considers pain and suffering and the indemnities as two compensable damages.

Second, following the civil law tradition, punitive damages are not allowed in China as a general rule, but they can be awarded in exceptional cases of product liability. Such punitive damages initially appeared in the Consumer Rights and Interests Protection Law,[37] passed in 1993. In Article 49, the law allows the court to award punitive damages equal to the price of the goods or services in addition to the compensatory damages to consumers where the seller or service provider engaged in fraudulent behavior. In the latest version of the law, amended in 2013, the punitive damages rise further to three times of the price.[38] In the Food Safety Law[39] promulgated in 2009, the amount of punitive damages was raised to ten times the price where the producer manufactures food products that do not conform to the food safety standard or where the seller sells such food products with prior knowledge of nonconformance. Article 47 of the Tort Liability Law provides for the imposition of punitive damages. The new rule affects two aspects of the previous punitive damages scheme. On the one hand, it expands the usage of punitive damages to cover all kinds of products besides foods, and nonconsumer victims are also entitled to punitive damages. Moreover, producers and sellers can be required to pay such damages insofar as the product defects are known, even if no active fraud is involved. On the other hand, however, the new law limits the award of punitive damages to cases where defective products have resulted in death or serious health injuries. This limit essentially bars the claims raised by consumer protection activists who purchase defective products on purpose to demand punitive damages but are not injured personally.

3.4.2 Raising the Amount of Damages

In terms of the assessment of damages, thorny problems usually arise in relation to personal injuries. The SPC Interpretation on Personal Injuries serves as a roadmap in this regard, and is largely followed in judicial practice even after the promulgation of the Tort Liability Law. This judicial interpretation is generally more favorable to victims than was the case under the previous rules. Damages for medical malpractices and high-voltage electric shocks are two good cases in this point.

With regard to medical malpractice, the Medical Accident Regulation introduced a set of rules on compensable damages that are separate from the Interpretation on Personal Injuries. The starkest differences between these two sets of rules exist with respect to the calculation of damages in cases involving death or disability. Where the victim died as a result of medical malpractice, the Medical Accident Regulation does not include death indemnity as the Interpretation on Personal Injuries does, but, instead, allows damages for pain and suffering. Though the Interpretation of Personal Injuries does not provide for damages for pain and suffering itself, the SPC Interpretation on Pain and Suffering does recognize such damages. Hence, courts frequently award both the death indemnity and the damages for pain and suffering in death cases when the Interpretation on Personal Injuries is applicable. The sum of these two items of compensation is much higher than the damages for pain and suffering acknowledged in the Medical Accident Regulation, which is capped at six years' average annual living expenses of local residents.[40] If the victim is disabled, both the Medical Accident Regulation and the Interpretation on Personal Injuries allow for the award of disability indemnity, albeit with the former employing a less generous calculation standard. The Medical Accident Regulation again sets the standard as the average annual living expenses of local residents while the SPC interpretation uses the average disposable income of urban residents or average net income of rural residents. In Shanghai, for example, the former is usually roughly 70 percent of the latter in recent years.[41] With respect to the living expenses of victims' dependents, the standard used in the Medical Accident Regulation is residents' minimum subsistence allowance whereas in the judicial interpretation it is the average consumption expenses of urban residents or the average annual living expense of rural residents.[42] Moreover, the dependent's living expenses are paid until the dependent turns 16 under the Medical Accident Regulation but 18 under the SPC interpretation.

Before the implementation of the Tort Liability Law, the relatively generous standards embodied in the judicial interpretation were said to be applicable only in the case of malpractices not amounting to medical accidents, whereas the more serious malpractices ascertained as medical accidents were oddly subject to the grudging calculation included in the Medical Accident Regulation (SPC 2003).[43] In medical malpractice cases this situation is referred to as the "dual track" of compensation (*eryuanhua*). It is intended that the passage of the Tort Liability Law should end this anomalous phenomenon (Wang 2010, p. 276). Despite the continuing ambiguity in rule selection, resulting from the circumstance that the Medical Accident Regulation has not yet been repealed, perhaps to most Chinese courts, the elimination of the dual track essentially means that, after the new law has taken effect, assessment of damages in medical malpractice litigations should always follow the provisions of the Interpretation on Personal Injuries.

The standards for damage calculation is also more generous in respect of cases associated with injuries from high-voltage electric shocks. In 2000, SPC issued the SPC Interpretation on Several Issues in Adjudication of Cases Concerning Personal Injuries Caused by Electric Shocks (*Zuigao Renmin Fayuan Guanyu Shenli Chudian Renshen Sunhai Peichang Anjian Ruogan Wenti De Jieshi*). Article 4 of this interpretation detailed the scope of damages in cases of electric shocks, which was later replaced by the Interpretation on Personal Injuries. The main difference between these two judicial interpretations relates to the standard for the calculation of death and disability indemnities. The former measure used the average living expenses as the standard for this calculation while the more recent SPC interpretation uses the alternative measure of the average disposable income of urban residents or the average net income of rural residents instead. As aforementioned, the former is usually much lower than the latter.[44]

The amount of damages payable to tort victims has also risen because of the changes made to the compensation caps in some special types of torts.

For example, the compensation limits for railway accidents used to be set at very low levels. Until 2007, for personal injuries the cap was only RMB 40,000 (about $6,800).[45] In 2007, the cap was lifted to RMB 150,000 (about $25,000) for personal injuries.[46] And these excessively low compensation limits were eventually repealed in 2012 under mounting pressure from the public, particularly in the aftermath of the disastrous high-speed train collision claiming 40 lives in July 2011.[47]

Finally, victims of traffic accidents also obtain higher levels of compensation because of the increased coverage of compulsory traffic accident liability insurance. The Safety Law mandated a compulsory liability insurance to cover damages in traffic accidents, essentially a no-fault insurance system. Therefore, following most traffic accidents, the insurance company should compensate the victim first within the compensation limit, and any remaining damages would then be handled according to the tort liability rules. The China Insurance Regulatory Commission (CIRC) is delegated with the power to determine the compensation limit of the liability insurance. CIRC initially set extremely low limits. In instances when the motorist is found liable, for example, the limits were RMB 50,000 for death and disability and RMB 8,000 for medical expenses. Obviously, such low limits were barely sufficient to cover victims' losses in traffic accidents, and had therefore been subject to bitter criticism (Civil Law Office 2010, p. 707).[48] In 2008, CIRC raised the compensation limits, in cases where the motorist is liable, to RMB 110,000 (about $18,300) for death and disability and RMB 10,000 (about $1,600) for medical expenses.[49]

4 Evaluating the Efficiency

In this section of the chapter, I will briefly evaluate the efficiency effects of the salient trend in the evolution of Chinese tort law to expand the protection of victims. By no means, however, do I implicate that efficiency has been a policy motivation underlying the change of law.

4.1 Deterrence Effect

In the realm of torts, efficiency requires a minimization of costs associated with tortious behaviors by optimally deterring imprudent activities (Calabresi 1970; Brown 1973). Indeed, the main reason to award tort damages is to incentivize people not to take actions that impose costs on others (Friedman 2000, p. 192). Generally speaking, where damages are below the level required for an optimal deterrence, an increase in damages creates better incentives for cautious behaviors, thereby lowering the costs of torts. As tort damages in China have historically been very low, they are unlikely to be close to the optimal level needed for cost minimization. Therefore, the general movement toward a higher level of protection for tort victims seems consistent with the efficiency requirement. However, a closer look at the efficiency effects entails a decomposition of a potential tortfeasor's *ex ante* cost of committing a tort into two components: the probability of being held liable and the amount of damages to pay in the event of being held liable.

Regarding the first component, the Chinese tort law has obviously opened a series of new sources of tort liability, as summarized in the previous section, thereby increasing the probability that a potential tortfeasor will be liable. But this change in law contributes to subduing inefficient tortious behaviors only when tort liability becomes more imminent for the party whose choice of action does affect the likelihood of harmful accidents. Conversely, when the probability of liability is raised for parties that have no impact on the occurrence of accidents, the total cost of accidents is at best unchanged, and it may even rise if the murkier rules of liability allow the externalizing of costs by the real culprit of accidents. Although many of the rule changes fit this general proposition reasonably well, some of them do not appear mindful of upgrading the liability for the right party. As an illustration, consider the extension of the joint and several liability. Whereas the joint and several liability usually does not sacrifice efficiency in cases of concurrent torts (Landes and Posner 1980), the inability to escape such a liability even when one has proved itself not to be a cause of the injury, as provided by Article 10 of the Tort Liability Law, does not help reduce the probability of accident to an optimal level. To make matters worse, it may well allow cost externalization by those who can really reduce the occurrence of accidents, leading to more injuries as a result. It creates, in effect, an inefficient fixed share strict liability rule according to Kornhauser and Revesz (1989)'s taxonomy. Similarly, restricting the comparative negligence defense claimable by injurers subject to strict liabilities discourages victims to act cautiously when their precaution can lower the probability of accidents indeed (Cooter and Ulen 2012, p. 204). And this seems to be what the rule change has done in the area of domestic animal injuries.

Efficient deterrence also depends on the right amount of damages awarded to tort victims. In brief, efficiency requires the complete internalization of the cost of actual harm inflicted by the injurer. Since the cost of accidental harm to the victim equals the damages that make the victim whole, optimal damages usually means full compensatory damages no matter whether the strict liability or the negligence rule is applied (Cooter and DePianto 2014). As stated above, the absolute amount of damages awarded in tort cases in China is increasing. However, the absolute amount awarded in an average case remains meager, especially with regard to the compensation for personal injuries. The calculation of death indemnities, for instance, is pegged to the uniform and rather low standard of annual disposable income for urban residents and to an even lower standard in the case of rural residents. If we use the income figures in Shanghai in 2012 as an illustration, the value of life for an urban resident in the most economically prosperous city in China would be set at approximately 853,760 RMB (about $142,290).[50] Admittedly, the compensation for personal injuries would be lower in developing countries like China than in the developed world due to the difference in subjective values individuals place on risks to themselves (Cooter and Schäfer 2012, pp. 180–184). Nevertheless, the current level of compensation for personal injuries prevailing in China is much lower than in other developing countries like India, where studies show that the value of a statistical life in India is approximately $1–1.5 million (in constant 2000 US dollars) (Viscusi and Aldy 2003, p. 28). The lesson from law and economics research is straightforward: When the amount of damages is set well below the cost of actual harm, injuries will continue to occur too frequently. In a nutshell, then, although the increase in damages over the years has probably channeled the tort law in China closer than before to the efficient objective, it remains far from that objective.

4.2 Administrative Costs

As the law becomes more favorable to victims, we predict that there will be an increase in the number of legal complaints filed, at least where the absolute amount of damages awarded is still relatively low (Cooter and Ulen 2012, pp. 420–421). This seems to be borne out by the experience in China. Although there are relatively few national-level statistics, the courts in Jiangsu province reported that during the 18 months' period immediately after the promulgation of the more pro-victim Tort Liability Law, the number of personal injury cases filed with the courts of first instance rose by 25.58 percent and that of property loss cases rose by 11.62 percent, compared to the same period immediately before the promulgation of the law (Gong 2012, p. 372). Other things being equal, higher damage awards may also lead to more litigation costs per case due to the higher stakes to litigate over (Friedman 2000, p. 209). Therefore, we might expect an increase in the total costs associated with the usage of the judicial system to resolve tort disputes as the tort law becomes more favorable to victims. However, the standardization of the damage awards in personal injury cases pursued in the SPC interpretation has streamlined the judicial decision on this issue, thereby reducing the administrative costs per case. Article 17 of the Interpretation on Personal Injuries listed 15 types of damages that were claimable in personal injury cases. And relatively clear guidelines have been spelled out to facilitate the calculation of these damages, based either on the actual costs incurred by the plaintiff or on certain clear-cut formulae. In addition to smoothing damage calculations for Chinese judges who have relatively little training, clear standards also help curb judicial corruption as it becomes harder to hide and easier to detect fraudulent court behaviors (Cooter and Ulen 2012, p. 190). As a whole, therefore, there is no reason to believe that the evolution of Chinese tort law has generated higher administrative costs.

In any event, the rise in administrative cost should be weighed against the savings from the elevated deterrence effect as a result of a more victim-friendly tort system. Eventually, an elastic supply of tortious behaviors supports the more generous protection of victims from the efficiency perspective (Friedman 2000, p. 209). In this regard, unfortunately, we can do no more than make an educated guess. To the extent that a potential tortfeasor's incentive is consistent with the logic of market competition, it will be more sensitive to the price change related to its behaviors resulting from the change in tort law. Conversely, when the tortfeasor's incentive is forged through nonmarket forces, such as bureaucratic control, the price signal will be a blunt tool in terms of having any effect on its behavior. Consequently, the higher expected damages payable to victims might bring about better welfare effects in areas such as traffic accidents, where injurers are more likely to behave like market agents, whereas efficiency benefit can be lower, considering the administrative cost, with respect to medical malpractice or railway accidents where the injurers, mainly SOEs, are likely to follow a bureaucratic logic.

4.3 Risk Allocation

The tendency of Chinese tort law to expand victim protection can be best understood as an effort to reallocate the risk in such incidents. As victims are more likely to win tort cases and get higher damages, the risk of accidents is reallocated from victims to injurers. In the Chinese context, however, the risk allocation achieved through tort compensation usually does not shift the risk completely from victims to injurers because of the prevailing low level of damages awarded by courts. Admittedly, in many situations the change of tort law in China has initiated a small-scale loss spreading between victims and injurers, which has slightly relaxed the risk concentration on victims, especially those suffering personal injuries. As detailed in the previous sections, some of the changes in tort law mainly impact the injurers that are enterprises while others involve individual injurers. The efficiency benefits of loss spreading are more pronounced in the former case, but it can be achievable even in the latter because people feel they suffer less when a large loss is spread broadly (Calabresi 1961, p. 517). This being said, when the risk is reallocated among individuals, the number of parties involved in such reallocation may have a crucial bearing on its efficiency. Whereas a widely based loss spread tends to be in line with an efficient allocation of risk, such as the rule applicable to objects falling off buildings, the efficiency of loss spreading is less certain when the risk is shifted to just a few individuals such as the guardians of minor injurers or individual employers. Furthermore, if loss spreading is a major concern, it could be handled more efficiently through the social insurance scheme, which has a much broader basis than the tort system to spread loss (Calabresi 1961, pp. 529–530). This idea of social insurance has recently been introduced into traffic accident law in China with the Safety Law of 2003 requiring the establishment of social relief funds for road traffic accidents. However, the law in this area has been tentative at best. For one thing, these funds are used to pay for victims' losses only in limited situations. For another, the relief funds spend a very small proportion making these payments,[51] and the average amount of each payment is usually set at a rather low level.[52]

Using the tort system to reallocate risk may be particularly meaningful in China where the private insurance market is in its nascence. Despite rapid growth in recent years, the development of insurance in China still lags well behind the average world standard, in terms of both insurance density and penetration (Sun and Zheng 2013, p. 2).[53] In addition, the structure of the Chinese insurance market is biased against the insurance products spreading risks of accidents as indicated by the minuscule proportion of the premium paid to the accidental personal injury insurance (Sun and Zheng 2013: 4).[54] The idea of relying on insurance for risk spreading is especially remote to the poor people in developing countries (Cooter and Schäfer 2012, pp. 187–189). Indeed, the moderate compensation for personal injuries might be deemed to be some sort of implicit insurance offered to the lower income groups among the population, those with the least access to the business insurance market, which could be most effective when combined with the contingency fee arrangement.[55] In any event, given the still relatively low levels of compensation, the alleged insurance crisis that motivated the tort reform in the United States (Priest 1987, 1991) is largely irrelevant in the Chinese context. In a country where there is little first-party insurance, and, in particular, where the population has little access to such insurance, a comparison between first-party insurance and the tort system in terms of efficient risk allocation is beside the point. In fact, even in places with a mature first-insurance market, a tort system may nevertheless be a better choice, when accompanied with effective third-party insurance, because of the lower risk of adverse selection and *ex post* moral hazard (Baker and Siegelman 2014, pp. 185–187).

5 Conclusion

In China, the law of torts presents a clear trend toward the more generous protection of victims. This trend has manifested itself in a variety of ways as discussed in this chapter. Many of these steps, including the expansion of joint and several liability and the increase of damages, appear to be in stark contrast to the tort reform prevailing in the United States (Dobbs 2000, pp. 1071–1075, 1085–1087). However, at least in certain areas, such as medical malpractice, the law appears to evolve similarly to victims' benefit at both sides across the Taiwan Strait (see Chapter 6).

The Chinese tort law has also presented a combination of the concentrated and distributed mechanisms, as pointed out acutely in Chapter 1, along its evolutionary path toward broader victim protection. Whereas the wider coverage of joint and several liability, for instance, represents the distributed mechanism, the higher level of duty placed on manufactures in terms of product liability is clearly one indication of the concentrated mechanism.

Given the exceptionally low point from which the increment of victim protection in tort law has started, the change of rules in China is, by and large, moving in the direction of cost internalization as required by efficiency. Moreover, the law also evolves to promote the spread of accident costs on a broader basis, which is desirable in terms of improving the efficiency of risk allocation, especially in a country with an underdeveloped insurance market.

Nevertheless, the potential improvement in efficiency is perhaps a by-product of the development of tort law in China. The motivation behind the rule change is more likely to be loss redistribution rather than any attempt to upgrade efficiency. This is evidenced by the lawmakers' timidity in awarding damages equal to actual accident costs and their apparent inconsistency in holding the right party to account. At the same time, a more serious concern about efficient risk distribution should have adopted a more targeted approach toward enterprise liability rather than an across-the-board shift of risk to individual as well as enterprise tortfeasors.

This chapter sketches the overall direction in which the formal law of torts in China has plodded over the past three decades, and outlines the efficiency implications of this evolution. The current work is mainly descriptive and does not attempt to offer an in-depth exploration of the impetus underlying this change. But we also see traces from the above description that defy a single-minded understanding of the rule change as a spontaneous convergence to efficiency. In light of the policy-implementing orientation of the Chinese legal system (Damaska 1991) and the collectivistic propensity rooted in the law of torts (Calabresi 1978), political and institutional perspectives can bring us better insights into the driving forces behind the changes of law. For instance, a wider spread of loss suffered by tort victims is seemingly in accord with the top Chinese leaders' pursuit of a stable and harmonious society. At the same time, the basic social structure characterized by state units (*danwei*) in Maoist China had been fundamentally altered during the "Open and Reform" era. A vacuum is left with respect to the social security functions that had once been performed by these units (Lieberthal 2004, p. 301). In this regard, a growing system of tort liability may well be deemed to be filling part of this gap. Further inquiries along these lines may be the basis of interesting agendas for future research.[56]

References in English

Baker, Tom and Peter Siegelman. 2014. The Law and Economics of Liability Insurance: A Theoretical and Empirical Review. Pp. 169–195 in *Research Handbook on the Economics of Tort*, edited by Jennifer Arlen. Northampton, MA: Edward Elgar.

Brown, John. 1973. Toward an Economic Theory of Liability. *Journal of Legal Studies* 2:323–350.

Calabresi, Guido. 1961. Some Thoughts on Risk Distribution and the Law of Torts. *Yale Law Journal* 70:499–553.

1970. *The Costs of Accidents: A Legal and Economic Analysis*. New Haven: Yale University Press.

1978. Torts – The Law of the Mixed Society. *Texas Law Review* 56:519–534.

Cooter, Robert and David DePianto. 2014. Damages for Incompensable Harms. Pp. 439–459 in *Research Handbook on the Economics of Torts*, edited by Jennifer Arlen. Northampton, MA: Edward Elgar.

Cooter, Robert and Hans-Bernd Schäfer. 2012. *Solomon's Knot: How Law Can End the Poverty of Nations*. Princeton: Princeton University Press.

Cooter, Robert and Thomas Ulen. 2012. *Law and Economics*. 6th ed. International Edition. Boston: Pearson.

Damaska, Mirjan R. 1991. *The Faces of Justice and State Authority: A Comparative Approach to the Legal Process*. New Haven: Yale University Press.

Dobbs, Dan B. 2000. *The Law of Torts*. St. Paul, MN: West Group.

Friedman, David D. 2000. *Law's Order: What Economics Has to Do with Law and Why It Matters*. Princeton: Princeton University Press.

Kornhauser, Lewis A. and Richard L. Revesz. 1989. Sharing Damages Among Multiple Tortfeasors. *Yale Law Journal* 98:831–884.

Koziol, Helmut and Yan Zhu. 2010. Background and Key Contents of the New Chinese Tort Liability Law. *Journal of European Tort Law* 1:328–361.

Landes, William M. and Richard A. Posner. 1980. Joint and Multiple Tortfeasors: An Economic Analysis. *Journal of Legal Studies* 9:517–555.

Lieberthal, Kenneth. 2004. *Governing China: From Revolution Through Reform*. 2nd ed. New York: W. W. Norton & Company.

Priest, George L. 1987. The Current Insurance Crisis and Modern Tort Law. *Yale Law Journal* 96:1521–1590.

Priest, George L. 1991. The Modern Expansion of Tort Liability: Its Sources, Its Effects, and Its Reform. *Journal of Economic Perspectives* 5:31–50.
Viscusi, W. Kip and Joseph E. Aldy. 2003. The Value of a Statistical Life: A Critical Review of Market Estimates Throughout the World. *Journal of Risk and Uncertainty* 27:5–76.
Zhang, Wei. Forthcoming. Understanding the Law of Torts in China: A Political Economy Perspective. *East Asia Law Review* 11.

References in Chinese and Japanese

Civil Law Office of the Legislative Affairs Commission of the NPC Standing Committee. 2010. *Qinquan Zeren Fa Lifa Beijing Yu Guandian Quanji [The Complete Collection of the Legislative Background and Opinions of the Tort Liability Law]*. Beijing: Law Press.
Gong, Pixiang (ed.). 2012. *Jiangsu Fayuan Sifa Diaoyan Chengguo Ji: 2007–2011 [A Collection of the Results of the Judicial Research and Investigation by the Courts in Jiangsu Province: 2007–2011]*. Beijing: Law Press.
Jiang, Bixin (ed.). 2014. *Daolu Jiaotong Shigu Sunhai Peichang [The Road Traffic Accident Damage Compensation]*. Beijing: Law Press.
Shanghai Municipal Finance Bureau. 2013. Annual Audit Report on the Financial Statements of the Social Relief Fund for Road Traffic Accidents in Shanghai 2013. Available at www.czj.sh.gov.cn/zlzy/jtsgshjzjj/tzgg/201305/t20130509_141661.html (last accessed: May 6, 2014).
Shenzhen Municipal Government. 2014. Detailed Expenditure of the Social Relief Fund for Road Traffic Accidents in Shenzhen 2013. Available at www.stc.gov.cn/SHJZ/SHJZQK/201401/P020140120404730626014.pdf (last accessed: May 6, 2014).
Sun, Qixiang and Zheng Wei. 2013. *China Insurance Market Report 2013*. Beijing: Peking University Press.
Uchida, Takashi. 1997. *Minppo II: Saiken Kakuron [Civil Law II: Special Provisions of "Obligations"]*. Tokyo: University of Tokyo Press.
Wang, Shengming (ed.). 2010. *Zhonghua Renmin Gongheguo Qinquan Zerenfa Shiyi [Explanations of the Tort Liability Law of the People's Republic of China]*. Beijing: Law Press.
Yichun Municipal Finance Bureau. 2013. Audit Report on the Social Relief Fund for Road Traffic Accidents in Yichun 2013. Available at: www.ycf.gov.cn/zwgk/czgz_11399/czjd/201304/t20130403_349830.html (last accessed: May 6, 2014).
Zhang, Xinbao. 2010. *Qinquan Zeren Fa [Tort Liability Law]*. 2nd ed. Beijing: Renmin University Press.

Notes

1 *Minfa Tongze.*
2 Except otherwise specified, "law" in this chapter is used in a broad sense, including any rules binding in courts' adjudication.
3 *Qinquan Zeren Fa.*
4 For the official ranks of sources of law, see the Legislation Law (*Lifa Fa*), Art. 79.
5 *Tielu Fa.*
6 *Yiliao Shigu Chuli Tiaoli.*
7 Interview with Judge Liu, July 4, 2013 (on file with the author).
8 For instance, the right of giving birth (*shengyu quan*) was recognized by a court in Sichuan, whereas the right of chastity (*zhencao quan*) found its support in Guangdong.
9 *Zuigao Renmin Fayuan Guanyu Queding Minshi Qinquan Jingshen Sunhai Peichang Zeren Ruogan Wenti De Jieshi.*
10 In particular, interests are said to be protected only when they are substantial, when the injurer acts with malice and when the causation is stronger between the tortious behavior and the harm (Civil Law Office 2010, pp. 166–67).
11 To be more accurate, here one action does not necessarily mean one single physical behavior, but also includes a series of behaviors that can be regarded as steps of one scheme leading to certain results from the conventional perspective of our society. The typical example of the latter is the activities of gangsters belonging to the same gang.
12 *Zuigao Renmin Fayuan Guanyu Guanche Zhixing "Zhonghua Renmin Gongheguo Minfa Tongze" Ruogan Wenti De Yijian (Shixing).*
13 *Zuigao Renmin Fayuan Guanyu Shenli Renshen Sunhai Peichang Anjian Ruogan Wenti De Jieshi.*
14 A typical example of common risk is a case where two hunters simultaneously, independently, and accidentally fired shots toward a passerby and killed him (Wang 2010, p. 63). Another type of common risk cases often involves harm caused by multiple polluters when it is impossible to clearly attribute the harm to each polluter's discharge in part or in total (Uchida 1997, p. 493). Most prominently, the potential injurers in a common risk case have to act independently without communication or coordination.
15 *The SPC Reply on Whether the Entity Allowing Usage of Its Name Should Be Liable After the Actual Vehicle Owner Caused the Accident* (*Zuigao Renmin Fayuan Guanyu Shiji Chezhu Zhaoshi Hou Qi Guakao Danwei Yingfou Chengda Zeren De Fuhan*) of 2001.
16 *The SPC Interpretation on Several Issues Concerning the Application of Law in the Adjudication of Cases on Compensation for Damages in*

Road Traffic Accidents (Zuigao Renmin Fayuan Guanyu Shenli Daolu Jiaotong Shigu Sunhai Peichang Anjian Shiyong Falü Ruogan Wenti De Jieshi) of 2012, Art. 3.

17 In this sense, the term is used slightly more broadly than its traditional meaning.

18 Here, negligence does not bear on inflicting harm on the victim, but on precluding a third party from inflicting such harm.

19 This means schools guarantee external personnel's payment to the extent of $(x^* - x)/x^*$ where x^* is schools' level of precaution required under the law while x represents schools' actual precaution level.

20 In China, minors under 10 are legally incompetent whereas those aged between 10 and 18 are usually of restrictive legal competence (General Principles, Art. 12).

21 Measures for Handling of Student Injury Accidents (*Xuesheng Shanghai Shigu Chuli Banfa*) Arts. 8, 12, 13 adopted by the Ministry of Education in 2002. This department rule ceased to be effective in 2010.

22 More accurately, the Traffic Accident Measures looked to the parties' violations of the traffic rules and deemed such violations as negligence per se.

23 *Daolu Jiaotong Anquan Fa.*

24 The Safety Law was furthered amended in 2011, but Article 76 remains the same.

25 *Chanpin Zhiliang Fa.*

26 *Huanjing Baohu Fa.*

27 *Minyong Hangkong Fa.*

28 *Zuigao Renmin Fayuan Guanyu Shenli Tielu Yunshu Renshen Sunhai Peichang Jiufen Anjian Shiyong Falü Ruogan Wenti De Jieshi.*

29 *Zuigao Renmin Fayuan Guanyu Shenli Sheji Jisuanji Wangluo Zhuzuoquan Jiufen Anjian Shiyong Falü Ruogan Wenti De Jieshi*, which was revised in 2004 and 2006, and finally replaced by the SPC Provisions on Several Issues Concerning the Application of Law in Adjudicating the Civil Disputes over Infringement of the Right of Information Dissemination on Networks (*Zuigao Renmin Fayuan Guanyu Shenli Qinhai Xinxi Wangluo Chuanbo Minshi Jiufen Anjian Shiyong Falü Ruogan Wenti De Guiding*) in 2012.

30 *Xinxi Wangluo Chuanbaoquan Baohu Tiaoli*, which was amended in 2013.

31 It is not clear from the law what is the scope of potential victims that should be protected by public accommodations as it uses a very general term, "another person." Nevertheless, given the purpose of this article, at least the victim needs to be injured on the premises of public accommodations. But ambiguity exists pertaining to trespassers and temporary

visitors not coming for public accommodation's business services (Wang 2010, p. 201).

32 Although the law says that managers of public accommodations shall assume the tort liability, this is not an individual liability, but an enterprise liability, as evinced in numerous court decisions.
33 Exceptions exist in emergency situations with the approval of authorized persons in charge (Tort Liability Law, Art. 56).
34 This proportion rises from 28 percent in 1990 to 36.7 percent in 2002 (Wang 2010, p. 319).
35 Due to space limitations, I will not elaborate on the scope of damages for property loss, which has remained relatively stable over the years.
36 Pain and suffering can also be compensated for torts against personality rights including name, likeness, reputation, honor, dignity, personal freedom, and privacy.
37 *Xiaofeizhe Quanyi Baohu Fa.*
38 The relevant article number is changed to 55 in the revised law.
39 *Shipin Anquan Fa.*
40 In Shanghai, for instance, the death indemnity alone can be above RMB 803,760 (about $133,900) for urban residents using the 2012 standard, but the six years' average annual living expenses of Shanghai urban residents in 2012 is RMB 157,518 (about $26,200).
41 Although the Medical Accident Regulation allows a maximum of thirty years' compensation of disability indemnity for victims under 60, that does not need to be the actual number of years used for assessment. In contrast, the Interpretation on Personal Injury generally uses a uniform twenty-year criterion to calculate disability indemnity for victims of the same age group. Based on the 2012 Shanghai income standards, therefore, any disability indemnity assessed according to the Medical Accident Regulation for urban residents, or for rural residents for a period shorter than 29 will be less than the assessment made under the judicial interpretation.
42 Again, using the 2012 Shanghai income numbers, we can see the minimum subsistence allowance is merely 26 percent of the average consumption expenses for urban residents.
43 *Notice on Adjudication of Civil Disputes over Medical Malpractices Referring to the Regulations on Handling of Medical Accidents (Guanyu Canzhao "Yiliao Shigu Chuli Tiaoli" Shenli Yiliao Jiufen Minshi Anjian De Tongzhi)* issued by the SPC in 2003.
44 Although it is a reasonable argument that the compensation standards in the Interpretation on Personal Injuries are more generous to victims as a whole, the previous interpretation did allow a greater multiplier when courts were calculating death indemnities for victims aged above 60.

45 *Provisions on Compensation for Damages to Passengers of Railway Transportation (Tielu Lüke Yunshu Sunhai Peichang Guiding)* adopted by the Ministry of Railways in 1994.
46 *Administrative Regulation on Emergency Rescue in and Investigation and Handling of Railway Traffic Accidents (Tielu Jiaotong Shigu Yingji Jiuyuan He Diaocha Chuli Tiaoli)* adopted by the State Council in 2007.
47 See the revised *Administrative Regulation on Emergency Rescue in and Investigation and Handling of Railway Traffic Accident.*
48 Ironically, the premium is higher for the compulsory insurance than for commercial insurance with a comparable coverage (Civil Law Office 2010, p. 708).
49 When the motorist is not liable, the caps are slightly higher.
50 The annual disposable income in 2012 was RMB 40,188, and the largest multiplier allowed to calculate death indemnity is 20. On top of that, the maximum damages for pain and suffering currently allowed in Shanghai is RMB 50,000. If the deceased has a dependent, usually his or her child, the maximum amount of awardable life support is RMB 472,554 (about $78,750) if the dependent is normal, or RMB 525,060 (about $87,510) if he or she is completely disabled in 2012 (see Shanghai Municipal Statistical Yearbook of 2013).
51 For instance, in 2012, the relief fund in Shanghai only spent less than 0.06 percent of its financial resource on emergency medical expenses (Shanghai Municipal Finance Bureau 2013).
52 For instance, this number in the rich coastal city of Shenzhen is RMB 47,189 (about $7,850) in 2013 (Shenzhen Municipal Government 2014), and RMB 44,990 (about $7,480) in the less developed inland city of Yichun in Jiangxi Province in 2012 (Yichun Municipal Finance Bureau 2013).
53 In 2012, the insurance density and penetration in China were, respectively, 27 percent and 46 percent of the world average.
54 In 2012, this proportion was 2.5 percent of the total premium income of the Chinese insurance industry.
55 See the *Regulatory Method on Lawyers' Service Fees (Lüshi Fuwu Shoufei Guanli Banfa)*, Art. 11.
56 Zhang (forthcoming) includes some of the initial insights in the political economy of the Chinese tort law legislation.

6 *The Evolution of Tort Law in Taiwan*

A Doctrinal-Economic Interpretation

TZE-SHIOU CHIEN*

1 Introduction

Taiwan's tort law, as a civil law system, comprises general provisions in the Civil Code and special statutes concerning liability for damages. Article 184 of the Civil Code provides that a person who is at fault of infringing another person's rights, or acting against good morals, or violating protective laws, is liable for the damage. The provisions from Article 185 to Article 191-3 are concerned with some forms of vicarious liability and strict liability. The scope of liability, according to Article 213 of the Civil Code,[1] is the restoration of the status quo prior to the injury, i.e., the compensation principle. In the case of damaged nonpecuniary interests that cannot be restored to the status quo ante, Articles 194[2] and 195[3] of the Civil Code give the injured a right to claim from the injurer pain and suffering damages. Statutes, such as the Consumer Protection Law, have been enacted to impose some form of strict liability on injurers. Like most modern civil law systems (for the German case, see Zimmermann 2005, pp. 24–27), jurists (see Chapter 8) and courts (Wang 2015, p. 5) have also played a significant role in the development of tort law in Taiwan.

In economically assessing Taiwan tort law, current standard economic theories of tort law are defective, however, because they are based on the principle of regulatory deterrence. Current standard economic theories (see, for example, Brown 1973; Landes and Posner 1987; Shavell 1987) have modeled tort liability as giving people incentives to raise their capability of reducing risks by imposing liabilities for the damage as sanctions. These models do not fit with the *ex post* essence of compensation in tort law. Tort liability is about allocating

* Research Professor, Institutum Iurisprudentiae, Academia Sinica; Professor, College of Law, National Taiwan University. Comments from Yun-chien Chang, Kan-Hsueh Chiang, Daniel Klerman, Dong Jin Lee, Thomas Merrill, and Ariel Porat are appreciated. Hsing-Pei Chen has much improved the English writing.

risks, rather than reducing risks, although a correct allocation of risks would necessarily lead to a reduction of risks (Section 5 of this chapter). Due to the high transaction costs arising from accidents, tort law as default rules would decide whether the injurer is responsible or not once the accidents occur. The damage, as Ronald Coase (1960) pointed out, is reciprocal. Therefore, according to the Hand formula (*United States* v. *Carroll Towing Co.*, 159 F. 2d 169 [2d Cir. 1947]), the injurer would not be liable for damage if he would have lost more than he would have reduced the expected loss if he had not taken the action. This formula would *ex ante* benefit both the injurer and the injured – that is why negligent torts liability, embodying the Hand formula, is a set of default rules!

The Hand formula represents an implicit contract (Cheung 2014, p. 815) made by the injured and the injurer. In the formula $B < PL$, because a claim for liability can only be initiated after the damage has been done, B represents the interests that cannot be realized if the injurer does not take the action, while PL stands for the expected amount of losses that can be reduced if the injurer does not take the action. This means that the more risky the activities in which the injurer engages, the more likely the injurer would be liable for the damage. The robustness of the Hand formula, however, needs a subjective dimension – negligence as a state of mind, i.e., the failure of recognizing the recognizable. The calculation of this formula should be recognizable to the injurer; otherwise it cannot be a norm guiding people's actions. The survival nature of human action dictates that the more risky the activities are, the more recognizable they are. This subjective understanding of the Hand formula would prevent tort liability from being seen as an instrument to deter people's actions and thus would connect tort law with contract law and would distinguish tort liability from regulatory fines and criminal sanctions. Tort law, as a part of private law, takes advantage of the decentralized nature of societal knowledge while unintentionally improving the welfare of society.

Based on this economic reasoning, this chapter will examine Taiwan's tort law. First, the fault principle will be explored. The objectification of negligence, the dualism of the negligence rule and strict liability, and the expansion of liability via violations of protective laws are the specific issues to be addressed in Section 2. Section 3 will clarify the confusion concerning tort liability and contractual liability. The regulatory deterrence thesis of tort liability renders contractual liability almost impossible and would thus destroy market order. Section 4 will fit tort liability into the context of the entire legal system, including property law, insurance law, and criminal law. Again, the regulatory deterrence thesis of tort law does not fit into the legal system. Section 5 will demonstrate why tort law is private law and how tort law unintentionally improves social welfare. The final section offers some concluding remarks.

2 The Fault Principle

2.1 Objectification of Negligence?

There are three categories of general tort in Taiwan: infringement of rights, acts against good morals, and violation of protective laws (Taiwan Supreme Court 2011 Taishangzi 1314 decision). Article 184(I) of the Civil Code provides: "A person who, intentionally or negligently, has wrongfully damaged the rights of another is bound to compensate him for any injury arising therefrom. The same rule shall be applied when the injury is done intentionally in a manner against the rules of morals." Article 184(II) further provides: "A person, who violates a statutory provision enacted for the protection of others and therefore prejudice to others, is bound to compensate for the injury, except when no negligence in his act can be proven."

Infringement of rights is the most general category of torts. Taiwan's courts and legal theorists have adopted a three-phase analysis to apply this general clause of tort law (Wang 2015, p. 113). They are: first, the fact that a right was infringed has to be found; second, there must be no negative factors to excuse this infringement; third, the injurer's intention or negligence has to be found. This is an outdated framework transplanted from German law (Markesinis and Unberath 2002, pp. 79–83). The problem concerned is the wrongful consequence approach in phase 2, which is not just purely a theoretical dispute with the wrongful conduct approach, as Markesinis and Unberath (2002, p. 81) said. This wrongful consequence approach would exclude the calculation of the Hand formula from determining the wrongfulness of the injurer's act and thus defer the calculation to phase 3 and objectify the negligence. Consequently, the key role of negligence as a state of mind in the development of private law has been lost.

Take as an example of how to determine the standard of negligent conduct for the less capable driver, such as the near-sighted or the elderly. If a less capable motorist drives into a person, under the current framework, he would be judged as infringing on another's rights with no excuse for the wrongfulness and then the question is simply whether he is negligent or not. Due to the lack of calculation of the Hand formula in phase 2, the calculation thus has to be done in phase 3, which was originally reserved for determining whether or not the calculation (risk) was foreseeable to the injurer. Therefore, the calculation of the Hand formula takes over the foreseeability in phase 3. Negligence loses its cognitive characteristic and becomes objectified. Usually, driving capability becomes the standard of negligent conduct. According to the standard, if a capable driver is liable for the injury, a less capable driver would definitely be liable too. However, this conflicts with the spirit of negligence rules, which would not impose liability on people whose compliance with the standard is beyond his capability.

The correct analysis should be as follows: the less capable driver is a more dangerous driver engaging in a riskier activity. Under the Hand formula $B < PL$, PL is higher for the less capable driver, meaning that if he drives slower, or if he does not drive at all, he would reduce more risks than would be the case for more capable drivers. Assuming that the value of driving is the same for all drivers, B (the benefits that the driver forgoes by driving slower or not driving) is equal for all drivers. Therefore, it is more likely for $B < PL$ to hold true for less capable drivers, meaning that they would be more likely to be found to have acted wrongfully. Finally, assuming that less capable drivers have the same cognitive capacity to recognize risks as normal drivers, negligence as a state of mind or foreseeability becomes a nonissue, and thus less capable drivers would be more likely to be held liable for the injury. In determining wrongfulness, the less capable driver has a higher rather than a lower standard of negligent conduct. The negligence rule does not impose a standard with which the less capable driver cannot comply, as the objectified negligence thesis would imply.

In the current economic analysis of tort law, negligence has also been objectified. On the law side, in contrast to Taiwan's tort law, which consists of separate elements for wrongfulness and negligence, negligence rules are independent types of torts in common law. On the economic side, liability as a regulatory instrument rather than as a means for compensation dominates the law and economics scholarship. In the example of the less capable driver, when calculating the standard of negligent conduct, Landes and Posner (1987, pp. 123–131) and Shavell (1987, pp. 73–77) would assign more costs to less capable drivers than to normal drivers due to the former's physical "difficulties" in preventing accidents and they would therefore give less capable drivers a lower standard of negligent conduct.[4] Both Landes and Posner (1987) and Shavell (1987) acknowledge the absurdity of this calculation. Landes and Posner (1987) resort to arguing that a higher standard would save court costs due to the information problem the courts would face in concrete cases. This cannot be right, however. The information costs might be high when distinguishing among the same category of drivers while the information costs would be low when distinguishing between the aged or near-sighted drivers and more capable ones. Shavell (1987) says that less capable drivers derive less benefit from driving, so a higher standard would deter their engaging in the activities in the first place. This is a big if. The theories of Landes and Posner (1987) and Shavell (1987) are ad hoc at best.

There is a reasonable person standard in common law that would not allow less capable injurers to be excused from tort liability. This standard has been said to be objective to the extent it might exclude any possibility of subjective standard of negligent conduct (e.g., Ben-Shahar and Porat 2016). This is a misunderstanding of the standard. Here is the oft-quoted statement of Oliver W. Holmes (1881, p. 108): "The law takes no account of the infinite varieties of temperament, intellect, and education which make the internal character of a given act so different in different men." This only means, however, that those individuals' elements cannot be made excuses for relieving the injurer's liability. It is not obvious, and indeed it is probably quite mistaken, to infer that the less temperamental, the less intellectual, or the less educated the injurer, the lower the standard at which the injurer is held to be accountable. Probably only utilitarians such as Landes and Posner (1987) and Shavell (1987) would adopt this position in the calculation of the Hand formula (see the previous paragraph). Tort law is not utilitarian after all. This is also the reason why they failed to develop a coherent economic theory of tort law. As the driving example shows, the less capable the driver is, the higher the standard of negligent conduct the driver will be held to. The standard of negligent conduct could be both "subjective," in the sense of depending on the individual's capability, and "objective," in the sense that it distinguishes between the subjective recognition of risks.

Negligence along with intention is a state of mind. Intention requires that the injurer foresaw that the accident would happen because he intended to let it happen. Negligence requires that the injurer should have foreseen, but did not foresee that the accident would happen. The foreseeability of the accident depends on its riskiness which depends, in turn, on the injurer's taking action with a given physical capability (safety measure) relevant to the accident. The moment at which the less capable driver increases his speed is when he begins engaging in a more risky activity. In other words, if he had slowed down, he would have engaged in a much less risky activity. In the Hand formula $B < PL$, the expected reduced loss (PL) would be larger for the less capable driver. Under the usual assumption that the benefit enjoyed by driving does not vary with differences in the driver's capability to drive, i.e., B being equal for all drivers, the less capable driver's standard of negligent conduct is higher, meaning that he has to drive at a lower speed limit. At the same driving speed, the less capable driver would be more likely to be seen as wrongful. How about his state of mind? Usually, the capability to drive does not correlate with the capability to acknowledge the fact that the less capable the driver is, the slower he should drive. Therefore, the more risky the activity the injurer engages in, the more likely he would be negligent and thus liable for damage. The so-called objectified standard of negligence is misleading – in fact, it is completely wrong. Negligence is subjective, as a state of mind. The requirement of negligence guarantees that the ruled would not be surprised by unforeseeable liabilities. It is for the reason of rule of law that a (subjective) negligence should be required!

2.2 *Violations of Protective Laws*

According to Article 184(II) of the Civil Code, a person who violates those laws enacted for protecting another and causes damage to another shall be liable for this damage. This provision expands the protection of tort liability to interests which are not covered by the preceding Article 184(I). This is so because in the former part of Article 184(I), the entitlements protected are absolute rights such as rights *in rem* or personal rights; and interests other than absolute rights, according to the latter part of Article 184(I), could only be protected on the condition that the injurer intentionally takes the action which is against good morals (Taiwan Supreme Court 2000 Taishangzi 2560 decision). This difference in protection of absolute rights and interests makes sense because interests other than absolute rights are usually not foreseeable to the injurer upon his taking concrete actions. The requirement that the injurer must have acted against good morals would further prevent injurers such as competitors in the market from being held liable for the rivals' damage from competition.

Article 184(II), prior to its 1999 modification, reads as follows: "A person who violates the laws of protecting others shall be presumed negligent." Judging from this text, it would be more appropriate to see this provision as a rule shifting burden of proof between the injurer and the injured rather than a rule declaring that tort is independent. In one case, however, the Taiwan Supreme Court(1975 Taishangzi 2263 decision) ruled that the employer, because he did not insure his employees as required by labor laws, was liable for the damage to the employees on the basis of Article 184(II). The legislative history of the 1999 modification of Article 184(II) shows without a doubt that this provision declares violation of protective laws to be an independent type of tort and distinct from infringement of rights and acting against good morals.

Taiwan's courts have sometimes misused Article 184(II) to bypass the more stringent Article (I) to make the injurer liable for the damage. First, the provisions of the Civil Code cannot be the protective laws of Article 184(II) as such. In a recent case (2011 Taishangzi 1012 decision), the Taiwan Supreme Court ruled that Article 794 of the Civil Code is the protective law of Article 184(II), and that therefore the injurer was presumed negligent and liable for damage (Chien 2012). Article 794 reads as follows: "In excavating the land or in constructing buildings, the landowner shall not cause the foundations of the adjacent land to be shaken or endangered, nor can he cause any injury to the building or other works of the adjacent land." It is clear that the foundations of the adjacent land, the building, or other works of the adjacent land are the (absolute) rights which are protected under Article 184(I). Article 794 is only a clarification and does not create the right. If a person kills or hurts another, whether he is liable or not is determined by Article 184(I), and consequently there is no reason that a building or land should be given more protection by Article 184(II). It is not necessary for a Civil Code to contain a provision such as Article 794. If there is an impending infringement of adjacent land, the landowner thereof can sue for injunction according to Article 767 of the Civil Code.[5] The bad consequence of misapplying this provision can be demonstrated in the case of Taiwan Supreme Court 2001 Taishangzi 26 decision. In this case, the preexisting building actually had been built on unstable ground, and, as a result, it was damaged by the later development of neighboring land. The court, indeed, did not invoke Article 794 for its judgment. The court must have known that it was the weak ground of the preexisting building rather than the development of neighboring land that was primarily responsible for the damage. The following reasoning of the common law case *Bryant v. Lefever* (4 C.P.D. 172 [1878–1879]) would shed light on this Taiwan case: "It is the plaintiff who causes the nuisance by lighting a coal fire in a place the chimney of which is placed so near the defendants' wall, that the smoke does not escape, but come into the house" (Coase 1988, p. 109).

Second, causation is still required for a person to be held liable for violating regulatory protective laws. In the age of the regulatory state, there exist many regulations which are intended to protect the interests of another. Take traffic accidents as an example. If an unlicensed driver violates traffic regulations, he would not be liable for damage if the damage was not caused by him. Taiwan courts, however, are too rigid in applying the traffic rule requiring cars to maintain a safe distance. In one case (1997 Taishangzi 833 decision), Taiwan's Supreme Court adhered to this rule and refused to consider the possibility that the injured party suddenly cut into the lane in which the injuring party was driving. The most distorted reasoning arising from this provision was a case (Taiwan Supreme Court 1997 Taishangzi 56 decision) in which a doctor was held liable on the ground that he had violated a regulation requiring a written agreement from the patient before surgery, rather than on the ground that he had performed a second surgical procedure without consent in an attempt to cover up the failure of the first surgery. It seems that courts in Taiwan try to be seen as rule-bound and to avoid making any value judgments (Chien 2003).

Third, the imposition of criminal penalty should not be used as a means of coercing the injurer to compensate the injured. In Taiwan, the victim of a criminal act can also seek compensation for his damage during the criminal procedure. According to the law of criminal procedure, the plaintiff, usually the prosecutor, has a higher standard of proving the defendant's guilt than in civil cases, i.e., beyond reasonable doubt rather than more likely than not. This difference in standard of proof, however, has been undermined by the addition of civil compensation for damage in the criminal procedure because courts distracted by civil compensation tend to leverage the criminal penalty in coercing the injurer to compensate the injured. This occurs particularly in cases concerning traffic accidents. The courts' decisions show that if the defendant settles with the injured on civil compensation for damage, they would hold the defendant on probation only. This compensation-oriented approach has distorted the law of criminal procedure, which was originally enacted for protecting people from being arbitrarily punished.

2.3 Strict Liability

It might seem a little surprising that this subsection, titled "Strict Liability," is arranged under the section titled "The Fault Principle." In this subsection, I will argue that strict liability is, in essence, a kind of negligence liability. As subsection 2.1 shows, the Hand formula of the negligence rule dictates that the more risky the activity the injurer engages in, the more likely the injurer will be held liable for the damage. Thus it can be inferred that the injurer certainly will be held liable when the activity he engages in is extremely dangerous. This is strict liability!

The current economic theories of strict liability, however, are complicated and distorted. The economic theories have modeled strict liability not as a legal doctrine, but instead as a decision of the court to hold the injurer liable for the damage. No liability, strict liability, and negligence have been compared on the same level. For example, Landes and Posner (1987, p. 62) have said: "No liability" is a liability rule in a sense – an economic sense – because it affects the incentives of the parties." They have further said (1987, p. 63): "Strict liability is symmetrical with no liability." While the determination of negligence can result in either liable or not liable for the injurer, this comparison of three "rules" is confusing. If there exists no "no liability" as an independent type of tort, "strict liability" in its opposite sense would not be an independent type of tort either.

Confusing as it might be, the comparison between negligence and strict liability and the choice between the two have been done. First, contrary to ordinary impression, strict liability would not lead the injurer to be overcautious by not taking action that he would have taken under the negligence rule (Landes and Posner 1987, pp. 64–65). Ironically, this reason would eliminate the most important factor determining the choice of negligence or strict liability in the regulatory deterrence-based model.

Second, the costs of administering the negligence rule and strict liability have been compared (Landes and Posner 1987, p. 65). There are two problems here: (1) For the choice of liability rule, using administrative costs, rather than behavior channeling as the key factor, is incoherent in a regulatory *deterrence-based* model; (2) The comparison of information costs and claim costs would be indeterminate because strict liability should be favored when information costs are high, while negligence rule should be favored when claim costs are high.

Third, "strict liability has a larger insurance component" (Landes and Posner 1987, p. 66). This insurance component can be derived without a regulatory deterrence-based model. Furthermore, the negative consequences of insurance such as moral hazard and adverse selection have to be taken into account and thus this component becomes indeterminate.

Fourth, strict liability would provide "the incentive to avoid accidents by reducing level of an activity rather than by increasing the care with which the activity is conducted" (Landes and Posner 1987, p. 66). However, this claim is only valid on the condition that negligence liability has been determined based on the level of care without taking account of the level of activity. In the real world, this artificial separation of level of care and level of activity is difficult, and probably even impossible. Again, take driving as an example. The driving speed is the standard of negligent conduct. It could be considered level of care. It could also be considered level of activity. A driver could stop driving because of either strict liability or the negligence rule. While the separation of level of care and level of activity might be possible in the (*ex ante*) regulatory deterrence-based model, it could not arise in *ex post* tort liability, in which the (level of) activity is the object to be evaluated in the Hand formula.

In Taiwan, strict liability has been regarded as equivalent to outcome liability, meaning that it is not necessary to prove fault for injurers to be liable for the injury. This dualism of liability has caused much confusion in Taiwan's tort law. Understood correctly, strict liability is a type of fault liability. As the Hand formula demonstrates, the more risky the activity the injurer engages in, the more likely the injurer will be liable for the injury; therefore, when the activity is extremely dangerous, i.e., when P of the Hand formula is close to 1, the injurer almost certainly will be liable for the injury. Article 191-3 of Taiwan Civil Code,[6] a general provision of strict liability, was added to the Civil Code in 1999, almost six decades after the Code came into force in 1930. This new stipulation, however, has not caused a "flood" of tort litigation as many people feared. This is so because this provision does not create a new tort and only clarifies the general provision of Article 184 of the Code. In common law, although negligence and strict liability are separate and independent types of torts, they are not opposite from each other – the fault principle governs not only negligence but also strict liability.

Intentional tort has the same economic structure as strict liability. In the real world, it is impossible to determine whether or not the injurer was acting with intent. The intention of the injurer has to be inferred from the riskiness of the activities he engages in. Intentional tort means that the injury would not have happened if the injurer had not taken the action on purpose. In the Hand formula, this means that P is close to 1. The more risky the activity, the more likely the injurer would recognize the risk. When P is close to 1, the injurer must have acted intentionally.

3 Tort Liability or Contractual Liability

3.1 Good Samaritan or Not

Whether a person should act like a good Samaritan would further reveal the defectiveness of the regulatory deterrence-based model. A Good Samaritan Law requires a person to help someone out of danger if he could easily do so. A regulatory model of tort law would make a person liable if he does not act like a good Samaritan. The reasoning behind this is as follows: in the regulatory model, the difficulties that a person faces are the costs of precaution (B), which is small, while the success rate of help is high, meaning P is high; therefore, $B < PL$ is established. This can be illustrated by what Shavell (1987, p. 74) asserts: "Thus, it may be desirable for a young, able-bodied person to clear a sidewalk of ice, but undesirable for an elderly individual to do so."[7]

In Taiwan's tort law, a person who does not act like a good Samaritan is not liable for the damage, and this is for sound reasons. First, how would the person know whether or not he is in a position to rescue the injured if the injury was not caused by him? In accident cases, it is the riskiness of the activity the injurer engages in which would naturally lead the injurer to recognize the risk. In good Samaritan cases, the "injurer's" recognition of "risk reduction" usually has not been taken into account. This would be illegitimate in private law.

Second, the person might believe that someone else would come to the rescue and therefore his inaction would not matter in the prevention of the injury. This means that in the Hand formula, P is close to 0 and $B < PL$ would not be established.

Third, the opportunity costs of the rescue for the person might be large, such as having to rush a patient to the hospital for emergency treatment, thus making B large, which makes $B < PL$ harder to be established.

Fourth, imminent danger is often present in these types of situations, making it impossible for the injurer and the injured to conduct transactions with each other, and therefore asymmetric information cannot be eliminated. This means that a person who does not lend his hand in another's dangerous situation must have good excuses (reasons 1–3), and any court intervention on the basis of the good Samaritan would always be a mistake.

If a person bears no affirmative duty of the Good Samaritan, he also should not be burdened with a contractual liability deriving from his affairs being intervened in by another even with benevolence in mind. Indeed, Article 176(I) of the Civil Code provides: "If the management of the affair is beneficial to the principal and is not against his expressed or presumptive wishes, and where the manager has, for the principal, made necessary or beneficial expenses, or assumed debt, or suffered injury, he is entitled to claim against the principal for the reimbursement of such expenses plus interest commencing from the date of outlay, or the payment of such debt, or compensation for the injury sustained." This provision explicitly does not grant the intervenor the right to remuneration for his management of affairs even beneficial to the principal.

The reasons for this law are parallel to the ones given for the abovementioned Non-Good Samaritan. First, remuneration would give a person the incentive to intervene in another's affairs even without benevolence in mind. Second, remuneration would give a person an incentive to intervene in another's affairs even if he is not the person best qualified to manage the affairs. Third, the person whose affairs have been intervened in might have subjective values that are not socially average. Fourth, a transaction eliminating this asymmetric information does not arise by definition. This means that there will be too many cases of remuneration-based intervention in another's affairs for which the courts are not suited in dissolving the difference between the intervenor and the principal.

On the one hand, the law does not want to encourage frivolous cases of intervention in another's affairs; on the other, the law also does not want to discourage benevolent cases that could greatly increase social welfare. Indeed, Article 175 of the Civil Code provides: "If the undertaking of the management of the affair is in order to avert an imminent danger which threatens the life, body or property of the principal, the manager is not responsible for any injury derived from his management, except in case of bad faith or gross negligence." The lower standard of negligent conduct for the benevolent intervenor would clear his concern for unexpected (liability) risks.

3.2 Faults in Contractual Liability

As a result of the high transaction costs, the law, depending on whether the injurer engages in risky activities which are beneficial to him, prescribes that a benevolent intervenor would bear a lower standard of negligent conduct for liability. Needlessly to say, this autonomy principle would also apply to contexts of contract. Article 220 of Taiwan Civil Code provides: "I. The debtor shall be responsible for his acts, whether intentional or negligent. II. The extent of responsibility for one's negligence varies with the particular nature of the affair; but such responsibility shall be lessened, if the affair is not intended to procure interests to the debtor." This provision will apply when the contracting parties do not explicitly allocate the risks in the contract. This provision is a restatement of liability rules in torts and for good Samaritans. In good Samaritan cases, no remuneration is "the affair not intended to procure interests to the debtor" of Article 220; the injurer, as a good Samaritan, would have a lower standard of negligent conduct for liability as provided for in Article 175. The structure of this general provision of contractual liability echoes the structure of tort liability. In tort liability, the more risky the activity the injurer engages in, the higher the standard of conduct the injurer would bear. In contractual liability, the more remunerative the activity the debtor engages in, the higher the standard of conduct the debtor would bear. As the Hand formula shows, the more risky the activity the injurer engages in (i.e., the higher the PL), the higher the unrealized benefits (B) of the injurer has to be in order not to let the injurer be liable for the damage. The purpose of tort liability, however, is to *ex ante* equalize the unrealized benefits (B) and the riskiness of the activity (PL). In contractual liability, this means that the smaller the unrealized benefits (B), the lower the riskiness of the activity (PL) the injurer is willing to engage in. This is why, in gratuitous contracts and good Samaritan cases, the injurer has a lower standard of conduct than the one in torts.

In a recent case (Taiwan Supreme Court 2014 Taishangzi 2070 decision) concerning medical malpractice (Chien 2015b), the Taiwan High Court ruled that doctors are obliged to follow standard medical guidelines *and* also to perform their contractual duties. The court, however, said that doctors' obligations of performing contractual duties are higher than the level set in the standard medical guidelines. This is an odd decision. In Taiwan, doctors are obliged to treat patients in an emergency without first signing any written contract. In this case, there is no information revealing that the patient has paid a higher than usual price. In addition, Taiwan's National Health Insurance Program has usually underpaid doctors and hospitals. According to Article 220 of the Civil Code, doctors would be liable for damage based on a lower rather than a higher standard of negligent conduct because they derive little benefit from the treatment. However, the Taiwan Supreme Court did not take issue with the Taiwan High Court and remanded it on other grounds.

3.3 Medical Malpractice as Products Liability

Products liability is a contractual liability. Accordingly, the principle of Article 220 of the Civil Code should be applied here. Article 7 of Taiwan's Consumer Protection Law,[8] however, provides that enterprises should be more or less strictly liable for the damage related to the product use.[9] As subsection 3.2 shows, strict liability as contractual liability would mean that the riskiness of the activity engaged in by the enterprise should not be too large otherwise there will exist no contract. A unique aspect of the Consumer Protection Law in Taiwan is that it also covers the liability of service providers. In literal terms, medical services would fall under the jurisdiction of this law. Taiwan courts have heavily debated this issue. In the end, the courts concluded that the strict liability provision of the Consumer Protection Law should not apply to medical services (Taiwan Supreme Court 2007 Taishangzi 2738 decision). In this debate, economic analysis of law was even put forward to support the position that strict liability should not be applied.

Taipei District Court (1998 Suzi 1521 decision) fired the first shot in 2001. The court first argued that the purpose of adopting strict liability is to reduce dangerous activities, in contrast to the negligence rule whose purpose is to increase the level of care of the actors. The court then opined that if strict liability is applied to medical malpractice, then the doctor would reduce his harm-causing activity, meaning that he would adopt defensive medication while forgoing the more suitable treatment such as surgery. The court concluded that this result would not be in the spirit of Article 1 of the Consumer Protection Law, which states, "The Consumer Protection Law is enacted for the purposes of protecting the interests of consumers, facilitating the safety of the consumer life of nationals, and improving the quality of the consumer life of nationals."

The main problem with this reasoning is that in emphasizing the difference between level of activity and level of care, the court ignored the more fundamental difference between contractual liability and tort liability and made the argument circular (Chien 2008). First, as the court said that the purpose of strict liability is to induce the injurer to engage in less dangerous activities rather than increase the level of care, then what is the court's reason for abandoning strict liability in favor of the negligence rule when doctors do forego risky treatments as a response to strict liability? Second, if reducing the level of dangerous activities is not the ultimate goal of the law, then why compare strict liability with the negligence rule? Third, if reducing dangerous activities is not the ultimate goal of the law, then strict liability would certainly not be a good rule.

The framework of level of care and level of activity is not a good tool for analyzing tort liability. First of all, level of care and level of activity cannot be meaningfully separated. Again, take driving as an example. Should driving speed, the key variable in determining the driver's responsibility, be considered level of care or level of activity? Once a speed limit is imposed, the degree of caution of the driver turns into level of care. The driver who falls asleep constitutes an insufficient level of care. But why does negligence have to be limited to this scope? If the driver increases his speed, his level of activity has increased, and even if he exercises an adequate level of care by not falling asleep, he would still be deemed negligent, so why is strict liability even necessary? There are varying standards of negligent conduct for the various types of medical treatment. Once a treatment method is selected, negligence must be determined based on its individual standard. But in an emergency situation, if medication is insufficient and surgery becomes the only option (even if the success rate is not 100 percent) and doctors choose not to do the surgery, they still will be held liable for the injury based on negligence rule regardless of the lower level of care or the lower level of activity.

It is absurd to apply a model based on reducing the level of activity to explain the contractual obligations of medical care, which reduces risks via increasing the level of activity. The inappropriateness of strict liability for medical malpractice is not that it would not decrease or that it would even increase harm, but that the reduction in risks is not sufficient. As the court stated, "defensive medical care" is a consequence of the imposition of strict liability – excessive care leading to a portion of cases receiving perfect medical care, but another portion being completely barred from receiving any medical care. Cases that receive medical treatment witness reductions in harm, but those that do not receive any medical care see no such reduction in harm. So even though the overall risks may be decreased, on the one hand, the distribution of the reduction is uneven, and on the other hand the reduction is suboptimal compared with the negligence rule. This is reflected in the decrease in medical malpractice litigation which some would say that strict liability has achieved its goal of deterrence. This observation is problematic.

The court also tried hard to distinguish between consumer products and medical services, but the criterion it used was mistaken. The use of consumer products and the provision of medical care both arise from contractual transactions, so in principle adopting strict liability (outcome liability actually) is inappropriate in both cases. The court was wrong when it argued that in medical care, strict liability is unable to encourage potential victims to increase their level of care to prevent the harm whereas in consumer products, it can. As long as strict liability (without contributory negligence) is adopted, regardless of whether it is applied to consumer goods or to the provision of medical services, it is never able to encourage potential victims to increase their level of care.

The primary difference between the purchase of consumer goods and the provision of medical services lies in the fact that the preexisting risks of patients would be transferred to doctors if the principle of strict liability is adopted. The Hand formula is both a normative criterion determining liability and a positive measure predicting people's behavior. In the case of medical services, P of the formula is large. Therefore, B has to be large to offset large P. This means that patients have to pay a high treatment fee to compensate doctors for accepting risks transferred from patients, otherwise doctors would not provide services in the first place. By contrast, the lack of preexisting risks in the purchase of consumer goods does not affect P. Therefore, strict liability (outcome liability) applied in this case would not do as much harm in product markets as it would to medical services.

4 The Law as a System

4.1 Rights in rem *versus Rights* in personam

The information-based interpretation of negligence also sheds light on the issue concerning the nature of rights *in rem*, which have priority over rights *in personam* when the two rights are in conflict. Taiwan's Constitutional Court, in Interpretation No. 349, overrode a precedent issued by the Taiwan Supreme Court, opining: "Legal actions under the Civil Code can be classified as actions *in personam* and actions *in rem*. Unless specifically provided by the law, the former shall have legal effect on persona certa while the later shall, upon notice being given to a third party through means of public announcement, have legal effect on any third party. Hence, means of public announcement, by delivery for movables and by registration for immovables, are essential conditions for the acquisition, forfeiture and alteration of rights and interests. This is to protect bona fide third parties. In the event that the third party actually received or ought to have received notification of the contract, its terms shall have legal effects on the third party notwithstanding that the contract may be in personam."

This is so because rights *in rem* get the *in rem* characteristic from their publicity by possession, recordation, or registration, while rights *in personam* cannot be easily recognized by the public (Su 2010; Chien 2011). Compared to tort liability, the priority of rights *in rem* means the injurer – the holders of rights *in rem* – is not liable for the damage – the inferiority of rights *in personam*. In the calculation of the Hand formula, this means that P is very small – it is very difficult for the holders of rights *in rem* to avoid the damage because rights *in personam* have not been publicized – therefore, $B < PL$ cannot be established. Conversely, from the perspective of holders of rights *in personam*, the Hand formula would also show that the holders of rights *in personam* are (contributorily) negligent and thus cannot claim superiority over rights *in rem*. It is very easy for the holders of rights *in personam* to avoid the damage because rights *in rem* are publicized – P of the Hand formula is very large and therefore $B < PL$ would be established. In the case of creating fraudulent rights *in personam* with the intent to dilute the rights *in rem* concerned, P is 1 and therefore $B < PL$ certainly will be established.

4.2 Tort Liability and Insurance

In standard law and economics, the goal of tort law is to deter people from engaging in activities that externalize their associated costs. Insurance for liability, therefore, would frustrate the deterrence goal. Furthermore, according to the deterrence theory of tort law, there would be no accidents that are not cost-justified because people would fully comply with the legal standard and therefore third-party liability insurance would not be needed. The fact that there is a demand for liability insurance indicates that the benefits the insured receives from engaging in the activity must be larger than the loss that he would have to compensate for via tort liability.

In Taiwan, the Compulsory Automobile Liability Insurance Act was "specially adopted in order to ensure prompt basic coverage for the injured parties in automobile traffic accidents that result in injury or loss of life and to maintain roadway traffic safety," as declared in Article 1 of the Act. Article 29(I)[10] also shows that the legislators of the Act did know that the liability for intentional torts or gross negligence cannot be insured; if it were people would have no incentive to engage in only those activities that are considered to be reasonably risky. Intentional torts and gross negligent conducts have to be deterred and cannot be insured while negligent conducts should be allowed and can be, and sometimes even have to be, insured.

4.3 Tort Liability and Criminal Sanctions

The Taiwan Criminal Code could further illuminate the nature of tort liability as a compensatory scheme rather than being deterrence-based. Article 12 of the Criminal Code provides: "I. A conduct is not punishable unless committed intentionally or negligently. II. A negligent conduct is punishable only if specifically so provided." Indeed, the provisions of the Criminal Code concerned with punishing conducts that cause damage to another's pecuniary interests, i.e., Articles 320 to 363, do not specifically provide that negligent conducts are punishable. The unpredictability of the intentional harm which depends on the injurer's internal will unobservable from outside is the rationale of criminal law (Fletcher 1985, p. 925). Negligence as a state of mind, by definition, is not as arbitrary as intention, meaning P in the Hand formula not close to 1, as intention is (see subsection 2.3). Therefore, criminal punishments should not apply to negligent conducts. Whereas for nonpecuniary interests, which by their very nature cannot be fully compensated by monetary damages (Geistfeld 2011), the injurer even only in cases of negligence thus has to be deterred by the law.

Furthermore, the fact that the standard of proof is higher in criminal cases than in civil cases also weakens the thesis of tort liability for the purpose of deterrence. The higher standard of proof means that the P in the Hand formula has to be higher otherwise the conducts cannot be proven to be negligent. It can be inferred that only conducts of intention or gross negligence can be punishable in criminal law. Ordinary negligent injurers would not be liable for criminal sanctions but only for civil damages.

As Calabresi (1997, p. 2204) said that one of the reasons why he wrote the now-classic article "One View of the Cathedral" (Calabresi and Melamed 1972) is that the economist Gary Becker did not distinguish criminal punishment from civil damages. Calabresi and Melamed's placing of tort liability in the category of liability rules, however, is a mistake. The characteristic of Calabresi and Melamed's liability rules is that the injured would lose his entitlements without his consent if the injurer would pay a price which is determined either by a third party or by the injurer himself. Eminent domain is a typical case. Tort liability is not like eminent domain. The outcome liability rule which would be a Calabresi and Melamed's liability rule has never been the principle for any modern tort liability regime. In tort liability cases, the first priority of the courts is to determine whether the injurer is negligent and liable for the damage. Tort liability as a Calabresi and Melamed's liability rule would gloss over the most important element of tort liability – negligence. Negligence liability is not an instrument or an incentive that can be manipulated by the courts to achieve some goals outside the injurer and the injured. The courts have to determine the tort liability based on negligence rules which are default rules allocating the risks between the injurer and the injured. Calabresi and Melamed (1972) may have saved tort liability from degenerating into criminal sanctions, but they put tort liability into another directive category of rules and thus the autonomous essence of tort liability has been buried.

5 The Invisible Hand of Tort Liability

From an economic perspective, the purpose of tort law is to minimize the added amount of precautionary costs and expected loss, as the Hand formula shows. The standard economic analysis, however, has adopted an *ex ante* regulatory deterrence-based model for the *ex post* tort liability. In this *ex ante* regulatory model, precautionary costs are the injurer's expenses to reduce risks associated with physical challenges or risks. In the case of driving, for example, drivers with weak eyesight have higher precautionary costs than normal drivers do; in the calculation of the Hand formula, weak-sighted drivers therefore have a lower standard of conduct for liability. This is absurd, obviously. Precautionary costs associated with reduced physical capabilities would make sense only if the goal of the law is to reduce risks by *ex ante* requiring that all drivers should have some level of eyesight. This means that the *ex ante* regulatory model could not apply to those actually occurring in concrete accidents because the information structure has changed through time (O'Driscoll and Rizzo 1996). The regulatory deterrence-based model therefore does not fit with *ex post* tort liability law.

Hayek (1948, p. 77) pointed out that "The peculiar character of the problem of a rational economic order is determined precisely by the fact that the knowledge of the circumstances of which we must make use never exists in concentrated or integrated form but solely as the dispersed bits of incomplete and frequently contradictory knowledge which all the separate individuals possess." The risks with which tort liability deals are a kind of this dispersed knowledge. Again, in the example of driving, whether the driver is weak-sighted or not per se becomes irrelevant because the driver can drive slower to compensate for his reduced capability, or because the benefits of this specific driving activity are larger than normal, such as in the case of getting a patient to the hospital. Indeed, Article 150 of the Taiwan Civil Code excuses the injurer's liability for damage if the injurer's action is intended to avoid the imminent danger to life, body, freedom or property of himself or others.[11] A regulatory interpretation of tort liability would lead to inefficiency in the real world or to ad hoc theories explaining nothing, such as ones offered by Landes and Posner (1987) and Shavell (1987).

Most importantly, although the *ex post* nature of tort liability would not directly address raising incentives for people to increase their capabilities and reduce risks as standard economic analysis of tort law does, there is a built-in mechanism in tort liability to induce people to take such actions. The core of tort liability is that the less capable the injurer is, the more likely he will be liable for damage. Therefore, people have real incentive to improve their capability of reducing risks because this improvement would allow them to engage in higher level of activities without being held liable for damage. This private adjustment of level of capability by definition would be socially more accurate than requirements prescribed by *ex ante* regulations.

6 Conclusion

As a civil law system, Taiwan's tort law is an integral part of its Civil Code and even of its whole legal system, including the Criminal Code and administrative laws. This means that the investigation of the compensation for damage in tort law has to be done under a systemic framework.[12] The current standard economic analysis of tort law –

the regulatory deterrence-based model – is too narrow for this task. The compensation by the injurer to the injured should not be considered as only an external incentive imposed on the injurer to correct his action.[13] This chapter has shown that this manner of classifying tort liability as a mandatory rule is mistaken. The default rule of tort liability is the negligence rule because it benefits both the injurer and the injured by allocating risks Pareto-efficiently. Strict liability is a form of the negligence rule. A unified theory of contractual liability and tort liability emerges. It explains why medical malpractice cannot be a form of product liability. The puzzle of rights *in rem* versus rights *in personam*is also solved quite simply. The limited coverage of insurance and the more stringent requirements of criminal liability are explained. The invisible "Hand" of tort liability, in the sense of Adam Smith's and the Hand formula, has been revealed. The evolution of tort law in Taiwan, of course, is not linear. It is hoped that the economic theory developed in this chapter would shed on the path travelled and give guidance to the future (Epstein 1997).

References in Chinese

Cheung, Steven N. S. 2014. *Economic Explanation*. Beijing, China: China CITIC Press.

Chien, Tze-Shiou. 2003. The Presumption of Negligence in Violating Protective Statutes: Economic Analysis and Judicial Misuse. *National Chengchi Law Review* 75:79–121.

2008. Doctor's Malpractice Liability and the Obligation to Disclose. *Cross-Strait Law Review* 22:38–52.

2011. The Problem of Right *in rem* Externality. *Academia Sinica Law Journal* 8:227–257.

2012. For What the Protective Laws Have Been Referred in Tort Law. *Court Case Times* 18:25–31.

2014. Negligence Rules as the Principle of Private Law. *Peking University Law Review* 15(1):155–173.

2015a. Law as Contractual Arrangements. *SJTU Law Review* 2015(2): 37–46.

2015b. The Contractual Nature of Medical Liability. *Court Case Times* 39:16–20.

Su, Yeong-chin. 2010. Freedom of Contract on Registrable Goods – Revisiting the Principle of Numerus Clausus in Property Rights from the Perspective of Chinese Civil Law on Both Sides of Taiwan Strait. *Nanjing University Law Review* 2010(Autumn):16–44.

Wang, Tez-chien. 2015. *Tort Law*. Taipei, Taiwan: Author.

References in English

Ben-Shahar, Omri and Ariel Porat. 2016. Personalizing Negligence Law. *New York University Law Review* 91:627–688.

Brown, John Prather, 1973. Toward an Economic Theory of Liability. *Journal of Legal Studies* 2:323–349.

Buchanan, James M. 1974. Good Economics – Bad Law. *Virginia Law Review* 60:483–492.

Calabresi, Guido. 1997. Remarks: The Simple Virtues of *the Cathedral*. *Yale Law Journal* 106:2201–2207.

Calabresi, Guido and A. Douglas Melamed. 1972. Property Rules, Liability Rules and Inalienability: One View of Cathedral. *Harvard Law Review* 95:1089–1128.

Chien, Tze-Shiou. 2013. The Legal Meaning of Coasean Economics. *Peking University Law Journal* 1:197–214.

Coase, R.H. 1960. The Problem of Social Cost. *Journal of Law and Economics* 3:1–44.

1988. *The Firm, the Market and the Law*. Chicago, IL: The University of Chicago Press.

Craswell, Richard. 2003. In That Case, What Is the Question? Economics and the Demands of Contract Theory. *Yale Law Journal* 112:903–924.

Epstein, Richard A. 1997. Law and Economics: Its Glorious Past and Cloudy Future. *University Chicago Law Review* 64:1167–1174.

Fletcher, George P. 1985. A Transaction Theory of Crime? *Columbia Law Review* 85:921–930.

Geistfeld, Mark A. 2011. The Principle of Misalignment: Duty, Damages, and the Nature of Tort Liability. *Yale Law Journal* 121:142–193.

Hayek, Friedrich A. 1948. *Individualism and Economic Order*. Chicago, IL: The University of Chicago Press.

Holmes, Oliver W. 1881. *The Common Law*. Boston, MA: Little, Brown and Company.

Landes, William M. and Richard A. Posner. 1987. *The Economic Structure of Tort Law*. Cambridge, MA: Harvard University Press.

Markesinis, Basil S. and Hannes Unberath. 2002. *The German Law of Torts: A Comparative Treatise*. 4th ed. Oxford, UK: Hart Publishing.

Mestmäcker, Ernst-Joachim. 2007. *A Legal Theory without Law: Posner v. Hayek on Economic Analysis of Law*. Tubingen, Germany: Mohr Siebeck.

O'Driscoll Jr., Gerald P. and Mario J. Rizzo. 1996. *The Economics of Time and Ignorance*. London, UK: Routledge.

Posner, Eric A. 2003. Economic Analysis of Contract Law After Three Decades: Success or Failure? *Yale Law Journal* 112:829–880.

Posner, Richard A. 2003. *Law, Pragmatism, and Democracy*. Cambridge, MA: Harvard University Press.

Shavell, Steven. 1987. *Economic Analysis of Accident Law*. Cambridge, MA: Harvard University Press.

Zimmermann, Reinhard. 2005. *The New German Law of Obligations: Historical and Comparative Perspectives*. Oxford, UK: Oxford University Press.

Notes

1 The article reads as follows: "I. Unless otherwise provided by the act or by the contract, a person who is bound to make compensation for an injury shall restore the injured party to the status quo before the injury. II. If the restoration of the status quo ante shall be paid in money, interest shall be added from the time of the injury. III. Under the circumstances of the first paragraph, the creditor may claim the necessary expenses for restoration instead of the restoration."

2 The article reads as follows: "In case of death caused by a wrongful act, the father, mother, sons, daughters and spouse of the deceased may claim for a reasonable compensation in money even if such injury is not a purely pecuniary loss."

3 The article reads as follows: "I. If a person has wrongfully damaged to the body, health, reputation, liberty, credit, privacy or chastity of another, or to another's personality in a severe way, the injured person may claim a reasonable compensation in money even if such injury is not a purely pecuniary loss. If it was reputation that has been damaged, the injured person may also claim the taking of proper measures for the rehabilitation of his reputation. II. The claim of the preceding paragraph shall not be transferred or inherited, except a claim for compensation in money has been promised by contract or has been commenced. III. The provisions of the preceding two paragraphs shall be mutatis mutandis applied when a person has wrongfully damaged to another's status based on the relationship to their father, mother, sons, daughters, or spouse in a severe way."

4 In the calculation of the Hand formula $B < PL$, this means that B is larger for less capable drivers, and therefore they are less likely to be negligent.

5 The Article reads as follows: "I. The owner of a thing has the right to demand its return from anyone, who possesses it without authority or who seizes it. Where his ownership is interfered, he is entitled to claim the removal of the interference; and where the ownership might be interfered, he is entitled to claim the prevention of such interference. II. The

provision of the preceding paragraph shall apply mutatis mutandis to the rights in rem other than ownership."

6 This article reads as follows: "The person, who runs a particular business or does other work or activity, shall be liable for the injury to another if the nature of the work or activity, or the implement or manner used [is dangerous] to another. Except the injury was not caused by the work or activity, or by the implement or manner used, or he has exercised reasonable care to prevent the injury."

7 Usually the law prescribes that the occupier of the house is responsible for keeping the sidewalk in front of the house ice-free (for the German case, see Wang 2015, p. 358). On the assumption that the elderly usually are richer and have larger houses than the young, it is the elderly who bear a higher burden of clearing the sidewalk because a larger house usually has a longer sidewalk.

8 The article reads as follows: "I. Business operators engaging in the design, production or manufacture of goods or in the provisions of services shall ensure that goods and services provided by them meet and comply with the contemporary technical and professional standards of the reasonably expected safety prior to the sold goods launched into the market, or at the time of rendering services. II. Where goods or services may endanger the lives, bodies, health or properties of consumers, a warning and the methods for emergency handling of such danger shall be labeled at a conspicuous place. III. Business operators violating the two foregoing two paragraphs and thus causing injury to consumers or third parties shall be jointly and severally liable therefore, provided that if business operators can prove that they are not guilty of negligence, the court may reduce their liability for damages."

9 Article 7-1 further provides, "I. Where business operators allege that when their goods launched into the market or at the time of rendering service were in compliance with the contemporary technical and professional standards, of reasonably expected safety, they are required to produce evidence in support thereof. II. Goods or services cannot be presumed inconsistent with the requirement of safety set forth in the first paragraph of the preceding Article simply because better goods or services are subsequently provided."

10 The article reads as follows: "When an automobile traffic accident involving an insured automobile occurs as a result of any of the following behaviors on the part of an insured, the insurer shall still bear liability for payment of insurance benefits as provided herein, provided that the insurer may be subrogated to the claimant's right of claim against the insured, within the amount of benefits paid: 1. Was driving the automobile after ingesting alcohol or another similar substance and had a breath

or blood alcohol concentration exceeding the standard set by any act or regulation governing road traffic. 2. Was driving after having taken intoxicants, hallucinogens, narcotics, or other similar controlled substances, as verified through a test. 3. Caused it through a deliberate act. 4. Was engaging in a criminal act or evading lawful arrest. 5. Was driving an automobile in violation of Article 21 or 21-1 of the Act Governing Management of Roadway Traffic and Administration of Sanctions."

11 The article reads as follows: "I. A person acting to avoid an imminent danger menacing the life, body, liberty or property of himself or of another is not liable to compensate for any injury arising from his action, provided the action is necessary for avoiding the danger and does not exceed the limit of the injury which would have been caused by the said danger. II. Under the circumstances specified in the preceding paragraph, if the person so acting is responsible for the occurrence of the danger, he is liable to compensate for any injury arising from his act."

12 Richard Posner (2003, p. 250) would criticize this as formalism.

13 For the critique of seeing law as incentive rather than as norm, see e.g., Buchanan (1974); Mestmäcker (2007). For the worthiness of this approach, see Craswell (2003); Eric Posner (2003).

7 *The Evolution of Chinese Property Law*

Stick by Stick?

SHITONG QIAO[1]

1 Introduction

Chinese land reform has managed to both maintain and disintegrate state and collective land ownership simultaneously by discarding the unitary conception of ownership. It is consistent with the idea that "property comprises a complex aggregate of social and legal relationships" (Heller 1999: 1191) rather than being "the simple and nonsocial relation between a person and a thing" (Alexander 1997, p. 321). Scholars disagree about whether property rights are *in personam* rights or *in rem* rights. Traditionally, the *in rem* nature of property was widely recognized. Most famously, Sir William Blackstone (1803, p. 1) defined property as "that sole and despotic dominion which one man claims and exercises over the external things of the world, in total exclusion of the right of any other individual in the universe." According to Blackstone, property is "a right of a person with respect to something that avails against a large and indefinite number of other persons" (cited in Merrill and Smith 2001a: 361). Later, however, legal realists succeeded in promoting a rival conception – that of property as a bundle of rights. Ronald Coase (1960) went one step further, conceiving of property as a list of particularized use rights that individuals have when it comes to resources, i.e., *in personam* rights. In recent decades, the "bundle of rights" view has come in for considerable criticism (e.g., Penner 1995; Merrill and Smith 2001a). Henry Smith (2011, 2015) further criticizes the *in personam* concept of property rights, explicitly proposing property as a law of things to theorize the *in rem* nature of property rights. Although this *in rem* versus *in personam* debate is a familiar one, its relevance to property reform in developing countries has not been explored fully (for an exception, see Qiao and Upham 2015).

Taking up the case of China, this chapter argues that the path of Chinese land reform better fits a "bundle of sticks" than a "law of things" view of property rights. Regardless of Chinese legal scholars' enthusiasm for, or leftists' hatred of, the idea of individuals having sole and despotic dominion over private property, the law- and policymakers of Chinese land reform have often taken a more pragmatic approach, reconfiguring land rights in China "stick by stick." The two main achievements of Chinese land reform, i.e., the establishment of land use rights (LURs) in the urban area and the establishment of land management and contract rights (LMCRs) in the rural area, are both examples of the stick-by-stick approach. The ideological debates over privatization, in contrast, has more often intensified conflicts within the country's political system. When such ideological enthusiasm dominates the law-making process, it hampers land reform, as exemplified in the making of the 2007 Property Law. It is misleading, therefore, to ask who owns and who prevails in the context of Chinese land reform. The better question is how the bundle of sticks is arranged among government, communities, and individuals. This bundle of rights metaphor, or conception of legal relations, as Heller (1999: 1191–1194) calls it, is useful because society is generating more forms of property than the simple thing–ownership metaphor captures. This chapter also examines the recent policy developments following the third plenum of the 18th Congress of the Chinese Communist Party (CCP) and finds that policymakers have adhered to the stick-by-stick approach. The chapter develops its arguments by reviewing the main property laws and policies over the past three decades to outline the basic contours of the Chinese property system.

The remainder of the chapter is organized as follows: Section 2 examines the concept of *in rem* property rights. Sections 3 and 4 investigate the competing concepts of property rights in the fable and reality of Chinese property law respectively. Section 4 the explores the status and meaning of public land ownership in the current system, as well as how individual sticks of property rights have evolved and become separated from public land ownership. Section 5 concludes.

2 *In Rem* Property

Who is eligible to serve as an owner of property? Individual persons, close-knit communities, and governments "all can and do own property" (Merrill and Smith 2010). But what is meant by "property rights"? Some scholars believe that property is a bundle of rights that indicates which designated individuals are entitled to engage in which uses of particular resources (e.g., Ellickson 2011; Epstein 2011; Baron 2014). This *in personam* approach defines property as social relations between persons with respect to resources, and is analogous to a bundle of rights. Another school of thought holds that "property is a distinctive type of right to a thing, good against the world" (Merrill and Smith 2001a). This *in rem* concept of property consists of three parts. The first part is emphasis on "property as the law of things" (Smith 2011). As Smith (2014) argues, "the definition of a thing and its role in mediating private interactions lie at the heart of property." The "thing" plays a role in depersonalizing and formalizing property relations. In general, this *in rem* concept views property as the relationship between human beings and resources instead of a web of social relations among human beings.[2] "First, it identifies particular resources ('things'), and specifies which person (the 'owner') is to act as the gatekeeper or regulator of the thing" (Merrill and Smith 2001b). Things are "modules" through which law can organize the complex relationships into "lumpy packages" of legal relations (Smith 2012).

The second part of the *in rem* theory of property is the emphasis on the right to exclude; that is, the right to exclude others from some definite thing is central to what the owner owns (Merrill and Smith 2010: 4–8. To describe someone as an owner of some thing is to say that someone has the right to exclude others' use of that thing. Merrill (1998) holds that the right to exclude is more than just one stick in the bundle of property rights: "Give someone the right to exclude others from a valued resource . . . and you give them property. Deny someone the exclusion right and they do not have property." However, Smith (2014) recently argued that "the right to exclude . . . is not quite a *sine qua non* of property." In the same essay, he addresses other property rights, such as the right to transfer and the right to use. Even more recently, Chang (2015) claimed that "ownership" is just one type of property right, labeling the right to transfer and the right to use, among others, as "subsidiary rights." Despite these recent elaborations, however, the *in rem* concept retains its long-time emphasis on the right to exclude as the natural consequence of defining property rights as a law of things. Under this view, then, the first question to ask remains who owns the thing, which generally means who is the gatekeeper and has exclusive control over it.

Merrill and Smith (2001a) argue that legal realists and legal economists have successfully replaced the traditional *in rem* concept of property rights with the bundle of rights picture. In their view, someone who believes that property constitutes a right to a thing might be mocked for being lack of sophistication. Nonetheless, the Blackstonian concept of absolute dominion still dominates our imagination of property rights. The standard trilogy of private, communal, and state property rights presumes the *in rem* concept of property rights and is evidence of the Blackstonian concept. "Theorists push reforms toward one type or the other, but none" has substantially challenged the trilogy itself (Heller 2001).

Private property, despite the inherent ambiguity of its boundaries, is the benchmark and starting point of this trilogy. Blackstone's sole and despotic dominion over the external things of the world is an *in rem* portrayal of property rights. Further, as Dagan and Heller (2001) argue, "comm[unal] property designates resources that are owned or controlled by a *finite* number of people who manage the resource together and exclude outsiders." Essentially, it is "a regime that holds some resources as a commons among a group of 'insiders,' but as an exclusive right against 'outsiders'" (Rose 1998). It is "commons on the inside, [private] property on the outside" (Rose 1998). State property, or centralized property, refers to property over which the state holds all rights of exclusion and is the sole locus of decision-making regarding the use of resources (Heller 2001). Like the definition of private property, the definitions of both communal and state property present a relationship between a thing and an owner, in which exclusion is the core.

The third component of the *in rem* view is the *numerus clausus* principle. Merrill and Smith (2000) develop the optimal standardization thesis and further develop the *numerus clausus* principle based on the *in rem* concept of property rights, which, on the whole, overemphasizes the role of law and downplays the role of social norms in the evolution of property rights. In the world of *numerus clausus*, law is the main source of property rights. Merrill and Smith (2001) argue that the government, particularly the legislature, should play a role in standardizing rights, an argument that is closely aligned with Bentham's (1831) supposition that without law there would be no rights. Smith's (2003) well-known analogy between language and property is apt here. He pointed out that the grammar of a language is standardized spontaneously, whereas the source of the standardization of property rights is different (Merrill and Smith 2000:38).

In rem property rights theory also dominates the evolution of property rights literature, the majority of which, following the path-breaking work of Harold Demsetz, focuses on the paradigmatic situation in which the evolutionary process begins with open-access or communal property and ends with private individualized property. Demsetz (1967) centers his discussion on the emergence of private property among the Indians of the Labrador Peninsula. Robert Ellickson (1993) explores the switch from group ownership to individual ownership over time using various empirical materials. Finally, Michael Heller (1998) investigates the postcommunist transitions of property regimes in Russia, the aim of which was a shift from government ownership to private ownership.

In summary, the Blackstonian idea of property rights, defined as the exclusive relationship between a thing and its owner, might be more powerful and persistent in legal research than scholars thought (Merrill and Smith 2001a). Its prevalence is likely owing to its clear-cut, intuitive nature (Ackerman 1978), which reduces information costs (Merrill and Smith 2000). The real world is more complicated (Qiao 2016), however. Hence, I examine the competing concepts of property rights in Chinese land reform in the two following sections.

3 The Fable of Chinese Property Law

At first glance, both Chinese property law and the public discourse on Chinese land reform adopt the *in rem* view outlined above and follow the *numerus clausus* principle closely. The 2004 Constitutional Amendment stipulates that "citizens' legal property shall not be violated," a statement that was broadly welcomed by commentators both inside and outside China as a landmark success in China's long march toward a market economy and constitutionalism based on private property (e.g., Buckley 2004). Article 5 of the 2007 PRC Property Law states that "the varieties and contents of real rights shall be stipulated by law," which is essentially the Chinese version of *numerus clausus* (*wuquan fading*).[3] The legislative interpretation is that the establishment of new kinds of property rights and the content of those rights can be stipulated only by law, i.e., cannot be left to agreement between parties. The underlying rationale, according to this legislative interpretation, is that property rights differ from contract rights in the sense that there are thousands of obligators, as a result of which the former cannot be decided by the parties concerned, only by law (Committee of Legal Affairs of Standing Committee of NPC 2007). This is a perfect match with Merrill and Smith's (2000) information cost theory. The legislators also considered that new property rights might emerge, and thus that property law should allow room for their development. However, again consistent with Merrill and Smith (2000), the Chinese legislators concerned concluded that new property rights can be sanctioned only by law (Committee of Legal Affairs of Standing Committee of NPC 2007).

The *in rem* picture of property rights in China is vividly exemplified in the mass media by the phenomenon of the nailhouse (*dingzihu*). A Chinese neologism that first appeared in the media in 2007, the term "nailhouse" refers to a "hold-out house" that stands in the way of urban redevelopment like a stubborn nail sticking up out of the floor. The first nailhouse was located in the city center of Chongqing in a case dating back to 2004, when the Chongqing government decided to redevelop the area in which it was located. Of the 281 households affected by the redevelopment plan, only one remained in September 2006, a so-called nailhouse owned by a couple who were demanding more compensation. The land developers began to reconstruct the demolished area surrounding the nailhouse and cut off its supply of water and electricity. On March 16, 2007, the National People's Congress of China passed the Chinese Property Law, the main purpose of which, according to the Chinese mainstream media, was to strengthen protection for private property (Xu 2007). On March 21, Yang Wu, the husband concerned, climbed onto the roof of his house, hoisted the national flag, and unfurled a banner reading "citizens' legal right to private property cannot be violated"(Xu 2007). Wu Ping, his wife, stood in front of their home with a copy of the Chinese Constitution in her hands, Article 13 of which stipulates the exact words written on the banner. Within 24 hours, this poignant scene had attracted national and even international attention. On March 22, reporters from around the world rushed to Chongqing to see "the coolest nail household in history."[4] The case was settled by offering more compensation to the owners, the amount of which remains a secret. This case was widely applauded as a great success in protecting private property against public power. In the words of the *New York Times*, "a simple homeowner stared down the forces of large-scale redevelopment that are sweeping this country, blocking the preparation of a gigantic construction site by an act of sheer will" (French 2007). Mainstream opinion attributed the couple's success to the power of law (Hong 2007), with many believing that the new Chinese Property Law and 2004 Amendment to the Chinese Constitution had enabled an ordinary couple to resist and prevent an abuse of public power (French 2007).

The public discourse on rural land reform also presents an *in rem* picture, focusing on whether rural land should be privatized, recollectivized, or even nationalized (Qin 2008). The privatization proposal emphasizes individual autonomy, liberty, and the necessity of securing private property for long-term economic development (Chen 2014), whereas the recollectivization proposal considers the decline of the irrigation system in the rural area and the overall insufficient supply of public goods to be the failure of the country's Household Responsibility System (HRS), and claims that recollectivized rural land would have an advantage in terms of economies of scale (Bai 2015). The nationalization proposal is more complicated: some proponents propose state land ownership for the purpose of preventing village collectives from violating individual households' land rights (Chen 2014), whereas others propose it as a strategy to modernize the agricultural sector through the creation of large-scale farm operations (Chen 2014). Although such proposals contest who should own rural land, they are consistent in their *in rem* view of land.

Who owns China's land? This question can be misleading because it is premised on an exclusive relationship between land and the state, the village community, or individuals/private entities. The conventional view further holds private "sole and despotic dominion" over real estate as the benchmark for comparison. As a result, several phrases have been invented to depict developments in Chinese property regime, such as "quasi-private property rights" (Kung 2002) and "incomplete property rights" (Bennett et al. 2011) However, Chinese land reform is not a simple privatization, i.e., the transfer of exclusive control from the state or collectives to individuals. Accordingly, the *in rem* view of property rights is inconsistent with Chinese reality. What is needed instead is examination of how the bundle of rights to Chinese land has been rearranged over the past three decades.

4 The Reality of Chinese Land Rights: The Sticks of Public-Owned Land

Chinese land reform is not done by changing land ownerships. More than three decades since the beginning of the market transition, China's economy is still built on public land ownership: generally speaking, urban land is state-owned whereas rural land is collectively-owned. Despite the conventional belief that private property is the key to economic growth (e.g., North and Thomas 1973; Cooter and Schäfer 2012), China's economy has become the second largest in the world in the absence of private land ownership. The seeming contradiction of the so-called "China problem" has compelled scholars to reflect on the role of property rights in economic development (e.g., Clarke 2003; Palomar 2004; Trebilcock and Veel 2008; Upham 2009).

In reality, the separation of LURs from land ownership is a central feature of the evolution of the Chinese land regime. This separation has resulted in the emergence of urban LURs ("ULURs") and the rural LMCRs ("RLCMRs"). In the 1980s, the Chinese government, which had set development as its supreme goal, consciously and pragmatically gave up the unitary conception of public land ownership and focused on restructuring the complex social and legal relationships surrounding property. Both ULURs and RLCMRs emerged, and they were gradually adopted into law as sticks detachable from the bundle of sticks of state-owned land and collectively-owned land, respectively. This process has involved the gradual adjustment of the rights and obligations between land owners (the state and collectives) and land users. Although the rights of both are listed as usufructuary rights (*yongyi wuquan*) in the 2007 Property Law, they are created by contracts between land owners and corresponding land users, and are still far from fee simple: the exercise, mortgage, and transfer of ULURs are subject to detailed restrictions in the assignment contract between the state and the initial user, regardless of whether the ULURs have been further transferred. And the transfer and mortgage of RLCMRs are still strictly controlled and subject to the approval of the collective land owners in many situations.

In the following section, I examine the continual confirmation of public land ownership in Chinese law, the emergence and legalization of ULURs and RLCMRs, and the nature and contents of both rights.

4.1 *Public Ownership Stays*

Public land ownership, including the state ownership of urban land and the collective ownership of rural land, still defines and shapes the Chinese land regime. Public land ownership remains in Article 10 of the 1982 Chinese Constitution and it has been consistently confirmed in a number of succeeding laws. Articles 73 and 74 of the 1986 General Principles of Civil Law (GPCL) stipulate state property ownership and collective property ownership separately, both of which were arranged before individual property ownership (Article 75) and before LURs and LCMRs in Article 80. Both public ownership and its priorities were kept untouched in the 2009 revision of the GPCL. Article 1 of the 1986 Land Administration Law (LAL) states that the law is intended to "strengthen land administration, maintain socialist public ownership of land, protect and develop land resources." Articles 6 and 8 of the 1986 LAL reiterate the state ownership of urban land and collective ownership of rural land separately. Subsequent revisions to the LAL in 1988, 1998, and 2004 have kept intact the law's purpose to maintain public land ownership. Both the 1990 Interim Regulations Concerning the Assignment and Transfer of the Right to the Use of the State-owned Land in the Urban Areas ("the 1990 Interim Regulations" hereafter) and the 1994 Urban Real Estate Administration Law were made to implement state land ownership. Finally, the 2002 Rural Land Contract Law (RLCL) also confirms the collective ownership of rural land.

Readers may question the meaning of such articles, just as they may question the validity of the communist ideology in the Chinese constitution. Does their meaning matter? Yes, the ongoing confirmation of public land ownership matters in two ways. The first way is via the expressive power of law (McAdams 2015), which includes the expression of a particular ideology, but goes beyond expressing an ideological preference. The aforementioned articles confirm the status of the state and collectives as land owners. Despite the decreasing sphere of both owners' rights to the land, all individual rights are from and subsidiary to public land ownership: except for those granted to individual entities, all rights remain in the hands of the state or collectives. The second way in which their meaning matters is more substantive and has posted an ongoing threat to individuals' land rights. What does land ownership actually mean? If it is superior to ULURs and RLCMRs, then the government can destroy individual land rights by exercising its land ownership. This is what happened in the land nationalization conducted by the Shenzhen city government in 2004 (Economic Information Daily 2013), in the sales of collective land by village heads in the name of the collective in Wukan, Guangdong in 2001, and in other places on many occasions (Ramzy 2011).

The significant meaning of land ownership also made it a focus of constitutional debate in the making of the 2007 Property Law. Professor Gong Xiantian of Peking University Law School sent a public letter to the Standing Committee of the National People's Congress (NPC), claiming that the entire Property Law draft under the NPC Standing Committee's review was unconstitutional because it lacked an article on the protection of public property. This letter extended the Law's review process and led to substantial revisions to the draft, including the addition of Articles 3 and 4 to emphasize the protection of public property. The state ownership of urban land and collective ownership of rural land are reiterated in Chapter 5, "State Ownership and Collective Ownership, Private Ownership," of the Property Law.

4.2 ULURs

The government of Shenzhen, China's first special economic zone (SEZ), created LURs under the influence of the Crown land lease model of Hong Kong. Although the practice was unconstitutional, it soon spread to other cities, and later triggered the 1988 constitutional amendment that sanctioned ULURs. On the one hand, ULURs can be transferred, leased, and mortgaged. On the other, their contents are specified in the ULUR assignment contract and run with the land. The 2007 Property Law includes the *numerus clausus* principle and lists the ULUR as a usufructuary right. However, ULUR assignment contracts leave sufficient room for both parties, the government in particular, to create well-tailored terms to control the use and development of the land without worrying about future ULURs holders changing those terms.

4.2.1 The Creation of ULURs

Before 1979, land was controlled by the state and used by various government units for free in accordance with Marxist principles stating that the price mechanism was inappropriate after the abolition of private property. However, following the implementation of China's reform and opening-up policies, the state ownership of urban land required a more nuanced understanding than that provided by Marxist orthodoxy. The cities at the frontier of the reform and opening-up policies blazed the trail for land use reform. On December 31, 1979, for example, the director of the Shenzhen City Construction Commission signed a contract with a Hong Kong investor according to which the Shenzhen city government contributed land, and the Hong Kong investor financed land development and shared in a fixed percentage of the profits (Feng 2006). On December 5, 1980, the Shenzhen City Construction Commission signed the first "land use fee" contract with a Hong Kong investor, which included the essential ingredients of today's standard contracts governing the assignment of state-owned LURs between local governments and real estate developers, including the term (30 years in this contract) and price of land use (HK$5,000 per square meter) (Feng 2006).

The practice of land use fees discussed above can be considered a prologue to land use reform because of their limited scale, but it ultimately served as the beginning of a norm cascade (Ellickson 2001; Sunstein 1996). The Shenzhen SEZ went one step further. In November 1981, Shenzhen created its own land use regulation that required domestic investors within Shenzhen, as well as foreign investors, to pay one-time land use fees.[5] However, in the absence of a land market, the standard land use fee was fixed by law and applied to all construction projects. Users who valued the land most had no opportunity to reveal their willingness to pay higher prices. Shenzhen, as the first city to charge land use fees, was the first to feel their constraints. After carefully studying the Crown land leases in Hong Kong (Nissim 2008), the Shenzhen government realized the revenue-generating power of land markets. It wanted to sell land, and it created a slogan in response to the CCP's call to build a "commercial economy with planning." Its slogan was: "No land market, no complete commercial economy." Shenzhen's desired reform faced an ideological challenge from Marxism: how could a socialist country that had abolished private property sell land? In response to this challenge, the reformers separated LURs from land ownership. A local reformer searched the classics of Marx and Engels page by page and found support from the latter. Engels wrote: "[A]bolishing private ownership of land does not require abolishing land rents; rather it requires submitting land rents to the society" (Lin 2015). Thus, selling LURs would not challenge state land ownership in China, but would allow the state to utilize land rents.

Shenzhen eventually held the first public auction of transferrable LURs in the history of the PRC on December 1, 1987, in direct conflict with the then effective LAL and Constitutional Law (Feng 2006). This public defiance led to the legal authorization of the transfer of LURs by the People's Congress of Guangdong Province (the province in which Shenzhen is located) on January 3, 1988, and, more importantly, by a Chinese Constitutional Amendment on April 12, 1988 and a similar amendment to the LAL on December 29, 1988.

The 1988 amendments to the Constitution and LAL removed the legal barriers to the sale of LURs by local governments. On May 19, 1990, the State Council promulgated the 1990 Interim Regulations detailing the rules governing the assignment (*churang*) of LURs from the government and their transfer (*zhuanrang*) among land users, which remains in effect today. The 1990 Interim Regulations confirm that the assignment of LURs is the responsibility of city and county governments.

4.2.2 The Content of ULURs

ULURs are a mixture of contract and property rights. On the one hand, ULUR holders are entitled to transfer (Article 19 of the 1990 Interim Regulations), lease (Article 28 of the 1990 Interim Regulations), and mortgage (Article 32 of the 1990 Interim Regulations) their rights, just like standard property owners. The maximum terms of ULURs range from forty to seventy years, depending on the land use (Article 12 of the 1990 Interim Regulations). ULURs are automatically renewed in the case of residential land, and the government should approve ULURs holders' renewal applications in other cases, except when there is a need to take back land for public use. On the other hand, what rights holders have are subject to the ULURs assignment contract, which follows a standard format but leaves considerable blank for negotiation with the state owner. First, regarding the use and development of the assigned land, the ULURs holder has little choice but to utilize the land according to the contract. If a ULURs holder does not follow the terms and conditions of the contract in land use and development, the land administration agency can issue a warning or fines and in extreme circumstances may even withdraw the ULURs (Article 17 of the 1990 Interim Regulations). In situations in which changing the agreed land use is justified, the ULURs holder needs to renegotiate a ULURs contract, including an adjustment to the ULURs assignment fees and registration of the new ULURs (Article 18 of the 1990 Interim Regulations).

Second, the initial holders of ULURs contracts (i.e., the assignees of ULURs contracts) cannot transfer their ULURs before satisfying the conditions specified in those contracts. A standard ULURs contract requires either finishing 25 percent of the investment or the fulfillment of other specified conditions (Article 20 of the 1990 Interim Regulations). It is interesting to note what is actually being transferred. As specified by law, what are transferred are the rights and obligations of the ULURs contract (Article 21 of the 1990 Interim Regulations). Therefore, it is not the *in rem* rights that are transferred, but rather the *in personam* contract rights. It is the same situation in the lease of ULURs, which cannot be leased without satisfying the conditions of investment and utilization specified in the contract (Article 28 of the 1990 Interim Regulations). Furthermore, when ULURs are transferred, any buildings on the land, built in accordance with the ULURs assignment contract, must also be transferred (Article 23 of the 1990 Interim Regulations). When the price of a transfer is significantly lower than the market prices, the government has the right of first purchase (Article 26 of the 1990 Interim Regulations).

We can see the contractual nature of ULURs more clearly by comparing it with the leading English case affirming what Merrill and Smith (2000) call the *numerus clausus* principle, namely, *Keppell* v. *Bailey*. In this case, the purchasers "covenanted on behalf of themselves and their successors and assigned to acquire all limestone required by the works from a particular quarry and to ship the limestone to the works on a particular railroad" (Merrill and Smith 2000). The Court of Chancery held that this type of agreement did not fall within the recognized types of servitudes enforceable against subsequent purchasers as a property right running with the land (Merrill and Smith 2000). According to Merrill and Smith (2000), inventing new modes of real property rights such as the covenants in *Keppell* and allowing them to be established as property rights would create unacceptable information costs for third parties. In the case of ULURs, the entire ULURs assignment contract "runs with the land," i.e., runs automatically with the land even when it passes into remote hands (Chang and Smith 2012, p. 35): the transfer of ULURs means the transfer not only of the rights and obligations specified in the registration documents, but also of those specified in the assignment contract.[6] A standard ULURs assignment contract allows specially tailored terms on the use of the land, which can be as specific as "commercial office (value-added telecommunication business) use"[7] and "the nature of the main constructions, the nature of affiliated buildings, floor area ratio, building density as well as height limits."[8] Such detailed agreements are as peculiar and idiosyncratic as the covenants in *Keppell*. Other than the specified land use written into the contract, the land cannot be used for any other purposes without rewriting the contract.

The importance of ULURs assignment contracts is also verified by the registration process. These contracts are required for the transfer and lease of ULURs. Article 21 of the 1990 Interim Regulations emphasizes that "rights and obligations in ULURs assignment contract and registration document are transferred when ULURs are transferred." Therefore, a ULURs assignment contract is not only the basis for ULURs certificates, but also an equally important document for verifying the rights and obligations running with the land. This requirement has been confirmed in various legislations since 1990.

This contractual nature of ULURs is determined by the strong will of the state to control the use and development of land, which arises from a combination of the legacy of the planned economy and also the current developmental state's strong hand in the market. The subsidiary role of ULURs is also reflected in the expropriation of urban housing. There is no compensation for ULURs. The State Council passed the Regulations on the Expropriation and Compensation of Housing on State-Owned Land in 2011 ("2011 Regulations" hereafter). The title reveals that these regulations concern housing alone, and there are no separate regulations concerning the expropriation of and compensation for ULURs. Article 13 of the 2011 Regulations states that ULURs are withdrawn when housing is expropriated in accordance with the law. Article 17 stipulates that compensation is restricted to the value of the expropriated house, moving and temporary accommodation costs caused by the expropriation, and expropriation-induced business losses (Article 17 of the 2011 Regulations). No compensation is to be provided for the loss of the involved ULURs. One could reasonably argue that location is considered in calculating the value of an expropriated house, and therefore that ULURs are at least indirectly considered. However, that is still different from recognizing the independent value of ULURs. The words of the 2011 Regulations suggest that the underlying logic is that ULURs return to the state land owner when the related housing is gone, which is consistent with the resilience theory of ownership in civil law (Chen 2004).

4.3 RLCMRs

It was Chinese farmers, rather than the government, that created RLCMRs, the first key institutional innovation in China's market transition. The Chinese government did the right thing by tolerating the emergence and development of such an institution, and it has been cautiously building legal institutions to secure people's expectations, to reduce the risk, and also to resolve disputes. It is a long process and one that has yet to be completed. Nevertheless, it is noteworthy that RLCMRs were not created by law, and its contents are still evolving beyond the strict boundaries of law.

4.3.1 The Creation of RLCMRs

The underlying system of RLCMRs is the HRS, the essence of which is to liberate Chinese farmers so that they can produce for themselves on individually allocated plots of land. The system was initiated by the actual practices of farmers, particularly those of farmers in Xiaogang Village in An'Hui Province in the early 1980s, but was not made constitutional until a 1993 constitutional amendment, by which time the system had been fully operational across the country for several years. The 1993 constitutional amendment legitimizes the HRS by defining it as a form of socialist collective economy. RLCMRs first appeared in law in the 1986 GPCL, Article 80 of which, under Section I, "Property Ownership and Property-Ownership-Related Property Rights" of Chapter Five, "Civil Rights" states that citizens' contract and management rights to collective-owned land are protected by law. The same article also states that land cannot be sold, leased, mortgaged, or transacted illegally in other ways. This article does not specify the content of RLCMRs, leaving room for future development. In the 1980s and early 1990s contract adjustments between individual households and village collectives occurred quite often. From time to time village collectives gave instructions and guidance to farmers on what and how to plant, and also reallocated the contracted land periodically in the name of equality (Zhu 2005). Further elaboration of RLCMRs had to wait until the 1998 LAL, which has a longer article dedicated to RLCMRs. Article 14, in addition to emphasizing that RLCMRs are protected by law, specifies that the term of RLCMRs is thirty years and that contract adjustments within that term need to be agreed by a two-thirds majority in villagers' meetings or by villagers' representatives. It was not until 2002 that the RLCL was made to fully specify the details of RLCMRs, including the rights and obligations of village collectives as contractors and individual households as contractees, the principles and procedures of contracting, the terms and contents of contracts, and the protection and transfer of RLCMRs. The 2007 Property Law further includes RLCMRs in Part III as one kind of usufructuary rights, together with construction ULURs, residential LURs, and easement.

4.3.2 The Content of RLCMRs

Like ULURs, RLCMRs, although recognized by the 2007 Property Law as property rights, are actually a mixture of property and contract rights. As the name implies, RLCMRs are created by land management contracts between village collectives and their members and concern the division of rights and obligations between contractor and contractee. Such rights are *in personam* in nature, context-specific, and inconsistent with the depersonalized "thing-ownership" concept (Heller 1999, p. 1189). First, RLCMRs are affiliated with holders' identity as members of a village collective and are unavailable to outsiders (Article 15 of the RLCL). When RLCMRs holders lose their collective membership by changing their *hukou* (household registration) from rural to urban, they need to return their land to the village collectives, resulting in the demise of their RLCMRs (Article 26 of the RLCL). In addition, when a woman marries a man from outside her village, she may also lose her RLCMRs after being granted RLCMRs in her husband's village (Article 30 of the RLCL). Second, assignment contracts between village collectives and individual households are subject to the approval of two-thirds of the village members or their representatives (Article 18 of the RLCL). The same two-thirds majority can also decide to adjust the land allocated to members in the event of natural disasters or some other special circumstances (Article 27 of the RLCL). Third, the contracted land can be used only for agriculture, which is a contractual obligation per se and requires no reference to the zoning of local jurisdictions (Article 16 of the RLCL). Finally, RLCMRs are created at the moment the corresponding contract is signed (Article 22 of the RLCL). Although this is, of course, not decisive evidence of the contractual nature of RLCMRs, registration is viewed as more of an *in rem* effect (Smith 2015). RLCMRs were initially treated as contract rights, but have gradually been sanctioned as property rights in the past three decades together with extending their terms and imposing restrictions on interference by village collectives (Chen 1996).

In the following, I examine the alienability and expropriation of RLCMRs in detail so as to elucidate both their contractual nature and the government's gradual adjustment of their content. I also examine the right to develop contracted land as a possible extension of RLCMRs in Chinese policy discussions.

(1) Alienability of RLCMRs

There are four main forms of RLMCRs transactions: subcontracting (*zhuanbao*), lease (*chuzu*), exchange (*huhuan*), and transfer (*zhuanrang*). Exchange refers to the exchange of RLMCRs between members of the same village collective. Transfer means the transfer of RLMCRs from one holder to another, and requires the approval of the contractor, i.e., the village collective. The transferee also needs to sign a new contract with the village contractor (Article 37 of the RLCL). In this case, the transferor loses its RLMCRs. Subcontracting means that the holders of RLMCRs subcontract the land to other members of the village, and lease refers to those holders leasing their RLMCRs to someone outside the village collective. In both subcontracting and lease arrangements, RLMCRs holders do not lose their RLMCRs, and only need to register their transactions with the village collectives (NPC Website 2003). All of the foregoing RLMCR transactions take a contractual approach and reflect the *in personam* nature of the RLMCRs. Procedures differ between transactions within and outside the community. What is transferred are contract rights to the village collectives, rather than *in rem* rights to the land. Whether a new contract is to be signed also serves as a key difference between different forms of transactions. Moreover, village collective members have the right to first purchase (Article 33 of the RLCL), which is *in personam* in nature because it is based on membership and is not connected to any specific plot of land of any particular villager.

The restrictions on the alienability of RLMCRs have both historical and political roots. In the early stages of reform, the government was leery of what might be seen as the logical next step: the free alienability of LMCRs. The CCP's No. 1 Document of 1982, for example, not only strictly prohibited alienation but also empowered the collective owner, i.e., the village, to cancel the contract if alienation was attempted (CCP No. 1 Document 1982). As early as 1984, however, the picture began to change, with the CCP Central Committee promulgating a notice allowing members of village collectives to subcontract their land with the collective's approval (CCP Central Committee 1984). The decades since have witnessed considerable toing and froing over an issue that is eloquent testimony to the central government's ambivalence about the full blossoming of the free exchange of farmland, of which the HRS may have been the first step. In 1988, a constitutional amendment and amendment to the LAL legalized the transfer of LURs, although it remained unclear whether alienability included rights to the collectively owned land contracted to individual households. Then, in 1995, the State Council explicitly recognized that the transfer of RLMCRs was an "extension and development" of the HRS, declaring: "Provided that collective ownership is retained and there is no change in the agricultural use of the land and with the approval of the contractor, a contractee may subcontract, transfer, exchange, or convert their land into shares of stock (*rugu*)."

In the subsequent years, however, the pace of liberalization has slowed. Although it has become conventional wisdom that the Chinese agricultural sector is in need of modernization, which would require some degree of land concentration, the central government remains suspicious of the long-term leasing and management of rural land by industrial or commercial enterprises (CCP Central Committee 2001). Instead, the transfer of agricultural land is supposed to take place among rural households to facilitate land concentration in the hands of the more productive farmers without diverting land from agricultural use (CCP Central Committee Document No. 1, 1984; CCP Central Committee 2001). The 2002 RLCL, confirmed by the 2007 Property Law, was the most recent statute to address the transfer of land contract rights. It maintained the requirement of village approval for transfer but converted the approval requirement for subcontracting, exchanges, and leases to simple registration.

In the wake of rapid urbanization and the flow of millions of farmers into cities, the need for agricultural land transfers has intensified in recent years. Since 2008, a number of central government documents have reiterated the goal of establishing "a market for RLMCRs." Nevertheless, substantial progress has yet to be made. The most recent reform plan delineated three redlines for any reform: land ownership must remain public; the amount of arable land should remain above the minimum necessary for national food self-sufficiency; and farmers' interests should be protected (Hong 2014). The ambivalence is understandable. Collective land ownership is ideologically central to a nation that still calls itself communist. Public ownership, furthermore, need not hinder gradual reform, as we have seen from the rise of the HRS, the development of an urban land market, and the reform of state-owned enterprises. The other two conditions are of more pragmatic importance. The protection of arable land is based on a strategic concern for food self-sufficiency that may be not only unattainable but, paradoxically, may even lead to gross inefficiencies. Self-sufficiency may also be contrary to the third condition. It is conventional wisdom that landless farmers in Chinese cities pose a serious threat to social order in times of economic downturn. Therefore, the retention of small household plots, no matter how inefficient in terms of economies of scale, is seen as serving as an essential social safety net for migrant workers, at least until the government builds a social welfare system in the countryside.

Farmers themselves seem to understand this. According to statistics from the Ministry of Agriculture, about one-quarter of agricultural land has been subjected to some form of transaction (Lin 2014). However, most of those transactions took the form of subcontracting and were agreed between villagers who were known to one another. Few migrant workers are willing to sever their connections to their home villages by selling their land. That is why the central government has emphasized that local governments should not promote the transfer of agricultural land against farmers' will (Li 2013).

(2) RLMCRs in Land Expropriation

As with the state ownership of urban land, the collective ownership of rural land also figures in cases of expropriation. Article 10 of the Constitution states that the state can expropriate land to serve the public interest as long as compensation is provided. Article 42 of the Property Law specifies the types of compensations required, including compensation for land, relocation cost, and structures and crops. The land compensation fee, according to the LAL, should be between six and ten times the land's average output in the three previous years. Relocation costs are calculated according to the number of rural household members. The total amount of the two types of compensation should not exceed thirty times the average annual output of the expropriated land in the past three years (Article 47 of the 2004 LAL). What is the standard and purpose of compensation? The purpose is to maintain the livelihood of farmers whose land has been expropriated and to protect their legal interests (Article 42 of the 2007 Property Law). That is why relocation assistance is provided, calculated according to the number of rural household members and subject to the future career arrangements of the farmers who are losing their land (Interpretation of the 2004 LAL, Article 47). Rural land ownership and RLMCRs do not include the right to develop rural land. Therefore, the legislative interpretation of the LAL explicitly rejects the idea of compensating farmers according to the price the government assigns ULURs. The same legislative interpretation also emphasizes that "land expropriation is a state act and not a land transaction... [Hence, compensation] is not subject to the negotiation between government and farmers or the 'market value'" (Interpretation of the 2004 LAL, Article 47).

Who is entitled to the land compensation fee? According to the legislative interpretation of the LAL, both land owners and land users are so entitled. Accordingly, Article 48 of the LAL states that local governments should listen to the opinions of village collectives and farmers whose land has been expropriated. Article 49 further states that village collectives whose land has been expropriated should make public the income from and expenses involved in the land compensation fee and accept monitoring from their members. There are no clear legal standards on how to divide the land compensation fee between the village collective and their members. In reality, it seems that village collectives receive the fee and decide how to spend it. How much is land ownership worth? How much are RLMCRs worth? The absence of any clear answers has led to the arbitrary allocation of land compensation fees between village collectives and their members, mostly to the advantage of the former and often serving the personal interests of village collective leaders.

Reforming the system of rural land expropriation has been under discussion for a long time. In 2012, the then-premier Wen Jiabao promised to issue a State Council Regulation on Expropriation of Rural Land and Housing, but he did not succeed in doing so (Wen 2012). Discussions of rural land expropriation have tended to follow the conventional wisdom on eminent domain and to focus on public interest and just compensation. However, such expropriation in China differs from eminent domain in countries in which *in rem* private land ownership is well established. I argue that the existing approach cannot work because it overlooks the bundle of rights structure of rural land for the following reasons.

First, "public interest" was designed to restrain the government's expropriation power but, in China, expropriation is the only way to convert rural land to urban land – only the latter can be sold and put to a variety of uses. Article 43 of the LAL requires that "any unit or individual that needs to use land for construction must apply for the use of state-owned land in accordance with the law," which means that city and county governments must expropriate rural land to satisfy the land needs of rapid industrialization and urbanization processes. It is thus no wonder that "public interest" has been interpreted in an extremely broad fashion. Therefore, defining "public interest" more strictly without changing the current land structure is a nonstarter. If urban users cannot buy land from farmers for nonagricultural use, there is no other way for them to buy land but to buy it from the government, and government land is simply rural land that has been expropriated.

Second, as previously noted, "market value" is clearly rejected by the legislative interpretation of the LAL. How, then, is compensation for farmers calculated? We need to investigate what rights they have, and whether they are entitled to the nonagricultural development value of rural land. Chinese farmers are acutely aware of the vast wealth produced by urbanization based on formerly agricultural land. Ignoring farmers' expectations carries a political cost. From the opposite perspective, however, granting farmers the full post-conversion market price would deny growing municipalities a substantial source of revenue (Qiao 2016). With no obvious immediate replacement, cities would be faced with falling even further behind in providing the public goods needed to accommodate a growing population of former farmers seeking a better life than is possible back on the farm. In any case, basing compensation on the post-converted market value of rural land would not constitute compensation for RLMCRs, but the granting of new rights or expansion of the content of RLMCRs, depending on how those rights are formulated.

(3) The Right to Nonagricultural Use

As noted, RLCMRs holders are not entitled to use the contracted land for nonagricultural purposes. Granting them the right to nonagricultural use can be understood either as expanding the content of RLCMRs or as moving one stick of the rural property rights from the state to farmers. Conflicts caused by rural land expropriation and the prevalence of illegal rural land development (Qiao 2015) have triggered policy discussions and experiments in this direction. The review of policy developments below provides another vivid example of the bottom-up, decentralized, stick-by-stick approach of Chinese land reform.

In early October 2008, the Third Plenary Session of the 17th Central Committee of the CCP for the first time in history proposed to "gradually unify the construction land use markets in urban areas and rural areas" and that "legally-acquired rural collectively-owned construction land should have rights equal to those of state-owned land" (CCP Central Committee 2008). It also emphasized that rural LURs must be transferred through a unified and *visible* market in a *public* way, a clear indication of the central government's concern with the *invisible* or *hidden* small-property market (CCP Central Committee 2008). Just one month later, the Ministry of Land and Resources issued a notice to its local branches on implementing the decision. The notice stated that the transfer of rural construction land has particularly important meaning to the protection of farmers' land rights, and also called for the establishment of institutions for the assignment and transfer of rural collective construction land that are compatible with the existing urban land use market (Ministry of Land and Resources 2008).

This foregoing proposal was reiterated five years later at the Third Plenary Session of the 18th Congress of the CCP and promulgated as two points on November 12, 2013: (1) establishing a unified construction land market, thus allowing rural collective construction land to be transferred in the same manner as state-owned land; and (2) granting more property rights to farmers by selecting several experimental sites and cautiously promoting the lien, mortgage, and transfer of farmers' property rights to their residential houses (CCP Central Committee 2013).

The 2014 No. 1 Document of the CCP Central Committee also has a paragraph on incorporating rural construction land into the market. It states that under the precondition of consistency with land use control and planning, rural construction land should be permitted to be transferred, leased, and converted to shares in the same way as state-owned land for the same rights and the same price (Xinhua News 2014b). Then, on December 2, 2014, the Leading Small Team for Deepening Reform of the CCP Central Committee promulgated an opinion on experiments in reforming rural land expropriation, incorporating rural construction land into the market, and rural residential land reform (Xinhua News 2014a). Although the full text of this opinion is not available, according to news reports the experiments should be finished by 2017, before which no transfer of rural construction land is allowed without authorization (Wang 2015).

Rural land reform is challenging, and the final institutions will be built on an evaluation of different experimental plans. As happened with the HRS, the property laws that will confirm the completion of such evaluation will come once effective practices have been recognized.

In summary, RLMCRs are subject to and subsidiary to both collective land ownership and the state's police power (i.e., a "state act," as stated in the legislative interpretation) in land conversion and expropriation. RLMCRs are still not strong *in rem* rights per se. Rather, as one stick in the bundle of collective property rights, they are entangled in the relationship among rights holders, collective land owners, and the state.

5 Conclusion

Understanding property as a bundle of sticks provides a logical basis for separating ULURs and RLCMRs from public land ownership, and also for rearranging the sticks to adapt to social and economic developments, which often run well ahead of the legislature. Despite the enthusiasm for private land ownership among scholars and the mass media alike, Chinese policymakers have taken the more pragmatic approach of adjusting the bundle of property rights cautiously and carefully while keeping land ownership public. This is not to say that they understand, or even know about, such scholarly jargon, but rather that when they try to accommodate new changes in reality in their daily work through gradual policy and legal reforms, they do not take property as an undivided concept but adjust the rights and obligations of the related parties with great care. This is now the bundle of rights idea has become rooted in the evolution of Chinese land laws. A recent policy development serves as another example of the stick-by-stick approach to land reform in China. To resolve the conundrum between protecting farmers' property rights and promoting farmland transactions, the current government proposed the separation of three rights: land ownership rights, land contract rights, and land management rights (Zhang 2014). The idea is that rural households will keep their land contract rights, which cannot currently be freely transferred, but will be able to transfer land management rights to agricultural companies, banks, and other entities outside village collectives to realize the market value of the land (Wu 2015). The proposal's details are still to be figured out, and the consequence of separating land management rights from land contract rights fully examined (Liu 2015). The stick-by-stick approach has its own problems, including the costs and uncertainty incurred by fragmented and unstandardized property rights (Ellickson 2012), the political maneuvering in the reform process (Qiao 2016), and the weakness of individual rights. Nevertheless, we can expect it to continue to dominate China's land reform, driven by pragmatism and incrementalism, for the foreseeable future.

References in Chinese

Bai, Yang. 2015. New Type of Collectivization Is the Only Way to Realize a Well-off Society for All Farmers. Available at www.wyzxwk.com/Article/zatan/2015/07/347950.html (last visited October 1, 2015).

CCP Central Committee. 1984. CCP Central Committee Document No.1 of 1984. Available at http://money.163.com/10/0126/18/5TVO4HML002544P9.html (last visited July 18, 2016).

2001. CCP Central Committee Notice on Guaranteeing the Circulation of the Farmers' Right to the Use of Contracted Rural Land. Available at http://news.xinhuanet.com/zhengfu/2002-11/05/content_618438.htm.

2008. CCP Central Committee's Decision on Several Crucial Questions about Promoting Rural Reform. Available athttp://cpc.people.com.cn/GB/64093/64094/8194418.html (last visited July 18, 2016).

2013. Decision of the CCP Central Committee on Several Crucial Questions about Comprehensively Deepening Reform. Available at http://news.xinhuanet.com/politics/2013-11/15/c_118164235.htm (last visited July 18, 2016).

Chen, Su. 1996. Propertization of Land Contract and Management Rights and the Establishment of Agricultural Land Use Rights System, Chinese Legal Studies, No. 3. Available at http://www.iolaw.org.cn/showArticle.aspx?id=150.

Chen, Rongwen. 2004. The Legal Nature of Ownership Retention. Available at http://article.chinalawinfo.com:81/article_print.asp?articleid=24921 (last visited October 1, 2015).

Chen, Shiqing. 2014. Nationalization of Rural Land Is Fundamental to Solve the Three Rural Issues. Available at www.21ccom.net/articles/economics/dongjian/20140908112762.html (last visited October 1, 2015).

Committee of Legal Affairs of Standing Committee of NPC. 2007. *Interpretation of the PRC Property Law*. Beijing: China Legal Publishing House.

Economic Information Daily. 2013. The Legacy of Land Nationalization Transition in Shenzhen Becomes Evident and the Complex Property Rights. Available at http://news.xinhuanet.com/house/2013–06/14/c_124853003.htm (last visited October 1, 2015).

Feng, Jie. 2006. Two Decades of Shenzhen Land Administration. Available at www.szpl.gov.cn/xxgk/gzdt/zwdt/200908/t20090825_46190.html (last visited October 1, 2015).

Hong, Bihua. 2007. The Legislative Background and Institutional Innovation of Chinese Property Law. Available at www.lawlib.com/Lw/lw_view.asp?no=8518&page=2 (last visited January 9, 2010).

Hong, Lefeng. 2014. Public Ownership of Farmland is the High-tension Cable in Red Line. Available at http://opinion.people.com.cn/n/2014/1204/c1003–26149221.html (last visited October 1, 2015).

Li, Haitao. 2013. Land Conversion Cannot Be Against Farmers' Will or Act Above the Law. Available at http://szb.farmer.com.cn/nmrb/html/2013–05/03/nw.D110000nmrb_20130503_3–02.htm (last visited October 1, 2015).

Lin, Lingdong. 2015. Shenzhen Real Estate: Hero or Sinner of Cities? Available at http://www.21ccom.net/articles/economics/dongjian/20150806127651_all.html (last visited September 9, 2016).

Lin, Yuan. 2014. The Area of Farmland Conversion in China Reaches a Quarter and Land Reform Will Promote the "Separation of Three Rights." Available at http://finance.sina.com.cn/china/20140114/011917938824.shtml (last visited October 1, 2015).

Liu, Shouying. 2015. Clarifying the Connotation of "Three Rights" of Farmland is Crucial. Available at http://china.caixin.com/2015–08–02/100835416.html (last visited October 1, 2015).

Ministry of Land and Resources. 2008. MLR Party Branch on Studying and Implementing the Spirit of the Third Plenary Session of the Seventeenth CCP Central Committee. Guotu Zidang Fa [2008]46, November 14.

NPC Website. 2003. Legislative Interpretation: The Transfer of Contractual Right of Land. Available at www.npc.gov.cn/npc/flsyywd/jingji/2003–10/28/content_323095.htm (last visited October 1, 2015).

Qin, Hui. 2008. At the Crossroad: Land System Reform in China. Available at www.aisixiang.com/data/21233.html (last visited October 1, 2015).

Southern Weekly. 2007. Party Secretary Zheng Hong: What Happened in the Fifteen Days? Available at http://news.enorth.com.cn/system/2007/04/12/001609237_01.shtml (last visited January 9, 2010).

Wang, Libin. 2015. Pilot Marketization of Rural Land to Be Completed by the End of 2017, Non-pilot Areas Not to Act Without Instructions. Available at www.jfdaily.com/caijing/new/201501/t20150111_1134127.html (last visited October 1, 2015).

Wen, J. 2012. Regulations on Rural Collective Land Expropriation Compensation to be Issued. Available at: http://news.sohu.com/20120314/n337716782.shtml (last visited July 18, 2016).

Wu, Jinglian. 2015. The Understanding of "Separation of Three Rights" in Farmland is Still Under Controversy. Available at http://people.chinareform.org.cn/w/wjl/media/201505/t20150522_225929.htm (last visited October 1, 2015).

Xinhua News. 2014a. Rural "Three Pieces of Land" Reform Direction is Clear: Farmers Who Pull Out From Homestead Might Be Compensated. Available at http://news.xinhuanet.com/politics/2014–12/03/c_127271189.htm (last visited October 1, 2015).

2014b. Several Opinions on Comprehensively Deepening Rural Reform and Accelerating the Modernization of Agriculture. Available at http://news.xinhua08.com/a/20140121/1295025_3.shtml (last visited October 1, 2015).

Xu, Baike. 2007. A Sample in a Demolition Era. Available at http://news.163.com/07/0328/08/3ALJ5BER00011SM9_2.html (last visited December 5, 2009).

Zhang, Hongyu. 2014. From "Separation of Two Rights" to "Separation of Three Rights." Available at www.npc.gov.cn/npc/xinwen/rdlt/sd/2014–01/14/content_1823604.htm (last visited October 1, 2015).

References in English

Ackerman, Bruce. 1978. *Private Property and the Constitution*. New Haven, CT: Yale University Press.

Alexander, Gregory S. 1997. *Commodity & Propriety: Competing Visions of Property in American Legal Thought, 1776–1970*. Chicago and London: University of Chicago Press.

Baron, Jane B. 2014. Rescuing the Bundle-of-Rights Metaphor in Property Law. *University of Cincinnati Law Review* 82:57–101.

Bennett, Michael T., Aashish Mehta, and Jintao Xu. 2011. Incomplete Property Rights, Exposure to Markets and the Provision of Environmental Services in China. *China Economic Review* 22 (4):485–498.

Bentham, Jeremy. 1831. Pannomial Fragments. Available at http://www.laits.utexas.edu/poltheory/bentham/pannomial/pannomial.c03.html.

Blackstone, William. 1803. *Blackstone's Commentaries*. Philadelphia: William Young Birch and Abraham Small.

Buckley, Chris. 2004. China Approves Amendments On Property and Human Rights. *The New York Times*. Available at www.nytimes.com/2004/03/15/world/china-approves-amendments-on-property-and-human-rights.html.

Chang, Yun-chien. 2015. The Economy of Concept and Possession. Pp. 103–127 in *Law and Economics of Possession*, edited by Yun-chien Chang. Cambridge: Cambridge University Press.

Chang, Yun-chien, and Henry E. Smith. 2015. The *Numerus Clausus* Principle, Property Customs, and the Emergency of New Property Forms. *Iowa Law Review* 100(6):2275–2308.

2012. An Economic Analysis of Civil Versus Common Law Property. *Notre Dame Law Review* 88(1):1–56.

Clarke, Donald C. 2003. Economic Development and the Rights Hypothesis: The China Problem. *American Journal of Comparative Law* 51: 89–112.

Coase, Ronald. 1960. The Problem of Social Cost. *Journal of Law and Economics* 3:1–44.

Cooter, Robert, and Hans Bernd Schäfer. 2012. *Solomon's Knot: How Law Can End the Poverty of Nations*. Princeton and Oxford: Princeton University Press.

Dagan, Hanoch, and Michael A. Heller. 2001. The Liberal Commons. *Yale Law Review* 110:549–557.

Demsetz, Harold. 1967. Toward a Theory of Property Rights. *American Economic Review* 57:347–359.

Ellickson, Robert C. 1993. Property in Land. *Yale Law Journal* 102:1315–1318.

2001. The Market for Social Norms. *American Law and Economics Review* 3:1–49.

2011. Two Cheers for the Bundle-of-Sticks Metaphor, Three Cheers for Merrill and Smith. *Econ Journal Watch* 8:215–222.

2012. The Costs of Complex Land Titles: Two Examples from China. *Brigham-Kanner Property Rights Conference Journal* 1:281–302.

Epstein, Richard. 2011. Bundle-of-Rights Theory as a Bulwark against Statist Conceptions of Private Property. *Econ Journal Watch* 8: 223–235.

French, Howard W. 2007. Homeowner Stares Down Wreckers, at Least for a While. Available at www.nytimes.com/2007/03/27/world/asia/27china.html?_r=0 (last visited October 1, 2015).

Grey, Thomas C. 1980. The Disintegration of Property. *Nomos: Property* XXII:69–85.

Heller, Michael A. 1998. The Tragedy of the Anticommons: Property in the Transition from Marx to Markets. *Harvard Law Review* 111:621–688.

1999. The Boundaries of Private Property. *Yale Law Journal* 108:1163–1223.

2001. The Dynamic Analytics of Property Law. *Theoretical Inquiries in Law* 2:79–95.

Kung, James Kai-sing. 2002. Choice of Land Tenure in China: The Case of a County with Quasi-Private Property Rights. *Economic Development and Cultural Change* 50(4):793–817.

McAdams, Richard H. 2015. *The Expressive Powers of Law: Theories and Limits*. Cambridge, MA: Harvard University Press.

Merrill, Thomas W. 1998. Property and the Right to Exclude. *Nebraska Law Review* 77:730–755.

Merrill, Thomas W., and Henry E. Smith. 2000. Optimal Standardization in the Law of Property: The Numerus Clausus Principle. *Yale Law Journal* 110:1–70.

2001a. What Happened to Property in Law and Economics? *Yale Law Journal* 111:357–398.

2001b. The Property/Contract Interface. *Columbia Law Review* 101:773–790.

2010. *The Oxford Introductions to U.S. Law: Property*. Oxford and New York: Oxford University Press.

Nissim, Roger. 2008. *Land Administration and Practice in Hong Kong*. Hong Kong: Hong Kong University Press.

North, Douglass C. and Robert Paul Thomas. 1973. *The Rise of the Western World: A New Economic History*. New York: Cambridge University Press.

Palomar, Joyce. 2002. Land Tenure Security as a Market Stimulator in China Contents. *Duke Journal of Comparative and International Law* 12:7–74.

2004. Contributions Legal Scholars Can Make to Development Economics: Examples from China. *William and Mary Law Review* 45:1011–1053.

Penner, James E. 1995. The Bundle of Rights Picture of Property. *UCLA Law Review* 43(3): 711–820.

Qiao, Shitong. 2015. Small Property, Big Government: A Focal Point Explanation. *American Journal of Comparative Law* 63(1):197–238.

2016. The Politics of Chinese Land: Partial Reform, Vested Interests and Small Property, *Columbia Journal of Asian Law*, 29(1):70–113.

and Frank Upham. 2015. The Evolution of Relational Property Rights: A Case of Chinese Rural Land Reform. *Iowa Law Review* 100:2479–2506.

Ramzy, Austin. 2011. Revolt in China: After Protests, a Village Gets Blockaded by Local Authorities. Available at http://world.time.com/2011/12/14/revolt-in-china-after-protests-a-village-gets-blockaded-by-local-authorities/ (last visited October 1, 2015).

Rose, Carol M. 1998. The Several Futures of Property: Of Cyberspace and Folk Tales, Emission Trades and Ecosystems. *Minnesota Law Review* 83:129–155.

Smith, Henry E. 2003. The Language of Property: Form, Context, and Audience. *Stanford Law Review* 55:1105–1160.

2012. Property as the Law of Things. *Harvard Law Review* 125:1691–1693.

2014. The Thing about Exclusion. *Brigham-Kanner Property Rights Conference Journal* 3:95–123.

2015. The Persistence of System in Property Law. *University of Pennsylvania Law Review* 163:2055–2083.

Sunstein, Cass R. 1996. Social Norms and Social Roles. *Columbia Law Review* 96:903–968.

Trebilcock, Michael and Paul-Erik Veel. 2008. Property Rights and Development: The Contingent Case for Formalization. *University of Pennsylvania Journal of International Law* 30:397–482.

Upham, Frank K. 2009. From Demsetz to Deng: Speculations on the Implications of Chinese Growth for Law and Development Theory. *NYU Journal of International Law and Politics* 41:551–602.

Zhu, Keliang, et al. 2005. Rural Land Question in China: Analysis and Recommendations Based on a Seventeen-Province Survey. *NYU Journal of International Law and Politics* 38:761–839.

Notes

1 The author thanks Yun-chien Chang, Donald Clarke, and Bob Ellickson for comments; Yicheng Su and Jie Zheng for research assistance; and the University of Hong Kong Seed Funding Programme for Basic Research (Project Code: 201411159056) for financial support. All errors are my own.

2 Note that Chang and Smith (2012) argue that "property is a *structured* bundle of relationships," which makes the distinction between the *in rem* and *in personam* concepts more nuanced.

3 For an introduction to how Chinese property scholars interpreted the *numerus clausus* principle, see Chang and Smith (2015, pp. 2301–2303).

4 Sixty-one reporters representing more than 40 media organizations participated in a press conference held by the local court on March 23, 2007. Numerous magazines and newspapers, including the *New York Times* and BBC News, reported the incident. See Southern Weekly (2007).

5 See Article 19 of Interim Regulations on Land Administration in Shenzhen Special Economic Zone (promulgated by The People's Congress of Guangdong Province, December 24, 1981).

6 See Article 22 of an English translation of the Contract on the Assignment of the Use Right of State-Owned Land. Available at www.sec.gov/Archives/edgar/containers/fix150/1269238/000119312508094260/dex421.htm.

7 See Article 4, *Id.*

8 See Article 11, *Id.*

8 *The Evolution of Property Law in Taiwan*

An Unconventional Interest Group Story

YUN-CHIEN CHANG*

1 Introduction

This chapter studies the evolution of statutory property law in Taiwan.[1] Specifically, Book III in the Taiwan Civil Code (the Book of Things) underwent large-scale overhauls in the period 2007–2010. This chapter examines the driving force behind the statutory change and evaluates whether the new law is more efficient than the old one. Unlike Demsetz (1967), Krier (2009), Levmore (2002), and other studies on the evolution of property *rights*, this chapter focuses not on why resources change from being held in commons to being held exclusively by one or a few private parties, but on why statutory property laws are amended,[2] which may or may not involve privatization.

Levmore (2002)'s analytical framework is the starting point for this chapter. Levmore (2002, p. S451) points out that "[t]he content of private property is itself a function of government, and virtually all legal moves need to be analyzed in terms of both transaction costs and interest groups." This chapter will examine whether the Taiwanese statutory amendment was driven by interest groups and to what extent the new law has increased economic efficiency. "Normative judgments about the role of government in maintaining and transforming property arrangements must depend on local evidence about given pieces of

* This paper has been presented at the 10th Annual Meeting of the Asian Law and Economics Association held at National Taiwan University College of Law on June 20–21, 2014, Asian Law Institute Annual Conference held at National Taiwan University College of Law on May 20–21, 2015, and East Asian Law and Society Annual Conference held at Waseda University in Tokyo, Japan on August 3–6, 2015. I thank Frank Bennett, Jianlin Chen, Tzu-shiou Chien, Brian Christopher Jones, Jonathan Kang, Saul Levmore, Ariel Porat, Shitong Qiao, Wei Shen, Tay-sheng Wang, and Yueh-ping Yang for helpful comments. Charline Jao, Alice Kuo, Hilary Tsai, Christine Yuan, and Chiehhan Wang provided valuable research assistance.

property, industries, and so forth" (Levmore 2002, p. S451). In order to unveil the driving force behind the Taiwanese amendment of property law, this chapter presents descriptive statistics and interviews, and delves into the archives of legislative hearings and meeting minutes of the task force in charge of proposing bills to the legislature.

The interest group versus transaction cost stories can be reformulated in another perspective: formal versus informal property rights. The transaction cost story more easily explains the emergence of informal property rights in "relatively close-knit, egalitarian communities" (Merrill 2002, p. S338), such as fur rights in Indian tribes (Demsetz 1967) and parking space rights in secondary streets in Chicago during storms (Epstein 2002). Social norm theory complements the transaction cost story (e.g., by adding a norm entrepreneur) in explaining the emergence of property customs (Ellickson 1991). By contrast, interest group theory more easily explains contemporary changes in formal property rights (particularly those through amendments of property-related statutes, such as land use regulations and civil codes).[3] Since interest groups are more likely to benefit from privatization or entitlement reallocations than devolution into commons (Levmore 2002, p. S429), and given that elected legislators generally do not amend laws to improve efficiency (Levmore 2002, p. S428), we expect changes in property statutes to benefit the politically powerful at the expense of the politically weak.

Nevertheless, the Book of Things in the Taiwan Civil Code is no ordinary statute. The Book contains many general and abstract doctrines, such as the doctrine of first possession, that are unlikely to significantly affect the wealth of many people. The costs of overcoming the collective action problem (Olson 2009) are likely to outweigh the tiny benefit each participant receives. Even for big landowners, statutes regarding property taxes, land use regulation, urban renewal, eminent domain, etc. involve higher stakes than the mostly "technical" stipulations in the Taiwan Civil Code. Thus, lobbying for amendments in the Taiwan Civil Code is not a productive use of time and resources for the politically powerful.

Against this backdrop, this chapter deals with the drivers of the legislative amendments in 2007–2010. Elected representatives, as part of the interest group politics, are unlikely to initiate the politically unattractive amendment of the Taiwan Civil Code, as that would likely dampen campaign contributions and votes in the next election. My story is that jurists in the task force drove the legal change. To be more exact, the scholarly judges[4] and property law scholars dominated the amendment process.

One of the oldest and longest debates in law and economics is whether and why the judge-made common law tends to become more efficient over time, while the legislator-made statutes do not (e.g., Posner 1973; Priest 1977; Rubin 1977; 1982; Parisi 2004; Fon, Parisi, and Depoorter 2005; Ponzetto and Fernandez 2008; Niblett, Posner, and Shleifer 2010; Zywicki and Stringham 2010; Garoupa and Ligüerre 2011; Posner 2011). In the United States, an alternative expression of this dichotomy is that private laws tend to be efficient whereas statutory regulations do not (Posner 2011, pp. 714–716)[5] – though efficient statutes exist. When applying this framework to civil law countries, where statutes are sources of private law, the first-order inquiry is whether private laws (civil codes) will be efficient because they deal with civil matters or whether they will be inefficient because they are enacted by legislatures. Another consideration in private law, regarding the same legal problem, is whether the doctrine in American common law or the one in civil law tends to be more efficient. Chang (2013), for example, finds that the code-stipulated property doctrine – access to landlocked land – in several European and Asian civil-law countries is more efficient than its US counterpart. Garoupa and Ligüerre (2011, pp. 308–321) contend the superiority of French law over American law in terms of efficiency. Arruñada and Andonova (2008, p. 83) point out that common law and civil law at their inceptions in the nineteenth century were both efficient adaptations to the local circumstances, and the civil law countries in the nineteenth century reserved more rule-making powers for the legislature, instead of the court, to preserve the market.

This study on the evolution of property law in Taiwan further complicates the debate. I find that the legislature rubber-stamped the proposed bill sent from the executive branch, and this highly technical and sophisticated bill is the brainchild of an official task force consisting of property scholars and judges. In other words, the depressing story often told by public choice theorists – that legislative changes reflect the narrow interests of lobbying groups and campaign funds donors – is not applicable here. If the prima facie case against statutes in terms of efficiency is lifted, can we make a general prediction as to whether statutes like this will be welfare-enhancing?[6] I am not ready to offer a grand theory. Yet my case study on the evolution of property law in Taiwan sings a positive note, as I observe that the amendments of the Book of Things are generally Kaldor–Hicks-improving. Of course, civil codes are special cases, so my findings may not be readily generalizable. But civil codes are important laws, so any theory on the general inefficiency of statutes should be able to explain them.

The structure of this chapter is as follows: Section 2 summarizes the current property law in Taiwan. Section 3 describes the changes of property law in 2007–2010. Section 4 discusses whether the new Taiwan Civil Code is more efficient than its predecessor. Section 5 concludes.

2 Overview of Current Property Law in Taiwan

The original Taiwan Civil Code was enacted in 1929 and came into force in 1930 when the Nationalist Government still ruled China. Since 1949, the Civil Code has been the private law of the land in Taiwan. The 1929 Civil Code was drafted with the assistance of Japanese consultants and was heavily influenced by German and Swiss civil codes (see, e.g., Tsai 2000, pp. 54–55). That said, both the original and the amended Book of Things in the Taiwan Civil Code are far from carbon copies of either the German or the Japanese Civil Code. The Japanese Civil Code treats possession as a right and contains comprehensive stipulations regarding priority rights (other than mortgage and pledge), for example, while the TCC conceptualizes possession as a fact (Chang 2015a) and does not have any priority right other than mortgage and pledge. In Japan and Taiwan, land and fixture are separate real estates, while under the German Civil Code, fixture is generally part of land. The drafters left out usufruct (such as easement in gross) and security interests (such as land charges) that were adopted in the German Civil Code but distant from property practice in China. Finally, the Taiwan Civil Code incorporated the "*dian* right," a traditional Chinese property right absent in Germany and Japan.

After decades of application in Taiwan, loopholes emerged, both big and small. The Taiwan Supreme Court, through its "selected precedent" system, filled in the holes while sometimes creating other problems. After two failed attempts to change the Book of Things in the Taiwan Civil Code, the Taiwan Civil Code eventually went through a major overhaul in 2007–2010 (for the scope and process of this reform, see Section 3 of this chapter; for evaluation of the reform, see Section 4 of this chapter).

One structural change worth highlighting here is that the pre-2009 Article 757 of the Taiwan Civil Code adopted a strict version of the *numerus clausus* principle (Merrill and Smith 2000; Hansmann and Kraakman 2002), but the 2009 amendment switched to a looser version under which property customs can create property forms. Though courts in Taiwan have not formally recognized customary property forms, they have done so implicitly (Chang and Smith 2015a).

The following sections briefly overview the property forms formally recognized in the Taiwan Civil Code as of 2015.[7]

2.1 *Ownership and Registration*

Like other civil codes influenced by the German Civil Code, the Taiwan Civil Code distinguishes ownership from possession (Chang 2015a). Under the Code, ownership is a full title to real or personal properties, while possession, defined as actual control, is a fact. As under the Japanese Civil Code (Article 86) and PRC Property Law, land and fixtures (such as buildings) are separate things and can thus be owned by different persons (as is frequently the case). There are three types of co-ownership: tenancy-in-common (Chang 2012), owners-in-common (similar to, but not exactly the same as, joint tenancy), and condominium. As a snapshot, on February 11, 2011, 20.5 percent of land parcels in Taiwan were co-owned, whereas 5.4 percent of apartments or houses were co-owned (see Figure 8.1 for the distribution of the number of co-owners).[8]

Ownership and limited property rights of real properties can be de jure transferred only after registration in the land registry. In this regard Taiwan, like Germany, adopts the Torrens registration system (Arruñada 2012, pp. 72–73).[9] Land registration is mandatory and the Department of Land Administration, Ministry of the Interior, has actively mapped land in Taiwan and put it in the registry. At the end of 2012, the total area of Taiwan is 36,192.82 square kilometers,[10] 34,937.12 square kilometers of which are registered.[11] That is, only 3.47 percent of land is unregistered (Figure 8.2), most of which is state land exempted by the Land Act for registration purposes. On the other hand, the registration of buildings is optional. For example, builders of their own houses can choose to leave their constructions off the

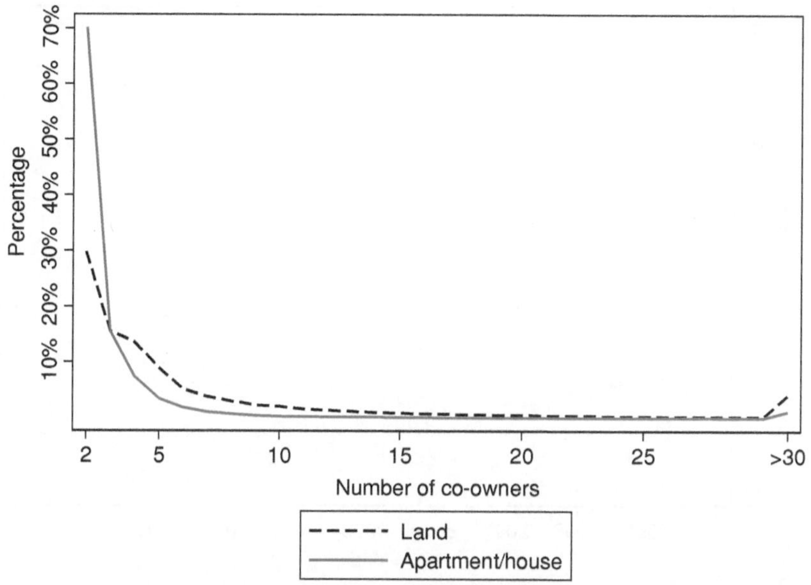

Figure 8.1 The number of co-tenants in co-owned land and apartment/house
Note: The unit for calculating co-owners in land is defined as a land parcel with its own unique "land number." The unit for calculating co-owners in nonland real properties is defined as one ownership right. That is, if the whole building is subject to one ownership right, such as a house, the statistics here describe how many people share that right of ownership. A building held in condominium form is divided into multiple apartments. Because each apartment is subject to one ownership right, the statistics here describe how many people share that right of ownership in one apartment, not the ownership of the whole building.

registry, at the expense of not being able to transfer titles or establish limited property rights de jure. Many developers failed to comply with the building code and thus cannot register even if they want to. These kinds of constructions, known in Taiwan as "illegal buildings" (Chang 2015c) and "small properties" in China (Qiao 2015) (see also Qiao's chapter in this book), cause courts in Taiwan a great deal of trouble: numerous illegal buildings exist and were exchanged, and yet, legally speaking, no formal property rights changed hands. In the late 1950s, the Taiwan Supreme Court was forced to create a new type of property right, called the "de facto disposal right." I discussed this informal property right in more detail in Chang and Smith (2015).

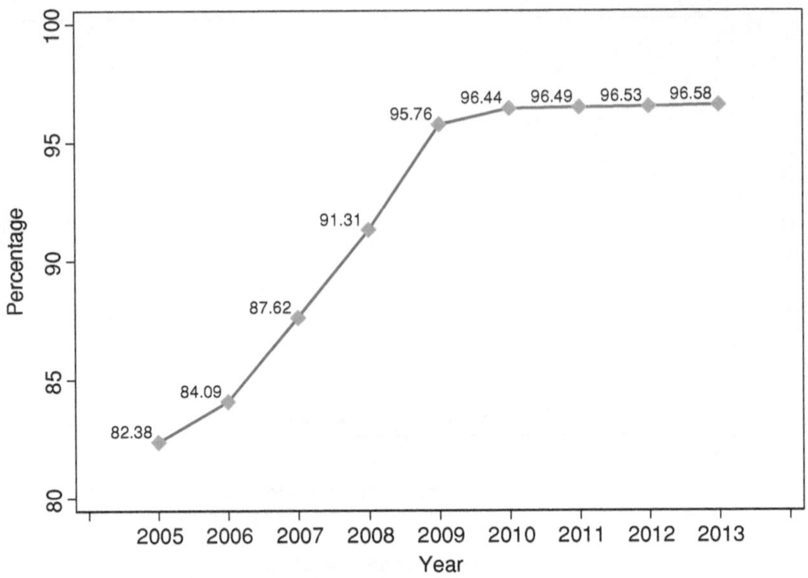

Figure 8.2 Changes in percentage of registered land in Taiwan, 2005–2012
Data Source: Ministry of the Interior Statistical Yearbook. Percentage is calculated based on the assumption that throughout the years the total size of Taiwan has always been 36,192.82 square kilometers.

2.2 Use Rights

The Taiwan Civil Code acknowledges three types of *usufruct*, or use rights: *superficies*, agricultural right, and easement. *Emphyteusis*, or permanent tenancy rights, a traditional form dating back to Roman law but rarely utilized nowadays (Hsieh 2007, p. 26; Figure 8.3),[12] was abolished in 2010 and replaced by a new agricultural right (more on this later). As noted above, land and buildings are separate real estates, which make *superficies*, or above-ground rights,[13] a crucial right in land use planning (lease is a type of contract under the Taiwan Civil Code). A building owner will need a *superficies* to legally use the underlying land. *Superficies* is legally effective upon registration. When contracting over temporary immovable property uses, many property owners still use leases, which have only *in personam* effect, resulting in lawsuits and disputes regarding building demolitions, owners of which do not have the right to use the underlying land.[14]

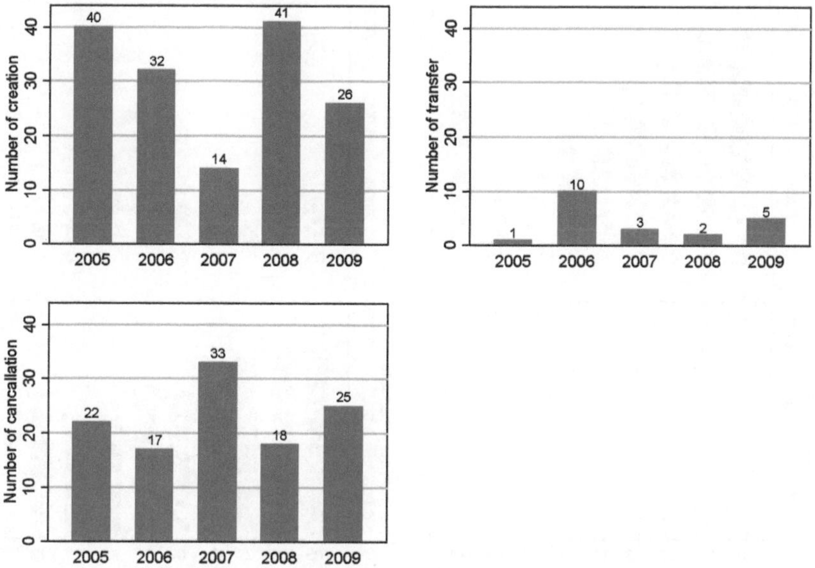

Figure 8.3 Number of *emphyteusis* registration, by registration type and by year
Data Source: Ministry of the Interior Statistical Yearbook.

Despite the ease of creating *superficies* and its *in rem* effect, in recent years, perplexingly, there was a downward trend in using *superficies* until 2012 (Figure 8.4 and Figure 8.5). The agricultural right, which has been implemented for less than five years, has yet to prove its usefulness (Figure 8.6). Before 2010, easements (or servitudes) could only be set between two land parcels. Now they can be set between any real property, such as between a house and a land parcel. Only easements appurtenant, but not easements in gross, is allowed (Su 2011, pp. 495–497). No-competition easement never took off in Taiwan; even passage easements are uncommon. As Figure 8.7 shows, easements are infrequently used,[15] though a big jump in registration in 2013 is worth noting. The amended Taiwan Civil Code (Articles 799-1 and 859-4) and Condominium Administration Act enable developers and residents to use covenants running with real properties in planning and managing condominium or large-scale neighborhoods. Doctrinally, this is a breakthrough, but the market has not picked up this tool.[16]

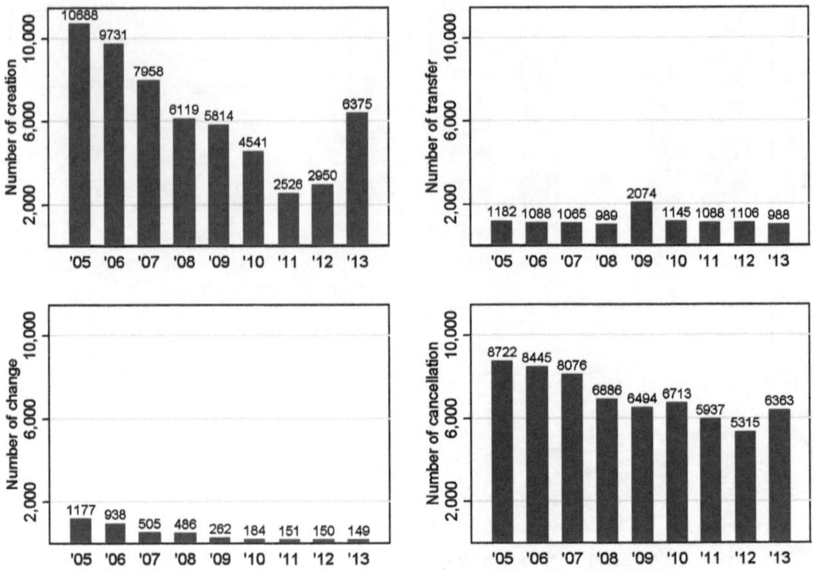

Figure 8.4 Number of *superficies* registration, by registration type and by year
Data Source: Ministry of the Interior Statistical Yearbook.

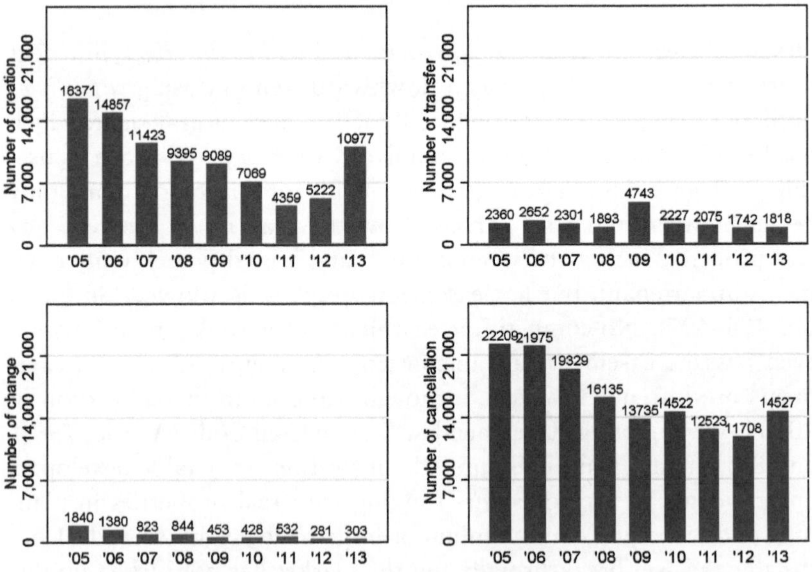

Figure 8.5 Number of land parcels affected by new *superficies* registrations, by registration type and by year
Data Source: Ministry of the Interior Statistical Yearbook.

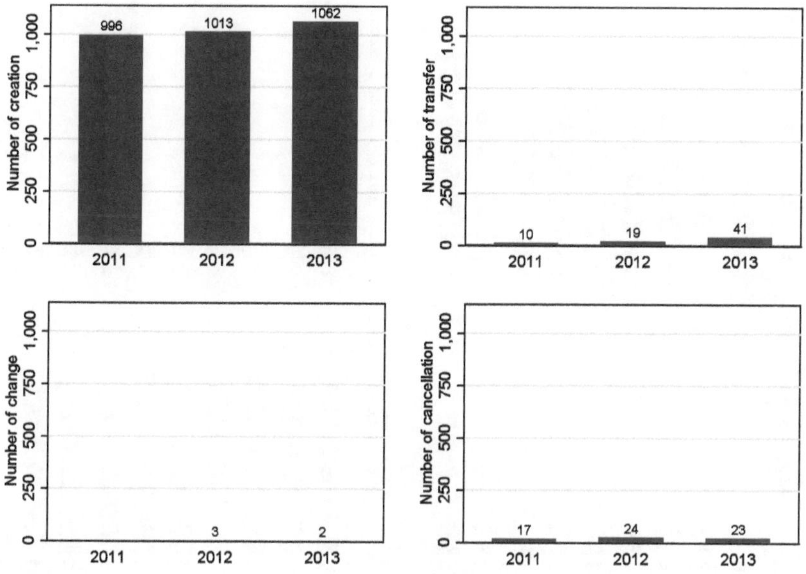

Figure 8.6 Number of agricultural right registration, by registration type and by year
Data Source: Ministry of the Interior Statistical Yearbook.

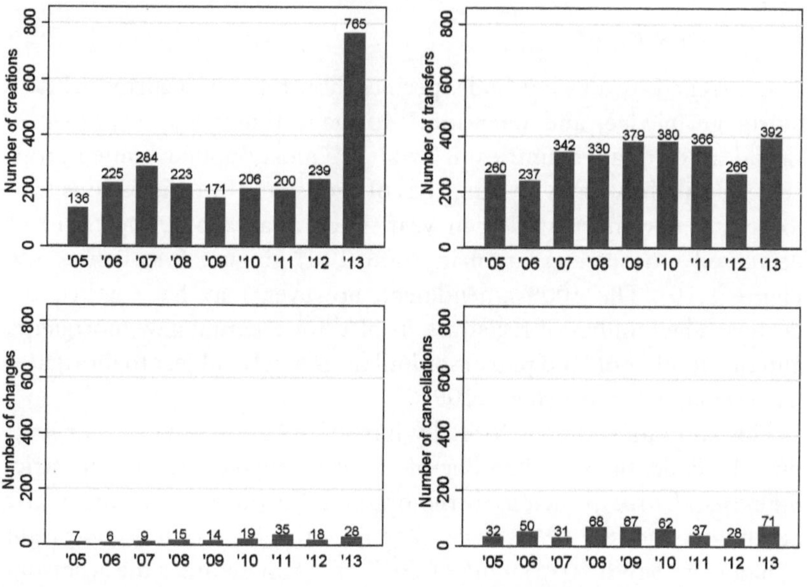

Figure 8.7 Number of easement registration, by registration type and by year
Data Source: Ministry of the Interior Statistical Yearbook.

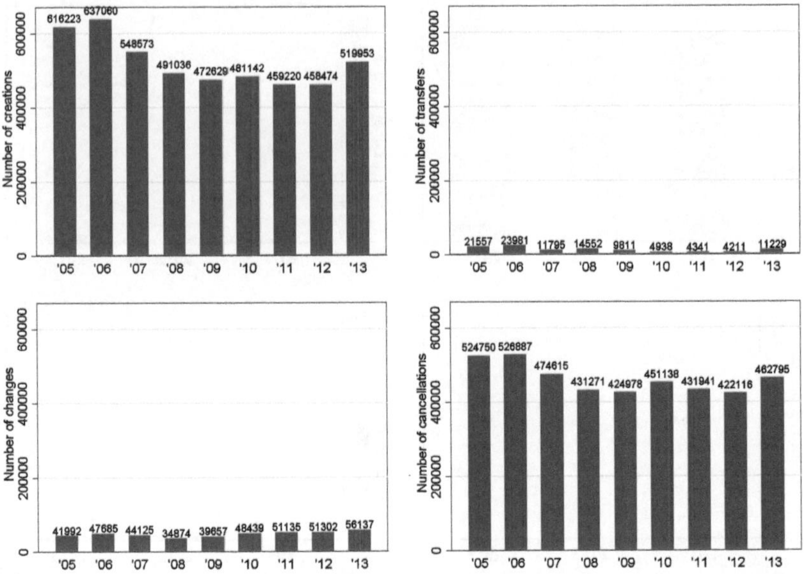

Figure 8.8 Number of mortgage registrations, by registration type and by year
Data Source: Ministry of the Interior Statistical Yearbook. Statistics include the number of ordinary mortgages and line-of-credit mortgages.

2.3 Security Rights

The current Taiwan Civil Code specifies three types of security rights:[17] mortgage, pledge, and retention. Mortgage (known as *hypothec* in European civil-law countries) is by far the most popular limited property right in Taiwan, with hundreds of thousands of registrations filed to create new mortgages each year. There was a puzzling trend of decreased mortgage creation in 2006–2009 (Figure 8.8, Figure 8.9, Figure 8.10). The 2009 amendment, however, may have halted the decline. The number of registrations filed for creating new mortgages, and the number of land parcels or buildings newly subject to mortgage, have remained stable since 2009.

The 2009 amendment formally introduced a subtype of mortgage into the code, the so-called line-of-credit mortgage. Despite the strict *numerus clausus* principle in the original Taiwan Civil Code, courts and banks since the 1960s have recognized this form of mortgage right (Chang and Smith 2015). Line-of-credit mortgage softens the accessory principle and allows both parties to stipulate the maximum amount of

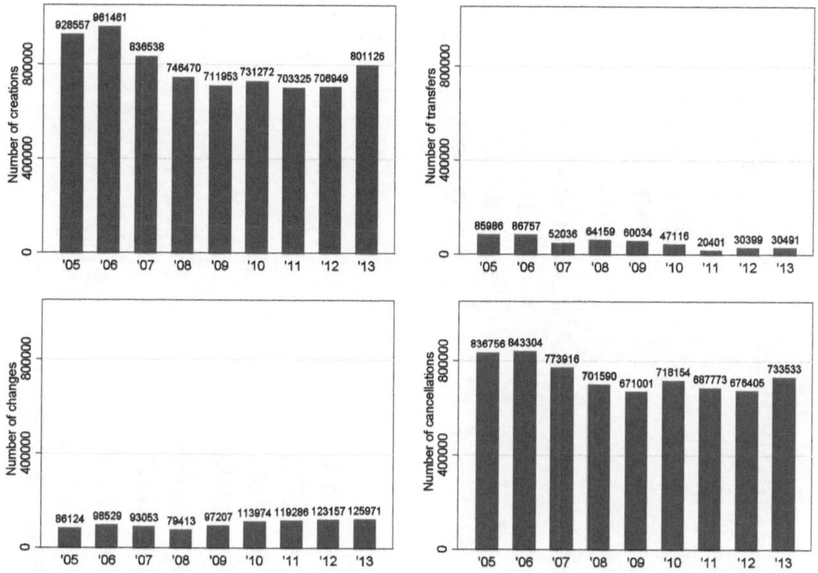

Figure 8.9 Number of land parcels affected by new mortgage registrations, by registration type and by year
Data Source: Ministry of the Interior Statistical Yearbook. Statistics include the number of ordinary mortgages and line-of-credit mortgages.

credit in the loan contract without requiring the lender to borrow out the full amount at the outset. Business lending often takes this form. By contrast, home mortgage is always in the form of a traditional mortgage. Home mortgage loans were heavily regulated even before the 2008 US Financial Crisis. As such, home mortgage payments are generally amortized.

The Taiwan Civil Code allows both pledges of things and pledges of rights, and thus the objects of property rights do not have to be corporeal. Pledge over rights is often used to borrow cash by pledging stocks. Pawning, the commercial pledge of things, was officially recognized by the Taiwan Civil Code in 2007 to be a special type of pledge subject to separate regulation. Pawn shops are to be found everywhere in Taipei City, Taiwan's capital, with advertisements that claim "everything can be pawned." Pawn shops are also in the business of chattel mortgage, which is recognized as a property form by the Personal Property Secured Transactions Act.[18] The legislators of this Act

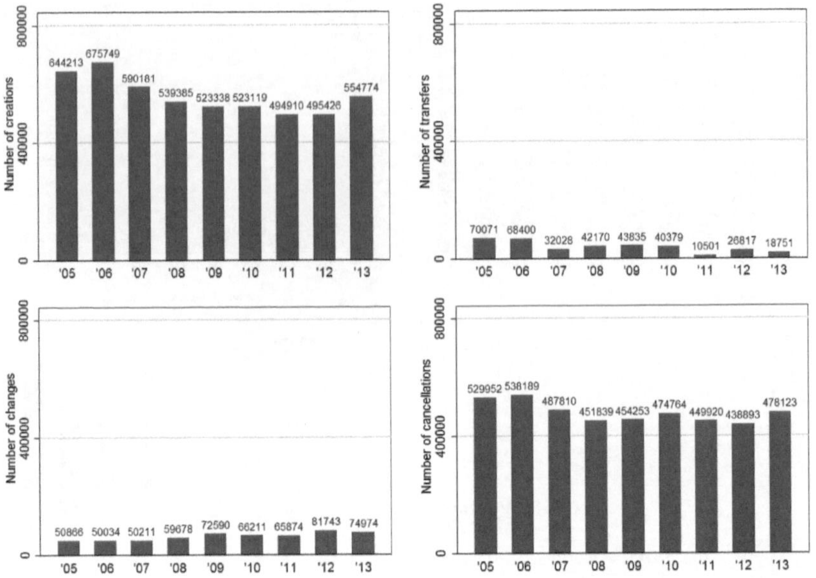

Figure 8.10 Number of apartments/houses affected by new mortgage registrations, by registration type and by year
Data Source: Ministry of the Interior Statistical Yearbook. For the definition of apartment/house, see the note accompanying Figure 8.1. Statistics include the number of ordinary mortgages and line-of-credit mortgages.

have borrowed this institution from the United States. Only certain registrable personal properties, such as motor vehicles and vessels, can be mortgaged.

Right of retention is, strictly speaking, a statutory pledge given to creditors who happen to be in possession of the lenders' movables when the latter defaults.

2.4 Dian, *a Hybrid Form*

A hybrid form, *dian* right, has been used only rarely in the past few decades. Under this system, a person pays another to use and profit from the latter's land; when the latter does not redeem the *dian* right within a prespecified period, the former becomes the owner. As Figure 8.11 demonstrates, *dian* rights are even more unpopular than the permanent tenancy right. Yet the legislature preserved this form and greatly amended the relevant stipulations in the Taiwan Civil Code,

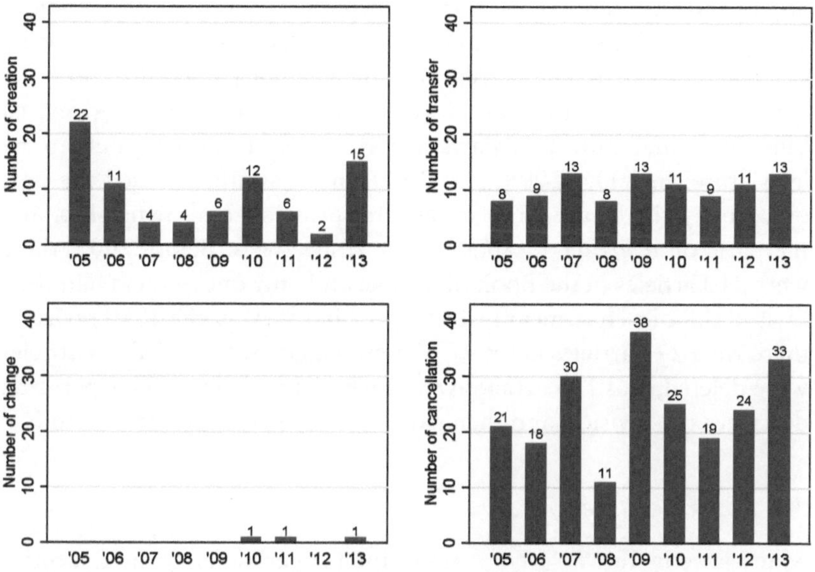

Figure 8.11 Number of *dian* registration, by registration type and by year
Data Source: Ministry of the Interior Statistical Yearbook.

hoping to rekindle interest in *dian* right (Hsieh 2007, p. 27). *Dian* right can be traced back to the Sung Dynasty in China (about 1000 years ago) (Huang 2001; Zhang 2011; Ellickson 2012), and was quite popular in Taiwan until 1923 (the later stage of the Japan colonization), when the Japanese government mandated conformation with the Japanese Civil Code (Tsai 2000, pp. 51–52; Wang 1997, p. 371; Wang 2010, p. 348), which does not recognize *dian* right. Unreported statistics (from the Ministry of the Interior Statistical Yearbook) would show that a majority of *dian* registrations from 2005 to 2012 took place in Kinmen County, an offshore island close to Mainland China and has never been ruled by Japan. Its isolation partly explains why *dian* rights are still used there.

3 The Reform in 2007–2010

The Ministry of Justice, Taiwan (hereafter MOJ), is in charge of the enactment and revision of many laws in Taiwan, including the Taiwan Civil Code. In 1988, the MOJ organized a task force composed of judges and legal scholars to draft the proposed revisions of the Book of Things in the Taiwan Civil Code. After 300 meetings over eight years, the bill was sent to the legislature but was not passed. In 2003, the MOJ organized another task force to improve the bill. This revised bill was divided into three parts which were sent out separately to the legislature. In 2007, 2009, and 2010, the legislature passed the part on security rights, the parts on general principle and ownership, and the parts on *usufruct* and possession, respectively. Before 2007, there were 210 articles in the Book of Things and only one of them had been revised since its enactment in 1929 in China.[19] After the 2010 revision, there were 277 articles in total – 82 new articles were added, 15 articles were deleted, and 135 articles were revised 137 times.[20] This part first describes the revision and then examines the driving force behind it.

3.1 Source of (New) Law

Many laws in Taiwan were revised upon suggestions by the Executive Yuan (the cabinet) or the Judicial Yuan (responsible for supervising judges, etc.). Either Yuan typically sends to the legislature a document starting with an executive summary, followed by a table that contains three columns: the current statutes, the proposed revisions, and the "underlying reasons" for amendment, article by article. These "underlying reasons" are not official (i.e. the legislature does not *pass* these reasons), but they are good sources for probing into the driving forces of legal changes.

Table 8.1 shows the typology of changes in the Book of Things. Among the 179 articles that were substantively amended, the underlying reasons for 102 of them (57 percent) indicate the influence of domestic scholarly theories, domestic court precedents, and foreign civil codes. According to my interview with Hon. Tsay-Chuan Hsieh,[21] the 77 articles that were substantively changed without a clear legal source may in fact have had an implicit source or two, but the task force considered such sources incomprehensive, ultimately leaving out the source references. Note that although a number of senior judges served in the task force – and citing court precedents as the "underlying reasons" to amend statutory laws is quite reasonable – court precedents are only cited in 18 underlying reasons.[22] By contrast, foreign laws are cited 59 times. Theories by law professors also feature in 45 underlying reasons.

Table 8.1 *Type of and Reason for Amendment in the Book of Things in Taiwan Civil Code*

Type of and reason for amendment	Frequency	Percent
Deletion	**15**	**5.0**
Textual amendment	**40**	**13.3**
Not amended	**67**	**22.3**
Substantive changes	**179**	**59.4**
Change without clear sources	77	25.6
Following scholarly theories	23	7.6
Following foreign laws	38	12.6
Following court precedents	6	2.0
Consistent with the civil code or other laws	8	2.7
Following scholarly theories and foreign laws	13	4.3
Following other combinations of scholarly theories, foreign laws, and court precedents	13	4.3
Total	**301**	**100.0**

Source: Author.

Figure 8.12 breaks down the sources of the foreign civil codes. Japanese Civil Code is the citation champion, but the number of citations actually overstates its influence, as 12 of the references concern the new property form – line-of-credit mortgage – that the Taiwan Civil Code imported almost wholesale from the Japanese Civil Code. The original Taiwan Civil Code was heavily influenced by German and Swiss Civil Codes, so their continued influence is unsurprising – references to German Civil Code concentrate on stipulations regarding ownership and general principle. The Quebec and Dutch Civil Codes inspire the task force partly because they are relatively new.[23] The underlying reasons accompanying stipulations regarding tenancy-in-common refer to multiple jurisdictions. In one case (the Taiwan Civil Code, Article 943), the task force amended an article to defect from the Japanese Civil Code to the German and Swiss Civil Code.

Chapter 2 of this book usefully categorizes convergence of law into several types: herding behaviors, legal competition among jurisdictions, coordination of legal systems, and voluntary and involuntary legal transplant. Voluntary transplant best explains Taiwan's further entrenchment of influences of foreign property laws. Herding

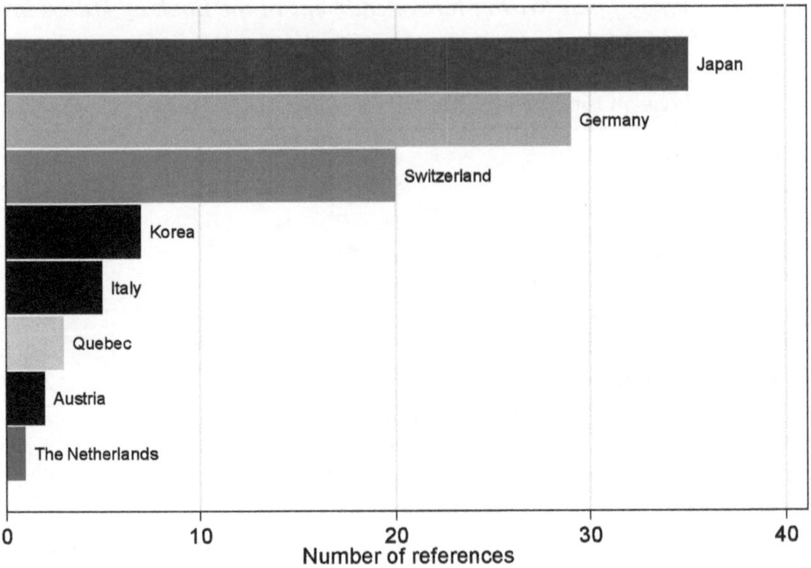

Figure 8.12 Number of references to foreign civil codes
Source: Author.

behaviors are not appropriate to describe a twenty-plus-year effort to modernize the civil code, and there is no preceding scandal or incident that has prompted the legislative reform. The notion of jurisdictional competition cannot explain recent developments in Taiwan, a centralized nonfederal regime. Property law (mostly about real estates) outside of trust law[24] hardly induces legal competition between neighboring jurisdictions, due to the immovable nature of land and buildings. The reform in 2007–2009 cannot be classified as coordination of legal systems because no international conventions, uniform laws, or model laws in East Asia are currently in place to facilitate harmonization in property law. Rather, importing "advanced" property stipulations from civil codes of developed civil-law countries – consistent with the Chinese saying "the foreign moon is rounder" (外國的月亮比較圓) – is the best descriptor of the legal changes in property law.

3.2 Legislature as Rubber Stamp

The two MOJ-convened task forces worked in a similar fashion (Hsieh 2007, pp. 18–19): they each met regularly to discuss the contents of the

Table 8.2 ***Legislative (re)action to the proposed amendment by the task force***

Legislative action	Frequency	Percent
Pass as proposed	226	75.1
Textual revision	1	0.3
Substantive revision	5	1.7
Amendment after own initiation*	2	0.7
Not amended	67	22.3
Total	301	100.0

* Strictly speaking, the two self-initiating amendments are independent of the efforts by the MOJ to revise the Book of Things, as these two amendments are quick reactions to the popular outrage over a law student who found a lost object and requested a 10 percent payment allowed by the original law.

Source: Author.

Book of Things. The first draft was circulated widely to call for comments from other government agencies, professional guilds and associations, and civil society. Based on these responses, they put together an amended second draft. The MOJ would then send the second draft to the Executive Yuan and the Judicial Yuan, which in only a very few circumstances made minor changes of their own before sending the legislative proposal on to the legislature. That is, the legislature was basically reviewing a bill that scholarly judges and scholars shaped.

Did the legislature reject the proposal as too ivory-tower in nature? As Table 8.2 shows, it did not. Of the 232 articles that the task force proposed to amend, 226 (97 percent) were quickly or eventually passed as proposed.[25] The legislature made all five substantive revisions in 2009 regarding mortgage. One explanation for the isolated activism is that a group of legislators proposed its own bill based on concrete proposals by an independent group of property researchers, so deviating from the task-force version is a low-cost alternative. Another possible explanation is that mortgage stipulations may greatly affect the business models and/or revenues for banks and real estate developers; thus, they may have lobbied under the table for or against certain revisions. Nonetheless, the big picture is that the legislature was only rubber-stamping[26] the proposal by the task force.

3.3 Legal Scholars as the Dominant Force

By now, it should be clear that scholarly judges and property professors (particularly the latter[27]) are the dominant force behind the evolution of property laws in Taiwan in 2007–2010.[28] Scant evidence, if any, exists to support the conjecture that interest groups from the business sector exerted significant influence over the amendment. Seemingly neutral and highly technical, the amendment of the civil code in Taiwan appears to constitute an atypical phenomenon in the eyes of public choice theorists.

From its inception, amending the Book of Things was the pet project of the legal elite, for doctrinal and other practical reasons, rather than being driven by any demand from civil society or the business world.[29] The Taiwan Civil Code was enacted in 1930 to govern resources in China. In the late 1980s it became clear that property transactions in modern Taiwan were wholly inconsistent with the assumption of a small-farmer, isolated economy implicit in the original Book of Things in the Taiwan Civil Code. One prominent example is when the second task force was formed, land registration was stored in electronic databases and almost all land parcels were registered. The capacity of the land registry has skyrocketed when compared with that in 1930. Negligible expenses and the huge accompanying benefits of lowering information costs make it sensible to open the door for more registrable information, and to make the registered information binding to third parties who are ignorant of the information.

By definition, a typical transaction cost story would suggest that the new Book of Things is more efficient, whereas a typical interest group story would cast doubt on whether the revised civil code increases social welfare. My story is an atypical interest group story. Law professors and scholarly judges could, of course, lobby for their own personal interests. But apart from being known as the new framers of the revised Book of Things, the personal stakes involved in shaping the new civil code are relatively low. As a result, the worldviews of these "framers" might have played a more important role. Their experience of pursuing a doctorate or master's degree in law in foreign countries (as was the case for most of them)[30] and the fact that the Taiwan Civil Code is modeled after European civil codes partly explains why foreign laws are frequently cited as authorities in the underlying reasons. Given that law professors greatly outnumbered judges in the second task force, the worldview story may also explain why "the conventional wisdom among legal scholars" is cited more often than Supreme Court precedents, which are legally more authoritative and practically more influential – albeit often criticized as flawed by scholars.

The worldview story is agnostic about whether the new code is more efficient than the old code. As at least two members in the task force (Yeong-Chin Su and Jer-sheng Shieh) frequently draw on property law and economics in their own writings, it is not unreasonable to hypothesize that changes in civil codes could be efficiency-improving. In the next part, I discuss whether the Taiwan Civil Code is evolving toward a more efficient system.

4 Toward a More Efficient Property Law

To render a conclusive evaluation of whether or not Taiwan is moving toward a more efficient property system is beyond the scope of this chapter. In the following sections, however, I shall offer a general observation and discuss in more detail two specific examples (boundary encroachment and stipulations regarding negligent good faith).

Generally speaking, the reform of the Book of Things increases efficiency. Most amendments "address local problems under local restrictions and specific determinants" (Garoupa and Ligüerre 2011, p. 291) and can be considered successful. Regarding security rights, particularly the widely used mortgage rights, the new law clarifies many doctrines and officially incorporates both the line-of-credit mortgage and the line-of-credit pledge of things. Legal certainty generally increases asset values. In addition, while the *numerus clausus* principle keeps information costs in check (Merrill and Smith 2000; Smith 2011), the number of property forms in Taiwan is so small that "frustration costs" are very high and desired transactions are hard to structure (Chang 2010). To make matters worse, without property-form trust and future interests, property law in Taiwan is hardly recursive (Smith 2011). Arguably, the number of property forms in Taiwan before 2007 was suboptimal. The 2010 amendment expanded the scope of easement (from between land parcels only to between all real estates[31]); created a new form of *superficies*, divided *superficies*,[32] which can be established on, above, and below surface; and eliminated the antiquated permanent tenancy right, replaced by a new agricultural right that arguably fits the current and future needs of residents in Taiwan. Moreover, the new legal servitude of passage doctrine excludes the applicability to land that becomes locked due to a voluntary act, greatly reducing the possibility of opportunistic behaviors (Chang 2016). Sections 4.1 and 4.2 of this chapter will discuss in more detail two examples of efficient amendment of the Taiwan Civil Code.

One might bring the task force to task for not going far enough. Easements in gross, reverse mortgages, real residential rights, etc. are not incorporated in the Book of Things. Trust and lease remain partway between contract and property. Despite the overly complicated stipulations regarding possession (Chang 2015a), the possession chapter in the Book of Things underwent no fundamental change. But considering the unprecedented large scale of reform and the many decades the task force took to finish the project, their due credit should not be taken away for these omissions.

Certain changes, however, are inefficient, and these changes appear to be correlated with ill-advised judicial precedents. (This is notably the opposite of the alleged tendency to produce efficient results by courts in common-law jurisdictions.) Regarding prescriptive acquisition of limited property rights on registered immovable properties, though it was implicitly disallowed under the original Taiwan Civil Code, a 1971 Supreme Court precedent recognized it. While it might have made sense more than forty years ago to twist the meaning of the law to allow such practice, given the comprehensive digitization of land records in Taiwan and the increasing popularity of Google Maps, Google Earth, and land-record apps developed by the Taiwan government, it arguably makes much less sense to deviate from the property rule as far as registered real estates are concerned (Chang 2014b). Yet the new Article 772 of the Taiwan Civil Code explicitly recognizes prescriptive acquisition of limited property rights on registered real properties.

Co-ownership partition lawsuits are numerous in Taiwan (with more than 1,000 lawsuits per year at the district court level; see Chang 2013). The original Taiwan Civil Code gave judges discretion to choose between partition in kind or partition by sale; partial partition such as partition in kind with owelty (i.e., compensation to some co-owners) is explicitly allowed, too. In the preamendment era, district courts have developed more than a dozen ways of partial partition methods and have used them quite frequently (Chang 2012, p. 536). The Supreme Court, however, has long preferred partition in kind. The 2009 amendment obeyed the wish of the Supreme Court, ignoring that partition in kind is not always the most efficient way to dissolve joint interests (Chang and Fennell 2014).

Finally, Section 2 of the newly enacted Article 826-1 allows covenants to use co-owned movable properties between the co-owners to run to transferees, as long as the transferees know or could have known the existence of such covenants. This stipulation codifies the doctrine invented by Judicial Interpretation No. 349 by the Constitutional Court of Taiwan.[33] The doctrine suffers from two problems (Chang 2011, pp. 1278–1280). First, for those co-owners who plan to contract for a covenant, the value of it is uncertain, as the covenant may not bind a good-faith transferee who could appear anytime. Second, many transacting parties who want no part of a restricting covenant will have to spend investigation costs to figure out whether any covenant exists (those who do not verify could be considered as the "could-have-known"). As far as movables are concerned, most of these investigations might be futile and a waste of costs.

4.1 Reducing Information Costs and Inducing Cost-justified Information Gathering

The task force does not explicitly emphasize the reduction of information costs (despite a few cameo appearances in the underlying reasons), but quite a few new stipulations do have this effect in practice.[34] In particular, the new Taiwan Civil Code allows several types of transactional terms (such as rent and limitations on the type of uses allowed) in *superficies*, servitude, agricultural rights, and mortgage to be registered,[35] and these covenants, once registered, have *in rem* effect and bind transferees. Although these stipulations cannot be used to create new property forms,[36] they better empower transacting parties to tailor their needs in an in-rem fashion, without overloading informational burdens on potential transacting third parties. This shall enhance efficiency.

Traditionally, a good-faith party is protected in property law, but the law and economic literature has started to distinguish between good-faith (without fault) and innocence (or negligently good-faith) (Landes and Posner 1996; Mackaay 2012; Sterk 2012; Chang 2014a). Innocent, or negligently good-faith, parties are those who could have known certain facts had they expended some costs in verification, when the expected benefit of verification is higher than the cost. The amendment of the Taiwan Civil Code is consistent with this line of research. In six new stipulations,[37] regarding both real properties and personal properties, parties who are either bad-faith or "good-faith out of gross negligence"[38] are treated equally – they are not protected. These stipulations shall induce relevant parties to verify titles and other information in a cost-justified way.[39]

4.2 Boundary Encroachment

The old Taiwan Civil Code contained one simple article on boundary encroachment. The 2009 amendment expanded it to three sophisticated articles (Articles 796, 796-1, and 796-2). In the optional law terminology (Calabresi and Melamed 1972; Ayres 2005; Chang 2015b), the old Taiwan Civil Code gives the encroached party the choice between Rule 1 (with a minor prerequisite) and Rule 2, and the new Taiwan Civil Code tinkers with the prerequisite and adds a "safety valve" (Smith 2009a, pp. 2128–2129; 2013) – courts can remove the option of Rule 1 after considering public and private interests.

Specifically, the new boundary encroachment doctrine is as follows: the entitlement of the neighbor whose land is trespassed is generally protected by the property rule when the encroachment is intentional or grossly negligent, as long as the neighbor objects to the trespasser as soon as she is aware of it. The entitlement, however, is only protected by the liability rule if the neighbor fails to promptly notify the negligent trespasser of her disapproval. And under the liability rule, the neighbor can either request the encroacher to purchase "the part of the trespassed land" and "the odd lot caused by the trespass" at a "reasonable price," or request payment for her losses. As a "safety valve," if the trespass is unintentional, the court, after taking into account public interests and both parties' interests, may switch from the property rule to the liability rule. The boundary encroachment doctrines apply to residential buildings and apply mutatis mutandis to other types of buildings that are "similarly valuable."

In Chang (2013d), I argued that the new boundary encroachment doctrine can better increase social welfare if the aforementioned stipulations are interpreted in the following ways: First, the prompt protest rule applies whether the construction is completed or not. Second, under the liability rule, the encroacher should pay rent, rather than torts damages, to the neighbor. Third, the reasonable price should be fair market value, rather than the underassessed official land value currently used by the court. Fourth, the precondition for the court to use the safety valve is that the encroaching part of the building is more valuable than the part of the trespassed land. The "public interest" that the court should take into account is the social benefits external to both parties' interests. Fifth, property owners usually attach subjective value to their residence. The "similarly-valuable buildings" that can be protected by the Taiwan Civil Code, Article 796 should have positive subjective value, too, whereas the "similarly-valuable buildings" that can be protected by Article 796-1 need to command a certain level of market value (with or without a positive subjective value).

It is worth noting that under the new doctrine, the prompt protest rule does not apply when the trespasser is acting in bad faith. This is an application of the *ex ante* viewpoint (Bebchuk 2001; Brooks and Schwartz 2005; Smith 2009b), which is emphasized by law and economics to increase long-term efficiency. One can reasonably either agree or disagree as to whether the exception should also apply to negligently good-faith trespassers. Given that verifying real estate information (including boundaries) in the registry has become extremely easy in Taiwan (Chang 2015b), and that an official survey, which is generally required before a builder applies for a building permit, is inexpensive (less than US$150 for most landowners) and definitive in setting land boundaries, trespassers who are unaware of the correct boundary should not be protected. A similar concern emerges as to whether the safety valve (a judicial taking of the neighbor's right to exclude) is desirable when the trespasser is innocent but not good-faith.

Although *ex post* analysis usually takes the back seat in law and economics, in a world of positive transaction costs, ill-advised entitlement allocation by courts can still decrease efficiency. With the broad and general language of the Taiwan Civil Code, Article 796-1, courts in Taiwan have wide discretion in determining whether to tear down the encroaching construction. Did courts exert this power so as to increase social welfare? Chang (2014b) observed that they did. Chang (2014b)'s empirical study uses a unique dataset that includes the population of all cases rendered pursuant to Article 796-1 since it became effective in 2009 (until 2012); at the time of writing there are 157 observations. Using descriptive statistics and a logistic regression model, Chang (2014b) finds that when the area of encroachment and the encroachment ratio is low, and the encroacher is not grossly negligent, courts tend to preserve the buildings.[40]

In sum, I argue that the new boundary encroachment doctrine,[41] if interpreted carefully, could be efficient as evidenced by recent practice. Compared to the *ex-ante*-centric old doctrine, the new doctrine tries to balance *ex ante* and *ex post* concerns. I do not claim, however, that the new law is more Kaldor-Hicks efficient than the old law, as more empirical evidence (regarding, e.g., judicial decision-making costs and transaction costs between the trespassing party and the encroached party) is required to underpin such an argument.

5 Conclusion

My analysis of the amendment of the Taiwan Civil Code in 2007–2010 contributes to the law and economics literature by demonstrating the following: legal scholars and judges can be effective in changing statutory laws. They can be considered an atypical interest group. As members of the task force, scholars and judges are semiofficial. On the other hand, their proposal in no way binds the legislature. Indeed, when another group of scholars proposed a bill of their own, the legislature made its only amendments to the task-force version of the bill. Hence, scholars and judges, particularly the former, could be considered an interest group. Frequent references to academic writings also serve as evidence that the task force behaves like an interest group.

To most, the term "interest group" has negative connotations, but interest groups do not always pursue narrow self-interest. With little personal stake in the substantive contents of the Book of Things, the task force clears away anomalous doctrines, updates an often-difficult-to-use code, and modernizes various stipulations. As a result of their efforts, the statutory amendment generally increases efficiency (yes, statutes can be efficient!). Ironically, in the few instances where the new law probably decreases social welfare, the task force drew on Supreme Court precedents as the rationales. This chapter does not argue that an exception in comparative law refutes the rule. Rather, this study should at least be counted as a cautionary tale to add new fuels to the debate on the relative efficiency of court-made law and legislature-made law.

References in Chinese

Chang, Wen-chen. 2013. An Empirical Study on the Reference of Foreign Laws and Precedents by Constitutional Court Interpretations: The Studying-abroad Backgrounds as the Key. Pp. 33–84 in *Empirical Studies of the Judicial Systems 2011*, edited by Yun-chien Chang. Taipei, Taiwan: Institutum Iurisprudentiae, Academia Sinica.

Chang, Yun-chien. 2010. Is Freedom of Property Form Principle Efficient? Interpretations of Article 757 of the Taiwan Civil Code and the Underlying Theory. *Technology Law Review* 7:119–168.

2011. An Economic Analysis of the Article 826-1 of the Taiwan Civil Code: The Distinction Between Property Rights and Quasi-Property Rights. *National Taiwan University Law Journal* 40:1255–1302.

2013c. An Empirical Study of Co-ownership Partition Cases in Taiwan: 2008–2010. Pp. 221–264 in *Empirical Studies of the Judicial Systems 2011*, edited by Yun-chien Chang. Taipei, Taiwan: Institutum Iurisprudentiae, Academia Sinica.

2013d. An Economic Analysis of Boundary Encroachment Law in Taiwan. *Academia Sinica Law Journal* 12:150–201.

2014c. An Empirical Study of Boundary Encroachment Litigation. *Academia Sinica Law Journal* 14:319–373.

2015c. Unlawful Buildings: A Theoretical Construction of the Right of De Facto Disposal. *NTPU Law Review*. 95:55–97.

Hsieh, Tsay-chuan. 2007. The Amendment of the Book of Things in the Taiwan Civil Code. *Taiwan Law Review* 100:17–33.

Su, Yeong-Chin. 2012. *In Search of New Civil Code*. Revised edition. Beijing, China: Beijing University Press.

Tsai, Ming-Cheng. 2000. The Development and Prospect of the Book of Things in the Taiwan Civil Code. Pp. 45-94 in *The Retrospect and Prospect of the Civil Code, Vol. 3*. Taipei, Taiwan: Angle.

Wang, Tay-Sheng. 1997. *Establishment of Taiwanese Legal History*. Taipei: Taiwan: Angle.

Wang, Tez-chien. 2010. *Property Law*. Taipei, Taiwan: Author.

References in English

Arruñada, Benito. 2012. *Institutional Foundation of Impersonal Exchange: Theory and Policy of Contractual Registries*. Chicago, IL: The University of Chicago Press.

Arruñada, Benito, and Veneta Andonova. 2008. Common Law and Civil Laws as Pro-Market Adaptations. *Washington University Journal of Law & Policy* 26:81–130.

Ayres, Ian. 2005. *Optional Law: The Structure of Legal Entitlements*. Chicago: University of Chicago Press.

Bebchuk, Lucian Arye. 2001. Property Rights and Liability Rules: The Ex Ante View of the Cathedral. *Michigan Law Review* 100:601–639.

Bell, Abraham, and Gideon Parchomovsky. 2001. Givings. *Yale Law Journal* 111(3):547–618.

Brooks, Richard R.W., and Warren F. Schwartz. 2005. Legal Uncertainty, Economic Efficiency, and the Preliminary Injunction Doctrine. *Stanford Law Review* 58:381–410.

Calabresi, Guido, and A. Douglas Melamed. 1972. Property Rules, Liability Rules, and Inalienability: One View of the Cathedral. *Harvard Law Review* 85:1089–1128.

Chang, Yun-chien. 2012. Tenancy in "Anticommons"? A Theoretical and Empirical Analysis of Co-ownership. *Journal of Legal Analysis* 4:515–553.

2014a. An Economic and Comparative Analysis of *Specificatio* (the Accession Doctrine). *European Journal of Law and Economics* 39(2):225–243.

2014b. To Tear Down or Not to Tear Down? An Empirical Study of Boundary Encroachment Cases in Taiwan. Pp. 144–158 in *Empirical Legal Analysis: Assessing the Performance of Legal Institutions*, edited by Yun-chien Chang. London: Routledge.

2015a. The Economy of Concept and Possession. Pp. 103–125 in *Law and Economics of Possession*, edited by Yun-chien Chang. Cambridge: Cambridge University Press.

2015b. Optional Law in Property: Theoretical Critiques. *NYU Journal of Law and Liberty* 9(2): 459–512.

2016. Hybrid Rule: Hidden Entitlement Protection Rule in Access to Landlocked Land Doctrine", *Tulane Law Review*, 91, forthcoming.

Chang, Yun-chien, Kong-Pin, Chen and Chang-ching, Lin 2016. Anchoring Effect in Real Litigations. Working paper.

Chang, Yun-chien, Weitseng Chen, and Ying Chieh Wu. 2016 forthcoming. *Property and Trust Law in Taiwan*. Alphen aan den Rijn: Wolters Kluwer.

Chang, Yun-chien, and Lee Anne Fennell. 2014. Partition and Revelation. *The University of Chicago Law Review* 81 (1):27–51.

Chang, Yun-chien, and Henry E. Smith. 2012. An Economic Analysis of Civil versus Common Law Property. *Notre Dame Law Review* 88 (1):1–55.

2015. The *Numerus Clausus* Principle, Property Custom, and the Emergence of New Property Forms. *Iowa Law Review* 100:2275–2308.

2016. Structure and Style in Comparative Property Law. Pp. 131–160 in *Research Handbook on Comparative Law and Economics*, edited by

Giovanni B. Ramello and Theodore Eisenberg. Cheltenham, UK and Northampton, MA: Edward Elgar.

Cheung, Steven N.S. 2008. *The Economic System of China*. 2nd ed. Hong Kong: Arcadia Press.

Demsetz, Harold. 1967. Toward a Theory of Property Rights. *American Economic Review* 57:347–359.

Ellickson, Robert C. 1991. *Order Without Law: How Neighbors Settle Disputes*. Cambridge, MA: Harvard University Press.

2012. The Costs of Complex Land Titles: Two Examples from China. *Brigham-Kanner Property Rights Conference Journal* 1:281–344.

Epstein, Richard A. 2002. The Allocation of the Commons: Parking on Public Roads. *The Journal of Legal Studies* 31(S2):S515–S544.

Fon, Vincy, Francesco Parisi, and Ben Depoorter. 2005. Litigation, Judicial Path-Dependence, and Legal Change. *European Journal of Law and Economics* 20(1):43–56.

Garoupa, Nuno, and Carlos Gómez Ligüerre. 2011. The Syndrome of the Efficiency of the Common Law. *Boston University International Law Journal* 29:287–335.

Hansmann, Henry, and Reinier Kraakman. 2002. Property, Contract, and Verification: The Numerus Clausus Problem and the Divisibility of Rights. *Journal of Legal Studies* 31:S373–S420.

Huang, Philip C. 2001. *Code, Custom, and Legal Practice in China: The Qing and the Republic Compared*. Palo Alto, CA: Stanford University Press.

Koo, Hui-wen. 2011. Property Rights, Land Prices, and Investment: A Study of the Taiwanese Land Registration System. *Journal of Institutional and Theoretical Economics* 167(3):515–535.

Krier, James E. 2009. Evolutionary Theory and the Origin of Property Rights. *Cornell Law Review* 95:139–159.

Landes, William M., and Richard A. Posner. 1996. The Economics of Legal Disputes Over the Ownership of Works of Art and Other Collectibles. Pp. 177–219 in *Essays in the Economics of the Arts*, edited by Victor Ginsburgh and Pierre-Michel Menger. Bruxelles: Université Librede Bruxelles.

Levmore, Saul. 2002. Two Stories about the Evolution of Property Rights. *The Journal of Legal Studies* 31(S2):S421–S451.

Lueck, Dean, and Thomas J. Miceli. 2007. Property Law. Pp. 183–257 in *Handbook of Law and Economics*, edited by A. Mitchell Polinsky and Steven Shavell: Amsterdam: Elsevier.

Mackaay, Ejan. 2012. Goof Faith in Civil Law Systems: A Legal-Economic Analysis. Pp. 103–132 in *Liber amicorum Boudewijn Bouckaert. Vrank en vrij*, edited by Jeff De Mot. Bruges: Die Keure.

Merrill, Thomas W. 2002. Introduction: The Demsetz Thesis and the Evolution of Property Rights. *The Journal of Legal Studies* 31:S331–S338.

Merrill, Thomas W., and Henry E. Smith. 2000. Optimal Standardization in the Law of Property: The *Numerus Clausus* Principle. *Yale Law Journal* 110:1–70.

Niblett, Anthony, Richard A. Posner, and Andrei Shleifer. 2010. The Evolution of a Legal Rule. *The Journal of Legal Studies* 39(2):325–358.

Olson, Mancur. 2009. *The Logic of Collective Action: Public Goods and the Theory of Groups*. Cambridge, MA: Harvard University Press.

Parisi, Francesco. 2004. The Efficiency of the Common Law Hypothesis. Pp. 195–198 in *Encyclopedia of Public Choice*, edited by Charles K. Rowley and Friedrich Schneider. New York, NY: Springer.

Ponzetto, Giacomo A. M., and Patricio A. Fernandez. 2008. Case Law Versus Statute Law: An Evolutionary Comparison. *Journal of Legal Studies* 37:379–430.

Posner, Richard A. 1973. *Economic Analysis of Law*. Boston: Little, Brown.

2011. *Economic Analysis of Law*. 8th ed. New York, NY: Aspen.

Priest, George L. 1977. The Common Law Process and the Selection of Efficient Rules. *The Journal of Legal Studies* 6:65–82.

Qiao, Shitong. 2015. Small Property, Adverse Possession, and Optional Law. Pp. 290–319 in *Law and Economics of Possession*, edited by Yun-chien Chang. Cambridge: Cambridge University Press.

Rubin, Paul H. 1977. Why Is the Common Law Efficient? *The Journal of Legal Studies* 6 (1):51–63.

1982. Common Law and Statute Law. *Journal of Legal Studies* 11:205–224.

Sitkoff, Robert H., and Max M. Schanzenbach. 2005. Juridical Competition for Trust Funds: An Empirical Analysis of Perpetuities and Taxes. *Yale Law Journal* 115:356–437.

Smith, Henry E. 2009a. Institutions and Indirectness in Intellectual Property. *University of Pennsylvania Law Review* 157:2083–2133.

2009b. Law and Economics: Realism or Democracy? *Harvard Journal of Law & Public Policy* 32: 127–145.

2011. Standardization in Property Law. Pp. 148–173 in *Research Handbook on the Economics of Property Law*, edited by Kenneth Ayotte and Henry E. Smith. Cheltenham, UK; Northampton, MA: Edward Elgar.

2013. An Economic Analysis of Law Versus Equity. Working paper.

Sterk, Stewart E. 2012. Strict Liability and Negligence in Property Theory. *University of Pennsylvania Law Review* 160:2129–2156.

Wyman, Katrina Miriam. 2005. From Fur to Fish: Reconsidering the Evolution of Private Property. *New York University Law Review* 80:117–240.

Zhang, Taisu. 2011. Property Rights in Land, Agricultural Capitalism, and the Relative Decline of Pre-Industrial China. *San Diego International Law Journal* 13:129–199.

Zywicki, Todd J., and Edward Peter Stringham. 2010. Common Law and Economic Efficiency (available at http://ssrn.com/abstract_id=1673968).

Notes

1 Official English translation of the Taiwan Civil Code is available at http://law.moj.gov.tw/Eng/LawClass/LawContent.aspx?PCODE=B0000001.

2 For the disconnection between the economics of property rights and the economics of property laws, see Lueck and Miceli (2007, p. 187).

3 Compare Wyman (2005)'s approach that emphasizes the role of political institution in establishing property rights (individual transferable quota in fishery) in order to increase economic efficiency.

4 I use the term scholarly judges to describe judges who either serve as adjunct law professors or publish legal textbooks.

5 Compare Rubin (1982, p. 207) which contends that the statute–common law distinction is one in time. That is, "in the early period most law was efficient and most law was common law. In the later period, most law was inefficient and most law was statute law."

6 Rubin (1982) has pointed out that there is no a priori reason for the inefficiency of statutes, but does not propose a general theory to predict the (in)efficiency of statutes.

7 Limited by space, this chapter is not able to fully explain the nature of each limited property rights. For a comprehensive account, see Chang, Chen, and Wu (2016).

8 I acquired a dataset from the Ministry of the Interior and calculated these statistics myself.

9 For a cliometric study that shows that introducing land registration in Taiwan under Japanese rule in the early twentieth century had increased legal certainty to title and thus increasing farmers' long-term investment, see Koo (2011).

10 Statistic from http://ebas1.ebas.gov.tw/pxweb/Dialog/Saveshow.asp (last visited 2014/2/5). Land in Taiwan at the end of 2012 was divided into 14,959,589 parcels.

11 Statistic from http://sowf.moi.gov.tw/stat/year/list.htm (last visited 2014/2/5).

12 Wang (2010, pp. 347–348) points out that the demise of *emphyteusis* should be attributed to the large-scale land reform in the 1950s, during which the land use laws stipulated that tenants received ownership –

through eminent domain and "givings" (Bell and Parchomovsky 2001) – after twenty years of leasing. Permanent tenants, as a result, essentially disappeared.

13 Above-ground rights are a literal translation. *Superficies* can, in fact, be established for developments below land surface. See the Taiwan Civil Code, Article 832.

14 The Taiwan Civil Code, Article 425-1: "The land and the house on such land belong to one person, he transfers only the ownership of land of the house to the other, or transfers the ownership of land and house simultaneously or in sequence to the different persons, the lease is presumed to be constituted between the transferee of the land or of the house and the person of transferor, or between the transferee of the house and of the land in the duration of the use of the house. The limitation of the period in the first paragraph of Article 449 shall not be applied."

The Taiwan Civil Code, Article 838-1: "Where the land and a building on such land are owned by the same person, a superficies is deemed to have been created and to exist at the time when the land and the building are thereafter sold by auction of compulsory execution to different bidder, and the rental, term, and scope of the superficies shall be determined by agreement between the parties. If such an agreement cannot be reached, the parties can apply to a court for a judgment determining these. The same rule shall apply when either the land or the building is auctioned."

15 In 1999–2004, easements were established less than 300 times each year (Wang 2010, p. 346).

16 My conjecture is that developers use *in rem* "condominium bylaws" (allowed by the Condominium Administration Act for two decades) instead of the new type of easement. In many scenarios, both function similarly.

17 Unlike many other civil law countries, the Taiwan Civil Code explicitly treats security rights as types of property forms, rather than contractual forms or intermediate forms (Chang and Smith 2016).

18 The official English translation of the Personal Property Secured Transactions Act is available at http://law.moj.gov.tw/Eng/LawClass/LawContent.aspx?PCODE=G0380024.

19 Article 942 was revised in 1995 to correct a typo.

20 Two articles regarding finders–keepers rules were amended twice each during this time frame. The second revisions were initiated by the legislators themselves, not the MOJ task force.

21 Hon. Hsieh is a former Grand Justice of the Constitutional Court and a member of the task force since 1988 (also chairing the 2003 task force).

22 I count the number of times using an article as one unit.

23 Interview with Hon. Hsieh.

24 See Sitkoff and Schanzenbach (2005) for jurisdictional competition in trust law in the United States. See Cheung (2008) for jurisdictional competition at the *xian* (county) level in China.

25 One might blame the task force for not being aggressive enough – not sending efficient but controversial proposals to the legislature. As a result, the legislature passes the uncontroversial as proposed. More on this later.

26 Note that by rubber-stamping, I do not make a normative judgment against the practice. If the task force proposed efficient or fairer revisions, why not take it wholesale? I point out the practice because rubber-stamping is unusual. I am not aware of any hard empirical evidence that proves this, but my prior research into legislative histories of various statutes in Taiwan leaves the impression that legislators often change the amendments proposed by the administrative agencies.

27 In the 2003 task force, most of the members were full-time property law professors.

28 In the past several decades, official task forces composed of legal scholars have been the driving force of most major legal reforms in Taiwan.

29 Compare Posner (2011, p. 719) who characterizes criminal codes are products of a "broad" interest group.

30 In her study on Constitutional Court Justices in Taiwan, W. Chang (2013) found that the experience of studying law abroad in a particular country statistically significantly affects which country's laws or cases a Justice cites in her concurring or dissenting opinions.

31 Note, however, that, according to my interview with an official responsible for real property statistics in the Ministry of the Interior, no local government since 2011 has reported any registration of easements between buildings.

32 See Articles 841-1–841-6 of the Taiwan Civil Code.

33 Official English translation of Judicial Interpretation No. 349 is available at http://www.judicial.gov.tw/constitutionalcourt/en/p03_01.asp?expno=349.

34 A law professor who served in the task force has emphasized the import of the expansion of registrable information (Su 2012, pp. 477, 493).

35 See the Taiwan Civil Code, Articles 836-1, 836-2, 838, 850-3, 859-2, and 873-1.

36 The Taiwan Civil Code, Article 826-1 allows registered covenants between co-tenants to run with the real properties (Chang 2012; Chang and Smith 2012). This can be used to create new property forms (Su 2012, pp. 475–480). For example, John, who wants to rent Mary's apartment for residential use in property form, can buy a small share of Mary's

apartment and use the co-tenant's covenant to arrange the residential rights.

37 See the Taiwan Civil Code, Articles 799-1(4), 826-1(2), 881(3), 899(3), 928(2), and 948(1).

38 Some articles use the phrase "could have known."

39 As noted above, the Taiwan Civil Code, Article 826-1(2) suffers from other problems, not shared by other stipulations listed in footnote 37.

40 In a sister article, Chang (2014c) finds that between 2002 and 2011, the encroaching constructions were mostly residential and nonresidential buildings, rather than fixtures like fences or extensions like garages. During that time frame, courts in Taiwan determined boundary encroachment cases in the following pattern: If part of the buildings encroached the land boundary, but tearing it down would not affect "the economic value of the whole building," courts would order the encroaching part removed. Courts rarely explicitly considered whether the trespasser was intentional, (grossly) negligent, or no-fault. It is difficult for the encroachers to persuade the court that the neighboring landowners failed to protest promptly. Courts consistently used the product of official land value and an ad hoc yield rate as compensation to the landowners. The official value, however, was much lower than market value, and the yield rates (from 1 percent to 10 percent, with 5 percent and 8 percent as the modes) do not appear to correlate with any legitimate index or standard (Chang, Chen, and Lin (2016) finds that courts suffered from the anchoring effect in determining yield rates, the anchor being plaintiffs' requests). Landowners seldom asked the trespassers to purchase the encroached land.

41 In Chapter 1 of this volume, Saul Levmore describes the new boundary encroachment doctrine as a further deviation from the "concentration strategy" to the "distribution strategy."

9 Evolution of Corporate Law in China: Mission Possible to Reform SOEs?

RUOYING CHEN*

1 Introduction

The evolution of law might take two basic paths: concentration of liability on a well-situated problem solver or, inversely, spreading or distribution of liabilities across a number of problem solvers (Chapter 1). Under such a framework, the emergence and development of law relating to business organizations in China, particularly that relating to corporations, is clearly more closely following the latter path. Among all the problem solvers, namely shareholders, creditors, and other entities represented by directors and other senior managers, shareholders are not always the ones who are to bear the ultimate risk. Meanwhile, the evolution of corporate law in China is similar to that in Taiwan, which fits well with the explanation of legal transplantation (Chapter 10) in the sense that many specific provisions borrow heavily from more advanced and mature economies. For a growth economy situated in the era of globalization to choose from an "existing menu" is not a surprising strategy. The use of such a strategy lends further support to the argument that the saving of transaction costs is the key merit of "harmonization" or convergence of laws (Chapter 2). However, China has not converged completely with either Anglo-Saxon law or German law, from which China borrowed many legal provisions

* I thank Jianlin Chen for presenting an earlier draft of this paper at the 10th Annual Meeting of the Asian Law and Economics Association held at National Taiwan University College of Law, June 20–21, 2014. I am grateful for valuable comments received from Jianlin Chen, Nicholas Howson, Yun-chien Chang, Saul Levmore, Wen Yeu Wang, and other participants at this conference. For excellent research assistance, I thank Peking University Law School graduate students, namely Jie Zheng, Thomas Smithurst, Di Huang, and Jean-François Maurice and exchange student David Kemp.

and institutional designs. It is hence interesting to inquire as to what is the driving force behind such a "pick-and-choose" approach, or selective divergence, especially in the presence of competing models and provisions.

In this chapter, I show that the driving force for these choices is a mixture of two potentially conflicting objectives. The first objective is to accommodate and unleash the power of investment from entities other than the government, such as foreign investors and later private entities. The second is to reform China's state-owned enterprises (SOEs) so as to maintain the dominance of the state-economy in China. Hence, corporate law institutions from other countries were adopted in their original form in China but only when they could serve the first general purpose. Once such institutions could potentially compromise the second objective, substantial amendment and adjustments were made.

To attain the aforementioned objectives, in addition to formal legislation and rules official announcements made by the Communist Party of China (CPC) are often used. Hence, to help understand the evolution of China's corporate law, we will refer to some key announcements made by the CPC at certain critical points in time.

To shed a new light on corporate law in China, this chapter also refers to legal and interdisciplinary empirical work. One valuable lesson that law and economics literature has taught us is that law often has unintended consequences and there are almost always gaps between law in book and law in action. We need therefore to make use of empirical tools to identify issues that have emerged from the actual operation of law. In this chapter, I introduce certain recent statistical and empirical studies on Chinese corporate law to expose issues in the actual law enforcement and implementation.

The rest of this chapter is organized as follows. Section 2 provides a brief review of the evolution of corporate law in China since the 1970s and outlines the main types of corporate entities. Section 3 addresses the rule of the piercing of the corporate veil and its judicial practice in China. Section 4 deals with three corporate governance issues, i.e., shareholders' supremacy, independent directors, and the dual-board structure. Section 5 analyzes two topics relating to the liability of corporate officers: the business judgment rule and shareholders' derivative suits. The chapter ends with a brief conclusion.

2 Reform of the Economy and the Emergence of Corporate Law

2.1 Pre-Company Law Era

For decades before the 1970s, both markets and the institutional conditions for market transactions were completely forbidden in China. After the central leaders decided to unleash the power of markets, following the sporadic and surprising emergence of market transactions, new laws were put into place to meet the needs of expanding investment and trade. In this process foreign investment was the first to be welcomed and encouraged, well ahead of purely private domestic investment. Meanwhile, law in this area has been used by the government to facilitate the reform of SOEs, turning them into more or less profit-driven business organizations rather than internal departments of the government run by bureaucrats. With a basic understanding of the goals set for corporate law, we can better appreciate why laws in this area started as fragmented sets of rules, each dealing with investment activities carried out by entities with different ownership structures: foreign-owned, domestically private-owned and state-owned. Since each of the three categories of enterprise in China had been exposed to market competition to different degrees, the purposes and goals of the rules corresponding to each category of enterprise diverged dramatically.

With domestic private enterprises and SOEs gradually catching up with foreign invested enterprises (FIEs) in China, the need for consolidation of the law also emerged. While foreign investment is still subject to certain restrictions enforced by entry permit regulations, it makes little sense to treat FIEs and domestic private enterprises differently in terms of corporate law. Meanwhile SOEs are still treated in a quite distinct manner by the government when it comes to the capital market, the financial market, the raw material market, and the labor market. This demonstrates the necessity to further reform SOEs, no matter how such reform is defined. Responding to this reality, business association law in Mainland China is converging rapidly with international practice while simultaneously remaining distinctive, as a result of its unique objective of facilitating the ongoing transition of SOEs towards becoming profit-driven entities.

From the establishment of the People's Republic of China in 1949 up until the Reform and Open-door Policy was formally implemented in the late 1970s, a substantial amount of investment was made by various government entities into enterprises wholly owned by the state. These enterprises can roughly be viewed as fully vertically integrated entities. In addition, both investment and production decisions were made more or less through government orders. It is unsurprising, therefore, that during this period the basic concepts found in the law of business organizations, such as the independence of legal persons, separate assets, limited liability, shareholders' rights, and fiduciary duty, were never referred to in Chinese law. When Chinese central leaders decided to open the economy to the outside world and to actually attract investment from outside the country, this created an urgent need for the establishment of a legal regime that was similar to that present in the investors' home countries, such as Hong Kong, Taiwan, and the United States. It is natural, therefore, that legislation in the area of business organizations first emerged to meet the needs of foreign direct investment in Mainland China at that time: the *Sino-Foreign Joint Equity Venture Law*, passed in July 1971, was effectively the first piece of corporate law since the beginning of China's opening and reform process. Subsequently, the *Foreign Equity Ventures Law* was adopted in 1986 and, in 1990, the former Ministry of Foreign Economic Relations and Trade promulgated the *Foreign Equity Joint Venture Implementation.*

Through the 1980s, parallel to the increase of foreign direct investment in China was the emergence of more private enterprises and the restructuring of SOEs. The rapid growth of township village enterprises in rural China came as a surprise to many and generated a substantial amount of new wealth and new jobs (Weizman and Xu 1994). Such a surprising success demonstrated the legitimate beneficial potential of business organizations in China and provided a strong reason to legally recognize private investment and to reform SOEs into modern business organizations. Accordingly, the Standing Committee of the National People's Congress and the State Council finally made the move to pass a company law. In 1983, the State Economic and Trade Commission and State Commission for Restructuring the Economic System prepared the first draft of a corporation law. In 1986, two draft laws were prepared: the draft *Limited Liability Corporation Law* and the draft *Share Stock Company Law.* In 1988, the State Council passed the *Private Enterprises Provisional Rules*, leaving various issues relating to SOEs for another time. Due to the same unsettled debates about how to reform SOEs, the attempt to create a general corporation law that would apply to all entities of different ownership structures was put on hold.

In 1992, Deng Xiaoping made his famous speech while visiting Shenzhen, the forefront of economic reform of China, thereby sending a strong message of getting the market-oriented reform back on track, especially with regard to SOEs. Subsequently, progress in corporate law legislation accelerated dramatically. On May 15, 1992, the State Council, together with the State Planning Commission, Ministry of Finance, the People's Bank of China, and the State Council Production Office, issued a number of joint documents outlining the framework for business organization: the *Share-System Enterprises Pilot Rules*, the *Share Stock Limited Liability Corporation Standardization Opinion*, and the *Limited Liability Corporation Standardization Opinion*. But ministry-level regulations were no substitute for national legislation, which was clearly required to protect investments, regulate internal affairs among investors and managers, and maintain economic and social order.

In August 1992, the State Council requested the Standing Committee of the NPC to review a draft *Limited Liability Corporation Law*. During the review, members of the NPC Standing Committee proposed that a corporation law covering a broad scope of entities was required to meet the needs of developing the "socialist market economy." The Legislative Affairs Commission of the State Council and relevant ministries were then ordered to produce a draft *Corporation Law*, based on the existing ordinances, standardization opinions, and the *Limited Liability Companies Law* draft.

The above brief history clearly indicates that the rules in the area for business association had been fragmented and were developed to different levels in terms of conformity with international practice, since enterprises with different ownership structures were receiving very differential treatment and were regulated by different government departments. When the reform of SOEs became a higher priority, a nationwide corporate law was called into place to turn SOEs into modern business associations that would be similar to existing modern enterprises, such as FIEs. Such a change in law, of course, benefits investment by private entities, but such collateral consequence is only a small part of the goal of the 1994 Company Law.

2.2 *The 1994 Company Law and the 2005 Company Law*

In November 1993, the CPC passed the *Decision on Establishment of a Socialist Market Economic System*, which had profound implications for China's economic and legal development over the following decades. This decision provided a clear direction to establish a modern enterprise system, noting that "to corporatize SOEs is a beneficiary experiment in establishing a modern enterprise system." This decision clearly hastened the introduction of a national law on modern business organizations. In December 1993, the NPC passed the *Company Law of People's Republic of China* ("*Company Law*").

The *Company Law* was subsequently amended on four separate occasions, in 1999, 2004, 2005, and 2013, respectively. The amendments made in 2005 were the broadest and most substantial. We hence focus on the 2005 *Company Law* but will also discuss the most recent amendment made in 2013, which touched only a particular provision with profound implications.

With the relatively narrow goal of facilitating the commercialization of SOEs and legalizing private investment, the 1994 *Company Law* was already out of date, to some extent, by the time of its official promulgation. In the ten years following the *Company Law*'s official promulgation at the end of 1993, both the Chinese market and Chinese society changed dramatically, increasing tensions between this piece of legislation and the reality of vigorous investment and trade by various entities in China. Instead of facilitating reform, quite a few provisions of the 1994 *Company Law* became impediments to further reform.

The required minimal registered capital amount to be contributed by investors in setting up a corporation was set at quite a substantial level under the provisions of the 1994 *Company Law*, with the intention of reserving the privilege of investment to SOEs. Such a high threshold made it extremely difficult for private enterprises to grow when such enterprises had been making impressive contributions to job creation and economic growth. It was therefore in the interest of the government, as well as of private entities, to have a lower threshold for setting up a business organization. Second, corporate governance rules were inadequate and the operation of these rules in China hardly supported the protection of private property and other basic promarket principles in the long run (Howson 2010). Many basic concepts of corporation law were missing, including the fiduciary duty of directors. Concurrently, limited liability protection was often abused at the expense of state-owned banks and other creditors. The absence of such concepts was particularly problematic to SOEs newly converted into limited liability companies, because the rather confusing relationship between shareholders and managers often resulted in the loss of SOEs' assets and huge losses for state shareholders. A related issue is the absence of mechanisms for protecting shareholders' interests, especially those of public shareholders in listed companies. While this issue was nearly not relevant back in 1993, the rapid growth of China's domestic stock market and the increasing number of overseas listings of Chinese companies had made this defect an increasingly pressing issue. Finally, the various restrictions and procedures set for share registration, transfer and listing of shares were simply too cumbersome to be compatible with the fast pace of a modern financial market.

Interestingly, during this period the pressure for change from the market was so intense that the first wave of recommendations for formal amendments actually came from an organization representing the voice and interests of both private entities as well as the state sector: in the "dual sessions" in March 2004, the National Chinese People's Political Consultative Conference (National PCC) members put forward certain recommendations for amending the *Company Law*. Subsequently, the State Council, ministries, a number of provincial governments, as well as enterprises and experts proposed amendments through a variety of channels. In October 2005, the NPC passed a new *Company Law* (the 2005 *Company Law*), together with a substantial amendment to China's *Partnership Enterprise Law* and the adoption of China's first securities law (the *Securities Law*), with an overwhelming majority. In many ways, this set of new legislations finally brought China in line with modern rules for business association and securities regulation, which are dramatically different from what was needed for the sole purpose of serving the reform of SOEs.

By now, SOEs have evolved from internal departments of government authorities to more or less independent commercial entities. All large-scale SOEs have implemented the corporate system and even have publicly listed shares on both international and domestic capital markets. In so doing, they have also established modern corporate governance structures (Lin and Milhaupt 2013). However, these enterprises have brought many challenges to the legal system, one of which is the lack of both effective control of, and effective incentives for the managers of SOEs.

The state-owned Assets Supervision and Administration Commission (SASAC) and its local branches are currently the controlling shareholder of 113 central-government-level nonfinancial SOEs and about 109,000 local SOEs, which hold about RMB 854 trillion (roughly US$133 trillion) in assets.[1] Financial institution SOEs are financial institutions that are similarly under the common control of the Ministry of Finance (MoF). Meanwhile, the senior management personnel of SOEs is controlled and managed by a special committee of the CPC. Hence, the CPC and the government not only control the appointment and dismissal of managers, but they also control much of the micro-level operation of companies. For example, the banking regulator in China directs the loans into or out of certain industries in order to implement macro-level economic control.

Such control has also created barriers to properly incentivizing the managers of SOEs. Since senior management members of SOEs are also part of the Chinese Communist Party and regular government systems, they are treated like civil servants, whose income level needs to be comparable with that of other public servants. For example, the SASAC and the MOF, the controlling shareholders of central-government-level SOEs and finance industry SOEs, prohibit the provision of equity incentives to executives of SOEs. The current remuneration of executives is not a true reflection of each enterprise's performance and each corporate executive's contribution. Some scholars have made legislative recommendations for the remuneration of SOE executives, including recommendations for an independent remuneration committee system (Jiang 2012). However, the incentive problem is difficult to resolve through traditional methods of incentivization. The lack of competition in the product market and capital market makes it difficult for shareholders and other external actors to see a causal relationship between corporate performance and individual executive performance (Sun, Liu, and Li 2005). With the above issues relating to SOEs remaining unresolved, laws concerned with commercial organizations in China will continue to evolve, generating new institutional arrangements and profoundly influencing market development.

2.3 Types of Corporations

The *2005 Company Law* provided for four types of companies, all enjoying the basic features of modern corporations commonly seen worldwide. Three of these are common to countries around the world: single-shareholder limited liability companies; limited liability companies with between two and 50 shareholders; and share stock companies. Listed companies must be share stock companies and are subject to a special set of rules set out in the *Company Law* and further specified in the 2005 *Securities Law*. The fourth type is rather peculiar to China: wholly state-owned companies. These companies do not have shareholders' meetings. Instead, the state-owned assets administration authorities in charge of these companies act as shareholders. In addition, union representatives must be appointed as members of the board of directors and at least one-third of members of the supervisory board must also be representatives of the union.

When multiple corporate investors with different ownership structures are involved, investors are free to choose between two forms of corporations: a limited liability company or a share stock company. Such a choice is not completely free, however, since share stock companies, which have a higher threshold for the minimal registered capital amount, a higher maximum number of shareholders, and more flexibility in terms of transferring shares, are often required for various purposes. For example, the form of a share stock company must be adopted in order to list and trade shares in a stock exchange. Many industrial regulators also require qualified candidates to take the form of share stock companies.

Outside the *Company Law*, legal instruments for business organizations can be divided into two broad camps: domestic enterprises and foreign-invested enterprises. In the case of domestic enterprises, three legislative instruments are available under the *Partnership Enterprise Law*:[2] partnership enterprise, individual proprietorship enterprise and individual industry and household business. Investors in these three forms of business organization do not enjoy the protection of limited liability. It is also worth noting that partnership enterprises in China do not enjoy *per se* tax advantages relative to the four types of companies created under the *Company Law*. Such a tax rule may explain why the use of partnership enterprises has not become as popular as in other jurisdictions.

For foreign-invested enterprises, there are also three instruments, all of which are governed by a set of national legislations implemented through a set of regulatory rules. The first one is the Sino-foreign equity joint venture company (EJV)[3] and the second one is the wholly foreign-owned equity joint venture company (WFOE).[4] Both are similar to limited liability companies under the 2005 *Company Law*. The third type is the Sino-foreign cooperative joint venture (CJV), which is created by contract and is not a separate legal entity from its investors. The EJV law was promulgated in 1979 and substantially amended in 1990 and 2001 subsequently. The WFOE laws almost went hand-in-hand with the EJV law. CJVs rarely have been used except in the case of greenfield projects in oil and gas exploration, given that this form does not generate separate legal personality and that the investors do not enjoy limited liability protection. The CJVs, EJVs, and WFOEs are often collectively referred to as FIEs.

The establishment of FIEs has been subject to discretionary approval by the foreign-investment regulators, in addition to any industry-wide regulatory approval necessary for both domestic enterprises and FIEs. The FIE regulation has been conducted according to an industry-specific catalogue, which divides industries into three types: prohibited, restricted, and encouraged. Such approval regime has been liberalized over the years, especially upon China's accession to the World Trade Organization in the year of 2001. Since the formation of the Shanghai Free Trade Zone in August 2013, China has been slowly moving toward the "negative list approach," i.e. lifting the regulatory requirements in general, except for a small number of listed industries. Such a trend is clearly consistent with the market-oriented reform of SOEs and the encouragement of the establishment of domestic private companies.

While FIEs have historically enjoyed enormous privileges, such as discounted tax rates, subsidized prices for land use rights, and even financial subsidies, such differential treatment is largely unavailable nowadays. The consolidation of corporate law rules applying to FIEs and other enterprises has started and is likely to accelerate over time.

3 Piercing of the Corporate Veil in Limited Liability Companies: Statutes and Judicial Decisions

The core task of any corporate law regarding limited liability companies is to protect insiders against outsiders, where information about such companies is difficult and costly to obtain for outsiders. In protecting outside creditors, China used to focus on *ex ante* measures, such as stringent minimal registered capital requirements, instead of *ex post* ones, such as piercing the corporate veil. But China has eliminated the minimal registered capital requirement in 2014, making measures of the latter category ever more important.

3.1 Statutory Rules

The term of "piercing the corporate veil" (Ci Po Gong Si Mian Sha) does not appear in any Chinese statute. However, the 2005 *Company Law*, for the first time in China, introduced the rules making it possible to achieve the same results as piercing the corporate veil: "if a shareholder of a corporation exploits the independent legal identity of the corporation and shareholder limited liability to evade debt, and in so doing seriously injures the interests of a creditor, such a shareholder shall bear several and joint liability for the debt of the corporation" (Art. 20). In addition, since the abuse of limited liability protection by insider shareholders is most common for single-person limited liability companies, Article 63 of the *Company Law* specifically addressed such a situation and shifted the burden of proof from creditors to the single-person shareholder: "if the shareholder fails to ensure that assets of the company are managed independently from his own assets, such a single-person shareholder shall be held liable for the debt of the company."

Almost a routine method in lawmaking in China, long before these principles were codified in the *Company Law*, the Supreme People's Court of China (the Supreme Court) had already been using "judicial replies," requesting lower courts to implement what essentially is the principle of piercing of the corporate veil. After the passage of the 2005 *Company Law*, existing judicial practice continued. In 2013, the Supreme Court also published a guiding case to provide more detailed guidelines for lower courts to follow.[5]

3.2 Judiciary interpretation

The Supreme Court shaped judicial practice of this principle through three circulars, issued in 1994, 2001, and 2002, respectively.[6] All such guidance was issued to enforce a rigid capital rule, which required each company to have a minimal amount of registered capital and all shareholders to contribute to a company's registered capital in certain statutory forms and in full. The purpose was to enforce such a rigid regime, which was a very sensible decision since nearly all creditors were then state-owned banks.

The 1994 guidance[7] dealt with the major issue of whether a corporate shareholder should be required to be liable for a company's debt when the enterprise has ceased to exist, either legally or as a business reality. It completely excluded the possibility of piercing the corporate veil when the debtor company was continuing to operate but is becoming an increasing concern to its creditors. Three separate scenarios were identified and dealt with in different ways. For the latter two scenarios, the basic measurement that emerged was whether the company's actual paid-in capital amount was no less than the minimal registered capital requirement under the law. This seemed a sensible choice, given that China had long been enforcing a regime of statutory minimal registered capital, abolished only in 2014. The doctrine of piercing the corporate veil had been applied to serve the purpose of enforcing this rigid regime of the minimal registered capital requirement set out in statutes.

The first scenario is where the business license of a corporation has been revoked. Even though the revocation of a business license almost always results from the failure of the business or from some form of corporate irregularities, the Supreme Court cited an Article of the *General Principles of the Civil Law* and affirmed the independent legal personality of the problematic corporation, including its ability to assume its own debt independent of its shareholders.

In the second scenario, the paid-in capital amount of a company is less than its registered capital amount, which is equal to, or greater than, the minimal registered capital amount required under Article 15 s (7) of the *Enterprise Registration Ordinance Implementation Rules* or other relevant rule. In absence of other factors affecting the legal independent personality of the company, the Supreme Court affirmed the independent legal personality of the company. However, it specified that the shareholders shall be liable for paying the company's outstanding debt, which is the difference between the actual paid-in capital and the registered capital, if the enterprise's assets are not sufficient to pay its debt at the time when its business license was revoked or when the company went out of business.

The third scenario is one in which a company either did not receive any contribution of capital from its shareholders or in which the actual paid-in capital amount is less than the statutory minimal amount of registered capital. The Supreme Court ruled that the company has lost its independent legal personality and that shareholders shall assume full liability for all the outstanding debt of the enterprise.

The Supreme Court also tried to deal with a widespread practice: shareholders often withdrawing or transferring funds or otherwise concealing property to prevent the company from repaying its debt. The Supreme Court ruled that such shareholders shall be required to return the funds so withdrawn or transferred or the property concealed, and shall cause the company to apply the returned funds or property to repay its debt.

Relating to the issue of independent legal personality, the Supreme Court affirmed the independent legal personality of companies properly set up by the military, police forces, a politico-legal authority, or political party. Mergers and acquisitions peaked in the period from the partial privatization of SOEs in the 1980s through to the 1990s. A recurring legal issue, which emerged at that time, was how to deal with the debt of the target entity being acquired. The Supreme Court affirmed that the controlling shareholder, who acquired the control through a recent acquisition of the target company's shares, should not be held liable for the debts of the target company. However, if withdrawal of funds or debt evasion by the company's controlling shareholder has caused the target company to be unable to repay its debt, such a controlling shareholder shall be liable for all the debts of the target company.

Following the passage of the 2005 *Company Law*, the Supreme Court published a guiding case on the "mixing of legal personalities," which essentially extended the application of the concept of piercing the corporate veil to affiliated firms such as sister companies, if it has become impossible to distinguish their respective assets. Under such circumstances, the affiliated companies are considered to have lost their respective independent legal personalities due to the mixture of employees, business, and financial matters. If the mixture of legal personalities has seriously damaged creditors' interests, these companies shall be both jointly and severally liable for each other's debts.

3.3 *Judicial Practice – Through the Lenses of Statistical Study*

Lower court decisions involving this issue seemed common, at least based upon two recent empirical analyses of such cases (Chen 2011; Huang 2012). It is, therefore, a fertile land for scholars to explore interesting questions, such as how lower courts reacted to the vagueness in the statutory provision and Supreme Court guidelines, or how to evaluate the basis upon which lower courts grounded their decisions on a normative basis. Study of these decisions might provide some clues to help in answering these questions. However, in the Chinese context the empirical study of judicial decisions can be tricky. Before January 1, 2014, Chinese courts were under no general obligation to make their decisions available to the public[8] and the implementation of this new requirement has not been automatic. Therefore, to identify a sizable dataset can be challenging, without even considering the various selection biases coming from all directions. Bearing in mind this caveat, however, it is still worth looking at the two empirical analyses of judicial decisions done by Chen (2011) and Huang (2012).

Chen (2011)'s study covers judicial decisions in 103 cases available to the public, which were issued between the years 2006 and 2010, with reference to Article 20 of the *Company Law* on piercing the corporate veil. He found that Chinese courts seemed twice as willing to pierce the corporate veil as US courts, with a proportion of 84.5 percent. On the other hand, practice in China presents some similarities with that in the United States. This is consistent with Huang's findings based upon a dataset of 99 judicial decisions: the rate of success in piercing the corporate veil was about two-thirds in China, compared with 40 percent in the United States, 47 percent in the United Kingdom, and 38 percent in Australia. However, the higher rate of piercing the corporate veil in no way implies that Chinese courts are more active than courts in other countries for at least one reason. When the controlling shareholder are either state-owned entities or the government itself, it is not hard to imagine the difficulty for creditors to litigate in court for the piercing of the corporate veil in such a case.

Chen (2011)'s study also suggested that lower courts seemed to be following the guiding case of the Supreme Court: in both arenas capital deficiencies and the confusion of corporate identity and assets emerged as the two main reasons cited by the courts in deciding to pierce the corporate veil, with each of these two reasons appearing in about one-third of the 103 cases respectively. In particular, in a few cases, the court concluded that one entity exercised excessive shareholder control over another company because they were "having two corporate brands but run by the same set of people." The "mixture of financial affairs" was found with evidence of a blurring of the distinction between the personal income and expenditures of shareholders with assets of the corporations, e.g. bank accounts opened in a shareholder's name being used for depositing revenue derived from corporate transactions. The third most popular reason claimed by lower courts, in about one eighth of the cases, has been that the shareholders failed in their obligation to properly liquidate the company, hence damaging creditors' interests.

The focus of both the Supreme Court and lower courts on the share capital of companies, as compared with the statutory minimal registered capital, has drawn very different reactions from scholars. Some argued that it is an understandable and actually reasonable measure, while others fiercely criticized it.

Xi (2011), for example, treats the *Company Law* provision and court practice as a given and offers an explanation regarding both how these decisions came about and what function the courts' opinions might be serving. In doing so, he painstakingly documented the "legislative" history of the statutory provisions and Supreme Court guidelines and told a convincing story of political compromise made by the court in front of powerful government and nongovernment entities in China. Such a case study is often regarded as being too hard to carry out in China, due to the relatively low level of transparency in legislative and government decision-making processes. Xi (2011)'s research stands out with rich and detailed facts and sharp analysis and shall be followed by more studies of a similar kind. Interesting questions remain to be answered – e.g., how such political interaction would shape the future of this rule as well as other corporate law rules. In the opposing camp, Ge (2011) proposes that the above criterion was flawed because the following possibility was completely ignored: that some shareholders may commit fraud against other shareholders. Ge hence argued that the courts were too favorable to creditors and too harsh to the innocent shareholders.

Another challenge faced by the court in applying the criteria of capital contribution is that the 2014 *Company Law* has essentially abandoned the requirement of a statutory minimal registered capital. The court would have to either completely give up the approach of looking at capital contributions by shareholders or face the thorny question as to whether any discrepancy between the paid-in capital and subscribed capital could warrant the piercing of the corporate veil. Choosing the latter would be a major deviation from current court practice.

In all, imposing statutory requirements regarding minimal registered capital and piercing the corporate veil are both tools with the objective of protecting the interests of outside investors in closely held corporations. The courts' attempt to enforce the *ex post* measure (piercing the corporate veil) through the enforcement of the *ex ante* measure (statutory minimal registered capital) is problematic. This paradox will eventually disappear with China's abandonment of the capital requirement in its most recent amendment to the *Company Law*. However, the question of how to protect outside investors (including outside creditors) in closely held corporations remains a substantial legal challenge in China, given that other protective tools remain largely undeveloped, such as the antifraud rule and reputational sanctions in the financial market. For this reason, it is worth paying close attention to how the court practice of piercing the corporate veil further develops.

4 Corporate Governance Structure

For companies with numerous shareholders, the core task of company law is to mandate a proper corporate governance structure. To a large extent, the 2005 *Company Law* achieved this goal by importing the basic corporate governance principles prevalent in the global market. Two examples are relevant here. The first is the adoption of the principle of shareholder supremacy. The other is the mandatory requirement of having independent directors. Meanwhile, certain unique justifications exist in China for seemingly global institutional design, and China produced certain institutional innovation, such as the dual system of a supervisory board and a board of independent directors.

4.1 Shareholder Supremacy or Director Supremacy?

Both as a statutory matter and as a strong tradition in judicial practice, China has clearly adopted the principle of shareholder supremacy. First, the Company Law leaves all residual power of decision-making in the hands of the shareholders. Second, members of the board of directors face disproportionate obligations and corresponding liability, even though they do not enjoy the ultimate decision-making power. Third, directors are not protected by anything akin to the business judgment rule (Deng 2013). Deng (2013) challenges the principle of shareholder supremacy and gives two convincing accounts of why adopting the principle is a mistake. First, China learned from other countries about corporate structures from a purely functional perspective, without any proper understanding of the corresponding institutional origins. Foreign precedents were introduced to increase China's wealth level and market force and no analysis about the rationale underlying the system design was carried out. In terms of research methodology, Chinese focused more on comparing texts of rules than on interpretation grounded in theory. Furthermore, Deng (2013) contends that the *Company Law* drafters cloned China's political decision-making structure into corporate law, which is clearly unsuitable for commercial entities. More specifically, the relationship between shareholders and directors mimics that of the National People's Congress and the State Council, because commercial decision-making in SOEs is a natural extension of the internal decision-making of the CPC.

Given the history of evolution of China's corporate law as set out in Section 2 of this chapter, the drafters of the *Company Law* clearly had SOEs in mind when they designed the ideal corporate governance structure. While modern theory of firms views the agency problem of corporate officers as a result of incomplete contract between entities of equal footing (Hart 1988), this is definitely not the case for shareholders and corporate officers of SOEs. For SOEs, shareholders and corporate officers are in a hierarchical relationship in the political structure. The shareholders' appointment of board members is not a contractual choice, but an administrative act of selection and appointment in a bureaucracy. Protecting the state shareholder's interests and ensuring the state shareholder's control of the enterprise are clearly of the utmost importance. These complex administrative relations and unique property interests of the state have been embedded in the *Company Law*.

Such a theoretical foundation and institutional origin created a strong tension between protecting the state-controlled shareholders and protecting the company's interests as a whole, not to mention the protection of the interests of minority and public shareholders. While it does make some sense to translate state supremacy into shareholder supremacy for SOEs controlled by the state, this is hardly the case when it comes to non-SOEs. The constraints and daunting liabilities faced by directors in non-SOEs are clearly producing a chilling effect and do not provide the right set of incentives for sensible business judgment and proper risk-taking activities by commercial entities.

4.2 Dual-Board Structure – Board of Supervisors and Independent Directors

The 2005 *Company Law* formally provided for a supervisory board and an independent board of directors to operate as a dual-board governance structure. A supervisory board is required for all SOEs and listed companies. An independent board of directors is a statutory requirement for listed companies. For SOEs and listed companies, the supervisory board is required to include union representatives.

It is worth noting that years before the passage of the 2005 *Company Law*, both systems had already been experimented with SOEs. The dual system reflected an interesting combination of the German-style two-tier board structure and the Anglo-Saxon model focusing on independent supervision of agency activities. Almost as if based upon a rather naïve intuition that combining the models would double the effect, the two systems were originally put into place together with the aim of dealing more effectively with serious agency problems in SOEs. Both boards were required to include representatives of the CPCs and state-assets regulatory authorities. Few discussions, however, were held as to whether the benefits of workers' participation would outweigh its costs (Hansmann and Kraakman 2001) and whether the effect would indeed be doubled or be cancelled out. Interestingly, we probably do not have to worry about any potential conflicting or offsetting effect between the supervisors/union representatives and independent directors, because the institutional orientation and function of unions in China are quite different from those in the West. Union officials are empowered by and responsible to the CPC and the government administration and thus may be discouraged from working for union members to maintain social stability and economic growth. Unions are not allowed to become strong enough to form an adversary power relative to the CPC. Concurrently, in order to promote economic performance and attract investors, especially foreign ones, government urges unions and workers to cooperate with rather than confront management (Metcalf and Li 2005).

Another rule that exemplifies the effort of drafters in using corporate law to reform SOEs is that the members of a state-owned corporation's supervisory board and board of directors must be appointed by the state assets management authority. In public companies in which the state is a controlling shareholder, such appointment authority translates into the right to nominate. Since the controlling shareholders do not have to abstain from voting on the appointment, they could effectively place their representatives on the boards, rendering it extremely difficult, or even impossible, for other shareholders to be involved in the composition of the board.

4.3 Independent Directors

Before the enactment of the 2005 *Company Law*, the China Securities Regulatory Commission (CSRC) had already imposed a mandate requiring all listed companies to appoint independent directors.[9] Under the *Company Law*, at least one-third of the board of directors of a listed company must be independent directors, including at least one qualified accountant. Any shareholder who individually or jointly holds more than 1 percent of the publicly issued shares in the listed corporation may nominate one candidate.

CSRC and the stock exchanges issued various rules to ensure the quality and independence of directors, including imposing a discretionary approval procedure for screening candidates to the position of director. Each listed company must seek approval from the CSRC and the stock exchange for every candidate to the position of board member. To get such an approval, the listed company must provide relevant information about the candidate in order to prove his/her qualification and independence. Only upon receiving the approval may shareholders proceed with voting on the appointment. An objection from the CSRC would constitute a veto against appointing the candidate as an independent director, though shareholders may still vote on appointing the candidate as a nonindependent director.

The effectiveness of independent directors is an empirical matter that may depend to a large extent on the actual circumstances of the economic and political background of a given society. China's economic and political setting, especially the extensive presence of SOEs, presented challenges with regards to corporate governance. The lack of detailed regulatory and judicial decisions made such a study particularly hard, but public information about listed companies has provided a unique source of information for this purpose. Even though these studies do not provide consistent and integrated conclusions, they at least showed what factors might be more effective. For example, the use of accounting experts and the curbing of transactions between related parties by independent directors are critical, while the number of independent directors seems not to make any significant difference. These valuable insights are certainly necessary for formulating amendments to law as well as new policies in the near future.

Xiaoping Xu (2011) applies regression models to a sample of companies listed during the period of 1999 to 2009 in China. He found that there is a positive correlation between the number of independent directors and the market value of the corporation, but that such correlation is not statistically significant, and that there is no sufficient reason to believe that the number of independent directors would enhance firm value. Xu (2011) also finds that independent directors have curbed the ability of management and majority shareholders to sacrifice investor interests for personal gains and have increased the firms' efficiency in using investors' capital. In addition, his study confirmed the possibility that an increase in the number of independent directors may strengthen corporate governance and protect investors.

However, other scholars reach less optimistic conclusions. For example, Wu (2010) studies all companies listed on the Shanghai and Shenzhen stock exchanges from 2005 to 2008 and finds that: (1) the relative proportion of the board made up of independent directors has little impact on corporate performance; (2) the higher the remuneration that the independent directors received, the more dedicated they were in providing service for the firms' development, proving effectiveness of incentive-based regimes for independent directors; (3) the presence of an audit committee, a remuneration committee, and a strategy committee correlates positively with earnings per share, but the presence of a nomination committee is irrelevant to earnings per share; and (4) the relative proportion of the board made up of independent directors has a limited impact on remuneration of directors and senior managers.

To access the effectiveness of independent directors, especially those with professional qualifications in accounting, Mao (2012) takes all the cases targeting A-share companies during the period of 2006–2009 where CSRC found irregularities in financial reporting. He finds that the proportion of accounting experts among independent directors and audit committee members of a listed company is positively correlated to more professional oversight and thus negatively correlated with financial reporting irregularities.

Gaoyan Xu (2011) studied nonfinancial insurance companies listed in the A-share market of the Shanghai and Shenzhen stock exchanges during the 2001 to 2007 period and used regression analysis to test whether independent directors could curb connected transactions, thereby improving both corporate governance and firm performance. He found that the reputation, the professional background, and the relative size of independent directors had a significant effect on curbing the connected transactions of higher value, but not the lower-value connected transactions. Second, the level of independence of the independent directors helped enhance firm value, even though such increases in value may not have been achieved simply through curbing connected transactions. While confirming the slight positive value of the independence of independent directors, his study revealed the prevalence of strategic behavior in the market in slicing big transactions into smaller ones.

5 Duties of Corporate Officers

Enforcement of the duty of corporate officials is critical to the success of any corporate law, and derivative lawsuits are a typical tool in realizing this goal. At the same time, however, we need to make sure that officers will not be deterred too much, thereby losing the incentives to make active judgment decisions that would profit shareholders, among other stakeholders. Current rules, at least in the book, are focusing too much on deterrence and not enough on incentives.

5.1 Business Judgment Rule

Fiduciary duty has been stipulated under the *Company Law* (Arts. 147, 148, 149), the *Securities Law* (Art. 152), and the *Bankruptcy Law* (Art. 125). Meanwhile, as Howson (2014) pointed out, many gaps in the law have now been filled not by judicial decisions but by the CSRC through regulatory rules.

Other than the liability for damage, the *Company Law* provides for the right of the company to recoup the personal gains made by directors, supervisors, and senior management when such gains have resulted from breaches in their fiduciary duty. If a director, supervisor, or senior manager of a listed corporation fails to fulfill his duty of care, causing a securities investment corporation to seriously infringe the law or regulations or to incur substantial risks, the CSRC could revoke his professional qualification and order the company to replace him. China's *Bankruptcy Law* stipulates that when a director, supervisor, or senior manager violates his fiduciary duty or duty of care, causing his enterprise to go bankrupt, he shall be liable for civil damages and may be barred from being appointed as director, supervisor, or senior manager for three years, starting from the completion of the bankruptcy proceedings. However, Chinese law does not have a statutory business judgment rule such as the one defined by Anglo-Saxon courts. Meanwhile, scholars indicated that Chinese courts were in fact implementing the spirits of such a rule in adjudication (Luo 2010).

5.1.1 Stringent Approach taken by Court and CSRC

With respect to the specific criteria of judicial review of duty of care of corporate officers, Chinese courts diverted dramatically from the American courts (Luo 2010). In particular, American courts have come to a consensus that courts shall only review the procedure of corporate decision-making, but Chinese courts tend to conduct a detailed review of substantive matters of corporate decisions.

In fact, the statutory criteria for breaching the duty of care have gone in the opposite direction from the liberating spirits of the business judgment rule. Chinese company law simply substitutes the subjective measure of business judgment by directors with objective criteria. Under China's *Company Law*, the duty of care would be regarded as being breached if: (1) the resolutions of the board of directors of the company violated the law, administrative regulations or articles of association; and (2) such a resolution caused serious losses to the company. However, a carve-out for liability for breach of duty of care is provided: if the meeting minutes recorded expressive objection to the relevant resolution by a party, said party shall be waived of any liability for breach of duty of care (Art. 113(2)). In other words, if one did not object to a certain resolution at the time of passing such a resolution, one will be held liable for breach of duty of care if the resolution is found, *ex post*, to be in breach of law, administrative regulations, or articles of association. Such an approach has been criticized as imposing too heavy a burden on directors, supervisors, and senior managers (Ren 2008).

According to Zhang and Shi (2013), the courts in China have taken just such a strict approach in their decisions. Even though the statutory provisions have ruled out factors other than legal compliance by the company and losses caused to the company, courts did take into account other factors in defining the scope of liability and in deciding the liability's monetary value.

Similarly, CSRC refused to recognize such a subjective criteria proposed by a sanctioned independent director and insisted instead on an objective criteria of due care. Such an approach would definitely cause serious chilling effects on potential candidates, especially those for the position of independent director.

5.1.2 Interpretation of the Adoption of Objective Criteria

Legislators, courts, and CSRC have all chosen an objective criterion in enforcing duty of care and have refused to provide a safe harbor for directors with respect to specific circumstances and the different level of skills of directors. One potential reason for this relates to the widespread existence and dominance of SOEs and the fact that corporate officers of SOEs are mostly appointed by the government rather than being selected through competitive mechanism in the labor market. For SOEs, corporate officers are appointees of the state shareholder, who are themselves state officers or quasi-state officers. Their appointment is usually not a result of market competition on the basis of their individual merits and capabilities, but that of a bureaucratic decision-making process. It is hence natural not to take into account the individual capabilities of corporate officers of SOEs when the court carries out *ex post* review of decisions made by such officers. Moreover, government interference at the level of day-to-day decision-making process is not an uncommon experience for SOEs. Government often implements policy initiatives and allocates resources by directing the investment of SOEs into certain types of projects or into certain regions. Therefore, corporate decisions are often made to meet such policy requirements or to take advantage of financial incentives provided by the government. These decisions can hardly be attributed to the attention and capability of individual corporate officers. Under such circumstances, an objective criterion probably makes more sense because it reflects the commonality rather than the difference among different corporate officers.

5.2 Shareholders' Derivative Suits: Rules and Practice

One widely appraised achievement of the 2005 *Company Law* is the creation of a shareholders' litigation regime (Art. 151). No threshold is imposed for shareholders of a limited liability company to bring such lawsuits. For a share stock company, the plaintiffs must, individually or jointly, hold more than 1 percent of the company's shares for more than 180 consecutive days, which is clearly in line with the continental European tradition (Wu 2015). A precondition is also imposed before a claim can be filed in court: the eligible shareholders must first file a written request to the supervisory board (or the supervisors in cases involving a limited liability company). In case a supervisor has violated his fiduciary duty under Art. 149 of the *Company Law*, the written request must be filed with the board of directors. The board is allowed 30 days to consider the issue, after which the shareholder can then file a claim to the court on behalf of the company, except in the case of an emergency situation involving irreparable damage. Even though some jurisdictions have limited the scope of defendants for shareholders' derivative suits to directors and other corporate insiders, China's *Company Law* also allows such suits against a vaguely described "third party," so long as the latter caused actual damage to the company (Art. 153(2)). Such a broad provision hence opens up the possibility to file lawsuits against liquidators, entities external auditors with alleged wrongdoings and purchasers of shares at alleged unusually low price, which have all been seen in real lawsuits (Wu 2015).

One critical issue affecting the incentives for parties to bring about derivative suits is whether the plaintiff is required to provide a bond for the suit. Currently, three different approaches are adopted in different jurisdictions. The first one is for law to be silent on this matter. This issue has never been formally addressed under Chinese law, which is consistent with the *Model Business Corporation Act*. The second approach is what was stipulated in a Supreme Court draft guideline: if the defendant in a "representative suit" proves that the plaintiff filed the lawsuit in bad faith and then requests the court to require the plaintiff to provide a bond for the lawsuit, the court shall do so. The amount of the bond shall be based upon the reasonable costs to be incurred in the lawsuit.[10] Such a different approach has been adopted, more or less, in the California Corporations Code Section 800. A third approach is for the court to generally require a bond upon request by the defendant. Due to one specific institutional design in China's litigation system, plaintiffs face essentially the same burden as if a bond had been required. In China, a plaintiff seeking damages must prepay court fees, which is, in most economic cases, equal to progressive percentages of the claimed amount of damage, ranging from 0.5 percent through to 2.5 percent.[11] Therefore, any plaintiff planning to bring a derivative suit will have to make this payment to the court for the course to be admitted, even though the defendant will be required to compensate the plaintiff for this amount if the plaintiff wins.

Scholars have criticized the above legal regimes for several reasons. First of all, the statute fails to impose a good-faith requirement upon qualified plaintiffs. Without such a qualification, the right can easily be abused by shareholders whose interests conflict with those of the company as a whole. Second, the statute fails to provide any guidance on who would count as "other defendants." As a matter of judicial practice, the courts allowed derivative suits against the controlling shareholder, the DFCP, promoters, and liquidators. One controversy that has been presented in front of the court is whether external auditors and accountants can be sued in derivative actions. Liu (2008) proposes to bar such suits, because these third party professionals are already subject to liability if they breach their professional obligations and ethics.

Hui Huang (2014) conducted an empirical analysis of all 60 derivative suits available in two databases, covering judicial decisions dated from January 1, 2006 through to the end of 2010. His study confirmed the existence of these suits in judicial practice in China. Based upon the judicial decisions, he criticized a gap in current law and proposed that shareholders of the parent company should be allowed to bring derivative suits against any wrongdoers damaging the interests of the subsidiary. One particularly interesting finding of Huang (2014) is that only one suit was against a joint stock company, with every other of the 59 cases were against limited liability companies. This finding stands in strong contrast with the circumstances prevalent in the United States, where more than 80 percent of the derivative suits were against joint stock companies. Huang (2014) regards this reality as a huge disappointment which defeats the very purpose of allowing derivative suits. One reason proposed by Huang to explain the disproportionate use of derivative suits with respect to limited liability companies is that minority shareholders used this mechanism to resolve deadlocks, due to the lack of any other effective way to do so.

Another potential reason might be the fact that courts are simply not the proper forum for the resolution of disputes between shareholders and other players for relatively big and sophisticated corporations, especially in China. Compared with market regulators, a Chinese court enjoys no advantages, in the form of either expertise or incentives to learn and work hard in sorting out facts and legal issues involved in complicated commercial transactions. For this reason, fewer derivative suits involving big companies might be a good sign, indicating that parties are making rational choices and seeking more efficient ways to protect themselves. A derivative lawsuit can be costly in the sense that the plaintiff would need to bear a heavy burden of proof, especially in cases taken against big companies, which are more likely to be complicated. If the court does not understand the corporate dynamic due to a lack of expertise and experience with respect to market transactions and business decisions, the time and resources spent in collecting such evidence are likely to be wasted. Meanwhile, shares in bigger corporations are usually more liquid than shares in smaller ones, hence providing cheaper exit for shareholders. Therefore, when the court is still in the process of accumulating expertise in understanding market transaction and business decisions, to exit is likely a more cost-effective way to protect shareholders interests, compared with the option of brining a derivative lawsuit.

Finally, at least one institutional feature of SOEs mentioned above has made derivative lawsuits an ill-suited tool for disciplining insiders in SOEs. Directors and other senior managers of SOEs are conducting multiple tasks, including maximizing corporate profits and implementing the policies of the CPC and the government. The latter task may cause them to make decisions that compromise the economic interests of shareholders. However, to hold them liable for such decisions in derivative lawsuits is seemingly misfiring and won't have any deterrence effect. In fact, it may lead to the unintended consequence of forcing rational managers to leave SOEs. There has been fear of such consequences, court might be cautious in allowing derivative lawsuits in general, especially against big and listed corporations, where SOEs are more often seen and dominant.

6 Conclusion

This chapter in no way defends the approach of designing corporate law to serve the purpose of reforming and empowering SOEs in China.

What I have suggested here is simply that keeping in mind this *de facto* policy goal as well as the reality of SOEs' dominance would help us better understand and interpret what we see in Chinese corporate law. Given that the dominance of SOEs has recently been enhanced but the mission to reform and empower SOEs is still an ongoing task for policymakers in China,[12] such a perspective would also help predict how Chinese corporate law may evolve in the future. Meanwhile, to assess the actual effectiveness of achieving this goal through corporate law or any other goals at all, we would need more research tools other than the doctrinal interpretation of rules. Instead, we should pay attention to the fast-growing literature in empirical studies of corporate law and securities regulation. In China, these studies are just burgeoning and probably more problematic than in other countries, which have a longer history of modern social science research and a higher level of transparency in decision-making by court and regulatory authorities. Nevertheless, these studies may light up dark corners and help identify unintended consequences of law and policy, which is essential for us to understand, challenge, and improve legislation, adjudication, and regulation.

References in English

Hansmann, Henry, and Reiner Kraakman. 2001. The End of History for Corporate Law. *Georgetown Law Review* 89:439–468.

Hart, Oliver. 1988. Incomplete Contract and Theory of the Firm. *Journal of Law, Economics and Organizations* 4:119–139.

Howson, Nicholas. 2010. Corporate Law in the Shanghai People's Court. 2002–2008. Judicial Autonomy in a Contemporary Authoritarian State. *East Asia Law Review* 5:303–442.

2014. "Quack Corporate Governance" as Traditional Chinese Medicine – The Securities Regulation Cannibalization of China's Corporate Law and a State Regulator's Battle Against Party State Political Economic Power. *Seattle University Law Review* 37(2):667–716.

Huang, Hui. 2012. Piercing Corporate Veil in China: Where Is It Now and Where Is It Heading? *American Journal of Comparative Law* 60:743–774.

Lin, Liwen, and Curtis Milhaupt. 2013. We Are the National Champions: Understanding the State Capitalism in China. *Stanford Law Review* 65:697–759.

Metcalf, David, and Jianwei Li. 2005. Chinese Unions: Nugatory or Transforming? An Alice Analysis, *Center for Economic Performance*

Discussion Paper No. 708. London: London School of Economics and Political Science: 4–5.

Weizman, Martin, and Chenggang Xu. 1994. Chinese Township Village Enterprises as Vaguely Defined Cooperatives. *Journal of Comparative Economics* 18(2):121–145.

Xi, Chao. 2011. Piecing the Corporate Veil in China: How Did We Get There. *Journal of Business Law* 5:413–430.

References in Chinese

Chen, Yuefan. 2011. Empirical Analysis of China's Piercing of the Corporate Veil Regime. (Master's thesis, Peking University Law School). (陈跃凡："我国公司法上刺破公司面纱制度的实证研究", 北京大学法学院 2011 年硕士学位论文。)

Deng, Feng. 2013. The Role, Functions and Theoretical Origins of the Board of Directors under Chinese Law: an Empirical Study. *China Legal Science* 3:98–108. (邓峰："中国法上董事会的角色、职能及思想渊源：实证法的考察",《中国法学》, 2013 年 3 期, 第 98–108 页。)

Ge, Weijun. 2011. On the Minimum Capital Requirement and Piercing the Corporate Veil. *Journal of the Shanghai University of Finance and Economics* 3:34–41. (葛伟军："论最低资本与揭开公司面纱",《上海财经大学学报》, 2011 年 3 期, 第 34–41 页。)

Huang, Hui. 2014. Shareholder Derivative Action in China: Empirical Study and Reform Proposals. *Renmin University Law Review* 1:232–264. (黄辉："股东派生诉讼制度研究",《人大法律评论》, 2014 年第 1 期, 第 232–264 页。)

Jiang, Jianxiang. 2012. Research into the Legal Regulation of State-Owned Enterprises' Executive Compensation. *Peking University Law Journal* 1:117–128. (蒋建湘："国企高管薪酬法律规制研究", 载《中国法学》2012 年第 1 期, 第 117–128 页。)

Liu, Fengwei, Zheng Sun, and Zengquan Li. 2007. Government Interference, Industry Competition, and Compensation Contracts – Evidence from State-Owned Listed Corporations. *Management World* 9:76–84. (刘凤委、孙铮、李增泉："政府干预、行业竞争与薪酬契约 – – 来自国有上市公司的经验证据",《管理世界》, 2007 年第 9 期, 第 76–84 页。)

Liu, Kaixiang. 2008. Judicial Practice of and Improvement to Legislation on Shareholders Derivative Suits: An Interpretation of Article 152 of the Company Law. *China Legal Science* 4 : 157–166. (刘凯湘："股东代表诉讼的司法适用与立法完善 – – 以《公司法》第 152 条的解释为中心",《中国法学》, 2008 年 4 期, 第 157–166 页。)

Luo, Peixin. 2010. An Empirical Analysis of Judicial Discretion Applied in Deciding Cases on the Duty of Care of Corporate Officers. *Securities*

Law Review 2:185–190. (罗培新："我国公司高管勤勉义务之司法裁量的实证分析",《证券法苑》, 2010 年 2 期, 第 185–190 页。)

Mao, Zhizhong. 2012. The Independence and Professionalism of Independent Directors and Corporate Financial Irregularities. *Journal of the Anhui University of Science and Technology* 26(6):106–111. (毛志忠："独立董事的独立性、履职能力与公司财务舞弊", 载《安徽科技学院学报》2012 年第 26 卷第 6 期, 第 106–111 页。)

Ren, Zili. 2008. Study of the Criteria for Duty of Care of Company's Directors. *China Legal Science* 6:83–91. (任自力："公司董事勤勉义务探析",《中国法学》, 2008 年第 6 期, 第 83–91 页。)

Sun, Zheng, Fenwei Liu, and Zengquan Li. 2005. Market Development, Government Interference and Corporate Debt Maturity Structure. *Economic Research Journal* 5:52–63. (孙铮、刘凤委、李增泉, "市场化程度、政府干预与企业债务期限结构：来自我国上市公司的经验证据",《经济研究》, 2005 年第 5 期, 第 52–63 页。)

Zhang, Hong, and Yifeng Shi. 2013. The Standard of Judicial Decisions on the Duty of Care of Directors of Listed Companies. *Oriental Law* 1:112–126. (张红、石一峰："上市公司董事勤勉义务的司法裁判标准",《东方法学》, 2013 年 1 期, 第 112–126 页。)

Wu, Caiyu. 2015. Qualification of Defendants in Representative Shareholder Lawsuits. *Western Law Review* 4:11–22. (吴才毓"论股东代表诉讼之被告适格",《西部法律评论》, 2015 年第 4 期, 第 11–22 页。)

Wu, Jie. 2010. An Analysis of the Effectiveness of Independent Director in Listed Companies in China (Doctoral thesis, East China Normal University). (吴洁："中国上市公司独立董事制度有效性分析", 华东师范大学 2010 年博士学位论文。)

Gaoyan, Xu. 2011. Independence of Independent Directors, Related Party Sale and Firm Value: Evidence from China Stock Market. *Journal of Audit and Economics* 26(4):77–84. (徐高彦："独立董事独立性、关联交易与公司价值 - - 基于沪深两市上市公司的经验证据",《审计与经济研究》, 2011 年 7 月, 第 26 卷, 第 4 期, 第 77–84 页。)

Xu, Xiaoping. 2011. Cash-Dividend Asset Valuation and the Effectiveness of Independent Directors. *Financial Research* 3:27–38. (徐晓萍 ："现金-股利资产估值与独立董事有效性", 载《财经研究》2011 年第 3 期, 第 27–38 页。)

Notes

1 See the Annual Report of the SASAC on enterprises supervised by the SASAC and its local branches for the year of 2013. Available on its official website: http://www.sasac.gov.cn/n86302/n326735/n326745/c1327899/content.html.

2 Partnership Enterprises Law, promulgated in 1997 and amended in 2006.
3 Sino-foreign Joint Equity Venture Law (promulgated in 1979 and amended in 1990 and 2001), with corresponding implementation rules (promulgated in 1983, and substantially amended in 1986, 1987, and 2001).
4 Wholly Foreign Owned Equity Law (promulgated in 1986, amended in 2000), with implementation rules (promulgated in 1990, amended in 2001 and 2014).
5 Supreme People's Court Guiding Case No. 15: Xugong Conglomerate Engineering Machinery Pty Ltd v. Chengdu Chuan Jiao Gong Mao Ltd (Contractual Dispute), approved by the Supreme People's Court judicial committee and published on January 31, 2013 (最高人民法院指导案例15号：徐工集团工程机械股份有限公司诉成都川交工贸有限责任公司等买卖合同纠纷案).
6 Reply Regarding Civil Liability When an Enterprise Set Up by Another Enterprise has been Cancelled or Gone Out of Business, [1994] Reply No. 4. Rules Regarding Several Issues Involved in the Adjudication of Disputes Arising from Military, Armed Police, and Politico-Legal Authorities Handing Over and Cancelling Enterprises and with Political Party Decoupling from Enterprises, [2001] No. 8. Rules Regarding Several Issues Involved in the Adjudication of Civil Disputes Arising from Restructured Enterprises, December 3, 2002.
7 Reply Regarding Civil Liability When an Enterprise Set Up by Another Enterprise has been Cancelled or Gone Out of Business, [1994] Reply No. 4.
8 See the Supreme Court Rules of Publishing Judicial Decisions on Internet, effective as of January 1, 2014.
9 Chinese Securities Regulatory Commission, *Guiding Opinion on the Establishment of the Independent Directors Regime in Publicly Listed Corporations* (Securities Regulatory Commission [2001] No. 102).
10 Article 47 of the Supreme Court Guideline on Corporation Related Law Suits (draft for public consultation, dated November 4, 2003).
11 See Article 13 of the Rules on Payment of Fees for Litigations issued by the State Council, effective as of April 1, 2007.
12 See the most recent policy announcement jointly made by the CPC and the State Council of China on Further Reform of the SOEs in China, dated August 24, 2015.

10 *The Evolution of Company Law in Taiwan*

A Focus on the Blockholder-Centric Model

CHING-PING SHAO*

1 Introduction

Three years after its establishment as the first constitutional republic in Asia in 1912, the Republic of China (ROC) issued the company regulation by executive order. In 1927, this company regulation was replaced by the code of Company Law, which was enacted by the Legislative Yuan, the lawmaking branch of the ROC. The outbreak of the Sino-Japanese War in 1937 meant that the Company Law was not given a full opportunity to evolve. As the war approached its end, the ROC government began to overhaul the Company Law to meet the needs of economic recovery; this amendment was finally passed in 1946. However, the Chinese Civil War soon erupted. The ruling party of the ROC, the Nationalist Party, lost China to the Communist Party and retreated to Taiwan in 1949.

Under the rule of the Nationalist Party, the Company Law and other codes were imposed on Taiwan. The Company Law was revised for the first time in 1966 and then on many subsequent occasions. In 2000, the presidential elections produced the first ever ruling party change in Taiwan. The Nationalist Party lost, and the candidate of the Democratic Progressive Party was elected president. An economic downturn occurred shortly after the inauguration of the new president and forced the new cabinet to prioritize the improvement of the legal environment for business (Tsai 2012, pp. 314–315). In addition, accounting scandals involving Enron and WorldCom, which were first exposed in 2001, offered an exogenous impetus for policymakers around the world to act (Chapter 2). Taiwan's regulators and lawmakers also followed suit.

* This paper has been presented at the 10th Annual Meeting of the Asian Law and Economics Association held at National Taiwan University College of Law on June 20–21, 2014.

In the years following the 2001 amendment, the Company Law and Securities Exchange Law (SEL) were further revised to promote the goal of strengthening corporate governance.

In the Company Law, there are four types of companies – unlimited company, limited company, unlimited company with limited liability shareholders, and company limited by shares ("corporation"). In terms of the number of organizations, the limited company is ranked at the top and the corporation is second. In practice, there are only a few unlimited companies and unlimited companies with limited liability shareholders. Because of the practical familiarity and administrative convenience, small business owners who are willing to take the risk of unlimited liability always prefer to adopt the form of partnership which is subject to the Civil Law. While the corporations are outnumbered by the limited companies, the corporation is unquestionably the most significant business organization when it comes to the development of economy and capital market. Thus, the evolution of Taiwan's Company Law can be seen, to a large extent, as the evolution of rules on corporation.

According to La Porta, Lopez-de-Silanes, and Shleifer (1999), corporate ownership structures in most countries are not widely held and Taiwan is no exception to this observation. Taiwan's corporations are typically controlled by family shareholders (Yeh, Lee, and Woidtke 2001). That being said, the corporate ownership in Taiwan may be less concentrated than expected. The seminal study by La Porta, Lopez-de-Silanes, Shleifer, and Vishny (1998) finds "this puzzling low concentration," and suggests it is because company law in East Asia, including Taiwan, is significantly influenced by the United States and thus strong in investor protection.

The company regulation issued in 1915 was based principally on Japanese corporate law (Lai 1984, p. 206). Taiwan's legal system belongs to the civil law tradition, which has affected the interpretation of the Company Law (Liu 2003, pp. 408–409). In recent decades, the legal system of the United States has exerted a powerful influence on Taiwan's lawmaking activities not only because of its hegemonic status in the world but also because of Taiwan's legal scholars' increasing familiarity with American laws (Wang 2015, pp. 191–195). It is now fair to say that the black letter of Taiwan's Company Law has been converging toward the shareholder-oriented model of the United

States' regimes, which Hansmann and Kraakman (2001) vehemently argue is the standard and efficient model of the corporate law.

It should be noted that Hansmann and Kraakman (2001) admit some deviations from the standard model may complement national differences and produce efficient nonconvergence. The mandatory cumulative voting rule in Russian company law is taken as an example. Cumulative voting is the centerpiece in the self-enforcing model that Black and Kraakman (1996) designed to meet the needs of Russian transitional economies. Hansmann and Kraakman (2001) also believe, as patterns of shareholding transform, Russia "will ultimately feel the need to conform its shareholder voting rule more closely to the rules found in" developed countries where cumulative voting rule is rarely mandatory.

Taiwan is one of the rare developed countries that has adopted mandatory cumulative voting in corporate elections. The shareholder-oriented rules borrowed from the United States, together with mandatory cumulative voting, in the Company Law could make Taiwan an exemplar of the Legal Origin Theory (Chapter 2) and legal convergence arguments mentioned above. However, this chapter demonstrates that in Taiwan's case mandatory cumulative voting is not complementary to other shareholder-oriented rules. The reverse is closer to the truth. The mandatory cumulative voting regime was picked and enacted by the authorities in order to meet the needs of shareholders with a significant block of shares ("blockholders"). In the recent process of legal transplantation, the shareholder-oriented rules have been modified to make them complementary to the model developed around the mandatory cumulative voting. In this light, Taiwan's Company Law is better seen as a blockholder-centric model rather than a shareholder-oriented model. The blockholder-centric model creates inefficiency as policymakers and bureaucrats become overly obsessed with blockholders' interests and tend to neglect the needs of shareholders as a group. In terms of the concentration strategy and the distribution strategy in legal evolution (Chapter 1), they decide to err on the side of the former and lose sight of the latter.

The remainder of this chapter is organized as follows: Section 2 describes the juridical-person director rule and the mandatory cumulative voting rule. While many functional features of corporate law are identical across jurisdictions (Hansmann and Kraakman 2001, pp. 439–40), these two rules are unique in terms of comparative corporate governance. Section 3 explains the change to these two rules brought about by the 2001 amendment. It shows that although the word of the law has been modified, it remains the same in practice. Section 4 then discusses the allocation of power between shareholders and the board as an example of the blockholder-centric model in action. Section 5 describes the revival of mandatory cumulative voting in 2011, which shows the resilience of the blockholder-centric model. Section 6 assesses the recent examples of legal transplantation, including shareholders' right of proposal, the institution of independent directors, and shareholders' right to nominate directors. In form, the newly added rules are touted as shareholder-oriented; in substance, they all fit the blockholder-centric model. Section 7 concludes that there is evidence in Taiwan of formal convergence toward the US model. However, although most of the legal rules are similar to those in the US regime, the few rules excluded from legal transplantation may be more essential than those borrowed from abroad.

2 Two Unique Corporate Governance Rules

2.1 Juridical-Person Director Rule

It should be noted first that the board structure in comparative corporate governance can be divided into two major systems, i.e., the one-tier board system and the two-tier board system. In the one-tier board system, the board is composed of directors who are elected by the shareholders. Taiwan's Company Law requires that a corporation have directors and supervisors, both of whom are elected by shareholders. This structure is often classified as a kind of two-tier board system (Lin 2011, p. 395). Unlike the institution of the supervisory board in China's Company Law (Chapter 9), supervisors of Taiwan's corporations are empowered to act individually, more like independent directors, and do not assemble on any other body than the board of directors. In Taiwan, supervisors can attend the meetings of the board of directors, but they do not have the right to vote in such meetings. In any case, in the two-tier system in the East Asian jurisdictions, supervisors' powers are generally limited (Kraakman et al. 2009, p. 56). Supervisors in Taiwan are often criticized for being perfunctory and not being able to fulfill their supervisory responsibilities (Gulinello 2003, p. 107; Lin

2011, p. 396; Liu 2014, pp. 545–546). Hence, while the institution of supervisors is often mentioned along with the institution of directors in the legal text that is analyzed in this chapter, it will not be specifically discussed for the purpose of brevity.

According to the 1946 Company Law, a company is permitted to be elected as directors and supervisors of a corporation (Article 21). Apart from companies, other forms of juridical persons are not expressly mentioned in the article. However, as a textual and contextual interpretation indicates (Articles 118 and 185), the government is also entitled to be a director or supervisor.

The uniqueness of the acceptability of juridical persons as directors further inheres in Article 185 in the 1946 Company Law, which states:

If the government or juridical persons are corporate shareholders, the number of directors to be designated by them shall be in proportion to the number of shares they subscribe as prescribed in the charter.

The director in the above Section, owing to his/her vocational capacity, may be replaced anytime.

The law empowers juridical persons that are shareholders to provide representatives that serve as directors and supervisors (Article 203) without being elected in shareholder meetings. The number of directors from the board that the shareholder can singlehandedly appoint is in accordance with the proportion of its shareholding in the total outstanding shares of the corporation. The designated director is removed when he or she is deprived of his or her representative capacity by the shareholding juridical person. The shareholding juridical person can then install a new face in the board simply by assigning such capacity to someone else.

While the proportional designation rule is an anomaly to modern corporate law principles, there may be some justifications to the efficiency behind it. To illustrate, imagine an example in which two investors negotiate to form a corporation. The very first issue they have to deal with is how many shares each should own and who should control the majority. The board membership is often allocated proportionately through their shareholders' agreement. As a result, the corporate election is a mere formality, which can be dispensed with under the proportional designation rule. This mandatory rule can effectively prevent the majority blockholders from reneging on his promise and expropriating all the board seats.

In Taiwan, the government adopted the proportional designation rule for reasons in addition to facilitating party autonomy. In the wake of the Sino-Japanese War, the ROC government intended to expand the state-owned enterprises and the planned economy at a rapid pace (Kirby 1990, pp. 128–132). At the same time, it needed to amass capital for industrial expansion and to recruit foreign investment. The Company Law of 1946 "emerged with a revised set of categories linking the interests of the state with those of prospective foreign investors" (Kirby 1995, p. 54). To put it another way, the proportional designation rule offered an incentive for wealthy investors to form the public–private partnership with the government. The more shares the investors obtained, the more directorship they can secure. Because board seats were always limited, investors with insignificant shareholding were given no chances of sitting in the board. In this light, this proportional designation rule was absolutely for the interests of blockholders, or blockholder-oriented.

In the 1966 amendment, Article 185 was revised and renumbered Article 27, and several changes were made pertaining to the directorship of juridical persons. First, the power of juridical-person shareholders to install directors was abolished; it was mandated that thereafter directors be selected by corporate election. Legislative justifications for introducing this change at that time could not be found and remained unclear. A reasonable guess is that the designation rule was finally found to be unacceptable as the notion of corporate democracy and corporate election became widely well received. Second, governments and other juridical persons were allowed to be elected as directors. They could choose to send one or several natural person representatives to participate in elections. By this means, such representatives were to be elected as directors in their own names rather than in the names of juridical-person shareholders. Directors could no longer be unilaterally installed, but juridical-person shareholders retained the right, as was allowed by the 1946 Company Law, to replace their original representatives with new representatives. Any who believed the proportional designation rule to be an anomaly to modern corporate law should also find the new rule unacceptable. According to the new rule, a representative-director who was elected by shareholders as a group could be removed on the order of the juridical-person shareholder who appointed the representative in the first place. It was clear that blockholders who could have their representatives elected were the parties most likely to take advantage of this new rule.

2.2 The Rise of Mandatory Cumulative Voting Rule

The corporate election for directors often makes use of two election methods – cumulative voting and straight voting. In straight voting, each directorship is a separate matter on which a shareholder votes. For example, in an election for nine directors, a shareholder who has one share is entitled to nine votes and must distribute the nine votes equally between the nine candidates. Thus, the election works as though there are nine separate contests for nine seats. Consequently, if there is a majority group which can control more than half of the outstanding shares, this group can always seize all of the seats on the board. Unlike straight voting, which is a "majority-take-all" rule, the original idea behind cumulative voting is that majority and minority electors should be represented in proportion to their numbers (Dalebout 1989, p. 1203; cf. Easterbrook and Fischel 1991, p. 73). To achieve the ideal combination, cumulative voting differs from straight voting by grouping the nine contests and distribution of votes that a shareholder can cast. In cumulative voting, the shareholder in the aforementioned example is allowed to allocate nine votes to either one or several candidates. Minority shareholders are empowered to allocate votes strategically and are thus in a more formidable position in cumulative voting than in straight voting. As a rule of thumb revealed by simple mathematics, the more the number to be elected under cumulative voting, the better the chance for the minorities to seize the seats in the election (Clark 1986, p. 364). It goes without saying that the operation of cumulative voting requires competing shareholder group to carefully calculate and allocate their votes (Mills 1968; Glazer, Glazer, and Grofman 1984).

In the 1946 Company Law, election methods for directors were not specified explicitly. Corporations were left to autonomously decide which election method to use. The 1966 amendment constituted the first incorporation of cumulative voting and made it mandatory for all corporations. Article 198, Section 1 of the 1966 Company Law reads as follows:

When an election for directors is held at the shareholder meeting, each share is entitled to the number of votes equal to the number of directors to be elected, and the votes can be assembled to support one person or allocated to support several persons. Persons who get more votes as represented by the ballots are elected as directors.

In addition to the seeming justification of minority shareholders protection, two explanations can be offered for the adoption of mandatory cumulative voting in the 1966 Company Law. The first one is a legal transplant explanation. Cumulative voting acquired considerable traction in the late 1940s in the United States, when 22 states made cumulative voting mandatory and another 15 states adopted permissive cumulative voting rules. The popularity of cumulative voting had declined since then, however (Gordon 1994, pp. 142–146). By the time Taiwan adopted cumulative voting in 1966, mandatory cumulative voting in the United States had been largely abandoned. This anachronistic adaptation is likely the result of the time lag in legal transplantation. Regulators began preparing the draft for the 1966 amendment in 1959 and produced it in 1960. This draft was later sent from the executive branch to the Legislative Yuan and was deliberated among lawmakers in 1961. Thus, Taiwan's techno-bureaucrats might just have caught the tail end of the cumulative voting trend in the United States when they began brainstorming for the reform of the Company Law. Relatively infrequent international interactions at that time might be the cause responsible for the time lag (Chapter 2).

The second one is a path-dependence explanation as "corporate rules at each point in time will depend on the economy's existing corporate structures at earlier points in time" (Bebchuk and Roe 1999, p. 157). When the designation rule was to be substituted for the election rule, the proportional representation structure in the board came under serious threat. Minority blockholders who could send their representatives to the boardroom might have no chance of winning any board seats under the straight voting regime. Minority blockholders as an interest group would certainly be mobilized against the change. Faced with this unavoidable legal import of corporate election, the government could adopt either the concentration strategy or the distribution strategy (Chapter 1) to re-create an efficient model of corporate law. Nonetheless, the government would find it very difficult to design a distribution strategy to have all blockholders behave as a team in the classical scenario of minority oppression. To defuse the corporate governance crisis, policymakers decided to take the concentration strategy and adopt the mandatory cumulative voting rule. The function of cumulative voting is to allocate board membership approximately in proportion to shareholding. Juridical-person shareholders could win broadly the same number of seats of directorship in the cumulative voting election as they could under the previous nonelection regime.

Besides, cumulative voting is made mandatory and majority blockholders are unable to opt out of it. As mentioned above, a juridical-person shareholder is allowed to replace at will any of his representatives-elected-as-directors to resume their directorship under the new Article 27. In sum, the combination of mandatory cumulative voting and the new juridical-person director rule makes the abolition of the power to install directors, as provided in Article 185 of the 1946 Company Law, more a change in form than a change in substance.

3 2001 Amendment and Aftermath

3.1 *Juridical-Person Director Rule Refined*

The juridical-person director regime is very convenient for blockholders. Unlike any individual shareholder, who can only be elected to occupy one board seat, one juridical-person shareholder can have more than one representative be elected as a board member as well as a supervisor. Representative directors run the risk of losing their positions if they disobey the orders of the legal person shareholder since the legal person shareholder has the power to replace the representative directors at his or her will.

The juridical-person director regime has long been the subject of severely attack by scholars but has always survived (Wang 2008, p. 193). Minor changes were made to this regime in the 2001 amendment, but its essence remains untouched. Progress was made in the 2006 amendment to the SEL, which applies only to public corporations and not to nonpublic corporations. This amendment contains the no-simultaneity rule which requires that representatives of any juridical-person shareholder can only be elected either as directors or as supervisors; the juridical-person shareholder of a public corporation can no longer send some of its representatives to be directors and others to be supervisors (Article 26-3). In 2012, Article 27 of the Company Law was revised in the same way and thus expanded the application of the no-simultaneity rule to all corporations. It is well known in Taiwan that an entrepreneur often controls several juridical persons as shareholding special purpose vehicles for convenience of business and tax planning. An easy division of labor for various juridical persons can render the no-simultaneity rule redundant. However, in the process of legal evolution, insignificance is often the exact reason why patchwork reforms can be done. On the one hand, entrepreneurs and blockholders who were found to be unaffected by this change did not insist on blocking the new rule. On the other hand, reform-minded scholars were not satisfied with the result which they deemed better than nothing. Bureaucrats were happy as long as something was being done smoothly.

3.2 The Fall of Mandatory Cumulative Voting Rule

Cumulative voting provides blockholders with the opportunity for representation on the board and possible access to corporate control. To obtain directorships, corporate raiders expend resources in purchasing stocks to create a toehold in target corporations (Williams 1955, p. 112). To ease opposition and avoid "scorched earth" battles inside the boardroom, majority shareholders and management may choose to play favorites with raider-blockholders (Choi and Talley 2002, pp. 285–310) and may listen to them in matters relating to corporate affairs. Sitting on the board provides such raiders greater access to corporate information and allows them additional leverage to collaborate with others in the fight for corporate control. Thus, hostile takeovers may occur more frequently with cumulative voting (Gordon 1994, p. 155; cf. Easterbrook and Fischel 1991, p. 73).

In the 1990s, the aforementioned scenario was particularly true in Taiwan. One of the most infamous cases involved the Kaohsiung Business Bank. As a local bank based in Southern Taiwan, this had long been controlled by major shareholders from three families. In the 1995 annual shareholder meeting, insurgent shareholders, who had acquired only a 0.03 percent shareholding of outstanding shares, made a huge purchase of proxies.[1] Under cumulative voting, they seized five of the 15 director seats in the election. They also formed a coalition with three other directors, meaning that they had majority control of the board and replaced the bank's management. Subsequently, loans of vast sums from the bank were offered to politicians and businessmen close to the coalition, and the corporation incurred substantial losses. In 1996, the family blockholders, who retained ownership 35 percent of the outstanding shares, finally called a special shareholder meeting and regained control of the bank. However, the bank was unable to recover from debts incurred under the previous management and it went bankrupt not long after. In 2002, the bank was taken over by Taiwan's Central Deposit Insurance Corporation.

The Kaohsiung Business Bank case, and other similar cases, show how insurgent shareholders can derail corporate management by means of cumulative voting. The question of whether cumulative voting should be mandatory was in the spotlight. The rigidity of the Company Law was strongly criticized; furthermore, the Company Law exacerbated the burst of the Internet bubble and the subsequent economic downturn in Taiwan at the beginning of the twenty-first century. Management teams in distressed firms were believed to be shackled with numerous restrictions imposed by the Company Law such that they could not effectively respond to the crisis (Liu 2003, pp. 414–417). Against this background, emulating the enabling model of Anglo-American corporate law was heralded as the goal of the 2001 amendment. Nearly half of the articles in the Company Law were affected in this overhaul of the corporate law system. The revised Article 198 reads as follows:

When an election for directors is held at the shareholder meeting, unless otherwise stipulated in the corporate charter, each share is entitled to the number of votes equal to the number of directors to be elected, and the votes can be assembled to support one person or allocated to support several persons. Persons who get more votes as represented by the ballots are elected as directors.

The revised Article 198 includes the text, "unless otherwise stipulated in the corporate charter," which renders this article no longer a mandatory provision, but an opt-out rule with cumulative voting as the default. This change of election rule could be expected to cause severe tension to block shareholders' relationship established under mandatory cumulative voting because it may not be difficult for majority shareholders to have the charter amended at a shareholder meeting. According to the Company Law, for nonpublic corporations, at least a two-thirds majority of shares must be represented in the shareholder meeting, which constitutes the quorum. More than half of the shares entitled to vote in this meeting must then be cast in favor of this amendment. For public corporations, if the two-thirds majority quorum is not met, a simple majority suffices. Under such circumstances, the number of votes required is increased to a two-thirds majority of shares entitled to vote (Article 277). In other words, majority shareholders who have two-thirds of outstanding shares siding with them have absolute power to obviate cumulative voting. If this occurs, incumbent directors who were elected with the support of minority shareholders will lose their positions in the next election.

Considering the concerns of minority blockholders, it is to be expected that additional requirements for the charter amendment of abolishing cumulative voting to take effect might be placed in the law in future. In this regard, the state of Ohio's transition from mandatory to permissive cumulative voting in 1986 offers one such example. The law categorizes Ohio corporations into two groups and establishes different conditions for charter amendments regarding cumulative voting. Most essential, in the case of nonpublic corporations, "an amendment to eliminate cumulative voting will not be adopted if shareholders opposing the change have sufficient voting power to elect even one director using cumulative voting" (Striegel 1987, p. 1282).

As minority shareholders of nonpublic corporations cannot easily follow the Wall Street Rule and sell their stocks, special protection for minority shareholders offered by the law is justified. By contrast, the 2001 amendment to the Company Law does not incorporate any such requirements. Regarding whether to adopt cumulative voting, minority blockholders are at the mercy of majority blockholders in Taiwan. One can logically predict that not long after the 2001 amendment, a certain number of corporations changed their charters and opted out of cumulative voting. Did the bureaucrats who are in charge of implementing the Company Law expect and prefer the extinction of cumulative voting when they proposed the amendment draft for the lawmakers' deliberation? Why were the minority blockholders who faced the "do-or-die" situation of being involved in corporate management unable to prevent this change? Was enough attention paid to this revised Article and full discussion devoted to its impacts during the legislative process of the massive legal overhaul?

Myths remain about the fall of mandatory cumulative voting, but what occurred in the wake of the 2001 amendment is crystal clear. In 2007, this author conducted a study of the Taiwan's top 1,000 corporations in order to assess the impacts of this change. Shao (2009, pp. 35–36) finds that only seven of them amended their charters to eliminate cumulative voting and adopted the straight voting rule. Obviously, in this instance, a change of law in books did not bring about a change of law in action.

The reasons for this business inertia are manifold. Because the long-term operation of cumulative voting often results in allocating board membership in proportion to shareholding, well-funded investors have strong incentives to acquire a block of shares in the invested corporation. It is not unusual, therefore, for the corporate ownership to be composed of several blockholders. If none of the blockholders owns a majority of outstanding shares, not opting out of cumulative voting may be the most favorable decision for each of them. In the words of Bebchuk and Roe (1999), this is rule-driven path dependence. Even if there is a group of majority shareholders that has sufficient votes for amending the charter in a corporation, initiating such a charter amendment and eliminating cumulative voting would be every bit as difficult as anticipated. Fierce opposition from other blockholders is unavoidable as they would be facing elimination from the corporate board. Therefore, retaining cumulative voting may also be deemed a form of shareholder favoritism from the standpoint of majority shareholders (Choi and Talley 2002). In addition, from the efficiency perspective, network externalities (Klausner 1995) developed based on the prevailing cumulative voting cause uncertainty in switching into another rule. This makes potential movers uneasy in opting for the relatively unfamiliar straight voting rule.

The government's attitude toward making cumulative voting a sticky default cannot be ignored. It may be inferred from the statutory change that the government was switching its strategy from one of concentration to one of distribution. But regulators' actions told another story. They always encouraged corporations to keep cumulative voting in the charter. In the then Corporate Governance Best Practice Principles approved by the securities regulators, Article 35 identified cumulative voting as the preferred method of election. As a matter of fact, up to its revival in 2011 the officials of Ministry of Economic Affairs made repeated proposals to restore the mandatory cumulative voting rule. One of the main arguments that is often given in favor of the system of cumulative voting is the perceived fairness represented by the proportional allocation of board membership in accordance with shareholdings.

4 The Blockholder-Centric Model in Action: Allocation of Power between Shareholders and the Board

Regarding the allocation of power between shareholders and the board, board hegemony has long been characteristic of US corporate law. The Delaware General Corporation Law vests the board with the power to manage the business and affairs of the corporation, except as otherwise provided in the corporate chapter. However, in accordance with Section 242(b)(1) of the Delaware General Corporation Code, the resolution to change the certificate of incorporation can be proposed only by the board. Thus, the power of the board clearly cannot be constrained without its own approval.

In Taiwan, the idea of board hegemony has been tested in two major amendments to the Company Law since 1946. In the Company Law of 1946, Article 196 is interpreted to lean toward shareholder primacy by stating that "business execution by directors shall be in accordance with laws, charter and resolutions of the shareholder meeting."

In the 1966 amendment to the Company Law, the aforementioned Article 196 was reassigned as Article 193, Section 2 and remains the same. In addition, Article 202 is presented below:

Execution of corporate business is decided by the board of directors. Except for the matters reserved for resolutions of the shareholder meeting as required by Company Law or the corporate charter, all can be done pursuant to resolutions of the board of directors.

To be sure, the wording of Article 202 is not uncontroversial. Whether this article reiterates the essence of shareholder primacy or deviates toward director hegemony is subject to interpretation. Shareholder primacy became the mainstream view only after Article 193 was taken into consideration.

The 2001 amendment to the Company Law, clearly emphasized the topic of the allocation of power. Article 202 is among those revised and currently reads, "execution of corporate business, except for the matters reserved for resolutions of the shareholders meeting as required by Company Law or the corporate charter, shall be done pursuant to resolutions of the board of directors."

As mentioned, mandatory cumulative voting was also revised in 2001. Both the permissive cumulative voting and board hegemony can be seen as products of legal transplantation from the US corporate regime. The legislative intent was clearly to distribute power between the shareholder meeting and the board. The word *shall* in place of *can* is at the core of the textual change. Because the corporate business *shall* be executed by the board, the shareholder meeting has lost most of its power to control. Article 193 was not changed in the 2001 amendment. Hence, regarding textual interpretation, Article 202 and Article 193 seem to conflict with each other. Article 202 favors board hegemony, while Article 193 still preserves shareholder primacy. Most people believe this technical complexity arises out of legislative negligence in not revising Article 193 concurrently. Expressing the latest legislative mandate, Article 202 should be offered deference.

The legal pendulum swung considerably toward a board hegemony regime in Taiwan until 2005 when another legal import of shareholders' proposal rights attempted to strike a new balance. Because Article 202 clearly states that the decisions of the board cannot violate the corporate charter, shareholders may still restrict the power of the board. Shareholders may find this path to regaining control illusory, however. Although the Company Law does not specifically require that any amendment to the charter be proposed only by the board, it prescribes that for a charter amendment to be valid when passed at a shareholder meeting, the motion of charter amending must be disclosed in the notice of meeting (Article 172). What should be written in the shareholder meeting notice was completely controlled by the board until the 2005 amendment placed the shareholder proposal right into the Company Law. Granted this right, shareholders finally had the power of initiation for charter amendment. However, as discussed in the Section 6 of this chapter, this right is often not exercised. Thus, Taiwan's corporate governance regime appears to be more of a board hegemony regime than of a shareholder primacy regime.

Taiwan's preference for the board hegemony regime may seem to be at odds with its long-standing cumulative voting rule. Based on the traditional principal–agent model (Jensen and Meckling 1976), it may be suggested shareholders, rather than agent-directors, should have ultimate power in the corporate hierarchy. Though counterintuitive, the board hegemony regime is often justified by theories that marginalize the role of shareholders. Nexus-of-contracts theory claims that a corporation is "a set of contracts." Shareholders of a corporation, like its directors, employees or creditors, are part of contracting parties. Thus, shareholders cannot be regarded as owners of the corporation. Maximizing the wealth of shareholders may remain the foremost goal of the board of directors, not because they are the principals that directors work for, but because this rule is favorable for every type of constituent of the corporation (Easterbrook and Fischel 1991; Bainbridge 2006). Comparably, the team production theory proposed by Margaret Blair and Lynn Stout (1999) refers to the corporation as a team production activity. Each constituent of the corporation (team member) makes a different contribution, and the outcome of their efforts is inseparable. Based on this theory, the board is granted the absolute power to manage the corporation simply because this arrangement is in the interest of all of the team members. The team members require a third party to solve team production problems. In their own words, the corporation works as a "mediating hierarchy." The board is the trustee of all of the team members rather than the agent of the shareholders. Thus, corporate social responsibility activities, which are often unwarranted under shareholder primacy norms, are justified by this theory. Nonetheless, a challenge remains for these theories. Both of the theories must explain why the members of the board are elected by shareholders, not by all of the contracting parties or team members. It might be argued that shareholder's voting right is practically meaningless in a public corporation with widely dispersed share ownership and that it therefore deserves little attention (Blair and Stout 1999, pp. 310–311). Another line of argument is that voting rights should be detached from the corporate decision-making structure. In reality, voting rights are not the power to review the decisions of directors, but an "accountability device of last resort to be used sparingly, at best" (Bainbridge 2006, p. 627).

These theories obviously cannot be effectively applied to the corporate governance regime in Taiwan. While the ownership structure in Taiwan is not as concentrated as some may expect, neither is it as widely dispersed as the ownership structure of the typical Anglo-American public corporation. Due to cumulative voting, among other reasons, there are shareholders with significant shareholding in many public corporations. The role of blockholders is so dominant that they cannot be treated equally with other constituents. More crucially, the election method of cumulative voting also induces the elected directors to regard themselves more as the agents of blockholders who vote for them and less as trustees of all shareholders. Against the backdrop of mandatory cumulative voting, the board hegemony rule in Taiwan counterintuitively ranks agents above principals. Moreover, under the traditional civil law system, the corporate control power might be considered one integral part of shareholders' rights (Chapter 9). An in-depth review suggested that blockholders may actually be in favor of the board hegemony rule. Cumulative voting makes the composition of a board similar to that of the proportional shareholding among blockholders. The board is often controlled by those who also own the majority of outstanding shares. Thus, the change from a shareholder-centric regime to a director-centric regime might not be opposed by blockholders because the decisions that the board makes should not differ from those that were made in the shareholder meeting. Moreover, the boardroom differs from the shareholder meeting with regard to how other shareholders are present and may intervene or participate in discussions. The board is a platform on which only directors (blockholders themselves or their representatives) can exchange opinions and bargain with one another. Vesting the power of control in the board can further marginalize the voices of individual shareholders and prove favorable to blockholders.

What if the decisions of the board deviate from the will of shareholders as a group? This unlikely situation may occur when the shareholding ownership structure changes. Because of share transfers or other reasons, the majority of the board may not constantly own a proportional number of shares in the corporation. Conflicts between the board and shareholders can therefore be expected. The blockholder-centric model predicts that the process of reelection is facilitated and the balance between shareholding and directorship is restored in this situation.

The Taiwan Supreme Court's verdict in the Fuhwa Financial Holding Company (Fuhwa) case may be reflective of the belief in the blockholder-centric model in spite of Article 202.[2] Fuhwa, a securities firm that turned into a financial holding company, was controlled by the Central Investment Holding Company (Central Investment). The second largest shareholder of Fuhwa was the Taiwan government. Yuanta Core Pacific Securities Company (Yuanta), a prosperous securities firm eager to transform itself into a financial holding company, was highly interested in acquiring Fuhwa and established its blockholding gradually. By 2005, the respective shareholdings of the "big three" in Fuhwa was 25 percent owned by Yuanta, 20 percent owned by Central Investment, and 14 percent owned by the government. To facilitate a friendly merger, Yuanta attained a consensus with the other two companies regarding power sharing on the board. Of the nine directorships on the board, Yuanta occupied four, Central Investment occupied three, and the government occupied two. However, the following negotiations toward the achievement of a friendly merger did not proceed as well as Yuanta had hoped. Gaining control of the board emerged as the only tactic for Yuanta to alter the situation. At the 2006 Fuhwa shareholder meeting, one shareholder, who was believed to be an ally of Yuanta, proposed on site to have the board convene for another shareholder meeting within the following 90 days and to hold an advance election of directors.

Because of the passage of this proposal at the shareholder meeting, Central Investment filed a lawsuit and requested that the court should declare the resolution invalid. Central Investment argued that the Fuhwa shareholder meeting intruded into the power of the board. Article 171 of the Company Law requires that, unless otherwise stipulated in this law, the shareholder meeting shall be convened by the board. In addition, based on Article 202, resolutions passed at shareholder meetings in this fashion are technically invalid. However, this viewpoint was not accepted by the court. The reasoning offered by the Supreme Court was that Article 202 applies only to *corporate business*. Convening a shareholder meeting, in the view of the Supreme Court, is not corporate business but noncorporate business. Although the board has the power of control over "corporate business," the shareholder meeting is the institution which has the final say regarding noncorporate business. Following this line of reasoning, the existence of Article 171 does not deprive shareholder meetings of the power to demand that the board calls another shareholder meeting.

The term *noncorporate business* is never used by lawmakers and was coined by the Supreme Court. Creating the noncorporate business category and empowering the shareholder meeting on such matters appears to conflict with the board hegemony regime established in the 2001 amendment. Whether corporate business and noncorporate business can be clearly defined is a question that may prove to be problematic for jurists in the future. The Supreme Court's standpoint can be justified only by considering the blockholder-centric model. The model centered on blockholders indicates that the board hegemony regime is favored by blockholders and lawmakers unless the shareholding structure among blockholders changes. The composition of the board should be changed to reflect the blockholder structure. A reelection should be facilitated, rather than hindered. Thus, the Supreme Court's holding should not be mistaken for the revival of the shareholder primacy regime, but should instead be considered to be an integral part of the blockholder-centric model.

5 The Revival of Mandatory Cumulative Voting Rule

The rare incidence of opting out of cumulative voting in the wake of the 2001 amendment suggests that majority shareholders consider it not cost-effective to initiate such an amendment. But the rationalist thinking also implies that majority shareholders will not hesitate to contend if conflicts among blockholders increase to such an intolerable level that the hope of maintaining an amicable relationship vanishes.

The Ta-I Inc. case is one such example. During the 2007 director election season, Yageo Inc., the insurgent shareholder, secured more than 40 percent of Ta-I Inc.'s outstanding shares and was expected to occupy nearly half of the seats on the board under the cumulative voting rule, whereas the Ta-I Inc. management group was expected to maintain a weak board majority. In the shareholder meeting notice sent to all of the shareholders, "charter amending" was listed on the agenda to be discussed in this meeting. However, no specific proposals on which of the articles of its charter would be revised were identified. When this motion of "charter amending" was in process, a shareholder abruptly proposed to amend the provision on the director election method in the charter. This extempore proposal was to eliminate the cumulative voting rule and adopt the straight voting rule. Yageo Inc. was caught off-guard. Despite strong opposition from Yageo Inc., the amendment was passed and in the immediate ensuing election, in which the straight voting rule was adopted, the Ta-I Inc. management group acquired all of the board seats, and Yageo Inc. left the meeting with none.

Be it fair or unfair for minority shareholders, judged from the perspective of legal technicalities, the manner in which the shareholder meeting of Ta-I Inc. was conducted complies with judicial and regulatory interpretations. According to the Taiwan Supreme Court, presenting extempore proposals on any provisions of the charter at a shareholder meeting is legal as long as the motion to amend the charter is included on the meeting notice.[3] An interpretation issued by the MOEA indicated that charter amendment takes effect immediately after the amendment proposal is approved in the shareholder meeting. However, Yageo Inc. demanded a fair election. The complaint was well received among scholars and regulators. To defend Yageo Inc., the quasi-governmental institution, the Securities and Futures Investors Protection Center,[4] filed a suit against Ta-I Inc. in an attempt to void its shareholder meeting resolutions and the election result. In the end, the Supreme Court did not overturn its prior decision and awarded a victory to Ta-I Inc.[5]

Whereas the procedures of the shareholder meeting were the core topic of the court case, the disproportionate allocation of board seats seemed to be the major reason that people were more sympathetic toward Yageo Inc. Regulators and lawmakers believed that only the revival of mandatory cumulative voting could prevent such an inequitable outcome. Because cumulative voting remained the prevailing norm, the change from a permissive rule to a mandatory rule would influence only a handful of corporations. Opposition to this revision proposal was rarely heard in the business community. By the end of 2011, the Legislative Yuan passed the revision of Article 198 and mandatory cumulative voting was reinstated in the Company Law.

6 Assessing Legal Transplant against the Blockholder-Centric Model

6.1 The Shareholders' Right of Proposal

Shareholders in a Taiwan's corporation did not have the right of proposal until Article 172-1 in the 2005 amendment was enacted. The current Article 172-1, Section 1 of the Company Law provides that

Shareholder(s) holding one percent (1%) or more of the total number of outstanding shares of a company may propose in writing to the company a proposal for discussion at a regular shareholders' meeting, provided that only one proposal shall be allowed, and in case more than one proposal are made, all the proposals shall not be included.

The threshold of 1 percent shareholding is an insurmountable challenge for nonblockholders in a public corporation. Although the rule issued by the MOEA has it that the 1 percent shareholding can be met by assembling the shareholding ownership of multiple shareholders, a collective action problem and rational apathy may prevent individual shareholders from coordinating such action. Consequently, only blockholders would consider it practical to initiate shareholder proposals.

Shareholder proposal right functions differently in Taiwan from its counterpart measure in the United States. First, because blockholders can often be elected as directors and voice their concerns in the board, attempting to persuade their fellow board members may be the most effective strategy to obtain what they seek. This right has seldom been exercised since its inception. By the end of 2013, the number of corporations whose shares are listed on the Taiwan Stock Exchange (TSE) or traded over-the-counter was 1,420. In 2013, the number of shareholder proposals proposed in these corporations was only a little more than 20.

Second, controlling shareholders occasionally use shareholders' right of proposal. This is certainly not what lawmakers anticipated when they borrowed this rule from the United States. Shareholders' right of proposal was created to provide shareholders with access to proxy material and the opportunity to put their proposals to a vote in shareholder meetings. Controlling shareholders, as their name suggests, should not require this right. However, the board is often divided under cumulative voting. Although controlling shareholders can dominate the majority of the board, the discussions of the board are not immune to opposition and obstruction. Alternatively, controlling shareholders can have the controversial proposals formed into a shareholder proposal. Legally, the board would have no choice but to accept the shareholder proposal. Because the board has no discretion, controlling shareholders would easily suppress the opposition in the board meeting and place the proposal in the shareholder meeting notice.

For example, in 2010, the Miramar Group (Miramar) and Nice Group (Nice) were two major shareholder groups in the Waterland Financial Holding Company (Waterland). On the 11-member board, Miramar held six seats and Nice held four. The remaining seat was seized by the Taiwan government, which is also a shareholder of Waterland. The two groups were in disagreement about nearly every major business decision. Before the shareholder meeting in 2010, a shareholder who was believed to have strong ties with Miramar submitted a proposal to remove three of the four directors supported by Nice. According to the Company Law, the removal of directors can be executed in the shareholder meeting only if this motion is clearly stated in the shareholder meeting notice. To meet the requirement, Miramar either had to make this suggestion when the content of the notice was under the discussion of the board or submit this proposal to the board by exercising the shareholders' right of proposal. By selecting the latter approach, Miramar avoided a board conflict, and a minority of the board members could do nothing regarding the removal motion proposed by the shareholders.

The removal proposal did not come to a vote in the end. Miramar had the shareholder withdraw the proposal soon after the Financial Supervisory Commission (FSC), the financial regulator in Taiwan, warned Miramar against such a proposal. One of the justifications that the FSC cited to intervene in this corporate control fight was that Miramar misused the shareholders' right of proposal, which is intended to protect small shareholders.

6.2 Institution of Independent Directors

In Taiwan's two-tier governance structure, a nonpublic corporation is required to have at least three directors and one supervisor and a public corporation is required to have at least five directors and two supervisors. Directors and supervisors are selected at a shareholder meeting in two separate elections and under a system of cumulative voting. In the same election procedure, fractional problems existing in the board can often occur among supervisors if there are several of them. In addition, the low number of supervisors results in a much higher threshold of votes for a candidate seeking election as a supervisor than one seeking election as a director. Although minority shareholders can seize one or more seats on the board, the acquisition of supervisorship is generally more difficult for them. If the majority of the board and all of the supervisors receive the votes required from the same blockholders, then it is probably unrealistic to expect the supervisors to monitor the board proactively. After all, both directors and supervisors may, at best, feel pressured from their supporters and may become dummies at worst.

How to reform the two-tier system has long been the subject of debate in Taiwan. The one-tier US-style governance structure has been introduced by scholars and gradually imported into Taiwan. Although the function of independent directors was seriously questioned in the aftermath of Enron and other corporate scandals at the beginning of this century, the Sarbanes–Oxley Act of 2002 (SOX) does not lose faith in the role of independent directors and further strengthens it (Romano 2005, pp. 1530–1532). Following the passage of SOX, Taiwan increased efforts to engage in legal transplantation regarding the role of independent directors. Since 2002, all of the companies to be listed on the Taiwan Stock Exchange or whose shares were to be traded over-the-counter were required by securities self-regulatory organizations to have at least two directors and one supervisor who met certain qualifications. These were *independent directors* and *independent supervisors* at that time (Liu 2003, pp. 421–422).

The formal legal transplantation of independent directors was implemented in 2006 when the SEL was amended. The SEL currently offers a mix of mandatory and enabling rules for independent directors. Furthermore, public corporations that are subject to the SEL can choose to amend their charters and include the role of the independent director. However, the FSC has the power to direct certain types of corporations to appoint independent directors. For a corporation governed by the FSC's mandate, the number of independent directors cannot be less than two nor less than one-fifth of the number of board members.

In addition to independent directors, audit committees were introduced into the SEL. Again, the current regime regarding audit committees is a mix of mandatory and enabling rules. A public corporation that has more than three independent directors can choose to create an audit committee. The audit committee comprises all independent directors and it is only made up of independent directors. In addition, the FSC can direct certain types of corporations to form an audit committee. Notably, the audit committee and supervisors cannot coexist in a public corporation. Corporations that choose to form an audit committee are required by the SEL to abolish supervisors. Thus, such a corporation would comprise only the board of directors and no supervisors.

Taiwan's lawmakers obviously intended to borrow from the US-style one-tier governance structure. However, considering the different election methods adopted in Taiwan and the United States, the effectiveness of such reform is doubtful. In cumulative voting, blockholders compete with each other for the maximal board membership they can obtain. Blockholders typically support themselves or their own protégés in corporate elections. Few would voluntarily allocate some of their votes to outsiders who meet qualifications for independent directors. This scenario was realized at the shareholder meeting of Taiyen Co. in 2003. Taiyen Co., a listed corporation, was required to select two independent directors and one independent supervisor by the TSE at that time, but none could be elected in the end. It took numerous negotiations and another shareholder meeting to have the independent directors chosen in the corporate election.

As reform was established consequent to the SEL amendment of 2006, the institution of independent director and audit committee were expressly granted legal status and specific powers by the law. Blockholders now can no longer risk ignoring and losing all independent directorships to their competitors. As a result, the fractional composition of the audit committee may resemble the fractional composition of the board. The fiercer the confrontation among blockholders, the less we can expect the independent directors to prevent their professional judgment from being tainted by corporate politics. In other words, the blockholder-centric model is by nature in conflict with the institution of independent director.

6.3 Shareholders' Right to Nominate Directors

The fates of legal rules on the right of shareholders to nominate directors in the United States and Taiwan differ markedly. Since 1942, the SEC has considered the feasibility of a proxy access rule that would enable shareholders to include their nominated director candidates on the proxy statement issued by a corporation. The SEC revisited this topic in 2003 in response to the outcry for the lack of accountability from directors following the events at Enron and in other corporate scandals. After the proposal was abandoned in 2003, the SEC's most recent attempt, which resulted in the adoption of Rule 14a-11, was initiated in 2009. The Dodd–Frank Wall Street Reform and Consumer Protection Act, which was enacted in 2010, explicitly authorizes the SEC to issue rules permitting the use by a shareholder of proxy solicitation materials supplied by an issuer of securities for the purpose of nominating individuals to membership on the board of directors of the issuer. Controversially, the SEC finally voted 3–2 to adopt this rule. Within approximately one month, a suit challenging the validity of Rule 14a-11 was filed. Based on the SEC's failure to assess economic effects and corporate governance impacts, the D.C. Circuit Court vacated the rule on July 22, 2011. The latest legal maneuver was ceased as the SEC decided not to appeal to the Supreme Court (Fisch 2012, pp. 440–452).

Inspired by the SEC's ill-fated proposal in 2003, Taiwan's regulators initiated efforts to incorporate into the Company Law the right for shareholders to nominate directors. The Executive Yuan proposed the draft in June 2004 to the Legislative Yuan, and the draft finally became law in June 2005. Article 192-1, Sections 1 and 3, respectively, provide as follows:

In case a candidates' nomination system is adopted for director elections by a public company, the adoption of such system shall be expressly stipulated in the Articles of Incorporation of the company; and the shareholders shall elect the directors from among the nominees listed in the roster of director candidates.

Any shareholder holding 1% or more of the total number of outstanding shares issued by the company may submit to the company in writing a roster of director candidates, provided that the total number of director candidates so nominated shall not exceed the quota of the directors to be elected. This restrictive condition shall also be applicable to the roster of director candidates nominated by the board of directors of the company.

It is worth considering why such right of shareholders is so controversial in the United States but well received in Taiwan. There are certainly differences between Rule 14a-11 and Article 192-1. However, the core characteristic of both regulations – that blockholders are empowered to have their director nominees placed on the ballot – remains the same. Because the proxy access rule is strongly opposed by the business community in the United States, providing shareholders with the right to nominate directors should incite controversy of a similar magnitude in Taiwan. It may be argued that the opt-in rule in the Company Law may help to reduce opposition from the business community. In terms of empowering shareholders through the corporate code, controlling shareholders and corporate management are expected to prefer the rule in a permissive form instead of the rule in a mandatory form. However, compared with adding a new, permissive rule into the law, the maintenance of the status quo should be the most favorable scenario for them. Lobbying to prevent this right from being part of the Company Law would have made the path to legislation laborious. In fact, this draft was enacted by lawmakers in less than a year. Little opposition or discussion intended to block this draft was raised.

The likely cause for this difference between the United States and Taiwan is the adoption of cumulative voting, a system in which proxies are always valuable. To obtain more seats on the board, blockholders must accumulate more shares and obtain more proxies. Consequently, blockholders frequently conduct proxy solicitations in Taiwan. This would be the norm even if a corporate charter grants blockholders the right to nominate directors. To be sure, placing their candidates on the corporate ballot can eliminate the expense of proxy solicitation for blockholders. However, without proxy solicitation, forecasting the turnout of proxies and distributing the votes to their optimal benefit would be difficult for blockholders. In other words, adopting the right to nominate directors would only slightly affect current proxy solicitation practice. It is enacted smoothly because it is complementary to the blockholder-centric model.

7 Conclusion

In terms of corporate governance rules, formal convergence toward the US model is evident in Taiwan. It may be suggested that Taiwan's case offers another piece of evidence supporting the argument that Hansmann and Kraakman (2001) made about the end of history of corporate law. However, although most of the legal rules are similar to those in the US regime, the few rules excluded from legal transplantation may be more essential. Both the juridical-person director rule and the mandatory cumulative voting rule in Taiwan are extremely unusual and persistent. By focusing on these rules, this chapter shows that blockholders are favored in this regime and encouraged to maintain the block shareholding. The shareholders' right of proposal and right to nominate directors, both of which are imported from the United States, are adjusted to fitting the blockholder-centric model. Taiwan's case can contribute to theories explaining why legal transplantation often does not work as expected.

Legal rules in the blockholder-centric model develop surrounding cumulative voting. To the extent that they are complementary to each other, they can produce efficient results. On the other hand, Taiwan's Company Law is inherently inefficient for corporations whose shareholders have a strong preference for election methods other than cumulative voting. Therefore, we should expect that the Company Law will evolve to allow investors with different preference to opt out of the blockholder-centric model. Whether and when this can be achieved remains to be seen.

References in Chinese

Lai, In-Jaw. 1984. Retrospect and Prospect of Chinese Company Legislation. *National Taiwan University Law Journal* 13(2):193–230.

Liu, Len-Yu. 2014. *Modern Corporate Law*. Taipei, Taiwan: New Sharing.

Shao, Ching-Ping. 2009. Recent Reforms and Developments in the US Corporate Director Election Regime–From a Comparative Law Perspective. *National Chung Cheng University Law Journal* 26:1–62.

Wang, Tay-sheng. 2015. *The Process of Legal Modernization in Taiwan: From "the Extension of Mainland" to "Independent Reception."* Taipei: Institute of Taiwan History, Academia Sinica and National Taiwan University Press.

Wang, Wen-yeu. 2008. *Corporation Law*. Taipei, Taiwan: Angle Publishing.

References in English

Bainbridge, Stephen, M. 2006. The Case for Limited Shareholder Voting Rights. *UCLA Law Review* 53(3):601–636.

Bebchuk, Lucian Arye, and Mark J. Roe. 1999. A Theory of Path Dependence in Corporate Ownership and Governance. *Stanford Law Review* 52(1):127–170.

Black, Bernard, and Reinier Kraakman. 1996. A Self-Enforcing Model of Corporate Law. *Harvard Law Review* 109(8):1911–1982.

Blair, Margaret M., and Lynn A. Stout. 1999. A Team Production Theory of Corporate Law. *Virginia Law Review* 85(2):247–328.

Chen, Ruoying. 2016. Evolution of Business Organization Law in China: More Than Meet the Eyes. In *Private Law in China and Taiwan: Legal and Economic Analyses*, edited by Yun-chien Chang, Wei Shan, and Wen-yeu Wang. Cambridge: Cambridge University Press.

Choi, Stephen J., and Eric L. Talley. 2002. Playing Favorites with Shareholders. *Southern California Law Review* 75(2):271–374.

Clark, Robert Charles. 1986. *Corporate Law*. New York: Aspen Publishers, Inc.

Dalebout, Richard S. 1989. Cumulative Voting for Corporation Directors: Majority Shareholders in the Role of a Fox Guarding a Hen House. *Brigham Young University Law Review* 1989(4):1199–1226.

Deffains, Bruno. 2016. Economics of Harmonization and Legal Convergence. In *Private Law in China and Taiwan: Legal and Economic Analyses*, edited by Yun-chien Chang, Wei Shan, and Wen-yeu Wang. Cambridge: Cambridge University Press.

Easterbrook, Frank H., and Daniel R. Fischel. 1991. *The Economic Structure of Corporate Law*. Cambridge, MA: Harvard University Press.

Fisch, Jill E. 2012. The Destructive Ambiguity of Federal Proxy Access. *Emory Law Journal*. 61(3):435–500.

Glazer, Amihai, Debra G. Glazer, and Bernard Grofman. 1984. Cumulative Voting in Corporate Elections: Introducing Strategy into the Equation. *South Carolina Law Review* 35(2):295–309.

Gordon, Jeffrey N. 1994. Institutions As Relational Investors: A New Look at Cumulative Voting. *Columbia Law Review* 94(1):124–192.

Gulinello, Christopher John. 2003. The Revision of Taiwan's Company Law: The Struggle toward A Shareholder-Oriented Model in One Corner of East Asia. *Delaware Journal of Corporate Law* 28(1):75–127.

Hansmann, Henry, and Reinier Kraakman, 2001. The End of History for Corporate Law. *Georgia Law Journal* 89(2):439–468.

Jensen, Michael C., and William H. Meckling. 1976. Theory of the Firm: Managerial Behavior, Agency Costs and Ownership Structure. *Journal of Financial Economics* 3(4):305–360.

Kirby, William C. 1990. Continuity and Change in Modern China: Economic Planning on the Mainland and on Taiwan, 1943–1958. *The Australian Journal of Chinese Affairs* 24:121–141.

1995. China Unincorporated: Company Law and Business Enterprise in Twentieth-Century China. *The Journal of Asian Studies* 54(1):43–63.

Klausner, Michael. 1995. Corporations, Corporate Law, and Networks of Contracts. *Virginia Law Review* 81(3):757–852.

Kraakman, Reinier, John Armour, Paul Davies, Luca Enriques, Henry B. Hansmann, Gérard Hertig, Klaus J. Hopt, Hideki Kanda, and Edward B. Rock. 2009. *The Anatomy of Corporate Law: A Comparative and Functional Approach*. Oxford: Oxford University Press.

La Porta, Rafael, Florencio Lopez-de-Silanes, and Andrei Shleifer. 1999. Corporate Ownership around the World. *The Journal of Finance* 54(2):471–517.

La Porta, Rafael, Florencio Lopez-de-Silanes, Andrei Shleifer, and Robert Vishny. 1998. Law and Finance. *Journal of Political Economy* 106(6):1113–1155.

Levmore, Saul. 2016. Concentrated and Distributed Law: Observations on Legal Evolution from China and Taiwan. In *Private Law in China and Taiwan: Legal and Economic Analyses*, edited by Yun-chien Chang, Wei Shan, and Wen-yeu Wang. Cambridge: Cambridge University Press.

Lin, Yu-Hsin. 2011. Overseeing Controlling Shareholders: Do Independent Directors Constrain Tunneling in Taiwan? *San Diego International Law Journal* 12(2):363–416.

Liu, Lawrence S. 2003. Global Markets and Parochial Institutions: The Transformation of Taiwan's Corporate Law System. Pp. 400–434 in *Global Markets, Domestic Institutions*, edited by Curtis J. Milhaupt. New York: Columbia University Press.

2008. The Politics of Corporate Governance in Taiwan. Pp. 255–277 in *Transforming Corporate Governance in East Asia*, edited by Hideki Kanda, Kon-Sik Kim, and Curtis J. Milhaupt. London and New York: Routledge.

Mills, Lewis R. 1968. The Mathematics of Cumulative Voting. *Duke Law Journal*. 1968(1):28–43.

Romano, Roberta. 2005. The Sarbanes–Oxley Act and the Making of Quack Corporate Governance. *Yale Law Journal* 114(7):1521–1611.

Shao, Ching-Ping. 2014. Representative Litigations in Corporate and Securities Laws by Government-Sanctioned Nonprofit Organizations: Lessons from Taiwan. *Asian-Pacific Law & Policy Journal* 15(1):58–93.

Striegel, June A. 1987. Cumulative Voting, Yesterday and Today: The July, 1986 Amendments to Ohio's General Corporation Law. *University of Cincinnati Law Review* 55(4):1265–1284.

Tsai, Chang-Hsien. 2012. Exit, Voice and International Jurisdictional Competition: A Case Study of the Evolution of Taiwan's Regulatory Regime for Outward Investment in Mainland China, 1997–2008. *Syracuse Journal of International Law and Commerce* 39(2):303–356.

Wang, Wallace Wen-yeu and Jian-Lin Chen. 2008. Reforming China's Securities Civil Actions: Lessons from PSLRA Reform in the U.S. and Government-Sanctioned Non-Profit Enforcement in Taiwan. *Columbia Journal of Asian Law* 21(2):115–160.

Williams, Charles M. 1955. Cumulative Voting. *Harvard Business Review*. 33(3):108–114.

Yeh, Yin-hua, Lee Tsun-sion, and Tracie Woidtke. 2001. Family Control and Corporate Governance. *International Review of Finance* 2(1/2):21–48.

Notes

1 In Taiwan, proxy purchase was allowed until 1998. Now "proxy rules permit listed companies to provide small gifts at shareholders' meeting as 'souvenirs,' thereby legalizing the collection of proxies while delivering souvenirs" (Liu 2008, p. 267).

2 See Zuigao Fayuan [Supreme Court], Civil Division, 96 Tai-Shang No. 2000 (2007).

3 See Zuigao Fayuan [Supreme Court], Civil Division, 72 Tai-Shang No. 113 (1983) (Taiwan).

4 A description of Taiwan's Investor Protection Center can be found in Shao (2014) and Wang and Chen (2008).

5 See Zuigao Fayuan [Supreme Court], Civil Division, 98 Tai-Shang No. 923 (2009) (Taiwan).

Conclusion

A Tale of Two Jurisdictions – Is it an End to the Divergence of Private Law?

WEI SHEN AND WEN-YEU WANG

This chapter aims to draw together the arguments presented across the book. The previous chapters present some interesting challenges to academics, and it is useful to present them here in a thematic way. This chapter is structured around three words: why, what, and how. That is: Why do we compare here? What is compared here? How can we understand and comprehend the comparison made here?

1 Why do We Compare Mainland China and Taiwan?

Comparative law studies have had a rich and lustrous history. A number of tasks or facets can be easily identified for comparative law studies. The first is to compare and investigate differences between legal systems. Broadly speaking, all legal systems are different. It is therefore important to distinguish between what might be called "real" and "artificial" differences. Most differences between systems are probably artificial as different rules can be enforced to achieve either similar or identical outcomes. Artificial comparisons, therefore, may only have a conceptual value. Comparing "real" differences, by contrast, is to unveil those driving forces that shape the divergent outcomes of the application of similar legal principles or convergent outcomes of different legal rules. The second dimension of comparative law is to trace developments in the relationships between legal systems and thus to explore tendencies of convergence or divergence (in terms of "real" differences), noting that in some areas convergence may be required while in other areas divergence may be justified. The third task is to explain and evaluate such developments: why do legal systems converge or diverge? And is convergence desirable or undesirable (Ogus 1999)? Accordingly, comparative law serves various functions. It builds bridges between legal systems and cultures. It is also a device to achieve a better understanding of everyone's own and foreign legal traditions and to enable the more reliable prediction that will result from legal development through law reforms introduced in national and other legal systems. Certainly, prediction and reform are probably the ultimate tasks for legal comparatists.

It is rare to compare legal systems that did not overlap in time and that are unlikely to have shared common influences or background. Uniformity among legal rules of different legal families or societies happens either due to common roots or because of unrevealed mysteries (Watson 1974). On the contrary, variety among the rules of different legal systems can be interpreted as a product of distinct cultural evolution or as a result of randomness. Comparatists are supposed to offer functional or behavioral explanations of variations in legal institutions.

Comparing the legal systems in mainland China and Taiwan is not the same as comparing oranges with apples. Rather, it is an interesting comparison exercise given the fact that mainland China and Taiwan share considerable similarities in legal origins, traditions, and cultures. According to the legal origin school (La Porta, Silanes, Shleifer, and Vishny 1997; La Porta, Silanes, Shleifer, and Vishny 1998; La Porta, Silanes, Shleifer, and Vishny 2002; La Porta, Silanes, and Shleifer 2006; Silanes, Djankov, La Porta, and Shleifer 2008; Silanes, La Porta, and Shleifer 2008), these two jurisdictions are supposed (or bound) to have the similar level of private rights protection. This is not the case, however, as the chapters in this book have indicated. Therefore, comparing the major branches of private laws in these two jurisdictions has some merit, and, more importantly, presents a conceptual challenge to the legal origin school, that is, in two similar jurisdictions with the same legal origins, what will be the major factors shaping convergence or divergence, and what will be the converging (or diverging) direction of these two jurisdictions when they develop their own legal systems. To paraphrase Fukuyama (1992) and Hansmann and Kraakman (2001), the puzzling question is whether there is an end of history for private law.

1.1 *Comparative Law in a Non-Western World*

This book has tried to avoid a Western-centric approach to the subject of comparative law. The traditional way of comparing law, and legal systems more generally, is to use Western law (or legal system) as a benchmark. The result of this comparative law approach is obvious – non-Western law is always perceived as backward, which is also a central feature of the neoclassical model of law as a command and control regime. Utilizing Western legal rules and standards as benchmarks to measure China's or Taiwan's legal system inevitably results in a simple conclusion that the Chinese or Taiwanese legal system lags behind Western countries.

The authors attempt to move away from this model toward that of a more transnational legal order. Recognizing the importance and uniqueness of non-Western countries and their legal systems enriches our understanding of law and legal orders, not only at the national but also at the global level. This awareness certainly also complicates our task of studying and comparing laws. While it is no longer a big surprise to see Asian legal systems have codes and statutes akin to Western countries, how these Western-originated rules work in Asian societies is still a mystery, if not a disappointment.

To Asia-based comparatists, the "outside influence" is usually an important topic, and, among others, the colonial influence has a historical importance (Klerman et al. 2011). Against this backdrop, the case of Taiwan shows this colonial (or postcolonial) element in legal development (e.g., Chapter 8). Colonial laws have been largely superseded in most Asian countries. But, in reality, many aspects of the legal reform in developing countries such as China are viewed as a colonialism, even in the absence of colonizers (Ruskola 2013). The opposite trend nowadays is to focus on the "inside influence" – i.e., the question of what driving forces in Asian countries made these countries so different from Western counterparts. Asian values and cultures, some authors contend, are worth being taken into consideration. These values and cultures are not law-centric even though they advocate some common virtues shared by Western countries. Meanwhile, Asian cultures place more focus on "collective rights," rather than a Western model of human rights. This technically makes legal transplants difficult as the cultural roots in Asian and Western societies are basically incompatible. The book sheds some light on this issue by offering some interesting materials and perspectives. The related but less explored question is how to make use of local resources such as cultural virtues in legal and societal development. Maximizing the utility of these virtues appears an optimal approach given its low switching cost. Nevertheless, this "invention of tradition" thesis has been largely overlooked, if not completely disregarded, by Asian countries largely due to the strong influence of globalization.

The value of this book is its comparative study of mainland China and Taiwan, an area which is rare in the comparative scholarship. The other value is that this book is written by "insiders" rather than "outsiders." Most of the authors for this book are "insiders," and they are extremely familiar with the domestic institutions and systems. As Émile Durkheim (1982) suggested strongly, local discourse does matter. Outsiders offer outsider perspectives and, due to the paradigm in Western legal scholarship, outsiders' theoretical and sometimes practical interests in Chinese and/or Taiwanese laws do not lead them to write on a Chinese and/or Taiwanese legal subject in a doctrinal manner. From a technical perspective, comparative jurists often have a preset mindset while conducting their comparative studies. They often start from their own jurisdiction with their distinctive doctrinal and analytical framework and ideology. Accordingly, their comparison can be biased. This remark is not intended to blame or downgrade any comparative jurists' academic value. It simply justifies the importance of an "insider" approach.

1.2 Shared Roots of Two Jurisdictions

There are quite a number of angles through which scholars can penetrate into the field of comparative law. Legal culture is a widely adopted approach in the study of comparative law with its intention being that the evolution of law and rules can be placed in a wider cultural context. Relevant to legal culture, the notion of the legal family is a dominant doctrinal framework in which civil law and common law are subjected to a thorough comparison. The law and finance school is built upon the key theme in legal families that the legal system adopted in many developing countries often shares a legal origin with its respective colonizer. It is further established that legal origin affects legal protections for investors and also the quality of enforcement. China and Taiwan are undoubtedly in the same legal family and share a similar legal culture. This common background merits a comparison between these two jurisdictions.

It is widely recognized that before 1949 there was a historical and cultural linkage between Chinese and Japanese laws. At the beginning of the twentieth century, the Qing Dynasty enacted statutes and codes which were heavily influenced by Japan. The subsequent legal reform introduced by the Qing Dynasty was more of a symbolic gesture than anything else as it only brought a Western type of legal framework into China while leaving most substantive laws unchanged or legal culture unshaped (Deng 2009). In other words, the enactment of Western-style statutes was not accompanied by a legal infrastructure in place necessary for the application of statutes.

After the founding of Communist China in 1949, Mainland China departed from a body of codes and statutes patterned after the civil law model and moved toward a Soviet-type legal system. Today, after a partial emancipation from ideology, Mainland China's legal system is a hybrid regime and it is probably no longer appropriate to classify it as a pure Socialist one (Chen 2011, pp. 81–112). In the past several decades, the legislature in China has turned to a combination of both classical continental and Anglo-American legal models. In private and commercial law, Anglo-American doctrines have been gradually incorporated into Chinese legislation. As a result, in China's legal system and rules the major distinctions between civil and common law systems have been blurred. This hybrid regime is justifiable due to the saved costs implied by the shortage of experienced lawyers and the slowness of the legislative work. While the common law rules are optimal in a more settled economy, a mixture of civil and common law processes in a transition economy is also optimal (Rubin 1994).

While Mainland China has been experiencing its zigzag in terms of shaping and reshaping its legal system, Taiwan maintains its close civil law tradition borrowed from Japan and Germany, except in the area of corporate law. The reception of more legal doctrines from the continental system by Mainland China in its economic reform era may have strengthened the cultural links between Mainland China and Taiwan through scholars and statutes. However, aside from the historical connection, Mainland China and Taiwan cannot be considered homogeneous in terms of their economic, political, and legal-cultural assumptions.

2 Moving Pieces and Missing Pieces in a Comparative Context

There are many issues surrounding or in relation to comparative law and an examination of all these issues is beyond the scope of a single book. There have been tremendous efforts by the scholars to have a comprehensive coverage of private and public law. A vast literature has been produced on comparative law and economics, involving both macro and micro analysis. Contracts, torts, property law, and company law have been the major areas of study for such comparative law and economics research. The reason for this is that these areas touch upon the foundational side of human life and affect the governance structure of a nation (Acemoglu and Robinson 2013). The missing component in such research is the connecting element between microeconomic and macroeconomic studies of comparative law. Significant differences have been studied at the macro level between different legal families (Siems 2008; Siems and Sithigh 2012; Gelter and Siems 2013). A large amount of research has also been conducted towards the analysis of more specific rules in almost all legal fields at the micro level. While the macro-level research does not have a micro-based theoretical foundation, the micro-level research lacks macro implications. There is a need to mitigate this gap even though the genetic relationship between the macro and micro level is not necessarily clear-cut. This book can be viewed as part of this great project.

2.1 Contract Law

Transactions through contracts are efficient in nature. The reason for this proposition is that contractual parties engage in mutually beneficial exchanges that are efficient. This may explain why the contract laws in mainland China and Taiwan are closer to each other than other private laws discussed in this book, because contract law, being a public good, must be conducive to the formation of contracts, from which economic growth may result. Against this notion, the more deviation there is from the mainstream contract rules, the more transaction costs are incurred by the transacting parties, which will thereby make most commercial transactions more costly and difficult.

While the trend of convergence is obvious, differences exist across jurisdictions. The use of consideration in contract formation and penalty clauses is controversial across legal families. Moving to remedies, from a comparative perspective, a common law system may prefer monetary damages while civil law jurisdictions such as China and Taiwan may normatively favor specific performance. Understanding this difference needs a contextual framework. Both the Chinese legal system and that of Taiwan are roughly homogeneous to have an intimacy with specific performance in their legal-cultural assumptions based on values rooted in the Confucian tradition. The concept of obligation in this tradition may have dominated the contractual jurisprudence. For instance, the assumption of bargaining in one's self-interest may be misplaced (Chen 1992). This may justify the initial legislative preference over specific performance in contractual enforcement. The cost–benefit analytical framework, however, as explained in Chapter 3, enhances a more pragmatic change in judicial practice favoring monetary damages. A social Darwinist could easily understand such a shift.

In terms of contract law, mainland China and Taiwan are still different, largely when it comes to the enforcement of contractual rights. Due to the premature market or tight regulation, in the Chinese context, there is a possibility of imperfect or asymmetric information. This may lead to the circumstance in which social benefits do not justify social costs of performance. As a consequence, they may justify more efficient breaches (or noncompliance). As the gains from using contract do not necessarily outweigh the costs, legal sanctions are rarely used or relied upon to enhance the exchange relationship (Macaulay 1963). This may explain why the volume of contractual breaches in China is not trivial, and, somehow related, why the relation-based transactions are widespread. The other way of considering this is through the value of institutions. The market itself is, of course, an institution. Without an effective market, it is hard for contracts and other contract-based business activities to be economically efficient.

China, like most developing countries, modeled its contract law code on CISG. This is a cost-efficient way of bringing domestic laws up to international standards, and the notion of desire for "prestige" (Graziadei 2006) as a motivation for imitation coincides with this idea. However, a calculus in contractual transactions also motivates such transplantation, and this may even be controlling in nature. Contracts are the most often used devices for transactions. Identical or similar contract law rules help to lower transaction costs, which, in turn, incentivizes local legislatures to transplant foreign or international rules. Taiwan's contract law, while predating the Chinese one and finding its roots from Japanese or German law, experiences the same transaction calculus. It is fair to claim, therefore, that contract law is the area in which we have seen the least divergence between China and Taiwan.

However, legal transplant does not complete convergence of contract law rules. In contract law, precontractual liability is the area that shows deviations in various legal families, indicating the difficulty of convergence even though globalization shortens the physical distance between transacting parties and removes the gap between jurisdictions.

2.2 Tort Law

Legal scholarship on torts, no matter whether in developed or developing jurisdictions, focuses on the same set of problems: the foundation of liability, the role of negligence and strict liability, causation, justifications, remoteness of damage, and compensation. The function of tort law is approached essentially within a consistent and homogeneous framework: compensation, deterrence, punishment, and interaction with other systems of compensation and welfare. China and Taiwan are no exceptions to this.

Tort law is placed in the legal system as a deterrent mechanism. Apart from the dispute over the nature of tort law either achieving retributive justice or distributive justice (Alexander 1987), the key topic in the economic study of tort law is the most efficient way of deterring accidents. Without effective deterrent mechanisms the social and economic fabric of any society is likely to deteriorate. Rules of remedies and liabilities are designed and used as a tool for the purpose of avoiding accidents or wrongdoing. In this sense, compensation can be viewed as the instrument to internalize accident costs or disincentivize the potential tortfeasors (Shavell 2004).

Tort law is also a strong means of internalization, having a significant impact on the economic system and market players. The introduction of negligence rules was one way to internalize social costs, and therefore reduce inequality in the liability-(re)distribution regime. For the same reason, negligent behavior is to be discouraged. Then the choice was between negligence and strict liability. In the evolution of tort law, judges and legislators first choose to impose the burden of proving negligence on the plaintiffs, thereby limiting the impact and the extension of tort law in the economic system.

It has been observed (if not generalized) that modern tort law is built upon a negligence foundation with exceptional strict liability rules. The rationale of the strict liability doctrine is that the society may be better off letting plaintiffs win without going through the burden of negligence suits. Conversely, the society is likely to be worse off if one defendant wins the case as the plaintiff's cost of losing the case is far outweighed by the savings in litigation costs.

Strict liability, as a market-sharing mechanism along with the deep-pocket argument, is probably the most efficient rule for market players in terms of dangerous activities. It will create an efficient level of precaution, lower the likelihood of harm, and deter less equipped market actors. Along with this line of thinking, some highly dangerous activities are subject to strict liability. These activities include blasters and spreading fires. Potential victims are often able to prove wrongdoing or bargain for alternatives with the tortfeasor. A socially desirable result may require the tortfeasor to prove the lack of abnormality or take precautionary steps beforehand.

The use of tort law varies from less developed societies to more developed societies. There may be different approaches to strict liability and negligence rules across jurisdictions. The initial approach was about a choice between negligence and nonliability. Unless there was a clear damage to rights, recovering damages through law was basically impossible (Lawson and Markesinis 1983). Thus, tort law became subsidiary to capitalism as the supremacy of economic growth requires a lower level of liability imposed on manufacturers and market players (Horwitz 1977). Industrialization, together with the notion of rights protection, gradually transformed the structure of tort law. These initial developments appear irrelevant to China and Taiwan when they come to the industrialization development. A lower level of liability, though lowering compliance costs, is likely to increase the reputational costs and push away potential consumers. As a result, today nonliability is no longer a policy choice for China and Taiwan. The strong consumerist movement, together with the technological developments, also calls for a higher level of liability to be imposed on manufacturers and distributors regardless of the economic growth stage and the potential deterrent effects on market players. This constitutes a common ground for the similar liability rules in China and Taiwan.

Tort law in China has been exposed to both social and economic pressure. Like other countries, either developed or developing, tort law in China already shows a complex evolution. In China, the choice between no liability (a negligence rule) and liability (a strict liability rule) for nonnegligent acts is more likely to be affected by a cost–benefit analysis in a nonindustrial economy. The choice, in turn, affects judicial practice as well as commercial behaviors. In this sense, a behavioral analysis of these rules can be a yardstick used to evaluate the sophistication of a given legal system.

The other area which may deserve attention is the rule of vicarious liability. Expanding vicarious liability can be either favored or criticized. The benefit of imposing a negligent liability on the employer, as occurs in Taiwan law, is that the principal is more likely to take precautionary actions for monitoring the agent in order to avoid the imposition of liability if the principal is more likely to be held liable. The increased cost involved in the departure from a general negligence rule to a strict liability rule may justify the society's adoption of a general negligence rule. Argued from both sides, it appears reasonable to claim that there is no best level of vicarious liability. Different legal systems may adopt various levels of such liability and all have good reasons to do so.

The problem of allocating liability and costs of risky (e.g., environmental or traffic) activities is another area. It is no surprise to see the imposition of civil (or even criminal) liability through an administrative-centered regulatory regime. This liability imposition practice shows one similarity that is shared by China and Taiwan – both are regulatory states rooted in paternalism. Tort law is developed by legislature and courts. Increased pollution in China may have been due to the effects of a regulatory failure, which can be attributed to a combined effect of various factors: prohibitively high costs in litigation and regulatory enforcement as well as ineffective enforcement mechanisms. The consequence of market and regulatory failures is a tragedy of the commons. The enterprises are likely to reduce precaution costs and leave losses to be borne by others. This practice therefore becomes standard in the market and leads to less precautions and failures of the deterrence potentiality of the system. These failures can only be cured by more rigid regulation and tort law, or even the introduction of criminal law.

The difference between liability standards in China and Taiwan may indicate the degree of wealth, even though it is difficult to quantify the magnitude of liability for negligently imposed injury. In tort law, wealth can be easily shifted from one party to the other due to the remedies for tort violations. These remedies can be quantified based on pecuniary damages. Pecuniary consequences may induce the parties to honor the precautionary behaviors, and compliance is more efficient than negligent acts. In this sense, wealth is a relevant objective indicator of a legal system's failure or success. In a broader context, the details of the variety can be a product of cultural influences, the attitude towards wealth distribution, or external influences. A society is unable to prosper without discouraging negligent or faulty behavior. Naturally, there is uniform imposition of liability for negligent or faulty acts. Based on this wealth-distribution line of thinking, it is unsurprising to see a similar movement in both China and Taiwan toward a more victim-friendly tort liability system. The Chinese ruling party's aim of shaping a more harmonious society can also be explained in an ideological context in which this liability development movement justifies a more rigorous liability system in a more concentrated mold.

2.3 Property Law

Property law rules are designed to achieve multiple objectives such as justice and efficiency. Maximizing property value and efficient allocation of property rights are two sides of one coin. It has been argued, mainly by economists, that importance of efficiency outweighs that of justice (Kaplow and Shavell 2002; Cooter 1989; Mattei 1994). Economic reforms in China, for example, have stressed the pursuit of utility and efficiency. A historical dimension may suggest, as Chapter 7 echoes, that the rules on ownership did not make sense of the inner workings of the system in the planned economy.

Property law is framed as a cure of externalities. Property law is bound to be efficient if externalities can be internalized through market mechanisms. It is full of instances, some of which explained and analyzed in Chapters 7 and 8, in which property law rules are put in place to reduce transaction costs either in property-related transactions or using property as collateral for development in the capital markets. By contrast, the spreading of efficient law is hindered by a number of factors such as tradition and path dependency (Chang and Smith 2012, 2016). In the Chinese context, property law seems less efficient. Externalities are unable to be internalized partly due to the widespread expropriation and, in part, because of the lack of adequate entitlements (Coase 1960). China appears to follow a civil law tradition by relying extensively on public law regulations and enforcement. As a result, private law and enforcement plays a weaker role partly due to the weak court system in China. The story of Taiwan's recent amendments to the Code of Things is a vivid example of legislative incident, which takes place throughout the long river of legal development in many jurisdictions. The preference of an interest group – in the case of Taiwan, scholars – in amending the law may accidentally switch the direction of legal development. Efficiency, rationality, or other virtues are hard to explain these accidental legal changes.

The development of property law rules in both China and Taiwan presents a free market paradox. Private ownership theoretically promotes rights protection, thereby creating wealth. Too much ownership, however, may have a side (if not damaging) effect by creating gridlock (Heller 2008). Ownership puzzles exist in a wide range of settings, especially in some transitional economies (Heller 1998). The transition in which the law of market is replacing that of Marx has resulted somehow in the creation of more problems, instead of solving the existing ones. The key to creating private property has something to do with clarity of property rights, less corruption, and the rule of law (legal infrastructure and courts per se) (Frydman and Rapaczynski 1994).

The clear definition of the initial endowment of property rights does not guarantee economic prosperity. The way in which the government creates property rights also has a stake in the property rights protection. Modern property theories recognize the modern view of property as a "bundle of rights" (Grey 1980). Transition regimes, however, often fail to endow any individual with a bundle of rights that represents full ownership of scarce resources. The Chinese government has been willing to turn socialist-era stakeholders to rights-holders in the market-oriented economy with the hope that property can be used and traded in a more productive and efficient manner. On the other hand, property rights have been endowed partially leaving the government with a tight grip over the property.

Partial endowment may explain a large number of disputes involving property and land in China. Endowment, in nature, is simply disaggregated rights other than coherent bundles of rights in scarce resources like land. It indicates the importance of conveying a bundle of rights to a single owner. A core bundle of rights allows the owner to fragment his ownership. The safeguard mechanisms in the legal system subsequently allow a rebundling of rights so that the property can be put in use soon. By contrast, endowment of rights of exclusion to multiple owners is not a cost-efficient arrangement. Anticommons property can become entrenched, and, more importantly, the market may have no adequate power to rebundle such rights (Michelman 1967; Hardin 1968; Buchanan and Yoon 2000).

The lesson the government may learn is to avoid creating anticommons property when defining new property rights. Transition or reform policy should focus on the content of property bundling and avoid the formation of anticommons property rights. Along with the privatization of land through endowing property rights to farmers is the possession of fragmented rights by the government. The legal system needs to remedy the policy failure through mechanisms inhibiting owners (or stakeholders such as the government) from fragmenting their rights too much for too long. But this effort always proves less fruitful. Two strategies may help turn the anticommons to private property: market or regulation. The market, however, may fail due to the prohibitively high transaction costs and possible strategic bargaining. Regulation may fail either due to the costs and regulatory complexity of compensation regardless of moral hazards potential investors may face while benefiting from the property reform without paying adequate compensation.

The limited experience of property law developments in China and Taiwan again proves the rule of thumb that property law rules are rooted not only in local contexts but also in legal institutions. Property law only has an impact on the market if structural institutions work effectively. The property law reform must take into account the tension between local peculiarities and structural characteristics. In other words, local factors are important in shaping property law. Property law only works in a legal system that has an independent court system.

2.4 Company Law

Corporate law attracts wide attention from legal economists. At the heart of the debate is the separation of ownership and control. The agency problem, therefore, constitutes a theoretical framework discussing dynamic relationships among various constituents within or outside of the company. At the macro level, the comparison is made between two shareholding structures: dispersed versus concentrated (cf. Chapter 1). In the Anglo-American system, the shareholding structure of the companies is generally more dispersed while the civil law countries generally see a more concentrated shareholding structure (Roe, Ramseyer and Romano 1993). Both China and Taiwan have a more concentrated shareholding structure. But Chapters 9 and 10 demonstrate different legal devices and legal reform packages for tackling this identical legal problem.

Law and finance, a new field in relation to the economic analysis of corporate law and financial regulation, has been developed to investigate the extent to which corporate performance, ownership, and organization is influenced by potential legal determinants (La Porta, Silanes, Shleifer, and Vishny 1998; La Porta, Silanes, and Shleifer 1999; La Porta, Silanes, Shleifer, and Vishny 2000; Armour, Deakin, Lele, and Siems 2009) or what forms of law enforcement provide a more successful regulation of the market for securities (La Porta, Silanes, and Shleifer 2006). A key theoretical component in the law and finance movement is the importance of institutions in promoting economic growth. In the context of China and Taiwan, the lack of a strong capital market has hindered equity transfers and corporate finance. For instance, in these countries sales and purchases have been the means and processes of diversifying state ownership. But a weak capital market is unable to facilitate such sales and purchases among investors. The shift of control from state ownership to management worsened the agency problem and raised concerns over efficiency.

There are two routes for the development of corporate governance regime: shareholder-based or stakeholder-focused. These two routes basically shape a country's corporate responsibility regime. While the shareholder-centered corporate governance regime follows the shareholder profit maximization theory, the stakeholder-oriented regime has a wider perspective considering multiple constituents and promoting the wellbeing of society. Common law jurisdictions lean towards a shareholder-centered regime (Bainbridge 2003; Hill 2005; Williams and Conley 2007), whereas civil law countries are more stakeholder-centered (Aguilera and Johnson 2003; Cappelli, Singh, Singh, and Useem 2010). Nevertheless, it is not yet clear how China and Taiwan will eventually shape their own corporate governance regimes. Their civil law roots may ultimately shape a pro-stakeholder framework, but the current corporate law regime appears heavily influenced by the shareholder-centered Anglo-American system.

In bankruptcy law, the macro-level comparison between the Anglo-American system and the French/German system rests with the difference between corporate reorganization and the focus of employee goals in the bankruptcy law. Bankruptcy law is also related to credit markets, contractual performance, and the business environment as a whole (Ayotte and Yun 2009). Often bankruptcy rules are discussed in the context of legal origins to identify more efficient bankruptcy norms (Djankov, Hart, McLiesh, and Shleifer 2008).

3 Some Preliminary but Forward-Looking Conclusions

3.1 Legal Sophistication and its Measurement

The point here is that the uniformity or diversity of these private law rules (Levmore 1987) discussed throughout this book does not necessarily reflect the sophistication of a given legal system. Comparison, while showing the varying degree of sophistication, may be biased or misleading, given the fact that the choice of a benchmark (a Western legal system) for a comparison (with a non-Western legal system) itself has a preset agenda. In policy evaluation analysis, a quantity measure is assigned to the quality of institutions. While quantitative values attached to institutional entities are facilitative to an empirical evaluation of institutions, an ambiguous measuring might led to wrong normative recommendations.

There has been a large body of so-called comparative economics literature quantifying the level of sophistication of a given legal system. World Bank's Doing Business Data (du Marais 2006), for example, consists of a set of ten indicators that measure the extensiveness of the regulation throughout the life of a firm. These indicators cover the regulation of starting a business, employing workers, getting credit, closing a business, enforcing contracts, protecting investors, registering property, paying taxes, dealing with licenses, trading across borders, and dealing with construction permits. This assessment of relative performance takes the form of a ranking. The underlying rationale is a market efficiency hypothesis. The more the market is left free from institutional constraints, the more it can benefit from an efficient resource allocation. The efficiency criterion is then used to rank alternative legal systems. This approach advocates low institutional burden and simpler procedures, thereby reducing transaction costs and encouraging party autonomy. Policymakers can therefore evaluate the desirability of a specific legal change. Based on this quantitative approach, China's legal system, not only its governance system but also private laws, has a lower ranking compared to other less developed jurisdictions.

The quantitative comparative evaluations should be scrutinized with caution (Davis and Kruse 2007; Woodruff 2006) given the numerous factors that could influence the observed dependent variables. Conclusions should not be pursued in a general manner due to the variations to the scope of application and limits of the existing techniques. Some empirical testing of a hypothesis sometimes leads to findings that are contrary to conventional economic theories. A variety of constraints and incentives affect human behavior and law is one of these factors. In addition, the number of regulatory constraints and their pervasiveness are likely to be a misleading proxy for institutional quality without considering the content and outcome of these regulatory perspectives.

Different from primitive legal systems, modern legal systems are bound to share more commonalities due to the relevance of legal transplants (Watson 1974, 1976) and the shared behavioral significance of these transplanted legal rules.

It is apparent that we are concerned with a reform of private law which may adequately support an efficient market. Meanwhile, the importance of legal infrastructure must be well recognized. At minimum, market actors must be provided with a set of legal remedies that are easy to enforce. Seen from this angle, this book is just a start as the enforcement of these private law rules has yet been thoroughly discussed.

3.2 Legal Transplant and its Limitations

Legal transplants raise several technical questions. First, in what scenario is the adoption of a solution available in the other jurisdiction better than the development of the rule in its own jurisdiction? China, as a developing country, displays the dynamics of a changing legal order. Transition economies like China, as well as Taiwan, should be able to develop original solutions for a different path. Even Western scholars have wisely cautioned against expansive expectations about conformity between China's legal order and the models from Europe and North America (Lubman 1999; Peerenboom 2002). As a consequence, legal transplant, as a device, should be used in combination with selective adaption (Potter 2004). Second, what will be an appropriate formula for the cost–benefit analysis? The costs here refer to internal costs of legal consistency and local preferences, while the benefits here are those benefits generated from international (economic or other) transactions. Transplants may not be efficient due to the externalities derived from the adoption of particular transplants. As a state-focused and top-down instrument for legal reform, legal transplant is not necessarily an efficient one. Third, what are the more important factors leading to a successful transplant? It has been advocated that predisposition and familiarity with the transplanted laws are more important than legal origins in assuring effective transplants (Berkowitz, Pistor, and Richard 2003). A related proposition is that local conditions for reception are more important than the country that supplies the law. Legal transplant of private law today is more often realized through legislative adoption, which is detached from both local actors and market players. The dynamic interaction between legal change and actors (or their epistemic assumptions) is thus easily ignored. From a supply–demand perspective, the key here is the social demand from the bottom, instead of a top-down chain of command (Vanderlinden 1989, p. 149) from the above, for legal transplants in recipient jurisdictions.

Putting aside these questions, legal transplant in general may be a cost-effective approach to transform and upgrade a nation's legal system. However, legal transplant may become unfruitful if used formalistically without considering the greater scheme involved. This is a real problem in the case of China, where the legislature often simplifies its legal reform by transplanting legal concepts and terminologies from other jurisdictions – first from Japan and Germany, and now more often from the United States and the United Kingdom, in order to fast-track the domestic legal reform. It ignores, however, the fact that law is often embedded in its legal culture. For example, in one piece of legislation, the Company Law (2005), adopted the veil-piercing doctrine, director's fiduciary duty, and shareholders' derivative actions almost overnight. These legislative changes amounted to a departure from China's civil law tradition. These changes were largely brought by Chinese comparative law scholars, who view the foreign laws, especially those from the United States, as advanced. Nevertheless, transplanting in these cases ignored other supportive or supplementary devices or doctrines a legal system should have had in place in order to make these transplanted doctrines work. With regard to the transplanted legal devices in the Company Law, for example, without an effective trust system, fiduciary duty becomes a shallow concept. With the dominance of state-owned enterprises in the marketplace, derivative action has been rarely used by minority shareholders to sue wrongdoers. These are good examples to show how comparative studies and legal transplants, when carried out superficially, would be merely a hollow hope. Throughout those application chapters in this book, we have seen many cases in which legal rules or doctrines transplanted from Western legal systems do not work as they are supposed to do. The main reason for this is the lack of supplementary or foundational legal framework which can be accommodative to the functioning of these transplanted rules or doctrines.

Urban land reform is the other area where a comparison can be easily made. Unlike its counterparts in Western countries, urban land use rights are not equal to title or ownership. In other words, the land use rights, the dominant form of land tenure, are less than full fee simple ownership. Using the full fee simple ownership as a benchmark, one immediate conclusion is that reprivatization is a necessary step for continued economic reform because such an incomplete ownership system must be improved before incomplete property rights drag on economic development (Clarke 2014). In practice, the legal protection afforded property "owners" in China far exceeds the theoretical underpinnings of the state as the sole owner of real property. While room for limited reform exists, the link between the land being owned by the people with the government acting as steward and the legitimacy of the one-party state are ideologically intertwined. In this context, reprivatization offers limited immediate economic value when weighed against its political costs and societal stability. While reprivatization may be a direction, it will not result in any constructive paradigm without political and ideological reform. As with land reform, Chinese and non-Chinese scholars hold opposing views on a variety of legal reforms in the sense that non-Chinese scholars are more insistent on Western-style legal reform while Chinese scholars may be more tolerant of informal arrangements. These ideological differences illuminate a stark distinction between a Western-centric and a China-centric viewpoint, or between legalism and pluralism, when it comes to the same legal issue within a changing context.

The harmonization of rules is used as a legal framework for the allegation of the convergence of legal systems worldwide. Convergence is more often seen in some facilitative areas of the law while local preferences remain in some more interventionist areas of the law which are not exposed to market pressure and regulatory changes. In the fields of contract law, tort law, company law, and property law, as

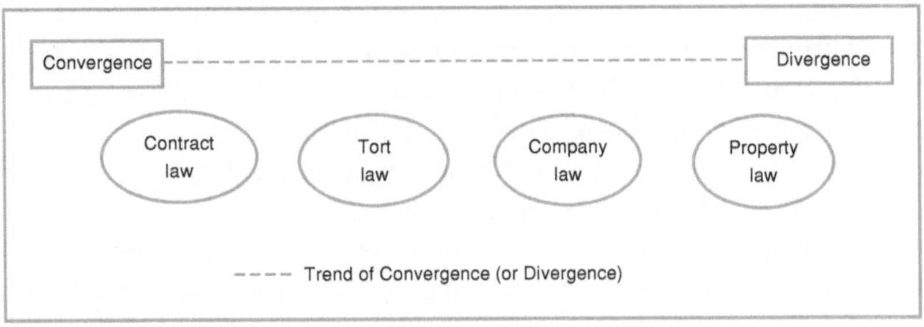

Figure C.1 The convergence (or divergence) spectrum

we may observe from textual (and empirical) perspectives, they can be placed in a spectrum of convergence (or divergence), as indicated in Figure C.1.

Trend of Convergence (or Divergence)

At one extreme of this spectrum is contract law which is the legal area that has experienced the highest degree of convergence. On the other extreme of the spectrum is property law which is clearly the most diverged legal area. The tort law is next to the contract law while the company law is closer to property law. Their places in this spectrum of convergence (or divergence) are determined by the transaction costs involved in divergent laws. For instance, if the contract law departs from the majority of contract law rules, transacting parties then would have to incur higher transaction costs, thereby hindering cross-border transactions. Also, transacting parties can opt out of the disfavored default rules anyway, making idiosyncratic doctrines a wasted effort. Legislature then has stronger incentives to move contract law rules closer to international standards. Property law involves fewer cross-border elements and more local flavors do not necessarily block potential transactions. Further, the shape of property law is often influenced by local factors, in particular, some extra-legal factors, such as political and even ideological factors, as the legislative history of China's Property Law of 2007 showed. Tort law can be understood as a de facto contract law either in an *ex ante* (meaning that the parties can negotiate the compensatory package through the contract in advance) or *ex post* (the compensation is awarded and then repackaged by the court to be a creditor-debtor relationship) context. Company law effectively deals with shareholder rights, which in nature is a form of property rights.

Then tort law and company law are closer to contract law and property law respectively. The jurisdictional competition theory (Romano 2002, pp. 64–73) may contend that the company law may diverge since some jurisdictions have more incentives to offer better company law rules in a race to the top (Romano 1985) to increase shareholder value (Daines 2001) in attracting corporate charter businesses while others may keep their company law rules less favorable given their lower capability of offering a higher level of shareholder protection.

The other way to explain this spectrum is the nature of the law. When the law is facilitative in nature, the rules tend to be more flexible. By contrast, the law tends to be more rigid if it is interventionist as the government and the law also needs to take into consideration the interests of other constituencies in the regulatory space. Consequently, more contract laws are indeed default rules while property laws are mandatory rules, which often involve a varying degree of regulation and monitoring as well as a redistribution of patriarchal privileges and economic entitlements. The fact that the PRC immediately passed the Land Reform Law in 1950, right after its founding, clearly demonstrates that the property law was utilized as the key device to redistribute the land and enhance the revolutionary fruits in a legalistic manner (Ruskola 2013). When regulation or the redistribution of privileges is the key element in shaping laws, rules tend to diverge as different governments may deploy a variety of regulatory devices based on completely nonuniform regulatory philosophies.

Applying this convergence (or divergence) spectrum to Chinese and Taiwanese law, two tentative conclusions can be drawn based on the comparative and analytical studies offered in the previous chapters. First, the "law in action" in China or Taiwan conform to this theoretical spectrum (Pound 1910). Contract laws in both jurisdictions are far closer compared to their varying property laws. Second, when we group China and Taiwan together and then compare this group with Western countries, it appears that contract laws and tort laws are more similar than company law and property law. Contract laws and tort laws play a similar function in these countries. In other words, contract law and tort law show a strong tendency of convergence while company law and property law diverge. Ultimately, we are likely to see quite different sets of property law rules in these jurisdictions. This brings us back to the puzzling question we raised at the beginning of this chapter: it appears reasonable to predict that there may not be an end of the history of private law, at least in some more interventionist legal areas. The rights protection movement may push for a more rights-centered legal regime in these legal areas. Additionally, path dependency and switching costs in these areas may hinder a complete convergence among different jurisdictions.

Convergence may encounter some obstacles such as local rent-seeking, in the uniqueness of local cultures and other forms of transaction costs (Ogus 2002) (i.e., the switching cost in path dependency). Along with legal convergence is the divergence of legal systems resulting from regulatory competition for more cross-border transactions and financial trading. Divergence is not necessarily a sign of inefficiency. Regulatory (or interjurisdictional) competition (Hara and Ribstein 2009) may justify and promote both divergence and convergence. Both legal convergence and divergence make sense to less developed countries which can extract benefits from both to improve their rule of law. This may explain why China's legal development path is a race to the top and to catch up the rest of the world, including Taiwan. This is particularly clear in the context of capital markets where China is trying to eliminate the gap between itself and Hong Kong by enacting more rigorous disclosure and accounting rules in order to attract more high-quality companies for domestic listings (Shen 2015).

Rationality and individualism are two of the assumptions underlying economic reasoning. Together with negligible transaction costs, they lead to a positive Coase theorem, based on which individuals tend to bargain between themselves for efficient results. The problem with the developing economies rests with the lack of both individual-centered and utility-maximizing perspectives. However, these economies may have a homogeneous (cultural) value system that constitutes a background framework for both economic growth and community development (Bohannan 1968; Deng 1971). Part of the economy, for instance, operates under a paternalistic or quasi-feudal regime (Lewis 1954; Little 1982), and nonmarket forces always play a role in a non-Western society (Nader 1965). These considerations help to explain those failed cases of legal transplants discussed in this book.

Comparative law appears less convincing now to rationalize or predict the current evolutionary path of legal development in the context of globalization. In other words, comparative law seems to lose its purposive character. This reminds us of the limitations of comparative law. The comparison made in the book dispels, to a certain extent, legal myths and fictions deconstructing the conventional boundaries of comparative law.

3.3 Demystifying the "China Myth"

Asian jurisdictions present some challenges and puzzles to legal comparatists. Conventional wisdom suggests such a proposition that economic development and prosperity would be impossible without institutional support. Law and development theory emphasizes the dominant role of law in a country's development. This is also the basic doctrine embedded in the law and finance theory. However, the rapid economic growth of China and others in Asia created a so-called "China myth," which becomes a counterexample disproving the correlation between rule of law and economic growth. China apparently lacks rule of law not only in a Western-centric positive sense but also in a thin/procedural sense. This "China puzzle" creates a headache to academics.

The rule of law presumably provides public goods such as transparency, certainty, and checks and balances, all of which constrain arbitrariness in both private and public law, thereby promoting property rights protection and economic development. In other words, a functioning legal system including an independent judiciary is a determinant of economic growth (La Porta, Silanes, Eleches, and Shleifer 2004). In the case of China, this common-sense type of positive correlation between rule of law and economic development turns to be a puzzle. The fastest-growing economy in this world actually does not have an effective court system. This reminds us that the interaction between the rule of law and economic development may be more complicated than anticipated (Glaeser, La Porta, Silaines, and Shleifer 2004; Kaufmann, Kraay, and Mastruzzi 2007).

Western scholars have tried hard to unveil this myth and have relied on the concept of "relationship" (*guanxi*) to explain this exceptionalism. A relationship-centred social order certainly explains the popularity of features such as relational finance, relational property (Qiao and Upham 2015), and reputational sanctions (Liebman and Milhaupt 2008) in China. This line of thinking supplements the deficient legal centralist model (Galanter 1981) and avoids the exclusive use of the legal centralist paradigm for normative description and policy design. In these four major fields of private law, there has been a strong convergence of substantive law (aside from procedure law and enforcement mechanisms). That is to say, China, while retaining many of its own characteristics, is not necessarily a jurisdiction without universalities. Its current legal system, albeit with inevitable defects, also has features of "modernity" even from the Western jurisprudential perspectives (Huang 2007). Its singularities are consistent with Durkheim's idea of local discourse, that is, human order and patterns of domination acquired a life from the people's own land.

Apart from the commonalities and differences in Chinese and Taiwanese laws, the comparison in these key fields of private law has flushed out the meaning and implication of the "Chinese characteristics" theory. In terms of legal infrastructure, China favors and makes use of less formal and extralegal dispute settlement and enforcement mechanisms. The court plays a less constructive role in China's rule of law development. Rather, arbitration and mediation are encouraged to be used through arbitration commissions. This preference over informal dispute settlement mechanisms may match the popularity of relationship in the Chinese business community. This also justifies the relational finance which guarantees a stable source of funding to private business sectors. The comparative setting is an interesting but convincing framework for understanding why China and Taiwan, two jurisdictions with the same legal origins and cultural backgrounds, are moving in two opposite directions in this respect.

Institution-wise, the "China myth" does not suggest that there have been no innovative institutional developments in either China or Taiwan.

Over the past several decades, China has gradually developed a system of judicial interpretations which is used and practiced to supplement civil law codes. The Supreme People's Court of China (SPC) may interpret points of law arising from the concrete application of the law in the adjudicative work of the courts. The legal basis of the SPC's power of judicial interpretation lies primarily in the Organic Law of the People's Courts (Article 33), although the origin of the SPC's power of interpretation of laws can be traced back to the 1955 Resolution of the National Committee of the Chinese People's Political Consultative Conference on Interpretation of Laws (Chen 2011b). The practice of judicial interpretations by the SPC was first systematically regulated by Several Provisions on Judicial Interpretation Work promulgated by the SPC in 1997, which had been replaced by the Provisions on Judicial Interpretation Work promulgated by the SPC in 2007 (Chen 2011b).

For instance, the three judicial interpretation documents promulgated by the SPC on the Contract Law primarily serve to address procedural, substantive, and technical details which the law itself does not clearly define, or which it stipulates only broadly. In other words, SPC judicial interpretation plays a quasi-legislative function in supplementing laws made by the legislature where ambiguities exist or new situations have rendered legal provisions inadequate in corresponding to changing social conditions.

With regard to the legal authority of SPC judicial interpretations, they are not legislative documents in nature but nevertheless serve a quasi-legislation function in judicial practice. This is because although they are not "laws" in the context of the legislative framework in the PRC, they shall be followed, by reference (*can zhao*) to, by lower courts in their trial activities.

As a matter of fact, since the 1980s, the practice of SPC judicial interpretation has developed rapidly, to the extent that its role and function have been elevated to the level of becoming the most important basis on which judges hear and make rulings. Judged by their quantity, the scope of areas covered, and their role in judicial practice, SPC judicial interpretations can be seen as a critical source of law, apart from laws (made by the NPC and its Standing Committee), administrative regulations (made by the State Council), and departmental rules (*gui zhang*, made by ministries and departments of the State Council).

In practice, the SPC not only defines its judicial interpretation documents as normative documents (in the sense of applicability as sources of law), but also has made them quasi-legislative in nature (in the sense of validity and authority in adjudicative practice). These promulgations not only bind lower courts in their trial activity, but also have become the authority in application of law to which courts must give priority consideration (Yuan 2003).

There are heated debates over whether the system of judicial interpretations should be abolished or reformed. For example, defenders of the system suggest that judicial interpretation documents are a useful supplement to legislation enacted by the NPC and its Standing Committee, which cannot possibly deal with the details of implementation. Critics point out that the practice of a lower court seeking a judicial interpretation from a higher court before the lower court decides the case renders the parties' right to appeal nugatory (Chen 2011b). In addition, critics also suggest that insofar as the SPC performs a legislative function when enacting judicial interpretation documents and creating new legal rules in a systematic and comprehensive manner, it usurps the role of the legislature (Chen 2011b).

Similarly for Taiwan, there is a judicial interpretation function in place for the Supreme Court to perform a similar quasi-legislative function, in which court decisions are selected by an internal process, stripping the decisions of its facts, in order to distill the legal standard proffered by the court. While interpretations dating back to 1927 (when the Supreme Court was established in Nanjing) may remain effective today, the court has not come up with new interpretations since the end of 2006 due to a similar concern regarding the usurpation of legislative power. As of June of 2015, there are a total of 4,350 effective interpretations regarding civil matters, ranging from contract laws to corporate laws, and even trademark law. As long as the Supreme Court can hear that case, there is a chance, at least prior to 2006, that the particular case be selected as a candidate for extraction of its legal essence.

In filling the void after 2006, the court has turned to another existing interpretive tool, the Civil Courts Resolution System, to offer guidance to the lower courts. While this type of interpretative guidance lacks any formal legal force to bind the lower courts to decide similarly, they are not completely toothless, and may be subject to constitutional review by the Justices of the Constitutional Court. It is clear that Taiwan's Supreme Court has continued, one way or another, its quasi-legislative agenda.

In late 2010, as a judicial reform measure, the SPC established a groundbreaking system in which certain Chinese court judgments are selected and reissued by the judicial committee of the SPC as de facto binding Guiding Cases ("GCs") to guide the adjudication of subsequent similar cases and ensure the uniform application of law. Judges are required to focus on the important points of GCs and use these points in similar cases while distinguishing the cases before them from GCs. The SPC released its judicial reform plan in 2013 and flagged the importance of the GC system by stressing that [it is to] expand fully the important role of GCs and cases for reference. The Communist Party of China expressed its approval for this GC system in its communiqué of the 4th Plenum of the 18th Central Committee of the CCP in 2014 by stating that [we should] strengthen and standardize judicial interpretation and case guidance, and unify standards of applicable law (CCP 2014). The benefits of putting this GC system in place are manifold. It helps strengthen the supervision and guidance of lower courts by higher courts through unifying the applicable of law and controlling judges' discretion, and improve the quality of adjudication by resolving the problem of similar cases decided differently. Although it is yet clear if this GC system will obtain a stare decisis-like status in the end (Yu and Gurgel 2012; Zhang 2012), the GC system has undoubtedly already reshaped China's judicial system with even stronger Chinese characteristics.

Returning to the discussion on legal convergence or divergence, for which we have identified transaction cost as the factor for convergence or divergence, it is the case that a divergence of laws can add to transaction costs for cross-border transactions. In addition, laws involving cross-border traits are encouraged and tended to converge, together with the convergence of economic and political values in a globalized context (Seita 1997), unless the subject of laws has "political colors" (a Chinese term that is used to describe political significance) such as the company law which, in the context of China, deals with the shareholding of state-owned enterprises. A similar analysis may be performed here regarding the constructive effect of the respective courts. In doing so, one may observe that due to the courts' positions in the respective regime, their interest may not lie with minimization of transaction cost. For example, personal reputation for the judges may outweigh any concern for collective economic efficiency, especially when such collective economic welfare runs counter to the perceived notion of societal justice and fairness. With this in mind, the law's shifting in the spectrum between convergence and divergence is further implicated by an additional factor.

The above judicial innovation stories show that China, in common with other non-Western jurisdictions such as Taiwan, has an effective institutional structure which includes a sustainable constitutional order (Lin 2015), which explains the model of China's growth and dynamic transformation. This requires us to take an unconventional look at the Chinese legal system and institutional order, which differ from those of liberal democracies (Lin and Ginsburg 2015). Apart from the institutional economics, both financing law (Shen 2014, 2016) and foreign investment law (Shen 2011) may shed some lights on this "China myth."

3.4 Large-Picture Narratives to Legal Comparatists

The new century brings us to the crossroads in a new sociopolitical era where the potential uses of comparative legal studies can be re-examined with a different agenda. The global contacts and confrontations as well as the times of economic and political crisis make comparison (judging legal systems and law's potential) more important. Today, new rules are assimilated across both national and supernational sources that differ in origin and kind. On the demand side, there is a spontaneous demand on the side of both legislatures and transacting parties. Even though the reception of law takes place in a fragmented and inconsistent manner, convergence becomes a trend and, as a result, domestic law is not as homogeneous as it may be supposed to be. However, as this book indicates, we probably will not see an end of divergence of private law in the near future, especially when it comes to the "living law" (Cotterrell 1992, p. 32). The on-the-ground reality is that international best practice can often be rejected, modified, or partially implemented (Peerenboom 2012, p. 199) when we come to the enforcement of law.

On the technical side, this book offers some insights into some of the processes by which reasoning and intellectual discovery occur. Currently, it has been well established to have two comparativist approaches: macro-comparison and micro-comparison (Cruz 2007). Meanwhile, there has been a positivist criticism on these mechanical comparative methods which were described as "a general failure of legal scholarship to invent and employ a method adequate to the task of realistically describing and effectively appraising a flow of authoritative decisions through time, that is, for making fruitful decisions through time" (McDougal 1952).

There are merits to the methodology in its proper domain of application. Much of the work in comparative law and economics builds on the economic analysis of legal issues in a comparative framework. Even with regard to the same legal problem, different jurisdictions may take different approaches, and economics provides techniques for assessing the comparative advantages and effects of alternative legal rules. Both conceptual apparatus and empirical methods of economics are deployed to the study of comparative law or legal systems.

Implication is probably an area this book can offer. Economic analysis has been utilized to understand and interpret legal issues related to the structural development of legal systems. Clearly, there is much room for more work inspired by law and economics on comparative legal issues from both positive and normative perspectives. There is a need to apply abstract methodological approaches to real-world institutional designs so as to either inform optimal choice or to frame an institutional structure for superior governance. Hypotheses generated by law and economics should be somehow tested empirically. Designing appropriate institutional frameworks for the growth and competitiveness is now central in comparative law and economics studies. Structural reform is the new horizon of legal comparative projects.

References in English

Acemoglu, Daron, and James A. Robinson. 2013. *Why Nations Fail: The Origins of Power, Prosperity and Poverty*. London: Profile Books.

Aguilera, Ruth V., and Gregory Johnson. 2003. The Cross-national Diversity of Corporate Governance: Dimensions and Determinants. *Academy of Management Review* 28:447–465.

Alexander, Larry. 1987. Causation and Corrective Justice: Does Tort Law Make Sense? *Law and Philosophy* 6:1–23.

Armour, John, Simon Deakin, Priya Lele, and Mathis M. Siems. 2009. How Do Legal Rules Evolve? Evidence from a Cross-Country Comparison of Shareholder, Creditor and Worker Protection. Centre for Business Research, University of Cambridge Working Paper No. 382.Available at http://ssrn.com/abstract=1431008.

Ayotte, Kenneth, and Hayong Yun. 2009. Matching Bankruptcy Laws to Legal Environments. *Journal of Law, Economics and Organization* 25:2–30.

Bainbridge, Stephen M. 2003. Director Primacy: The Means and Ends of Corporate Governance. *Northwestern University Law Review* 97:547–606.

Berkowitz, Daniel, Katharina Pistor, and Jean-Francois Richard. 2003. Economic Development, Legality and the Transplant Effect. *European Economic Review* 47:165–195.

Bohannan, Paul. 1968. *Justice and Judgment among the TIV*. London: Published for the International African Institute by the Oxford University Press.

Buchanan, James M., and Yong J. Yoon. 2000. Symmetric Tragedies: Commons and Anticommons Property. *Journal of Law and Economics* 43(1):1–14.

Cappelli, Peter, Harbir Singh, Jitendra Singh, and Michael Useem. 2010. The India Way: Lessons for the US. *Academy of Management Perspectives* 24:6–24.

Chang, Yun-chien, and Henry E. Smith. 2012. An Economic Analysis of Civil versus Common Law Property. *Notre Dame Law Review* 88(1):1–55.

2016. Structure and Style in Comparative Property Law. Pp. 131–160 in *Research Handbook on Comparative Law and Economics*, edited by Theodore Eisenberg and Giovanni B. Ramello. Northampton, MA: Edward Elgar.

Chang, Yun-chien. 2015. The Economy of Concept and Possession. Pp. 103–125 in *Law and Economics of Possession*, edited by Yun-chien Chang. Cambridge: Cambridge University Press.

Chen, Albert H. Y. 2011a. The Law of Property and the Evolving System of Property Rights in China. *The Development of the Chinese Legal System – Change and Challenges*, edited by Guanghua Yu. London and New York: Routledge.

2011b. *An Introduction to the Legal System of the People's Republic of China*. 4th ed. Hong Kong: LexisNexis.

Clarke, Donald. 2014. China's Stealth Urban Land Revolution. *American Journal of Comparative Law* 44(2):323–366.

Coase, Ronald. 1960. The Problem of Social Cost. *Journal of Law and Economics* 3(1):1–44.

Cooter, Robert D. 1989. The Best Right Laws: Value Foundation of the Economic Analysis of the Law. *Notre Dame Law Review* 64:817–837.

Cotterrell, Roger. 1992. *The Sociology of Law: An Introduction*. London: Butterworths.

Cruz, Peter de. 2007. *Comparative Law in a Changing World*. 3rd ed. London and New York: Routledge Cavendish.

Daines, Robert. 2001. Does Delaware Law Improve Firm Value? *Journal of Financial Economics* 62: 525–558.

Davis, Kevin E., and Michael B. Kruse. 2007. Taking the Measure of Law: The Case of the Doing Business Project. *Law & Social Inquiry* 32(4):1095–1119.

Djankov, Simeon, Oliver Hart, Caralee McLiesh, and Andrei Shleifer. 2008. Debt Enforcement Around the World. *Journal of Political Economy* 116:1105–1149.

du Marais, Bertrand. 2006. Methodological Limits of "Doing Business" Reports. Available at http://ssrn.com/abstract=1408605.

Durkheim, Émile. 1982. *The Rules of Sociological Method and Selected Texts on Sociology and Its Methods.* translated by W.D. Halls, edited by Steven Lukes. New York, NY: The Free Press.

Frydman, Roman, and Andrzej Rapaczynski. 1994. *Privatization in Eastern Europe: Is the State Withering Away?* Oxford: Oxford University Press.

Fukuyama, Francis. 1992. *The End of History and the Last Man.* New York, NY: Avon Books.

Galanter, Marc. 1981. Justice in Many Rooms: Courts, Private Ordering, and Indigenous Law. *Journal of Legal Pluralism* 19:1–47.

Gelter, Martin, and Mathias M. Siems. 2013. Language, Legal Origins, and Culture before the Courts: Cross-Citations between Supreme Courts in Europe. *Supreme Court Economic Review* 21(1):215–269.

Glaeser, Edward L., Rafael La Porta, Florencio Lopez de Silanes, and Andrei Shleifer. 2004. Do Institutions Cause Growth? *Journal of Economic Growth* 9:271–303.

Graziadei, Michele. 2006. Comparative Law as the Study of Transplants and Receptions. *The Oxford Handbook of Comparative Law.* Oxford: Oxford University Press.

Grey, Thomas C. 1980. The Disintegration of Property. *Nomos: property* 22:147–152.

Hansmann, Henry, and Reinier Kraakman. 2001. The End of History for Corporate Law. *Georgetown Law Journal* 89:439–468.

Hardin, Garrett. 1968. The Tragedy of Commons. *Science* 162:1243–1248.

Heller, Michael A. 1998. The Tragedy of the Anticommons: Property in the Transition from Marx to Markets. *Harvard Law Review* 111(3):621–688.

2008. *The Gridlock Economy: How Too Much Ownership Wrecks Markets, Stops Innovation, and Costs Lives.* New York, NY: Basic Books.

Hill, Jennifer G. 2005. The Persistent Debate about Convergence in Comparative Corporate Governance. *Sydney Law Review* 27:743–752.

Horwitz, Morton J. 1977. *The Transformation of American Law.* Cambridge, MA: Harvard University Press.

Huang, Philip C.C. 2007. Whither Chinese Law? *Modern China* 33(2):163–194.

Kaplow, Louis, and Steven Shavell. 2002. *Fairness Versus Welfare.* Cambridge, MA: Harvard University Press.

Kaufmann, Daniel, Aart Kraay, and Massimo Mastruzzi. 2007. Governance Matters VII: Governance Indicators for 1996–2007. *World Bank Policy Research Working Paper* No. 4280. Available at http://ssrn.com/abstract=999979.

Klerman, Daniel M., Paul G. Mahoney, Holger Spamann, and Mark I. Weinstein. 2011. Legal Origin or Colonial History? *Journal of Legal Analysis* 3(2):379–409.

La Porta, Rafael, Florencio Lopez de Silanes, Andrei Shleifer, and Robert W. Vishny. 1997. Legal Determinants of External Finance. *Journal of Finance* 52:1131–1150.

La Porta, Rafael, Florencio Lopez de Silanes, Andrei Shleifer, and Robert W. Vishny. 1998. Law and Finance. *Journal of Political Economy* 106:1113–1155.

La Porta, Rafael, Florencio Lopez de Silanes, and Andrei Shleifer. 1999. Corporate Ownership Around the World. *Journal of Finance* 54:471–517.

La Porta, Rafael, Florencio Lopez de Silanes, Andrei Shleifer, and Robert W. Vishny. 2000. Agency Problems and Dividend Policies Around the World. *Journal of Finance* 55:1–33.

La Porta, Rafael, Florencio Lopez de Silanes, Andrei Shleifer, and Robert Vishny. 2002. Investor Protection and Corporate Valuation. *Journal of Finance* 57:1147–1170.

La Porta, Rafael, Florencia Lopez de Silanes, Cristian Pop Eleches, and Andrei Shleifer. 2004. Judicial Checks and Balances. *Journal of Political Economy* 112:445–470.

La Porta, Rafael, Florencio Lopez-de-Silanes, and Andrei Shleifer. 2006. What Works in Securities Laws. *Journal of Finance* 61:1–22.

Lawson, Frederick Henry, and Basil S. Markesinis. 1983. *Tortious Liability for Unintentional Harm in the Common Law and Civil Law*. Cambridge: Cambridge University Press.

Liebman, Benjamin L., and Curtis J. Milhaupt. 2008. Reputational Sanctions in China's Securities Market. *Columbia Law Review* 108:929–983.

Levmore, Saul. 1987. Variety and Uniformity in the Treatment of the Good Faith Purchaser. *Journal of Legal Studies* 16:43–65.

Lewis, W. Arthur. 1954. Economic Development with Unlimited Supplies of Labor. *Manchester Sch. Econ. & Soc. Stud.* 22:139–191.

Lin, Yan. 2015. Constitutional Evolution through Legislation: The Quiet Transformation of China's Constitution. *International Journal of Constitutional Law* 13(1):61–89.

Lin, Yan, and Tom Ginsburg. 2015. Constitutional Interpretation in Lawmaking: China's Invisible Constitutional Enforcement Mechanism. *American Journal of Comparative Law* 63(2):467–492.

Little, Ian Malcolm David. 1982. *Economic Development: Theory, Policy, and International Relations*. New York: Basic Books.

Lopez-De-Silanes, Florencio, Simeon Djankov, Rafael La Porta, and Andrei Shleifer. 2008. The Law and Economics of Self-Dealing. *Journal of Financial Economics* 88:430–449.

Lubman, Stanley B. 1999. *Bird in a Cage – Legal Reform in China After Mao*. Stanford, CA: Stanford University Press.
Macaulay, Stewart. 1963. Non-contractual Relations in Business: A Preliminary Study. *American Sociological Review* 28:55–67.
Mading, Francis. 1971. *Tradition and Modernization: A Challenge for Law among the Dinka of the Sudan*. NewHaven: Yale University Press.
Mattei, Ugo. 1994. Efficiency as Equity: Insights from Comparative Law and Economics. *Hastings International and Comparative Law Review* 18:157–173.
1997. *Comparative Law and Economics*. Ann Arbor, MI: University of Michigan Press.
McDougal, Myres S. 1952. The Comparative Study of Law for Policy Purposes: Value Clarification as an Instrument of Democratic World Order. *American Journal of Comparative Law* 1:24–57.
Michelman, Frank I. 1967. Property, Utility and Fairness: Comments on the Ethical Foundations of "Just Compensation" Law. *Harvard Law Review* 80(6):1165–1258.
Merrill, Thomas W., and Henry E. Smith. 2001. What Happened to Property in Law and Economics? *Yale Law Journal* 111:357–398.
Nader, Laura. 1965. The Anthropological Study of Law. *American Anthropologist* 67:3–32.
North, Douglass Cecil. 2009. *Institutions, Institutional Change and Economic Performance*. Cambridge: Cambridge University Press.
O'Hara, Erin A., and Larry E. Ribstein. 2009. *The Law Market*. Oxford: Oxford University Press.
Ogus, Anthony. 1999. Competition Between National Legal Systems: A Contribution of Economic Analysis to Comparative Law. *International and Comparative Law Quarterly* 48(2): 405–418.
Ogus, Anthony. 2002. The Economic Base of Legal Culture: Networks and Monopolization. *Oxford Journal of Legal Studies* 22(3): 419–434.
Peerenboom, Randall P. 2002. *China's Long March Toward Rule of Law*. New York: Cambridge University Press.
2012. Between Global Norms and Domestic Realities: Judicial Reforms in China. Pp. 181–201 in *Law and Development and the Global Discourses of Legal Transfers*, edited by John Gillespie and Pip Nicholson. Cambridge: Cambridge University Press.
Potter, Pitman B. 2004. Legal Reform in China: Institutions, Culture, and Selective Adaption. *Law & Social Inquiry* 29(2):465–495.
Pound, Roscoe. 1910. Law in Books and Law in Action. *American Law Review* 44:12–14.

Qiao, Shitong, and Frank Upham. 2015. The Evolution of Relational Property Rights: A Case of Chinese Rural Land Reform. *Iowa Law Review* 100(6):2479–2506.

Roe, Mark J., J. Mark Ramseyer, and Roberta Romano. 1993. Some Differences in Corporate Structure in Germany, Japan and the United States. *Yale Law Journal* 102:1927–2003.

Romano, Roberta. 1985. Law as a Product: Some Pieces of the Incorporation Puzzle. *Journal of Law, Economics and Organization* 1(2):225–283.

2002. *The Advantage of Competitive Federalism for Securities Regulation.* Washington, DC: AEI Press.

Rubin, Paul. 1994. Growing a Legal System in the Post-Communist Economies. *Cornell International Law Journal* 27(1):1–47.

Ruskola, Teemu. 2013. *Legal Orientalism: China, the United States, and Modern Law.* Cambridge, MA and London: Harvard University Press.

Seita, Alex Y. 1997. Globalization and the Convergence of Values. *Cornell International Law Journal* 30:429–491.

Shavell, Steven. 2004. *Foundations of Economic Analysis of Law.* Cambridge, MA: Harvard University Press.

Shen, Wei. 2011. Protection of Foreign Investment in China. Pp. CHN1–145, in *International Protection of Foreign Investment.* 2 ed. Huntington, NY: Juris Publishing.

2014. *The Anatomy of China's Banking Sector and Regulation.* Hong Kong: Wolters Kluwer.

2015. *Investor Protection in Capital Markets – The Case of Hong Kong.* London: Sweet & Maxwell.

2016. *Shadow Banking in China: Risk, Regulation and Policy.* Cheltenham, UK: Edward Elgar.

Siems, Mathias M. 2008. Legal Originality. *Oxford Journal of Legal Studies* 28:147–164.

Siems, Mathias M., and Daithi Mac Sithigh. 2012. Mapping Legal Research. *Cambridge Law Journal* 71:651–676.

Silanes, Florencio Lopez De, Rafael La Porta, and Andrei Shleifer. 2008. The Economic Consequences of Legal Origins. *Journal of Economic Literature* 46(2):285–322.

Smith, Henry E. 2011. Property Is Not Just a Bundle of Rights. *Economic Journal Watch* 8(3):279–291.

Vanderlinden, Jacques. 1989. Return to Legal Pluralism: Twenty Years Later. *Journal of Legal Pluralism and Unofficial Law* 28:149.

Watson, Alan. 1974. *Legal Transplants: An Approach to Comparative Law.* Charlottesville, VA: University Press of Virginia.

Watson, Alan. 1976. Legal Transplants and Law Reform. *Law Quarterly Review* 92:79–82.

Williams, Cynthia A., and John M. Conley. 2007. Triumph or Tragedy? The Curious Path of Corporate Disclosure Reform in the UK. *William & Mary Environmental Law Journal* 31:317–361.

Woodruff, Christopher. 2006. Measuring Institutions. Pp. 105–126 in *International Handbook on the Economics of Corruption*, edited by Susan Rose-Ackerman. Cheltenham, UK: Edward Elgar.

Yu, Ping, and Seth Gurgel. 2012. Stare Decisis in China? The Newly Enacted Guiding Case System. Pp. 142–158 in *Reading the Legal Case: Cross-currents Between Law and the Humanities*, edited by Marco Wan. Oxford: Routledge.

Zhang, Taisu. 2012. The Pragmatic Court: Reinterpreting the Supreme People's Court of China. *Columbia Journal of Asian Law* 25(1):1–61.

Reference in Chinese

CCP. 2014. Communiqué of the 4th Plenum of the 18th Central Committee of the CCP. Available at http://news.xinhuanet.com/politics/2014–10/23/c_1112953884.htm (last visited on January 6, 2015).

Chen, Wenhua. 2011. Transactional Customs in Statutory Interpretation: From the Perspective of the PRC Contract Law. *Western Law Review* 2:31–36.

Deng, Feng. 2009. A Law and Economic Analysis of Legal Change in the Qing-end Era: Why Did China Only Learn from Continental Law? *Peking University Law Journal* 21(2):165–186.

Yuan Mingsheng. 2003. Exploring the Quasi-Legislative Nature of Judicial Interpretation. *Studies in Law and Business* 94(2):3–12.

Index